More praise for the second edition of
Alterations of Consciousness

A marvelously readable, wide-ranging, and insightful book that makes the case that we consider to be "normal" consciousness is—to paraphrase William James—just one out of a wide spectrum of different states. Altered states have a massive amount to tell us about the nature of reality and the limitations of our normal awareness, and this book guides us expertly through them.

—**Steve Taylor, PhD,** author of *The Leap* and *Spiritual Science*

Barušs gracefully covers eight diverse topics of consciousness with a clear and concise style that will appeal to beginners, yet the material is thoroughly cited for the experts, to broaden their horizons as well.

—**Paul Kalas, PhD,** Adjunct Professor, University of California, Berkeley; author of
   The Oneironauts: Using Dreams to Engineer Our Future

Full disclosure . . . I have been an admirer of the work of Imants Barušs for many years now. The broad range of his interests runs contrary to the current trend of simple specialization within narrowly defined fields. His forays into complex questions (can you pick a more difficult problem to study than consciousness?) produce a synthesis of ideas ranging from hard empirical data to grand philosophical questions. After reading this, the world you thought you knew will never seem quite the same again.

—**William Bengston, PhD,** President, Society for Scientific Exploration

Controversial, thought-provoking, and accessible, this new edition of *Alterations of Consciousness* is one of the most intriguing books you will read this year. It is a must-read for anyone interested in learning more about the nature of reality and what lies on the fringe of human experience.

—**Robert Horvath, BA (Psychology),** King's University College at Western
   University Canada, London, Ontario; **MA (Philosophy),** Katholieke Universiteit
   Leuven, Belgium

D1295435

Alterations of Consciousness

Alterations of Consciousness

An Empirical Analysis for Social Scientists

SECOND EDITION

IMANTS BARUŠS

 AMERICAN PSYCHOLOGICAL ASSOCIATION

Published by
American Psychological Association
750 First Street, NE
Washington, DC 20002
https://www.apa.org

Order Department
https://www.apa.org/pubs/books
order@apa.org

In the U.K., Europe, Africa, and the Middle East, copies may be ordered from Eurospan
https://www.eurospanbookstore.com/apa
info@eurospangroup.com

Typeset in Meridien and Ortodoxa by Circle Graphics, Inc., Reisterstown, MD

Printer: Sheridan Books, Chelsea, MI
Cover Designer: Beth Schlenoff Design, Bethesda, MD

Library of Congress Cataloging-in-Publication Data

Names: Barušs, Imants, 1952- author.
Title: Alterations of consciousness : an empirical analysis for social
    scientists / Imants Barušs.
Description: Second Edition. | Washington : American Psychological
    Association, 2020. | Revised edition of the author's Alterations of
    consciousness, 2003. | Includes bibliographical references and index.
Identifiers: LCCN 2020003852 (print) | LCCN 2020003853 (ebook) |
    ISBN 9781433832673 (paperback) | ISBN 9781433833748 (ebook)
Subjects: LCSH: Altered states of consciousness.
Classification: LCC BF1045.A48 B37 2020 (print) | LCC BF1045.A48 (ebook) |
    DDC 154.4—dc23
LC record available at https://lccn.loc.gov/2020003852
LC ebook record available at https://lccn.loc.gov/2020003853

http://dx.doi.org/10.1037/0000200-000

Printed in the United States of America

10 9 8 7 6 5 4 3 2 1

CONTENTS

PREFACE

I used the first edition of this book as a textbook for a popular psychology course about altered states of consciousness that I have been teaching every year to undergraduate students from across the spectrum of disciplines at a large Canadian university. Students have frequently told me that they have enjoyed reading the book and, in some cases, that their parents have enjoyed reading it as well! My goal has been to present the current scientific knowledge about altered states of consciousness in an accessible style, and I have continued that with the second edition. College and university professors who are using this book as a textbook are welcome to contact me through my website, baruss.ca, for additional resources that could be of use to them for their teaching.

No previous knowledge of psychology or physiology is necessary in order to read this book. I have kept the language as simple as possible, introducing technical terms only when they are commonly used or necessary, and defining them explicitly when their meanings are not transparent from the context. I have included descriptions of technical material, such as the activity of neurotransmitters, in such a way as to allow a reader to visualize that which is being described in sufficient detail for the purposes of the discussion without unnecessarily complicating matters. At the same time, I have been careful not to simplify in such a way as to misrepresent that which is complex in reality.

In writing the first edition, I had to make decisions about what to include and what to leave out of a brief overview of altered states of consciousness. A standardized list of topics has not yet been developed, so there was considerable latitude for choice. Some topics clearly needed to be included, such as sleep, dreaming, hypnosis, and psychedelic drug use. There were some topics it was reasonable to consider, such as daydreaming, sensory restriction, meditation, mystical experiences, and near-death experiences. But I also included some puzzling states that clearly involve alterations of consciousness, although they are not usually discussed in the context of the psychology of consciousness, namely, shamanism, possession, dissociative identity disorder, alien abduction experiences, and past-life experiences. I left out a number of alterations of consciousness, including most psychopathological states, drug-induced states other than those induced by the classical psychedelics, and perceptual anomalies such as synesthesia and blindsight.

For this second edition, I have included more neuroscience, because of its current prominence in our understanding of the psyche, but have done so as gently as possible. I also tried to capture some of the significant advances in research since the first edition by adding, for instance, sections about mind wandering, shared dreaming, and veridical near-death experiences. I have refrained from some other popular trends such as the increased use of Bayesian statistics, which is beyond the scope of an introductory overview. Otherwise, I have strategically updated the material in the book where such updating substantially adds to the understanding of the subject matter. The net result is that the reader will find a large number of citations from work that was done prior to the publication of the first edition in 2003, with a smaller number of citations from books and papers that have appeared in more recent years.

Because this book is an introduction, I have included much well-known material, such as John Lilly's invention of the flotation tank, Kenneth Parks's somnambulistic homicide, and Walter Pahnke's Good Friday experiment in which divinity students were given psilocybin prior to a Good Friday service. What I have done, however, for readers with some familiarity with the subject matter, has been to try to cover such ground in a fresh manner, for instance, by discussing the experiences of one of the participants in the Good Friday experiment based in part on my conversations with him.

If it is not already apparent, it will become so quickly in Chapter 1 that much of the material in the book is controversial. In particular, the frequency of anomalous phenomena increases with alterations of consciousness relative to the ordinary waking state. I included anomalous phenomena in the first edition but merely suggested that they imply that consciousness has nonlocal properties. Since then, careful evaluation of the relevant evidence has further verified that consciousness does have nonlocal aspects, so I simply treat that as any other psychological fact. At any rate, the examination of controversial material provides a good exercise in critical thinking.

Finally, in keeping with my interest in the fundamental questions about reality, I have made a point of raising existential, ontological, and similar questions whenever they surface in the context of altered states of consciousness. Indeed, 11 thematic threads based on such questions are introduced in Chapter 1, woven throughout the text, and then gathered up in the conclusion. It is my hope that these threads inspire the reader and ignite a sense of wonder about the nature of consciousness and reality.

ACKNOWLEDGMENTS

I am grateful to all the people who have told me about their altered states experiences and, in some cases, helped me to collect additional data about them. Four of those accounts have made it into this book: The example of contemporary North American channeling in Chapter 6 is by Isabella Colalillo-Kates; comments about his experiences in the Good Friday experiment, described in Chapter 7, were provided by Mike Young; Allan Smith reflected on his experience of cosmic consciousness in Chapter 8; and the report of an out-of-body experience toward the beginning of Chapter 9 is by Lydia Bristow.

I am grateful to King's University College at Western University for a teaching schedule and research funds that have allowed me to write this book and its revision. I thank Shannon Foskett for research assistance, critical comments, and assistance with editing the book. I also thank my acquisitions editor, Susan Reynolds, for requesting the second edition and everyone at American Psychological Association Books for their contributions, patience, and unwavering support for my work. Finally, I want to thank my students, my colleagues, the members of our Consciousness Club, and everyone else with whom I have engaged in vigorous discussions about consciousness over the years.

Alterations of Consciousness

1

Introduction

We are used to the everyday world being there for us, day after day, and we know from its monotonous regularity what it is that is real and what is not. At night, we sleep. And perhaps we dream. And while we dream, we think we know that what we dream is real, but upon awakening, we realize that it is not. And sometimes, while apparently we are awake, the everyday world disappears, and what we thought was real is gone, and we are confronted with that which is not supposed to be real. And afterward, perhaps we come to think that that which is not supposed to be real really is real, or we no longer know what is real and what is not.

What is real? What is imaginary? What is true? Alterations of consciousness pose fundamental questions that can challenge our ideas about the nature of reality.

AN EXAMPLE OF ALTERED CONSCIOUSNESS

Terence McKenna had an unusual experience at dawn after a night of rumination while sitting on a flat stone by a river at La Chorrera in the Amazon. He noticed a mist at some distance from him that "split into two parts" with each of those parts splitting again so that he was "looking at four lens-shaped clouds of the same size lying in a row and slightly above the horizon, only a half mile or so away" (T. McKenna, 1993, p. 157).

http://dx.doi.org/10.1037/0000200-001
Alterations of Consciousness: An Empirical Analysis for Social Scientists, Second Edition,
by I. Baruš

Then they coalesced in reverse of the manner in which they had divided. "The symmetry of this dividing and rejoining, and the fact that the smaller clouds were all the same size, lent the performance an eerie air, as if nature herself were suddenly the tool of some unseen organizing agency" (T. McKenna, 1993, pp. 157–158). The clouds grew darker, swirled inward, and formed what appeared to be a waterspout. McKenna "heard a high-pitched, ululating whine come drifting over the jungle tree tops" (T. McKenna, 1993, p. 158). He tried to shout, but no sound came out as he was gripped by fear. And then everything seemed to speed up as the cloud formed into "a saucer-shaped machine rotating slowly, with unobtrusive, soft, blue and orange lights" (T. McKenna, 1993, p. 158).

The flying saucer passed overhead and disappeared from sight. It was identical in appearance to the UFO in an infamous photograph widely assumed to be a picture of a vacuum cleaner end-cap. By having appeared "in a form that [cast] doubt on itself," it threw McKenna off more than it would have had "its seeming alienness [been] completely convincing" (T. McKenna, 1993, p. 159). In the end, McKenna did not know what to think. Perhaps it was a product of his imagination. After all, this early morning adventure occurred after weeks of ingesting psychedelic drugs. But what he saw "did not fall into any of the categories of hallucinated imagery" with which he was familiar. Rather, McKenna has suggested, what he saw was real, perhaps "the manifestation of something which in that instance chose to begin as mist and end as machine, but which could have appeared in any form, a manifestation of a humorous 'something's' omniscient control over the world of form and matter" (T. McKenna, 1993, p. 159).

Hallucinations are perceptions that do not correspond to physical reality (cf. Bentall, 2000; R. K. Siegel, 1975; Simons, Garrison, & Johnson, 2017). But can such misperceptions nonetheless occasionally be perceptions of possible nonphysical events from other dimensions of reality intruding into our subjective experience? Ordinarily we are locked into a particular way of thinking about reality. Our everyday world seems so real to us. Sometimes alterations of consciousness can open us to something unusual. As McKenna suggested, sometimes, perhaps, to something that appears to manipulate ordinary physical manifestation.

I have deliberately chosen an example of an experience in altered states of consciousness whose reality is ambiguous. There will be other examples of unusual experiences that appear to be products of the imagination and still others that are arguably veridical. What does the reader think? Was McKenna's perception a true hallucination or a sensation of something that truly exists? McKenna had recently not only been ingesting psychedelic drugs, he was also sleep deprived and emotionally aroused; he had been absorbed all night in his own thoughts; and perhaps he had entered a trance of some sort. But are such physiological and psychological factors the source of unusual experiences, or do they form a doorway into reality that is usually concealed from us? Conversely, are the physiological and psychological factors that lead to the ordinary waking state reliable mechanisms for encountering that which is real, or are they, rather, the source of experiences that obscure the real? This book is about alterations of consciousness, the vistas that they open for us, and the questions that they raise.

CONSCIOUSNESS

There are several things we need to do to get the conversation about alterations of consciousness off the ground. We need to define "consciousness" and "alterations of consciousness." However, even prior to that, it is helpful to identify the perspectives from which the study of consciousness is approached. And once we get going, I want to say a bit about the neuroscience of consciousness and anomalous phenomena. As we can see from the opening example, alterations of consciousness turn out to be more interesting than perhaps we expected.

Perspectives on Consciousness

There are three perspectives from which consciousness can be approached: the physiological, the cognitive, and the experiential. Each of these perspectives not only defines a domain of inquiry with its attendant epistemological approaches but is usually also associated with particular ways of thinking about consciousness.

The *physiological* perspective is concerned with the physiological processes involved in consciousness as studied usually within neuroscience using methods appropriate for the biological sciences. For instance, data could be gathered using brain imaging techniques to identify the parts of the brain that are involved in various cognitive tasks, including, for instance, practicing particular types of meditation. Those who engage in this type of research frequently also believe that brain processes, in some way or other, give rise to consciousness.

A somewhat separate aspect of the physiological perspective is that of *quantum mind*, a rubric for the conceptualization of possible direct links between subatomic processes and mental events as described by quantum mechanics or quantum field theory (e.g., Baruš, 1986, 2008b, 2008c, 2009; Lockwood, 1989; E. H. Walker, 2000). I will say a little bit more about this shortly but will not have an opportunity to develop it in any depth in this book.

The *cognitive* perspective is concerned with cognitive processes involved in consciousness, such as attention, perception, thinking, memory, decision making, and creativity. This perspective falls largely within cognitive science and the disciplines of psychology, philosophy, and computer science, whereby knowledge of cognitive events is acquired through the observation of behavior, including verbal behavior, and rational inquiry. Sometimes the assumption is made that cognition of any sort is the result of computational processes of a calculating device, such as the brain or a computer (cf. Ruffini, 2017).

The *experiential* perspective is concerned with the conscious experiences that people have for themselves. This perspective toward consciousness has sometimes been taken in psychology, philosophy, anthropology, and religious studies, and depends upon *introspection*, a person's examination of their own experiences, as its primary method of investigation (cf. Baruŝs, 2000a). This can also be regarded as a *phenomenological* perspective in that phenomena, as they are experienced, are considered as inherently meaningful events without reification necessarily into computational or neurological processes.

But such a tripartite division of discourse concerning consciousness raises questions. How do specific experiential events occur as cognitive processes? In turn, what are the physiological mechanics corresponding to specific cognitive processes? Obviously there are interconnections. For example, exposure to marijuana affects a person's brain, which in turn affects cognition and experience. But these interconnections can be quite complex given that, for example, some seasoned marijuana users can experience the effects of marijuana intoxication upon smoking marijuana cigarettes from which the main psychoactive ingredient has been removed (Jones, 1971). A person's belief that they are smoking a marijuana cigarette appears to be enough to provide them with an appropriate experience of marijuana intoxication. Our understanding of the processes in the brain corresponding to different phenomenal contents keeps improving (Havlík, 2017). Yet explanatory gaps remain between these domains of discourse. In particular, it is not clear how subjective experience could arise from computational or neural processes, a quandary that has sometimes been dubbed *the hard problem of consciousness* (cf. Chalmers, 1995; Jackendoff, 1987; Shear, 1996).

I think that it is important to engage all three perspectives, including their associated research strategies, as much as possible when trying to understand consciousness. Hence, all three approaches are used in this book. I will say more about the physiological perspective in a bit, but its inclusion in this book will be as user-friendly as possible, without assuming any knowledge of physiology on the part of readers. The experiential perspective receives more emphasis, so as to adequately document the varieties of alterations of consciousness and to open up a discussion of fundamental questions concerning their meaning, epistemology, and ontology.

Definitions of *Consciousness*

We use the word *consciousness*, but what do we mean by it? The word has four common meanings, which I distinguish primarily by numbering them with subscripts. Thus, *consciousness$_1$* refers to the registration of information and acting on it in a goal-directed manner; *behavioral consciousness$_2$* refers to the explicit knowledge of one's situation, mental states, and actions demonstrated behaviorally; *subjective consciousness$_2$* refers to the experiential stream of events that occurs subjectively for a person; and *consciousness$_3$* refers to the sense of existence of the subject of the experiential stream (Baruŝs, 1987). Let us look more closely at each of these definitions in turn.

Sometimes we are interested in distinguishing between an unresponsive state of an organism and one in which it is functioning normally within its environment. Such normal functioning is characterized by the ability to make discriminations among various stimuli, to process that information, and, at least minimally, to act in a goal-directed manner. That is the meaning of consciousness$_1$. To avoid arguments about how minimal or extensive the processing should be, let us say that the referent of the term consciousness$_1$ is a variable, of which there can be more or less. There is also no reason to restrict the term to biological organisms, so let us apply it also to computers, mechanical contrivances, and anything else that meets the criteria (Barušs, 1987). This definition is most closely associated with both the physiological and cognitive perspectives on consciousness.

If the processing of information is so sophisticated that an organism demonstrates substantial explicit knowledge of its own situation, internal states, and actions, then we say that it has behavioral consciousness$_2$. Ordinarily, this would apply to human beings but eventually could also apply to computers. However, this definition stems from an effort to capture from the outside the events of the experiential stream that occur on the inside, as it were, for individuals. Thoughts, feelings, and sensations occur for us in a streamlike manner within the confines of our subjective experience as noted by William James, one of the founders of modern psychology, whose ideas we will consider in Chapter 2. Subjective consciousness$_2$ refers to that experiential stream. Even though, for historical reasons, I have designated both of these definitions of consciousness as consciousness$_2$, the referent of the behavioral definition does not necessarily coincide with that of the subjective one. In particular, it could be possible for a person or a computer to demonstrate behavioral consciousness$_2$ but not to have subjective consciousness$_2$. The behavioral and subjective definitions belong, respectively, to the cognitive and experiential perspectives, thereby providing another way of characterizing the two sides of the explanatory gap that exists between those perspectives (Barušs, 1987, 2000a, 2008a).

The meaning of consciousness$_3$ is the most difficult to conceptualize. The word *consciousness* is sometimes used to try to capture the inimitable quality of being that one may have for oneself. This is a feeling of existence associated with being oneself that accompanies the contents of one's experience. If we use the word *qualia* to designate the feeling aspect of perception, then we could refer to the feeling of existence as *existential qualia* (Barušs & Mossbridge, 2017). The point is that this feeling is precisely not a feeling in the sense of being a content of one's experience, but rather the ground for there being any existence at all (Barušs, 1987). This referent of consciousness belongs to the experiential perspective on consciousness.

To illustrate the meanings of the word *consciousness*, we can imagine that we are driving a car when a traffic light turns red. Noticing the changed light and stopping the car would be consciousness$_1$. If we demonstrated that we explicitly realized that the light had turned red and that we had stopped the car, for example, by saying that the light had turned red and that we had moved our foot from the gas pedal to the brake pedal, then that would indicate the presence of behavioral consciousness$_2$. Whatever is going on in our experiential stream at the time would be subjective consciousness$_2$. Perhaps we are thinking about the changed light and the pedals. Or perhaps we are having a conversation about the previous Saturday's football game, and not about the light or the pedals. Consciousness$_3$ refers to the fact that we experience an experiential stream at all, irrespective of what we are thinking about. Notice that these distinctions need to be made since, for instance, from the point of view of subjective consciousness$_2$, consciousness$_1$ is usually not conscious. When I use the word *consciousness* without subscripts in this book, I will usually mean subjective consciousness$_2$ in the context of consciousness$_3$.

Neuroscience of Consciousness

Now that we have definitions of consciousness, we are in a better position to state the hard problem of consciousness. The hard problem of consciousness is the inability to explain how qualia and, in particular, existential qualia, could emerge from computational or neurological processes. So, that raises the question, what is the relationship of the brain to subjective consciousness$_2$ and consciousness$_3$? And what are the *neural correlates of consciousness* (NCC), as they have come to be called?

The obvious approach to finding the NCC is to use brain imaging techniques to see which parts of the brain are active only when consciousness is present. I will give a striking example of the power of such imaging in a bit. And the result? In my 35 years of reading the academic literature about consciousness and attending consciousness conferences, I have probably seen about 35 variations on which parts or functions of the brain are associated with consciousness, such as the front, the back, the middle, the left side, specific networks, specific frequencies of neural activity, electromagnetic activity, activity in microstructures of the brain, degree of connectivity, complexity, and so on. Let us just say that the question has not been settled (cf. Brogaard & Gatzia, 2016; Cavanna, Vilas, Palmucci, & Tagliazucchi, 2018; Demertzi et al., 2019; Havlík, 2017; Liu et al., 2017; Mateos et al., 2018; Tabatabaeian & Jennings, 2018).

I want to mention one recent candidate for the NCC, the *default mode network* (DMN). Suppose that I just sit here with my eyes closed without attending to sensory stimuli. Using brain imaging, a pattern of neural activity has been identified that appears to be "the baseline of neural activity" (Havlík, 2017, p. 75) and that is correlated to "the endogenous stream of subjective experience composed of self-directed cognitive content" (p. 76). In other words, a pattern of neural activity can be identified that corresponds to ruminations about ourselves, other people, the past, the future, and so on. We will consider this in greater detail in Chapter 2. But what, exactly, does this pattern of activity have to do with existential qualia? Good question. Note that we are looking from the outside, so the best we can ever do is to establish the neural correlates of behavioral consciousness$_2$.

But how likely is it even that subjective consciousness$_2$ and consciousness$_3$ emerge from a neural substrate? I have seen that assumption increasingly called into question. For instance, "Subjectivity is too radically different from anything physical for it to be an emergent phenomenon" (Koch, 2012, p. 119) although it could still, somehow, be a "physical" entity or process. Maybe we are just at the wrong level. I have been talking about neural activity. Neurons are cells in the body that are specialized for transmitting a signal. Why should those chemical "signals" be associated with existential qualia? Maybe we need to go down a level, especially if we are true reductionists (e.g., Churchland, 1980). Maybe the interface of consciousness and the brain is at the quantum level (Hameroff, 1994; Penrose, 1994; E. H. Walker, 1970). But then, the lines between matter and mind start to get a little blurry, so that, rather than explaining the mind using matter, we could end up explaining matter as mind (Baruss, 2006, 2008b, 2008c; Baruss & Mossbridge, 2017).

There are practical applications of neuroscience, as shown by the following example. Suppose that we have a patient in a so-called vegetative state whereby they are alive but unresponsive in any meaningful way to sensory stimuli. Could they still, nonetheless, be aware of what is going on, but be locked-in so that they are simply unable to generate a motor response to indicate their awareness? What if we use brain imaging techniques to see what is happening in such a person's brain when we present them with meaningful tasks? So we ask them to imagine that they are playing a vigorous game of tennis. Then we ask them to imagine that they are walking around from room to room in their residence. In a healthy person, an imaginary motor task and an imaginary navigation task are subsumed by different patterns of brain activity. That is also the case with some patients in a vegetative state! In other words, these patients can hear and understand the instructions, and comply with them. Now we could say, "Playing tennis means 'yes,' and walking around in your residence means 'no.' Are you in pain?" And we have established the presence of behavioral consciousness$_2$ and communication with the patient through the medium of the brain imaging technologies. Variations on these experiments have been carried out at several universities (Abdalmalak et al., 2017; Monti et al., 2010; Owen et al., 2006).

We clearly need neuroscience. But perhaps the physiological domain is not the critically important one for understanding the fundamental nature of consciousness. The journey of discovering the nature of consciousness could be more remarkable than we expected.

ALTERED STATES OF CONSCIOUSNESS

Let us turn now from consciousness to altered states of consciousness and consider some definitions and issues that their occurrence raises. How are we to define them? Altered states of consciousness have been studied for over 50 years by Charles Tart, whose edited book *Altered States of Consciousness* has become a classic in the psychology of consciousness (Tart, 1972a). Tart (1975) pointed out that we know what it is to be conscious in our everyday waking state. But suppose now that we were to fall asleep, or become hypnotized, or ingest psychoactive drugs, or meditate, or almost die. Our neurophysiology could change, our thinking could change, and our experience could be quite different from what it is in our everyday state. From the point of view of the person for whom it occurs, an *altered state of consciousness* is "a qualitative alteration in the overall pattern of mental functioning, such that the experiencer feels his consciousness is radically different from the way it functions ordinarily" (Tart, 1972c, p. 1203; see also Ludwig, 1966). From the point of view of an external observer, the presence of a radical shift of consciousness would have to be inferred from changes to a person's physiology and behavior (cf. Tart, 1972b). Note that, for Tart, an altered state of consciousness has been defined as a self-determined deviation away from a person's usual state of consciousness.

We could define altered states of consciousness more generally by specifying changes away from the ordinary waking state along some dimensions that we consider to be important. There is no single dimension or collection of dimensions that are considered to be the "correct" dimensions along which to look for the deviations (Schmidt & Berkemeyer, 2018). Here are some examples. Given that we have introduced three perspectives concerning consciousness, we can say that altered states of consciousness are stable patterns of physiological, cognitive, and experiential events different from those of the ordinary waking state. In order to be more precise, we can use our definitions of consciousness to say that altered states of consciousness are changes to the registration of information and acting upon it in a goal-directed manner (consciousness$_1$); the explicit knowledge of one's situation, mental states, and actions (behavioral consciousness$_2$); the stream of thoughts, feelings, and sensations that one has for oneself (subjective consciousness$_2$); and the sense of existence of the subject of mental acts (consciousness$_3$).

On the basis of responses from participants in a study who had been asked how they identified a state of consciousness in which they found themselves, Tart (1975) organized the resultant "experiential criteria for detecting an altered state of consciousness" (p. 12) into 10 categories, such as sensing the body, time sense, and interaction with the environment. There have also been proposed, among others, a "componential analysis of consciousness" (Hobson, 1997, p. 383) consisting of 10 components, a phenomenological mapping whereby altered states of consciousness are to be compared along 12 dimensions (Walsh, 1995), a phenomenological inventory for measuring changes to consciousness along 12 dimensions (Pekala, 1991), and a list of 14 dimensions of consciousness within which are included, attention, perception, imagery, inner speech, memory, decision-making, problem-solving, emotions, arousal, self-control, suggestibility, body image, personal identity, experience of time, and meaning (Farthing, 1992). Given that there is no standardized set of dimensions that is used for characterizing altered states of consciousness, in this book I use whichever dimensions seem most appropriate for the phenomena that we are discussing.

Alterations of Consciousness

Sometimes I will want to emphasize the stability and distinctiveness of specific patterns of physiological, cognitive, and experiential events, in which case I will use the terminology *altered states of consciousness*. Often, however, there is some question regarding the identification of a specific stable pattern of psychological functioning or the distinctions between apparently different states of consciousness disappear, so that I will use the looser expression *alterations of consciousness*. For example, is hypnosis a phenomenon in which there is a definite switch into a special state, or does it lie on a continuum with phenomena in the ordinary waking state (Woody, Drugovic, & Oakman, 1997)? In what state is a person who is asleep according to physiological measures but aware that they are asleep and able to communicate through observable behavior with those watching them (LaBerge & Gackenbach, 2000)? What of John Wren-Lewis (1988), who inadvertently ate poisoned candy, went into a coma, almost died, and has subsequently been in an almost continuous transcendent state of consciousness? Was his a drug-induced, near-death, or transcendent state? And what of McKenna's account given at the beginning of this chapter? In what state was he?

There is also a problem with the baseline for altered states. What is the ordinary waking state against which changes take place? If we accept Tart's definition of an altered state as subjectively different from a person's ordinary experience, then one person's ordinary waking state could be someone else's altered state. Wren-Lewis's transcendent state of consciousness is his ordinary state of being. The experiences of whole societies of people may be quite different from the experiences familiar to Western intellectual traditions. Such may have been the case, for example, with the native people who were living in parts of what are now Mexico and Central America before contact with Europeans (cf. Tompkins, 1990). We can also think of the ordinary waking state as the state of mind usually experienced in Western societies while awake. It turns out, however, that that state itself is not homogeneous but varies, sometimes dramatically, along the same dimensions that have been proposed for identifying altered states of consciousness (cf. R. Broughton, 1986). This leads to questions about whether alterations in the flux of waking consciousness, such as strong emotions or daydreaming, should be considered altered states of consciousness (cf, Farthing, 1992). In other words, the state of consciousness which is to be taken as the baseline is neither universal nor uniform but could itself be conceptualized as a collection of altered states (cf. Csikszentmihalyi & Nakamura, 2018).

It should be noted as well that the moniker *altered state* is not an explanation for psychological events but a shorthand description of the complexity of psychological processes characterizing any given altered state. In other words, the discussion is about psychological events anyway, whether or not they are labeled as "altered," so that the use of the term *altered state* is not essential. But stripping the moniker *altered state* from patterns of psychological functioning raises another point. Privileging the ordinary waking state in these definitions appears to add unnecessary value judgments about the "normality" of the ordinary waking state relative to other states. If we think about it, were it not for these definitions, the ordinary waking state would just be one of many "altered states" (cf. Facco, Agrillo, & Greyson, 2015; but see also Revonsuo, Kallio, & Sikka, 2009).

For the reasons given here, it seems to me that it is not always necessary to try to identify discrete, stable states but enough to just talk about alterations of consciousness. Sometimes I will use the term *altered state* to emphasize the distinctiveness and stability of a pattern of psychological functioning and alteration when the pattern of psychological functioning is less well delineated or more fluid.

Altered States and Psychopathology

There has been a tendency in the past, in Western cultures, to regard the ordinary waking state as the optimal state and all other states, except for that of sleep, as forms of mental illness (cf. Baruš, 2000b; Tart, 1972b). Certainly, some alterations of consciousness, such as those that occur in the mental disorder schizophrenia, fall within the pathological range, but that is quite a different matter from regarding alterations of consciousness themselves as symptoms of schizophrenia or some other pathology. For example, a shaman in an indigenous culture may undertake a soul journey in order to resolve a problem in the community. Their journey may involve the deliberate cultivation of an altered state of consciousness, separation from their body, traveling in a world different from that of ordinary reality, encountering spirits, searching for information or power that can resolve the problem, reentering their body, and implementing the results of their journey in the community (Walsh, 1995). Or at least, that is how the shaman would describe the events of their journey. We might say that these events transpire within the realm of their imagination. But in the past, we have gone further and labeled the shaman's experiences as symptoms of "epilepsy, hysteria, [or] schizophrenia" or regarded the shaman as an "imposter or con man" (Walsh, 2007, p. 94). However, as we shall see in Chapter 6, careful comparisons between schizophrenia and soul journeying, for instance, reveal that they are not the same.

Analyses of autobiographical accounts of experiences in schizophrenia, psychedelic drug intoxication, mystical experiences, and the ordinary waking state reveal that they are more different from one another than alike and that whereas "the description of the schizophrenic experience points to a devalued, negative sense of self, both of the other 'altered states' are associated with a vocabulary connoting a sense of self-enhancement" (Oxman, Rosenberg, Schnurr, Tucker, & Gala, 1988, p. 406). As we examine different alterations of consciousness in the course of this book, we will frequently consider the extent to which they are pathological, since that is a question that naturally arises.

That experiences in altered states of consciousness are not to be regarded as necessarily pathological does not mean that they cannot, nonetheless, disrupt a person's life. For example, disruption often occurs after near-death experiences (NDEs), which are events sometimes reported by a person to have occurred around the time that they were close to death. They may report having experienced a feeling of peace, separation from their body, witnessing of events occurring within the vicinity of their body, encounters with deceased relatives or spiritual beings, the presence of a loving light, and a panoramic life review. Subsequently a person may come to believe that death is not the end of life, that our usual concerns about our material well-being are unimportant, and that the purpose of life is to love one another. Despite the positive nature of most NDEs, a person may experience anger and depression at having been brought back to life, career interruptions, fear of ridicule and rejection, alienation from their relatives and acquaintances, and broken relationships including divorce. Many of these problems appear to result from the experiencer's inability to reconcile their altered sense of reality and changed values with the materialistic concerns of the people with whom they must interact (Atwater, 2007; Holden, Greyson, & James, 2009).

I think it is important to point out one more thing as we begin our discussion of altered states of consciousness, and that is their importance for understanding the psyche more generally. Consistent with what we have already been discussing, the ordinary waking state is just one of a range of alterations of consciousness, yet the academic understanding of consciousness and the psyche are almost exclusively based on what can be learned through an examination of events during the ordinary waking state of consciousness. This necessarily creates a distorted knowledge base about the psyche, which can be rectified by taking into account information gathered from alterations of consciousness (Barušs, 2012).

ANOMALOUS PHENOMENA

Anomalous phenomena are phenomena that fall outside the explanatory range of normative beliefs about reality (cf. Barušs & Mossbridge, 2017). They are more likely to occur in the context of altered states of consciousness (Honorton, 1974; Krippner & George, 1986; cf. Luke, 2011). What reaction do you have, as a reader, to these types of phenomena? Let us look at the range of beliefs about reality that underlie our ideas about what is possible, and then consider the evidence for some of these types of phenomena more carefully.

Material Versus Transcendent Beliefs

Robert Moore and I found in a survey of 334 academics and professionals, who could write about consciousness in the academic literature, that there is a material-transcendent dimension within Western intellectual traditions. The *material* or *materialist* pole is represented by the notion that reality is entirely physical in nature, apparently in the sense that the world is essentially a machine that functions in a deterministic manner. For the materialist, all phenomena, including consciousness, result from physical processes. Transcendent beliefs had two gradations, which we labeled as *conservatively transcendent* and *extraordinarily transcendent*. For those tending toward the conservatively transcendent position, spirituality and meaning are important. They are dualists, who believe that there is a mental aspect to reality as well as a physical one. Those tending toward the *extraordinarily transcendent* position claim to have had experiences that science cannot explain, such as transcendent or out-of-body experiences. For them, the physical world is a manifestation of consciousness rather than consciousness being a by-product of physical processes. Materialists, those who believe that the world is a physical place, would likely be interested in the physiological and cognitive aspects of consciousness and think of consciousness as an emergent property of the brain or a computing device, or as information in an information-processing system. Those who would be identified with a conservatively transcendent position tend to emphasize the subjective, experiential aspects of consciousness and believe that consciousness gives meaning to reality and provides evidence of a spiritual dimension. Those identified with the extraordinarily transcendent position seem to be less interested in the ordinary waking state and emphasize altered states of consciousness. For them, consciousness is the fundamental reality to be understood through a process of self-transformation (Barušs, 1990, 2008a; Barušs & Moore, 1989, 1992, 1997, 1998; cf. Reggia, Huang, & Katz, 2015).

Moore's and my use of the word *materialist* to designate a particular empirically derived cluster of beliefs is consistent with the use of that term in philosophy (e.g., Lycan, 1987). Sometimes it appears that materialists conceptualize the world as made up of tiny colliding particles that behave in predictable patterns like billiard balls on a billiard table and believe that everything can ultimately be explained by such interactions. Such a conceptualization is *mechanistic* and *deterministic*. Others, who could be called *physicalists*, maintain that everything is physical in whatever way physicists will eventually determine that to be. Usually, there appears to be an accompanying assumption that what physicists will find will not depart too greatly from one's normative conceptions of what it means for something to be physical. A materialist position is *reductionistic* in that psychological phenomena, such as consciousness, are considered to be ultimately dependent on physical processes even if the details of such reductions, in principle, remain opaque to the investigator. These are also the *conventional* ways of thinking about the nature of reality that are widely accepted within science (cf. Barušs, 1996; 2001a; Barušs & Mossbridge, 2017). In this book, while one or another of these more specific expressions will be used when such precision is necessary, in general the term *materialist* will be used to designate the belief that the world is ultimately physical in nature, whatever the details of that conceptualization may be.

Notice that we have directly contradictory beliefs about the nature of reality—reality is entirely physical versus reality is entirely mental—with variations in between. At some point, something has to give. Historically, within science, transcendent ideologies have given way to materialist ideologies. However, it turns out that there are a number of problems with materialist interpretations of reality, suggesting that the scales could tip in the other direction. It is materialism, in fact, that has poor goodness-of-fit to the data. The following are some of the arguments that have been made against materialism (Baruša, 1993; Baruša & Mossbridge, 2017).

First, it turns out that matter, at subatomic levels, violates our everyday intuitions about its nature and does not behave in the mechanical fashion that we might suppose that it would (Baruša, 1996). In an odd reversal of character, "the universe begins to look more like a great thought than like a great machine" (Jeans, 1937, p. 186). Second, there is a philosophical problem. All that we can ever know directly are our experiences, which appear to go on for us within our subjective domains. From our experiences, we must infer the independent existence of an objective world if materialism is to be correct. And such an inference is not automatic (Lipson, 1987). Third is a problem that we will encounter repeatedly in this book, namely, the need for any materialist theory to adequately account for anomalous phenomena (Baruša, 1993), a problem about which there has been considerable controversy (e.g., R. S. Broughton, 1991, Cardeña, Lynn, & Krippner, 2000; Irwin, 1994; Kurtz, 1985; Radin, 1997; Zusne & Jones, 1989). To illustrate the problem posed by anomalous phenomena, let me use as an example a series of studies that was done to try to detect the presence of the transfer of information through some mechanism other than sensory perception—in other words, to try to find extrasensory perception.

Anomalous Information Transfer

A series of studies was conducted over the course of 6½ years in which a method called the *Ganzfeld procedure* was used in order to try to demonstrate the existence of extrasensory perception. Suppose that extrasensory perception consists of the mental detection of a weak signal that is ordinarily masked by internal somatic and external sensory stimulation. The idea behind the Ganzfeld procedure is to seek to minimize the somatic and sensory noise. This is done by having a participant in the study, the receiver, recline in a chair in an acoustically isolated, electrically shielded room. "Translucent ping-pong ball halves are taped over the [receiver's] eyes and headphones are placed over [their] ears" (Bem & Honorton, 1994, p. 5). A red floodlight is directed toward their eyes and white noise is played through the headphones in order to produce a visually and acoustically "homogeneous perceptual environment that is called the *Ganzfeld*" (Bem & Honorton, 1994, p. 5). Before turning on the floodlight and noise, the receiver is led through a 14-minute relaxation exercise whose purpose is to lower internal somatic stimulation. Then the receiver is subjected to the Ganzfeld for 30 minutes while they report aloud their thoughts and images to the experimenter who is in the room together with them. In the meantime, there is a sender in a separate acoustically isolated, electrically shielded room, in many cases a friend of the receiver brought along to the experimental session for the purpose of acting as sender.

Prior to the beginning of the series of Ganzfeld experiments considered here, 160 potential targets had been prepared, 80 of which were still pictures and 80 of which were video segments with sound of about 1 minute in duration. The groups of static and dynamic targets had each been arranged in 20 sets of four in such a way as "to minimize similarities among targets within a set" (Bem & Honorton, 1994, p. 9). At the time of a Ganzfeld session, a controlling computer randomly selected a target from one of the 40 sets of targets and repeatedly presented it "to the sender during the ganzfeld period" (Bem & Honorton, 1994, p. 9). Following the Ganzfeld period, the computer randomly ordered the four potential targets in the set from which the actual target had been drawn and presented them to the receiver on a television monitor to be judged by them with regard to their resemblance to the thoughts and images that had occurred for them during the Ganzfeld period. Once the receiver had judged the images, the sender came into the receiver's room and "revealed the identity of the target to both the receiver and the experimenter" (Bem & Honorton, 1994, p. 10).

The experiment has been designed in such a way that there is no possibility that either the receiver or the experimenter could know the identity of the target that has been used, or even the target set from which it has been drawn, until the actual target has been revealed to them at the end of the Ganzfeld period by the sender. Several dozen researchers, including known critics of this type of research, have examined the automated Ganzfeld protocol and "expressed satisfaction with the handling of security issues and controls" (Bem & Honorton, 1994, p. 10). In addition, two magicians who specialize in the simulation of psychic phenomena have examined the automated Ganzfeld system and declared that it was secure from deception by subjects. In a review of methodological issues in a number of research areas, the Ganzfeld studies were found to "regularly meet the basic requirements of sound experimental design" (Bem & Honorton, 1994, p. 9). In other words, whatever the results that may be found, they should not be attributed to inattention to proper experimental procedures.

In the series of Ganzfeld studies discussed here, there were 240 receivers, 140 women and 100 men, with a mean age of 37 years, who participated in a total of 354 sessions of which 329 were used for the primary data analyses. Whereas one would expect about 25% of the targets to be correctly identified by chance, that is to say, about 82 targets, in fact 106 targets were correctly identified, giving a statistically significant hit rate of 32%. Dynamic targets proved to be more effective than static ones, with hit rates of 37% and 27% for the dynamic and static targets, respectively. In 20 sessions, 20 undergraduate students in drama, music, and dance from the Juilliard School in New York City correctly identified 10 of the 20 targets for a hit rate of 50%, thereby suggesting the presence of a relationship between creativity or artistic ability and performance on extrasensory perception tasks. The 32% overall hit rate is just below the postulated level at which a careful observer could see the effect with the naked eye without recourse to statistical analyses. It corresponds to an observer witnessing a correct identification about every third session rather than about every fourth session, as would be the case if the results were occurring by chance. These findings demonstrate the high probability of the presence of anomalous information transfer, that is to say, extrasensory perception, when using the Ganzfeld procedure (Bem, 1994; Bem & Honorton, 1994).

Despite the apparent care with which this series of studies was carried out, the conclusions drawn from them as well as from other Ganzfeld studies have been contested on various grounds (e.g., Hyman, 1994; Milton, 1999; Milton & Wiseman, 1999). But the objections to the conclusions have also been contested (Bem, 1994; Storm & Ertel, 2001). I leave it to the interested reader to consult the details of the arguments and make up their own mind. If the results are sound, as indeed they appear to be, then they need to be explained; they pose, by their nature, a challenge to the materialist interpretation of reality.

Military Remote Viewing

There is a certain luxury being an academic who can ponder whether or not something is really happening or not, in the sense that there are no direct consequences of protracted pondering. For military personnel, however, it is a different matter. There is continuous pressure to improve military capabilities. So, for instance, if there were to be ways in which intelligence gathering could potentially be improved, then it is reasonable to act quickly to research and develop them.

So it was that Hal Puthoff, a physicist at Stanford Research Institute involved in laser research, was minding his own business one day in 1972 when a couple of "visitors" from the Central Intelligence Agency (CIA) showed up (Puthoff, 1996, p. 65). The Soviet Union appeared to be funding paranormal research, and the CIA wanted to know whether the United States was missing out on anything that was really happening. This led to a secret research program at SRI by Puthoff and his physicist colleague Russell Targ, which had $49,909 in funding. They decided that the usual monikers, such as *extrasensory perception*, carried too much ideological baggage, so they came up with the term *remote viewing* as a descriptor for the apparent perception of events that are inaccessible to the physical senses (Schnabel, 1997; cf. P. H. Smith, 2011).

Among other methods, they used a straightforward research protocol, whereby an "outbound" agent would go to a site in the San Francisco Bay area, chosen randomly from a longer list, while a remote viewer in the lab would describe whatever impressions they had (Schnabel, 1997, p. 148). Independent judges matched the descriptions to potential targets. In some cases, the CIA monitors themselves functioned as the remote viewers and were sufficiently successful to conclude that "there was something to remote viewing" (Puthoff, 1996, p. 66).

As they continued with their research, Puthoff and Targ found that some people were just better at remote viewing than others. In particular, one of their remote viewers, Pat Price, could produce strikingly accurate information. In a variation of the previous protocol, called *coordinate remote viewing*, Price was given the latitude and longitude of a target of "ongoing operational significance," as well as being told that it was "an R&D test facility" (Puthoff, 1996, p. 69). Price had the impression that he was lying on his back, on top of a building, looking up at a large gantry crane that ran on parallel tracks, one on each side of the building (Targ, 1996). He then drew a sketch of the gantry crane. The site turned out to be a "super-secret Soviet atomic bomb laboratory at Semipalatinsk" in the northeast corner of Kazakhstan (Targ, 1996, p. 82). Price's sketch closely matches the image of a gantry crane on a tracing of a satellite photograph of the site (Targ, 1996). It is now known that more than 110 nuclear weapons were detonated above ground at that site between 1949 and 1963, with ongoing concern about the long-term effects of radiation poisoning on the people living downwind from it (Yan, 2019).

Remote viewing research and operations continued to develop (May, 1996), with some of these activities becoming declassified in 1995 (P. H. Smith, 2011). Some of the participants wrote popular books about their experiences (e.g., Graff, 2000; Morehouse, 1996; cf. Mandelbaum, 2000). All of that led to considerable popular interest in remote viewing and the founding of the nonprofit, volunteer International Remote Viewing Association in 1999 (P. H. Smith, 2011).

Subsequently, protocols similar to the outbound remote viewing protocol were used at the Princeton Engineering Anomalies Research (PEAR) laboratory at Princeton University, where a method of scoring was devised that allowed for the assignment of a level of statistical significance to the correspondence of a description to its target. At the PEAR lab, a total of 336 formal trials resulted in highly statistically significant results ($z = 6.36$, $p < .00005$; Dobyns, 2015; Nelson, Dunne, Dobyns, & Jahn, 1996).

I have used the PEAR protocol a number of times as a demonstration for students by sending a research assistant to a location of their choice and having the students fill out the PEAR scoring sheets. It is an interesting experience for students to see what happens when they try remote viewing for themselves. In addition, one of my undergraduate students carried out a remote viewing research project with assistance from one of the officers who had been involved in the clandestine activities, and I have had extensive conversations with several of them to fill in the details of the nuances of these phenomena.

THE SCIENTIFIC STUDY OF CONSCIOUSNESS

The evidence for the occurrence of at least some types of anomalous phenomena, such as remote viewing, is overwhelming. In fact, Julia Mossbridge and I wrote an entire book, *Transcendent Mind* (Baruss & Mossbridge, 2017), in which, among other things, we carefully review the evidence for the occurrence of anomalous events and conclude unequivocally that these sorts of things really are happening. And we are not the only ones who have reached this conclusion (cf. Bem, 2011; Braude, 2007; Cardeña, 2018; Goertzel & Goertzel, 2015; Roe, Sonnex, & Roxburgh, 2015; S. A. Schwartz, 2015; Tart, 2009; Watt & Tierney, 2014). The purpose of science is to follow the evidence, but there has frequently been considerable resistance to even examining the evidence; so what is going on here (Barušs, 1996)? To understand that, we need to go back to beliefs about reality and then consider the politics of science.

Transcendent Beliefs

The thrust in the past has been to characterize those who believe in the reality of anomalous phenomena as cognitively inferior to disbelievers. In a study in which undergraduate university students were required to critically evaluate favorable or unfavorable study reports of extrasensory perception, researchers found that "those participants who received a report which challenged their own *a priori* beliefs rated the study as of poorer quality than did those whose beliefs were in sympathy with or neutral towards the paper's conclusions" (Roe, 1999, p. 92). There was no support for the contention that believers are less proficient at critical thinking than nonbelievers. Note that this is just an instance of the *confirmation bias*, whereby a person seeks out and accepts only those ideas that conform to their previously held beliefs and avoids encountering and rejects any information that could challenge those beliefs (cf. Barušs & Mossbridge, 2017).

One of my undergraduate thesis students found some evidence to suggest that, among university undergraduate students, transcendent beliefs are associated with a personality characteristic called "understanding" that is essentially concerned with interest in the pursuit of rational knowledge about the world. Furthermore, she found that those who tend toward a conservatively transcendent position are "more curious about the world, more open to experience, strive more conscientiously toward goals in life, and are less concerned about what others think of them than those with materialist beliefs," while those tending toward an extraordinarily transcendent position "are not only more curious, open to the world, and unconcerned about others perceptions of them, but they also tend to be unorganized, adventurous, and spontaneous" (Jewkes & Barušs, 2000, p. 97). A correspondence between transcendent beliefs and understanding was again found in a replication study at another university, although the results were weaker and were found only for a sample of undergraduate students and not for participants solicited through the internet (E. James, 2001).

However, this does raise a question. Understanding is a facet of the personality trait "openness." And there is a known positive correlation between openness and intelligence. So, is transcendence related to intelligence? In order to test this relationship, another one of my undergraduate thesis students administered the Beliefs About Consciousness and Reality Questionnaire, designed by Robert Moore and myself, as well as an intelligence test, the Jackson Multidimensional Aptitude Battery—II, to 39 undergraduate students from the participant pool at our university college. The result is yes. All of the statistically significant scales and subscales had positive correlations between transcendence and IQ; none was negative. In particular, a key item of the questionnaire "There is no reality other than the physical universe" had a strong negative correlation with Full Scale IQ ($r = -.48$, $p = .002$, two-tailed). For this small sample of undergraduate students, intelligence was strongly correlated with believing that there is more to reality than the physical universe (as quoted in Lukey & Baruss, 2005, p. 265).

The Politics of Science

Science is an open-ended exploration of reality based on logical thinking about empirical observations. *Scientism*, as it has sometimes been dubbed, is the adherence to a materialist version of reality that confines investigation to those sorts of things that are permitted by materialism (Baruss, 1996). But materialism presents an obstacle to the study of consciousness. I have already noted some of the problems with materialism, described a series of studies concerning anomalous information transfer, and mentioned the ubiquity of reports of anomalous phenomena in alterations of consciousness. In other words, there are challenges to materialism that appear to become particularly pronounced with the study of consciousness. Hence it seems ill-advised that a discussion of alterations of consciousness begin with the assumption that materialism is the correct interpretation of reality.

Insistence on a materialistic approach may be due in part to the *politics of science* (cf. Kellehear, 1996), whereby "major segments of public and private policy and expenditure for research, development, construction, production, education, and publication throughout the world" are controlled by those who are "consumed with refinements and deployments of mid-20th century science" (Jahn, 2001, p. 24) so that, among other things, conventional interpretations of data are encouraged. Indeed, I myself have experienced censure for failing to conform to materialist beliefs. Yet it seems to me that in spite of political pressure to do so, it is counterproductive to insist that phenomena associated with consciousness always be reified in physical terms.

Is anything changing? Is there really a "sea change," as Julia Mossbridge and I have suggested (Baruss & Mossbridge, 2017, p. 3)? That is difficult to assess. It seems to me that materialists still get to play in the central circus ring, while those of us who challenge materialism get to be sideshows (e.g., Holvenstot, 2011; see also Sommer, 2014). This raises the question of who has the power to set the agenda. At the moment, the power still lies with materialists, so that a consciousness researcher can either opt in or be left out (Baruss & Mossbridge, 2017). There have been efforts to change that. The Academy for the Advancement of Postmaterialist Sciences was founded in 2017 for the purpose of normalizing and promoting postmaterialism in the academy (G. E. Schwartz et al., 2018). It remains to be seen whether anything will actually create a shift in power.

There is another variation on thinking about these issues, and that is to introduce the notion of a *boggle threshold*, or "the degree to which a person is willing to deviate from normative beliefs" (Barušs & Mossbridge, 2017, p. 24). Each person appears to have a boggle threshold, with some people being willing to accept the possibility of the occurrence of specific anomalous phenomena more so than others. Science appears to have little to do with this, although appeals to science are common when one insists that something is not happening, for instance, by simply labeling any research demonstrating whatever it is that is not supposed to be happening as *pseudoscience* (Barušs & Mossbridge, 2017). Ironically, forgoing actual empirical investigation in favor of preconceptions in the name of science is not science, but real "pseudoscience." And some of those who call themselves "skeptics" are not skeptics but, more accurately, *true believers in materialism*. But these can all be seen as differences in the settings of the boggle threshold, so that there is no point in arguing with someone who already thinks they know what is and is not possible.

The problem is that we cannot have a balanced discussion of alterations of consciousness if we begin by insisting that people's experiences cannot possibly be what they appear to be whenever they fail to conform to our beliefs about the world. Some version of materialism may yet turn out to be correct, but such an explanation has to follow from the data and cannot be insisted upon at the outset. We need to set aside personal predilections and political pressures so that we can objectively examine the evidence. The purpose in this book is not to convince the reader of any particular interpretation of reality, but rather to present for their consideration a variety of phenomena that occur during alterations of consciousness along with some of the explanations, materialist and transcendentalist, that have been proposed for them. Perhaps the reader's boggle threshold will be challenged. But in the end, they will, of course, make up their own mind.

OVERVIEW

We now have the context for our empirical investigation of alterations of consciousness. Before getting started on them, let me briefly give an overview of the topics that we will consider and introduce 11 thematic threads that run through the material in this book.

Outline

We started out in this chapter by discussing the study of consciousness and circumscribed the subject area of alterations of consciousness. We noted that consciousness researchers range along a material–transcendent dimension of beliefs about consciousness and reality. Problems with materialism, including challenges posed by anomalous phenomena, such as anomalous information transfer in the Ganzfeld studies, remind us that we need to remain open-minded when considering alterations of consciousness as required in the practice of science.

In Chapter 2, we will consider the ordinary waking state, starting with the question of access and then working our way deeper and deeper into the nature of the experiential stream of consciousness. Thus, we will start by examining introspection, then discussing the characteristics of thinking, daydreaming, mind wandering, uses of the imagination, and the pronounced interior experiences of sensory restriction. In the process of examining the ordinary waking state we will see that it already embodies some alterations and presages phenomena found in altered states. In Chapter 3, we will consider the prototypical altered state of consciousness, namely, sleep, beginning with physiological and phenomenological descriptions of the sleep stages, and then go on to discuss the remarkable benefits of sleep, the effects of drugs on sleep, and some of the sleep disorders. The study of sleep itself is relatively uncontroversial. However, such is not the case with the study of dreams, the subject matter of Chapter 4. In our discussion of dreams we will consider dream theories, dream research, working with dreams, lucid dreaming, precognitive dreaming, and shared dreaming.

The second half of the book is concerned with particularly controversial alterations of consciousness starting with Chapter 5, hypnosis. We will consider what it is like to be hypnotized, research concerning hypnosis, explanations of hypnosis, the apparent hypnotic enhancement of memory, and practical applications of hypnosis. Some of the phenomena associated with hypnosis are found again in shamanism, channeling, dissociative disorders, and alien abduction experiences, discussed in Chapter 6. In Chapter 7, we will consider drug-induced alterations, particularly those induced by the classic psychedelics, and some of the drawbacks and benefits of their use. At the end of Chapter 7, we will also discuss the Good Friday experiment as well as a follow-up replication of it. This will lead us, in Chapter 8, into various accounts of events in transcendent states of consciousness including persistent transcendent states of consciousness, along with some explanations for them and methods such as meditation aimed at inducing them. In Chapter 9, after considering alterations of consciousness associated with death, such as out-of-body experiences, near-death experiences, and past-life experiences, we will consider the possibility of the survival of consciousness after death. In Chapter 10, we will have an opportunity to reflect back on the phenomena discussed in the earlier chapters, to present an alternative theory of consciousness, to draw some conclusions, and to indicate directions for further research.

Thematic Threads

There are 11 thematic threads running through the book associated with fundamental questions about the nature of consciousness, some of which reflect some of the controversies regarding alterations of consciousness. We have already considered some of these thematic threads. The first is concerned with the perspective taken when approaching consciousness, whether that is *physiological, cognitive,* or *experiential.* The second is that of *material* versus *transcendent* beliefs about consciousness and reality. Both of these threads pervade the various altered states. The third thread is concerned with the question of whether events that occur in alterations of consciousness are *delusional* or *veridical.* For example, was McKenna hallucinating, or did he see something that was really present? The fourth thread is related to the third in that it is concerned with whether a phenomenon is actually *mundane* or *extraordinary* in nature. Are near-death experiences interesting but ultimately mundane in nature, or is there something extraordinary about them?

The fifth thread is concerned with whether or not a phenomenon is *meaningless* or *meaningful.* This applies, for example, to the question of dreams: Are dreams meaningful? But then, if some events are meaningful, are they meaningful in the same manner as meaningfulness is established during the ordinary waking state, or is there an increased depth of meaning such as that which apparently occurs during transcendent states? We will refer to these two dimensions constituting the sixth thematic thread as *lateral* versus *vertical.* Using the example of shamanism, we have already considered the question of whether experiences that occur during alterations of consciousness are pathological or normal. But they could also be instances of exceptional well-being. Thus we have the seventh thread of *psychopathology* versus *well-being* concerning the degree of psychopathology, normality, or exceptional well-being associated with specific experiences. Related to the seventh thread is the eighth concerning the extent to which alterations are *dangerous* versus *beneficial.* Are some altered states dangerous, such as intoxication with psychedelic drugs, whereas others are beneficial, such as sleep? The ninth thread is concerned with the *nature of the self.* For example, is the self a homogeneous aspect of our psyche as we ordinarily think of it, or is it fragmented as it appears to be in some dissociated states. Or does it even exist? The 10th thread is concerned with whether or not the psyche is *open* or *closed.* The Ganzfeld studies, among others, raise the question of whether consciousness is skull-bound or not. And, finally, with the 11th thread, *volition* versus *surrender,* we are concerned with the degree with which volition is experienced in altered states, such as during hypnosis. And surrender has sometimes been regarded as a therapeutic strategy during dysphoric psychedelic experiences, and as a prerequisite for experiencing transcendent states of consciousness.

These 11 thematic threads, sometimes identified as such, will recur as we make our way through the material in this book. My thesis is that paying attention to such fundamental questions about alterations of consciousness forces us to reconsider our ideas about the nature of consciousness and reality. Perhaps the world is a more interesting place than we usually think.

2

Wakefulness

In this chapter, we briefly examine the ordinary waking state of consciousness. It is something that we take for granted, but do we know what it really is like? What is the nature of our ordinary waking consciousness? Well, that is perhaps too broad a question. We would have to summarize considerable tracts of current psychological research in order to answer it, since the ordinary waking state is implicitly the subject matter of much of the discipline of psychology. Perhaps we can ask the more circumscribed question of what it is that goes on for us ordinarily in our experiential stream when we are awake. What are the contents of subjective consciousness$_2$? How are those contents structured? What are their dynamics? I suppose we could say that it is thinking that goes on, as our experiential stream has often been characterized (cf. Holyoak & Spellman, 1993; Markman & Gentner, 2001), but it encompasses, more generally, thoughts, perceptions, feelings, emotions, imaginings, and so on.

Note that by alluding to an experiential stream we are adopting the experiential perspective. We are considering consciousness from the inside. So we need to look at the methodology, introspection, that we are going to use in order to gather information about inner experience. Let me do that by considering introspection in the context of the history of the study of consciousness. Then go back to the late 19th century to look at what introspection revealed to William James, one of the founding figures of the discipline of psychology. From there we will pursue an investigation of the breadth and depth of our inner experience by looking at the contemporary study of the dimensions of thinking,

http://dx.doi.org/10.1037/0000200-002
Alterations of Consciousness: An Empirical Analysis for Social Scientists, Second Edition,
by I. Barušs

daydreaming, mind-wandering, the unexpected impact of our mentation on our bodies and the bodies of those around us, and finally, states of sensory restriction, in which sensory input has been attenuated.

As we proceed, the richness of our inner life will become revealed, and we will see how readily consciousness can be altered so that there is nothing ordinary about the ordinary waking state. It is really just another alteration of consciousness. Clusters of our thematic threads surface in this chapter, in the history of the study of consciousness, and again when considering the relationship of the imagination to immune function. and, at the end, in a discussion of sensed presences. As we shall see, challenging questions about consciousness and reality are raised even without entering the dramatic altered states of consciousness of the later chapters of this book.

INTROSPECTION

Introspection has had a long and troubled history as a method for studying the mind. Let us go not too far back, just to the time of the founding of psychology and the modern beginnings of introspection and the study of consciousness, then consider the more recent deconstruction of inner experience by behaviorists and computationalists, and end with some practical guidelines for using introspection for the investigation of consciousness.

Modern Beginnings

Wilhelm Wundt, a German professor with a background in physiology, has often been touted as the founder of psychology as a laboratory science in the late 19th century. Although Wundt recognized that the data of science about objective phenomena were derived from the experiences of scientists, he rejected the notion that scientists could understand experience itself through the unaided self-observations of others. Rather, his procedure of "experimental introspection" (Hilgard, 1987, p. 44) was confined to research concerning sensation and perception in which laboratory instruments were used to vary the stimuli. The result was that the stimulus conditions were so controlled and the demands on the observer so limited that the process of observation "came to resemble in all important respects external, ordinary perception" (Lyons, 1986, p. 4). In practice, for example, Wundt would present a participant in a study with a simple colored shape using a tachistoscope (a device for presenting visual stimuli for brief time periods) and ask questions about the shape's size, intensity, and duration.

The method of introspection used by Wundt was a version of what Franz Brentano had called *inner perception*, the discrete noticing of what was happening to mental events as they occurred without interfering with them. Mental events, so it was believed, "by their very nature forced themselves into our notice" (Lyons, 1986, p. 4). The idea was to perceive indirectly, out of the corner of one's mental eye, as it were, "mental phenomena as they went about their business" (Lyons, 1986, p. 4). The alternative to inner perception was *inner observation*, the direct focusing on one's inner mental life. This, according to Brentano, would not work because attention would be drawn away from the "mental life of thoughts, feelings, and volitions" (Lyons, 1986, p. 4), thereby devitalizing or destroying the very mental events that one was trying to observe.

But not everyone was enthusiastic about such a constrained research program. "There is little of the grand style about these new prism, pendulum, and chronograph-philosophers," said William James (1890/1983, p. 192). He accused the experimentalists of being boring. For James, "*Introspective Observation is what we have to rely on first and foremost and always.* The word introspection need hardly be defined—it means, of course, the looking into our own minds and reporting what we there discover" (W. James, 1890/1983, p. 185; italics in original). No mere noticing for James, but looking. However, James was not insensitive to the various problems associated with inner observation, so he ended up with the notion that mental states could only be examined and reported once they had already occurred. In other words, James's introspection was *retrospection*, whereby a person examines their memory of that which has previously transpired (Lyons, 1986). James acknowledged that such a method was "difficult and fallible," but he maintained that "the difficulty is simply that of all observation of whatever kind" (W. James, 1890/1983, p. 191, emphasis removed).

There were other approaches to introspection at the time, but in psychology the whole discussion about introspection was extinguished in the early part of the 20th century with the rise of behaviorism. Psychologists became interested in the behavior evoked in an organism by specific stimulus situations and the manner in which stimulus–response associations could be changed (Hilgard, 1987). In his 1919 book, John Watson said that "the reader will find no discussion of consciousness" nor reference to any mental activity given that Watson had found that he could "get along without them both in carrying out investigations and in presenting psychology as a system to [his] students" (Watson, 1919, p. viii). Until the 1950s, and, in many cases until much later, psychologists by and large dismissed consciousness and introspection as myths or, at least, regarded them "as items that were not amenable to investigation by a scientific psychology" (Lyons, 1986, p. 47). Such a conclusion is relevant to our fifth thematic thread, in that internal, subjective events are regarded as being meaningless. Philosophers continued to discuss introspection, as a process by which one part of the brain scans another, for example, but the theories that they advanced were also not without problems.

The Computational Approach

The development of information theory and the advent of computing machines in the 1950s brought new ways of thinking about the psyche that revitalized psychology (Hilgard, 1987). It was thought that just as a computer can process information on its hardware, so too the human brain can process information on its wetware. Thus, *mental processes* were conceptualized as operations on *mental representations*, the information that is in the brain (Jackendoff, 1987). Although such a computational approach brought renewed interest in memory, language, problem-solving, and other cognitive processes (Hilgard, 1987), consciousness initially failed to be readmitted into mainstream psychology (Natsoulas, 1983a). Furthermore, in "a review of the evidence bearing on the accuracy of subjective reports about higher mental processes" (Nisbett & Wilson, 1977, p. 233) the authors concluded that introspection was not possible. That conclusion has subsequently been challenged (White, 1988), but the idea has persisted that what we come up with when we believe that we are introspecting is not any actual knowledge about our mental life but an imaginative reconstruction of what we think our mental life should be like based on perceptions of our own and others' behavior (cf. Lyons, 1986). Despite this conclusion, at the close of the 20th century there was an explosion of academic interest in consciousness along with the assertion that introspection needs to be used as a means for its investigation. Indeed, although it does not need to be so, the computational model of the psyche largely underlies the cognitive perspective of consciousness.

Although the computational approach has been productive, particularly for research concerning human cognition, aspects of the psyche that cannot readily be conceptualized as calculations, such as the imagination or emotions, have been downplayed (Aanstoos, 1987; Hilgard, 1987). Furthermore, despite its overall utility, the computational interpretation of psychological events has caused problems, given that it is unlikely that the brain actually instantiates formal logical states as does a properly programmed computer (Barušs & Mossbridge, 2017; Barwise, 1986). Nor is it clear how information processing can give rise to subjective experience (Chalmers, 1995; Barušs & Mossbridge, 2017; cf. Eccles, 1966). Hence, to the extent that computation is an account of cognition, we have the presence of explanatory gaps among the physiological, cognitive, and experiential perspectives of consciousness. Computation has alternatively been conceptualized as proceeding in an idealized network of processing units (Rumelhart, Hinton, & McClelland, 1986), although that approach comes with its own difficulties and also does not solve the problem of the explanatory gaps (cf. Hanson & Burr, 1990; Smolensky, 1988). Nonetheless, a computational way of thinking about the mind has remained dominant in psychology and hence will recur throughout this book as a possible rationale for the phenomena associated with alterations of consciousness.

Practical Applications

As we can see from our selective overview, introspection seems to refer to a number of somewhat different putative processes. There is so little agreement among psychologists, philosophers, neuroscientists, and others, that it is not even clear whether introspection should be regarded as a perceptual or cognitive process (cf. Schwitzgebel, 2016). Of course, trying to make that distinction reveals how little we know about the phenomenological difference between perception and cognition. Is there one? The problem is that we need to proceed and cannot wait for an accepted theory of introspection—or of consciousness. Indeed, knowledge about consciousness and knowledge about introspection are interdependent, so that we are going to need to address them simultaneously.

At the most basic level, the question is, can we simply tell what is happening in our minds? From a computational point of view, whereby our minds consist of the churning of computing machinery that occasionally crosses a threshold into awareness, the prospects do not look good. However, we can reframe the problem of introspection by asking about the scope of *metacognition*, our ability to know something of our own cognitive processes (cf. Metcalfe & Shimamura, 1994). For instance, as I get older, I have noticed that I tend to forget things more frequently. I have made an observation about my memory. That is metacognition. And it is not just metacognition but a first-person observation that can, in principle, be verified through third-person observations, for instance, by companions noticing that I have become more forgetful. But, wait, am I really more forgetful, or do I just think that I am more forgetful because I am getting older, and I, and my companions, misremember all the times I forgot things before I was older? That, too, is empirically testable through longitudinal studies. It gets complicated. However, the point is that, within a cognitive framework, at least some knowledge of one's own internal states—in this case, memory—is possible.

Switching from the cognitive to the experiential perspective, the answer as to whether we can know something of our minds appears to be obviously "yes." Consciousness, in the sense of subjective consciousness$_2$ and consciousness$_3$, is already awareness. In fact, "Conscious states are often held to be in some sense self-intimating, in that the mere having of them involves, requires, or implies some sort of representation or awareness of those states" (Schwitzgebel, 2016). Notice the pervasiveness of a computational approach in that, even in this quotation, self-intimation is reframed in computational terms. However, such self-intimation is not even usually regarded as introspection, given that introspection is typically characterized as being effortful (Schwitzgebel, 2016). The point is that we can know something of our own minds by the very nature of how our minds function for us.

Suppose I imagine unicorns frolicking in a sunlit meadow, unaware perhaps, that my mind has wandered and that I am fantasizing. Wait a minute, I think, I am supposed to be writing a revised edition of my book, not thinking about unicorns. If you were to ask me what I had just been thinking about, I would give a verbal report and say that I had just been thinking about unicorns. I would report the contents of my experience as I recall them in memory. This notion of introspection appears to encompass the experimental introspection of Wundt as well as the introspective observation of William James. All that we have is experience of various sorts that goes on for us. Normally, it just goes on, but some of the time the contents of our experience can refer to pre-vious contents as having been experiences for us. Thus, introspection is part of the normal process of our consciousness whereby we explicate what it is that is occurring in our awareness (cf. Howe, 1991a, 1991b).

Even this experientially straightforward version of introspection is not without potential problems. Although it seems self-evident, I cannot be certain that I had really been thinking about unicorns. Perhaps I have incorrectly recalled what occurred. Rather than imagining playful unicorns I might have been seeing actual sinister extraterrestrials, but the truth was so awful that I hid it from myself behind a screen memory of playful unicorns. In that case, do I know that I thought that I had been thinking about unicorns? In other words, can I recall my metacognition? The point is that our experience is precisely that of which we are aware so that introspection, to the extent that it involves knowing what is happening in our minds, is just the awareness of our own experience. It is possible that there is imaginative reconstruction of our experience and further problems with making verbal reports of our experience, but these problems are usually thought not to be prohibitive (Farthing, 1992; Pekala & Cardeña, 2000). Or at least, it can be argued that these problems are not greater than those associated with data collection in science more generally, given that empirical observation ultimately depends on scientists' reports of their experiences, as noted previously with regard to Wundt.

At any rate, from a practical point of view, people are asked to report what goes on for them as a matter of course in psychology. Any time someone is asked to respond to the perception of a sensory stimulus, to report one's expe-rience, or to fill out a questionnaire about oneself, introspection is involved. More specifically, in the *experience sampling method*, participants wear an electronic pager that goes off at random intervals as they go about living their lives. When the pager goes off, participants "give a high-resolution descrip-tion of their mental states right as these are happening" (Csikszentmihalyi & Csikszentmihalyi, 1988, p. 253) by filling out a self-report booklet in which information is collected about the "main dimensions of consciousness" (p. 253), such as affect and intrinsic motivation, as well as "the main contextual dimen-sions that influence the state of consciousness" (p. 253), such as "where a person is [located], with whom, [and] doing what" (p. 253). Indeed, much of our understanding of thinking comes from studies using some variation of the experience sampling method.

As a second example, Ronald Pekala and his colleagues have developed a *Phenomenology of Consciousness Inventory* (PCI; Pekala, 1991) with which to measure changes in subjective experiences associated with alterations of consciousness. Participants in an altered state of consciousness of interest to an investigator would be asked to experience the state in which they find them-selves for some specified length of time. Subsequently they would be asked to fill out the 53 items of the PCI. The PCI would be scored along 12 dimensions and 14 subdimensions such as "Positive affect . . . Altered time sense . . . Altered meaning . . . Visual imagery . . . Attention . . . Internal dialogue . . . [and]

Volitional control" (Pekala, 1991, p. 133). For example, "altered time sense addresses the extent to which 'the flow of time changed drastically' or whether it seemed to 'speed up or slow down'" (Pekala, 1991, p. 132).

So, introspecting the content of the experiential stream, including some metacognitive elements, is at least doable. However, the process of introspection becomes more muddied if we ask not about access to the contents of people's experiences but about the structure and dynamics of their minds. Can we determine, for example, what it was that led us to the solution of a puzzle (e.g., Nisbett & Wilson, 1977)? Or how an object of perceptual awareness can have presence to our consciousness (cf. Natsoulas, 1999)? Or whether and how pure consciousness without contents is possible (e.g., Shear, 1996)? And what about our convictions? The feelings of knowing that accompany some mental events, particularly those that occur in altered states of consciousness, such as the certitude with which we appear to recall forgotten events during hypnosis? What are these feelings of knowing and how well do they affirm the correctness of what we think we know? Can we determine through intro- spection the correctness of our judgments about correctness (cf. Koriat, 2000; Metcalfe, 2000; Rosenthal, 2000)? Can neurological correlates help us out? Is there some combination of first-person and third-person observation that could be productive (Barušs & Mossbridge, 2017)? Here we are in a more difficult situation.

To rule out the possibility of answering any of these questions because that seems implausible is an ideological stance that is contrary to scientific investigation. The task becomes one of determining the extent to which, and the means whereby, answers may become possible. One avenue of research would be to investigate the relationship between interoception, the internal sensory perception of our own bodies, and introspection (e.g., Louchakova- Schwartz, 2017). Another would be to apply remote viewing to look at our minds. What would happen if we were to do that? What could we learn? Is that what we are already doing when we introspect? Can we use remote viewing to look at the minds of others? Can we "see" their experience? Or "experience" their interoception? Or experience their experience? There are various possibilities that could be investigated. At any rate, in this book we will report straightforward accounts of experiential contents as a matter of course but exercise caution with regard to more extensive introspective claims.

THINKING

I have found that sometimes there is an expectation that those who profess to know something about consciousness be familiar with the writings of William James, so let us briefly consider James's (1890/1983) influential characteriza- tion of thinking from his famous textbook, published in 1890, *The Principles of Psychology*. In fact, Allan Leslie Combs (2009) argued that at its founding in the late 19th century, psychology was on the right track but lost its identity when it took the trajectory that I described at the beginning of this chapter. Then we will skip forward in time to Erik Klinger's characterization of thinking derived from empirical investigations.

Characteristics of Thinking

Perhaps the first thing to note when reading James is that the language of representations is missing (cf. Haye & Torres-Sahli, 2017). For James, there is just an unmediated flux of thinking that intertwines with itself to create "stability, unity, and continuity" (Cresswell, Wagoner, & Hayes, 2017, p. A4). And for James, *thinking* is not the only word that he uses. The words "thought, experience, subjective life, feeling, state of mind, and consciousness are used interchangeably" (Haye & Torres-Sahli, 2017, p. 49). Later he rejected the word *consciousness* (W. James, 1904a) and preferred *pure experience* (W. James, 1904b, 1904c). Whatever it is that goes on for us subjectively is the subject matter of James's analyses.

James listed five characteristics of thinking, the first of which is that "every thought tends to be part of a personal consciousness" (W. James, 1890/1983, p. 220). For James, thoughts do not float freely but are always owned by someone, thereby presupposing the experienced presence of a personal self implied in consciousness,. But after emphasizing the "*existence* of personal selves" (W. James, 1890/1983, p. 221) James went on to deconstruct the self until the self ends up being interpreted as a passing thought that appropriates previously aggregated ideas about what one is like. Or to put it another way, the flux of thinking is the primary phenomenon whose interactions with itself through a "fallible process of unification and differentiation of experience create the experience of a personal self" (Haye & Torres-Sahli, 2017, p. 50).

This is consistent with notions of the self in cognitive science, whereby the self is conceptualized as the biological organism that a person actually is along with the mental representation of the biological organism and its attributes within a person's information processing system. The sense of self arises from the use of that mental representation. There are no other referents of the word *self* in reality (cf. Flanagan, 1992; Natsoulas, 1983b). We can, of course, question these interpretations and, indeed, the ninth thread running through this book is concerned with the nature of the self.

Second, "within each personal consciousness thought is always changing" (W. James, 1890/1983, p. 220). For James, "*no state once gone can recur and be identical with what it was before*" (W. James, 1890/1983, p. 224; italics in original). The things that we think about may be similar to things we have thought about in the past, but the brain changes as a result of experience and hence is not the same at the time of a later event as it was at the time of an earlier one. Changes in the brain translate into changes in experience. "For to every brain-modification, however small, must correspond a change of equal amount in the feeling which the brain subserves" (W. James, 1890/1983, p. 227). Well, no. "There are almost certainly neural changes that do not affect either nonconscious or conscious mental functioning (in any interesting way)" (Flanagan, 1992, p. 161). The converse is generally accepted as true in cognitive science, namely, that "any change at the level of consciousness must be explicable in terms of changes at the neural level" (Flanagan, 1992, p. 161). But James's point here appears to be to direct us back to the relational flux of thoughts as the primary, ever-changing existent; "there are no complete organisms or selves in a given moment" for whom states can recur (Haye & Torres-Sahli, 2017, p. 50).

Note that there is an implicit understanding of the nature of time underlying this contention regarding thinking. But time itself can apparently change in some alterations of consciousness, for instance, in the case of some psychedelic drug-induced experiences where experiencers appear to be looking-in at temporally dislocated events (Shanon, 2002). Or cases of future memory, in which a person who has had a near-death experience appears to prelive her future (Barušs & Mossbridge, 2017). Do the same states recur at different times, in some sense, in those experiences?

The Stream of Consciousness

Third, "within each personal consciousness thought is sensibly continuous" (W. James, 1890/1983, p. 220). Consciousness spans time gaps in that thoughts that follow a time gap feel as though they belong together with those that preceded it. Furthermore, James has argued at length that differences in content between successive thoughts are no more breaks in thinking than the joints in bamboo are breaks in the wood. Consciousness "is nothing jointed; it flows. A 'river' or a 'stream' are the metaphors by which it is most naturally described. *In talking of it hereafter, let us call it the stream of thought, of consciousness, or of subjective life*" (W. James, 1890/1983, p. 233). This metaphor has become so pervasive in our culture that we have already been using it in this book as a characterization of subjective experience.

According to James, the stream of consciousness has both substantive and transitive parts such that an object about which one thinks constitutes the substantive part and a *"fringe of relations"* (W. James, 1890/1983, p. 249; italics in original) of that object to other objects constitutes the transitive part within which the substantive part is embedded. While a succession of words and images may be discrete, the fact that such contents of thought are "fringed" (W. James, 1890/1983, p. 262), according to James, means that our thoughts are continuous. In other words, the substantive and transitive elements of thinking combine to form a stream. Through the use of these relations between thoughts, anticipatory projection of future events creates *feelings of tendency* so that we experience a continuity of consciousness. And the meanings of our thoughts are not usually part of their attentional focus but, rather, flow along the fringe (Haye & Torres-Sahli, 2017).

The notion of a fringe is an important one. Much of psychology has been concerned with the study of the objects of attention, so that reading James reminds us of the importance of also addressing the fringe. Feelings of knowing belong to the fringe. We know that we know something, such as a person's name, but cannot recall the information itself (e.g., Fiacconi, Kouptsova, & Köhler, 2017). *Feelings of reality* are feelings that what is going on is real. Feelings of reality can be diminished, such as in the pathological condition derealization disorder (American Psychiatric Association, 2013). Or they can sometimes be enhanced, as we shall see, during dreaming, transcendent experiences, and near-death experiences (Barušs, 2007c).

Because feelings of reality can be disconnected from actual reality, whatever that might be, they are not necessarily a good indicator of what is actually real. That should give us pause. We are usually confident that our experience in the ordinary waking state is real, in part, presumably, because we are using our feelings of reality to make judgments about actual reality. But hallucinations can also feel real. And, as one of my students found, the events during near-death experiences can feel real—or realer than real. So if we relinquish feelings of reality as a criterion of reality, then what is left (Barušs, 2007c; Dokic & Martin, 2017)? And how real are the events that make up the ordinary waking state? In this way, our third thematic thread surfaces: what is real, and what is delusional?

Intentionality

Fourth, James asserted that thought "always appears to deal with objects independent of itself" (W. James, 1890/1983, p. 220). The first part of this characterization, that thought appears to deal with objects, is the contention that consciousness is structured in such a way as to be about something, although, for James, such structure is secondary to the flow of pure experience (Haye & Torres-Sahli, 2017). This quality of aboutness, whereby mental phenomena exhibit the property of having "a direction upon an object" (Brentano, 1874/1960, p. 50), has been called *intentionality*. This use of the word *intentionality* should not be confused with the more common usage of *intentionality* to mean deliberateness (cf. Dennett, 1978). Intentionality does raise a question, though: What is the nature of the mind when the contents of thought apparently disappear, "leaving *consciousness* alone by itself" (Shear, 1996, p. 64), as can occur during meditation or self-development?

The second part of James's fourth characteristic of thinking is the contention that the things about which we think appear to have an existence independent of our thoughts themselves. In other words, it appears that there is a real world out there that we can encounter in our thoughts. That seems obvious from our everyday way of thinking about reality and is, of course, taken for granted from a materialist perspective, but becomes problematic upon reflection. What makes us think that there really is anything out there? Our feelings of reality? James noted that the recurrence of some object of thought leads us to "take the object out of [our past and present thoughts] and project it by a sort of triangulation into an independent position" (W. James, 1890/1983, p. 262). The repetitive presence of objects of thought is not enough to prove the existence of an objective reality, but for all practical purposes, it can suffice in order for us to act as though there were an objective reality without resolving the ontological status of objects of thought (Lipson, 1987). James, it appears, grew skeptical of the existence of an independent material reality and dropped this fourth characteristic of thought from his 1892 version of the book (E. Taylor, 1981). Is it possible that there are objective realities that are not material (cf. Mavromatis, 1987b)? Or is there anything objective about reality at all, in which case what is the nature of objects of thought?

Fifth, "[thought] is interested in some parts of these objects to the exclusion of others, and welcomes or rejects—*chooses* from among them, in a word—all the while" (W. James, 1890/1983, p. 220). We selectively attend to some parts of objects rather than others, and emphasize and unite some impressions but not others, so that we are always in a process of choosing between alternatives and, in doing so, leaving behind the alternatives not chosen. "The mind, in short, works on the data it receives very much as a sculptor works on his block of stone" (W. James, 1890/1983, p. 277). Indeed, given that the senses act as a data reduction system and that, furthermore, we are conditioned by cultural influences and, of necessity, choose to direct our attention toward some objects and not others, "ordinary consciousness is an exquisitely evolved personal construction" (Ornstein, 1972, p. 45; see also Hoffman, 1998).

But James has not just described a process of selective attention. He has said that thought is "interested" and "welcomes or rejects" specific contents, thereby suggesting an ongoing evaluative process. We are already always interested in some things and not others, and shift the flow of the ongoing stream so as to move in the directions of interest. Even in this regard, James's characterization of thinking has held up well, as we shall see in a moment (see also Flanagan, 1992).

Dimensions of Thinking

Let us turn to a more recent characterization of thinking by Eric Klinger and his colleagues who have studied thinking using a version of the experience sampling method. In these studies, participants were asked to record the last thoughts that went through their minds whenever a beeper went off at irregular intervals as they were going about their everyday lives (Klinger, 1990; Klinger & Kroll-Mensing, 1995). As a result of this work, a number of dimensions have been identified along which thinking can vary.

To begin with, thinking can be deliberate or spontaneous. *Deliberate thinking* is thinking that consists of specific content that is intentionally directed toward the attainment of certain goals (Klinger & Kroll-Mensing, 1995). Conceptually related to deliberateness is *controllability*, so that thinking can be "accompanied by a sense of volition, [be] checked against feedback concerning its effects, [be] evaluated according to its effectiveness in advancing particular goals, and [be] protected from drift and distraction by deliberately controlling attention" (Klinger, 1978, p. 235). Notice the exercise of volition here, referencing our

11th thematic thread. *Spontaneous thinking* consists of thoughts that "just pop into our minds" (Klinger, 1990, p. 76). Klinger and his colleagues have found that "about two thirds" of their participants "rated a majority of their thoughts as mostly deliberate, but nearly a third rated a majority of their thoughts as mostly spontaneous" (Klinger, 1990, p. 78). Overall, about one third of a person's thoughts are more spontaneous than deliberate.

Thinking can be either externally or internally focused. That is to say, we can be either *externally focused* paying attention to what is going on in the environment around us or we can be *internally focused* on thoughts away from what is happening in our environment. About one third of the time our thoughts are "focused on another place or on the past or future" (Klinger, 1990, p. 80). There can, of course, be combinations of deliberate versus spontaneous and externally versus internally focused thoughts. Suppose that I were listening to a song on my sound system. Trying to make out the lyrics of the song would be an example of deliberate, externally focused thinking. Realizing that it is difficult to figure out the lyrics would be an example of spontaneous, externally focused thinking. Trying to remember the name of an actress in a movie while listening to the music would be an example of deliberate, internally focused thinking. And worrying about an exam the following day while hearing the song would be an example of spontaneous, internally focused thinking.

Our thoughts can be *strange* along one of three dimensions. First, thoughts can be *fanciful* or *realistic*. Fanciful thoughts are ones in which "important social role expectations or current versions of natural laws" (Klinger, 1978, p. 241) are violated. Imagining that I am sailing my bicycle over the rooftops of the neighborhood houses would be an example of a fanciful thought. About 21% of thoughts depart at least to some degree from being physically possible (Klinger, 1990, p. 73). Second, thoughts can inexplicably jump from one to another so that nearly half the time participants in Klinger's (1990) studies rated their thoughts as being at least somewhat *disconnected*. More generally, the median length of a thought segment, "defined as a thought that is thematically homogeneous and ends when the topic shifts," is only 5 seconds, so that about 4,000 thought segments occur while one is awake each day (Klinger, Marchetti, & Koster, 2018, p. 218). Third, thoughts can be either *well-integrated* or become *degenerated* as they do in dreams whereby "images often flow without respect to beginnings or endings, shift gears drastically in the middle, interweave different concerns with one another, and offer images that seem to be the fused representatives of different basic ideas or forms" (Klinger, 1978, p. 241). In one of the thought-sampling studies, about 25% of thoughts contained "at least a trace of dream-like mentation" (Klinger & Cox, 1987, p. 124). Thus, thoughts can be strange in that they can be fanciful, disconnected, or degenerated.

Using the beeper methodology, Klinger and his colleagues found a number of other characteristics of thoughts. The single most common feature is the presence of *self-talk*. We are silent in only about a quarter of our thoughts, and half the time we converse with ourselves in "fairly complete statements or running commentaries" (Klinger, 1990, p. 69). Visual imagery, at least in fragmentary form, occurs in two thirds of our thoughts while half the time visual elements that usually include some color and movement are prominent. "About half of our thoughts include some sound apart from our own voices" (Klinger, 1990, p. 70). About one quarter of the time we think "about other people and relationships" (Klinger, 1990, p. 85). And 3% of the time "we focus on anxiety-provoking or worrisome thoughts" (Klinger, 1990, p. 85).

Emotions are often part of our multidimensional subjective experiences either accompanying or triggering thoughts. For example, we may feel shame upon remembering our reprehensible behavior toward someone or recall thoughts of being given flowers by someone we love because of the positive emotions that were associated with that event (Klinger, 1990). In explanations of emotions theorists have often regarded them as being made up of components. Thus, emotion experience itself can be thought of as consisting of what it is like to have a particular emotion and that of which one is aware during an emotion. This could be thought of as a distinction between consciousness$_3$ and subjective consciousness$_2$ applied to emotions. The level of a person's physical arousal and her bodily location in a spatial environment are other components of emotions as are feelings of pleasure or displeasure and tendencies to take action. Cognitive components could include appraisals of emotion triggers, evaluations of one's situation, and plans for action, which could proceed at the level of consciousness$_1$ or consciousness$_2$ (cf. Lambie & Marcel, 2002). For example, an encounter with an extraterrestrial alien in one's bedroom could trigger fear and an effort to escape. Reappraisal of the situation could lead one to conclude that escape is impossible or perhaps that one is in some sort of altered state of consciousness and that the alien is just a figment of one's imagination. In fact, as this example suggests, changes of emotional expression can be associated with alterations of consciousness (Ludwig, 1966).

Sometimes we suppress our thoughts in the sense of trying not to allow them to be part of the stream of subjective consciousness$_2$. However, studies have shown that we appear to monitor how well we are able to keep unwanted thoughts outside of our awareness so that, ironically, the suppressed thoughts have not disappeared but, indeed, surface again when we cease to try to suppress them or when there are multiple demands being made on our cognitive resources. Thus, suppression of pain can result in greater pain, suppression of substance cravings can increase them, suppression of awareness of one's unwanted personal characteristics can lead to projection of those characteristics on others, and trying not to be like someone else can result in becoming like them. It has also been found that "relationships that remained a secret were more likely to occupy a person's attention than previous public relationships" (Wenzlaff & Wegner, 2000, pp. 78–79) and that "individuals who suppress thoughts on a chronic basis show a pattern of physiological responses that [is] consistent with anxiety" (p. 76). *Thought suppression* appears to be a clumsy way of managing our thoughts; it raises the question of the degree to which more effective means could be used for mental control. Some forms of meditation, considered briefly in Chapter 8, for example, have had as their purpose the control of the mind.

PLAYING WITH THE IMAGINATION

There appears to have been a tendency in our Western cultures to conceptualize our subjective life as consisting of rational thinking devoted to mentally solving problems by carefully following the rules of classical logic with, perhaps, an occasional unfortunate lapse into irrationality. However, as we have seen thus far, our subjective life does not conform to such a preconception but is richly variegated. In fact, using the beeper technology, Klinger and his colleagues found that participants in one study were engaged in "active, focused problem-solving thought" (Klinger, 1990, p. 91) only 6% of the time. It would make more sense to say that our subjective life consists of irrational thinking with occasional patches of reason. So what is the nature of this irrational thinking, and of what use is it to us? We will start by looking at mind-wandering along with its benefits and drawbacks and then consider the use of guided imagery and its applications to healing efforts.

Mind Wandering

In Chapter 1, we briefly considered the default mode network of the brain, which we associated with endogenous activity that arises spontaneously when not attending to sensory stimuli (Havlík, 2017; Sripada, 2018). That would be the territory of the *imagination* perhaps (A. Abraham, 2018, p. 43). Such spontaneous activity has recently been studied under the rubric of *mind wandering*. Note the slight difference here with Klinger's definition of spontaneous thinking, which includes the occurrence of spontaneous thinking in the context of vigilance tasks in which a person is attending to a stimulus. In fact, somewhat analogous to the subject matter itself, there are serious discrepancies among definitions in the mind-wandering literature so that it is sometimes difficult to aggregate information across studies (cf. Andrews-Hanna, Irving, Fox, Spreng, & Christoff, 2018; Irving & Thompson, 2018; Stan & Christoff, 2018). So, with that in mind, "spontaneous thought can be defined as thought that arises relatively freely due to an absence of strong constraints on its contents or on the transitions from one mental state to another" (K. C. R. Fox & Christoff, 2018, p. 4). In addition to spontaneity, mind wandering is usually also associated with a "phenomenal quality of ease" (Stan & Christoff, 2018, p. 47) so that experiential content "moves freely as it unfolds" (K. C. R. Fox & Christoff, 2018, p. 4).

What is the content of mind wandering? For Klinger, the answer is *current concerns*. These are issues that are relevant to goals that are present for a person from the time that they commit themself to those goals until such time as those goals have been attained or abandoned. Mind wandering helps keep us organized by reminding us of the current concerns that are most important to us (Klinger, 1978, 1990; Klinger et al., 2018). And progress toward personal goals is associated with positive affect (Klinger et al., 2018, p. 216). So we note the temporal displacement of the content of mind wandering in that it is characteristically, although not always, future-oriented (Stawarczyk, 2018). We also note that this is consistent with James's notion that thought is always interested, in particular, for Klinger, interested in current concerns.

A number of other phenomenological features of mind wandering have been found. First, mind wandering is most likely to occur in the form of "visual images" or "inner speech" (Stawarczyk, 2018, p. 204) rather than in other modalities. Second, the content of mind wandering has a slightly positive emotional tone. Third, the content is usually realistic and related to specific events and actions (Stawarczyk, 2018, p. 205). Fourth, mind wandering usually occurs in an unintended manner, although sometimes people do also deliberately mind wander. Fifth, in a minority of cases, thought segments can be sequential, such as forming an argument about something, but they are more likely to be fragmented, particularly if they occur while one is performing a difficult task. Sixth, thoughts during mind wandering can be repetitive, especially if they are concerned with personal goals. Seventh, the visual perspective adopted during mind wandering tends to be a first-person one rather than a third-person one. Eighth, our thoughts during mind wandering "frequently focus on other people and social situations" (Stawarczyk, 2018, p. 207).

We should keep in mind that these features have been established using different definitions of mind wandering, that they are based on statistical norms, and that there are also large individual differences. There are also aspects of mind wandering that have not been adequately investigated. For instance, one of my students studied spontaneous musical imagery by giving a questionnaire that he developed to 67 participants. He found six dimensions, including the degree to which the music is persistent and the degree to which it is distracting (Wammes & Baruss, 2009). It is not clear how the music playing in our heads is necessarily related to current concerns.

Mind wandering and daydreaming have clear benefits. Daydreaming, in Klinger's sense of spontaneous or fanciful thoughts, helps to keep us organized by reminding us of the current concerns that are emotionally most important to us. By replaying events from the past, daydreaming allows us to learn from them, whereas anticipating and rehearsing possible future scenarios enables us to better prepare for and make decisions regarding the future. "Daydreaming is a channel of information about ourselves to ourselves" (Klinger, 1990, p. 7) in that it helps us to know what we want, what we fear, and, sometimes, what we do not want to know. Daydreaming can be used to assist with personal growth and to contribute to creative expression. "Finally, daydreaming can serve as a way to change our moods—to relax and to entertain ourselves, providing a way to have fun with life" (Klinger, 1990, p. 8).

But there can be drawbacks. *Rumination* is a form of mind wandering whereby spontaneous thoughts "become mired in affectively salient and entrenched problems" (DuPre & Spreng, 2018, p. 517). During rumination, "bottom-up" constraints appear to have been placed on mind wandering so that it no longer wanders freely (Andrews-Hanna et al., 2018).

In some cases, this could be helpful, but such thinking has typically been associated with negative affect and is implicated in depression (DuPre & Spreng, 2018). For instance, an "impaired disengagement factor" could interfere with "control of attention," thereby weakening "an individual's ability to switch from a stream of negative repetitive thoughts to something more constructive that might help to dispel the negative mood" (Klinger et al., 2018, p. 224). In such cases, some form of "cognitive control training" could be helpful (Klinger et al., 2018, p. 225).

Guided Imagery

Is it possible to deliberately harness the benefits of mind wandering and daydreaming while avoiding its drawbacks? One way to do that would be to engage in *guided imagery*, a process of actively directing images in a symbolically meaningful sequence. The visualization of symbols has been extensively used in a form of psychotherapy called *psychosynthesis*, which was developed by Roberto Assagioli beginning in 1910 with a critique of Sigmund Freud's psychoanalysis (Hardy, 1987). According to Assagioli, nonconscious aspects of our psyche include not only a *subconscious*, which is the source of primitive drives and residue from past events, but a *superconscious*, which is the source of ethical imperatives, altruistic love, inspiration, and genius (Assagioli, 1965). One way of accessing the superconscious was thought to be through the use of guided imagery such as the following inner-dialogue exercise.

Imagine yourself in a meadow on a warm, sunny morning. Become aware of the environment around you—the whispering of the breeze in the grass and its touch against your face, the fragrance of flowers, the sight of the sky, blue, above you. Now imagine that there is a majestic mountain rising in front of you. You decide to climb it and set out on a path into a forest at the base of the mountain. You feel the coolness of the shade among the trees and hear the sound of a stream beside the path. The path leaves the forest and begins to rise steeply. The ascent becomes arduous as you use your hands as well as your feet in order to climb. The air has become more rarified and invigorating. As you pass through a cloud you can barely make out your hands on the rocks in the mist. You emerge from the cloud with the sun shining brightly above. Climbing feels effortless as you near the summit. You find yourself on a plateau at the top of the mountain. There is perfect silence around you. In the distance you see a luminous point that takes on the shape of a person as it approaches you. You find yourself face to face with a loving and wise being. You can talk about anything you wish and listen to anything that the wise being has to say in turn. Perhaps the wise being has a gift to give you before you leave to come back down the mountain (cf. Ferrucci, 1982).

The idea in this exercise is to try to create a psychological effect through the use of symbolic imagery. Ascending a mountain represents a refinement of consciousness, and encountering a wise being is a personification of whatever latent wisdom we may possess. Deliberate thinking is involved in the directed sequence of specific images, with spontaneous thinking supplying the details of those images and any apparent response on the part of the wise being. But getting back to one of our thematic threads, does any of this play of the imagination actually mean anything? Are we accessing a superconscious or just fooling ourselves? Indeed, we may end up with spontaneous images that are fragmented, self-deprecating, and meaningless—that is to say, images that have nothing wise about them. However, at other times, the spontaneous images may be accompanied by a sense of rightness, understanding, and joy, even though the presence of such qualities does not guarantee that they are objectively true or necessarily wise (cf. Ferrucci, 1982).

Some research has been done to establish the effectiveness of the use of guided imagery (e.g., Feinberg-Moss & Oatley, 1990; Sell, Möller, & Taubner, 2018). For instance, in one study with 48 participants, it was found that, although participants improved in both conditions, "nature-based" guided imagery was more effective at reducing anxiety than "urban-based" guided imagery (Nguyen & Brymer, 2018). There has also been evidence that, in addition to regulating emotions, the imagination can be used to induce neural plasticity, activate parts of the brain that are responsible for perception and motor activity, enhance "real-world performance," and support "the prediction of future events" (Reddan, Wager, & Schiller, 2018, p. 994). In our case, imagining a wise being can be a way of trying to generate some interesting ideas, and techniques such as the inner dialogue exercise can be a means of attempting to harness our daydreams for creative expression, problem-solving, and personal growth.

Psychoneuroimmunoendocrinology

Whether or not we can create psychological changes as a result of working with imagery, it appears that sometimes our thoughts can have effects on our immune systems as found in a field of investigation that has come to be known as *psychoneuroimmunology* (O'Regan, 1983) and, more recently, with recognition of the additional role of the endocrine system, as *psychoneuro-immunoendocrinology* (Moraes, Miranda, Loures, Mainieri, & Mármora, 2018; cf. Lotti & França, 2019). In a study by Robert Ader and Nicholas Cohen, rats were given a saccharin-flavored drink 30 minutes before being injected with cyclophosphamide, a drug that suppresses the immune system. Subsequently, these same animals, when given the saccharin-flavored drink alone, had suppressed immune functioning even though they were no longer receiving any immunosuppressive drugs (Ader & Cohen, 1975). In other words, an association had been formed between the way something tasted and the activity of the immune system. Other studies have confirmed links between a variety of stimuli and physiological processes (Ader & Cohen, 1982, 1993). These results carry over to humans, with associations between psychological parameters and measures of immune functioning having been demonstrated (Adler & Matthews, 1994). For example, in one study, participants who had been asked to suppress their thoughts had significantly decreased levels of white blood cells (Petrie, Booth, & Pennebaker, 1998).

Other studies have shown that thoughts can have positive physiological effects. John Schneider and his colleagues did a series of 10 studies in which they examined the effects of guided imagery on the immune system, with particular interest in white blood cells known as *neutrophils*. Neutrophils have a property called *adherence*, which is capable of being increased and which has been hypothesized to be related to their ability "to migrate from the blood stream to a particular [site] of infection" (Schneider, Smith, Minning, Whitcher, & Hermanson, 1990, p. 181). In one of the studies, 16 healthy students "who believed they could influence their immune function" (Schneider et al., 1990, p. 182) were recruited from classes at a medical school and given a lecture and slide presentation about "neutrophils and their function in the immune system" (p. 184) and "two two-hour imagery training sessions" (p. 184). The participants were asked to imagine that their neutrophils were responding as if there were a crisis so that the neutrophils would be expected to increase their adherence and migrate out of the bloodstream to the site of the imagined crisis. Blood was taken from the participants before and after the experimental condition, and changes in the total white blood cell count, neutrophil count, and adherence were measured. The investigators found a significant 60% drop for the number of neutrophils but not for other white blood cells, and, contrary to expectation, they found a significant decrease in the adherence of the neutrophils. The investigators also found correlations between the immune system changes and the participants' self-reported effectiveness of their imagery along various dimensions.

Although the decrease in neutrophil count had been expected in the imagery study, what was troubling to the investigators was that the adherence of the neutrophils had decreased, and that the size of the decrease had been greater precisely for those participants who had rated their imagery as having been more effective. Was it possible that so many neutrophils had left the bloodstream that only those with low adherence remained in the bloodstream to be counted? To check this possibility, the experiment was repeated with 27 medical and graduate students who were asked to keep the neutrophils in their bloodstream while increasing their adherence. This time there was no change in the white blood cell count, but there was a significant increase in the adherence of the neutrophils and a positive correlation between increased neutrophil adherence and the quality of imagery ratings (Schneider et al., 1990).

What Schneider's studies demonstrated is the ability of a specific type of white blood cell to conform to imagined changes. If the immune system can be affected by guided imagery in healthy people, this raises the question of the scope of the power of the mind to create physiological and psychological changes also in cases of illness (e.g., Baron, 1989). In fact, it is now generally acknowledged that the interaction of psychological, neurological, immuno-logical, and endocrinological functioning, modulated by signaling molecules, needs to be taken into account in both healthy and diseased states (González-Díaz, Arias-Cruz, Elizondo-Villarreal, & Monge-Ortega, 2017; Lotti & França, 2019). In psychiatry, for instance, such an approach has ostensibly led to "progress that has . . . exceeded all expectations" (Halaris et al., 2019, p. 235) in understanding treatment resistance. In one review of relevant studies, it was found that practices such as yoga and meditation lowered levels of stress hormones and reduced inflammatory processes, although only "one study evidenced significant effects on a disease progression" (Moraes et al., 2018, p. 635). Such interactions are also at play in the *placebo* and *nocebo effects*, benefitting and harming the body, respectively, as a result of psychological factors such as expectations (Benedetti, 2009; Dodd, Dean, Vian, & Berk, 2017). All of this is related to our eighth thematic thread, the beneficial versus harmful effects that could occur in altered states of consciousness. We shall return to some of the beneficial effects in Chapter 8 when we consider meditation.

But there is a further question. If consciousness has nonlocal properties, such as those evidenced in the Ganzfeld studies, are the effects of the imagi-nation confined to the body of the person who is doing the imagining? Or can they apply to someone else's body? Is the mind open or closed? We have seen in this section that there is a more intimate connection between the physio-logical, cognitive, and experiential aspects of our nature than we might suppose, and it turns out that that connection can extend beyond a person's body.

Noncontact Healing

One of the more striking examples of noncontact healing has been demon-strated by the sociologist William Bengston in a series of experiments using mice with transplanted cancer. For instance, in a series of four experiments with 33 mice, 29 of the mice were healed. These are mice that typically die within 14 to 27 days of being injected with the cancer (Bengston & Krinsley, 2000). What happened?

Bengston's treatment consisted of a person placing their hands on the mouse cages for an hour a day for a month while engaging in *cycling*, a mental technique that Bengston developed for the purpose of healing. To "cycle," a person initially creates a list of situations that they find desirable and then practices going through that list, item by item, over and over again, until the process becomes quick and automatic (Bengston, 2007). When this was done during the experiments, the tumors became blackened, ulcerated, imploded, and then closed, so that the mice were healed. If mice were reinjected with the same cancer, the body of the mouse would reject the cancer, suggesting a role for the immune system in the disappearance of the cancer (Bengston & Krinsley, 2000).

There were onsite and offsite control mice. Eighteen of 26 onsite mice were healed, whereas all eight of the offsite mice died. Why are the onsite control mice not dying? Are these just "bad" mice? No. The strain of breast cancer that was used with that strain of mice makes spontaneous remission "highly unlikely" (M. M. Moga, personal communication, February 9, 2016). The healing effect appears to have extended somehow to some of the control mice that appeared to have become meaningfully entangled with the experimental mice.

But it is more complicated than that. In Experiment 3, the healing was carried out by five student volunteers who had been taught Bengston's technique. Each student received "one mouse to treat in the laboratory and one mouse to treat at home" (Bengston & Krinsley, 2000, p. 360). All the at-home mice remitted. "But in the laboratory, *all three of the experimental mice treated by the biology majors died within the expected time frame*. Only the sociology and child study majors were able to remit their mouse in the laboratory" (Bengston & Krinsley, 2000, pp. 360–361, emphases in original). Six control mice were "in an adjacent laboratory in the same building" (Bengston & Krinsley, 2000, p. 360). Three of those control mice died. But then, the biology students started visiting the remaining mice, and those mice remitted. Four mice sent off-site to another city died. The healing phenomenon appears to follow the contours of the participants' psyches. Control mice remit when someone involved in healing pays attention to them. On the other hand, experimental mice die in the laboratory when treated by biology students, perhaps reflecting those students' beliefs that this sort of healing is supposed to be "impossible."

In my discussions with him, Bengston is no longer interested in replicating the results, which he has done about a dozen times with different strains of mice and different transplanted cancers, but rather is trying to understand the mechanism involved (e.g., Beseme, Bengston, Radin, Turner, & McMichael, 2018). How is it that "cycling" allows for healing to take place? Or is the "cycling" just a distraction that serves to preoccupy the healer's nonconscious mind so that the healing effect can take place? I have speculated that the results could be explained by extending meaning beyond the human and by positing the existence of *meaning fields*, which intelligently structure physical manifestation and with which we can interact, in this case, in such a way as to remit mice who fall within the meaning field of healing (Barušs, 2018a). This line of research has clear implications for possible future advances in health care.

SENSORY RESTRICTION

Usually, our ordinary waking state of consciousness includes sensations of the environment around us, as reflected in the external versus internal dimension of thought, so that we can pay attention to what is going on around us or to what is going on in our minds. But what would happen if we were to restrict sensory input either by attenuating it or by substantially removing the variability of sensory stimuli? What if we were to force attention, in a sense, to the internal aspects of the stream of consciousness? What would happen? We already saw an example of sensory restriction with the Ganzfeld technique described in Chapter 1. In that case, sensory restriction was thought to promote the possibility of anomalous information transfer. What we find more generally is that some of the phenomena associated with the more dramatic alterations of consciousness already occur with sensory restriction, making it valuable not only as perhaps the most pronounced expression of ordinary waking consciousness but, paradoxically, as an example of an altered state of consciousness.

Early Research

John Lilly wanted to know what would happen if sensory input were to be reduced as much as possible. He thought about all of the ways in which sensory variations are created in the body and came up with the idea of using water flotation as a way of minimizing them. He devised an underwater breathing mask and rubber supports to hold up his arms and legs in the water while being "minimally stimulating to the skin" (Lilly, 1978, p. 102). One day in 1954, he put on the mask and the arm and leg supports, and immersed himself in a tank filled with tap water that was situated in a dark, soundproof room. He discovered that "this environment furnished the most profound relaxation and rest that he had ever experienced in [his] life" (Lilly, 1978, p. 103). He found, furthermore, "that there were many, many states of consciousness, of being, between the usual wide-awake consciousness of participating in an external reality and the unconscious state of deep sleep" and that he could experience events in his fantasy that seemed so real that "they could possibly be mistaken for events in the outside world" (Lilly, 1978, p. 103). Then one day, Lilly injected himself with 100 micrograms of LSD before getting into the tank. But that is a story for Chapter 7.

Lilly continued his flotation research, and in the 1970s he invented a flotation tank in which a person could float in a "warm solution of Epsom salts" (Suedfeld & Coren, 1989, p. 20) for the purposes of relaxation. Around the same time, it was found that "stimulus reduction, either alone or combined with other techniques, was a highly effective treatment in habit modification" (Suedfeld & Coren, 1989, p. 20) such as smoking cessation. As a result, among investigators, sensory restriction began to shed the initial image it had had as a form of torture, and increased research was undertaken to explore its further therapeutic applications to habit modification. What had been known as perceptual isolation or sensory deprivation was reconceptualized as *restricted environmental stimulation technique* and *restricted environmental stimulation therapy*, depending upon the context and, in either case, abbreviated as *REST*.

Two versions of REST have been used. In *flotation REST* a person floats on their back in a pool or tank of water filled with enough Epsom salts so that the face and surface of their body are above the waterline. Substantial effort is required to turn over, with the result that the person can daydream or sleep without being concerned about their safety. The pool or tank is itself in a dark and quiet room with an intercom connecting the person with a monitor. The usual time spent in a flotation tank is about 45 minutes, although a participant can leave at any time before then. In *chamber REST* a person lies on a bed in a completely dark room with reduced sound for a number of hours, with 24 being a frequently used time period. "Food, water and toilet facilities" (Suedfeld & Borrie, 1999) are available inside the room. Again, there is an intercom that "permits a monitor nearby to respond to questions or requests, and to help the subject leave the chamber before the scheduled end of the session if desired" (Suedfeld & Borrie, 1999, p. 546). A version of chamber REST known as *darkness therapy* has showed up in Europe, whereby participants spend a week in a dark room, usually interacting with a psychotherapist on a daily basis (Suedfeld, Rank, & Malůš, 2018, p. 566).

Effects of Sensory Restriction

As expected, REST has provided relief from the stressors in a person's environment, with increases in relaxation found on physiological and self-report measures "from before to after flotation sessions" (Suedfeld & Borrie, 1999, p. 553). Participants have sometimes indicated that the time spent in REST was an opportunity for them "to think more deeply than usual" (Suedfeld & Borrie, 1999, p. 557) about their life problems and to come up with solutions that were successfully implemented afterward. These solutions have included subsequent increased health-related behaviors such as initiating exercise programs or reducing the intake of unhealthy foods, as well as improved interpersonal relations with family members and colleagues at work. In some cases of serious self-examination, participants could uncover disturbing aspects about themselves, such as self-destructive patterns of behavior. Although such discoveries can be distressing, they can also be therapeutically productive. Sometimes individuals who are depressed may not benefit from REST, given that it provides them with an opportunity for increased rumination about their woes if they tend to have self-deprecatory thoughts (Suedfeld & Borrie, 1999). Some types of anxiety, though, have been found to improve with floatation REST (Feinstein et al., 2018; Jonsson, 2018). In general, however, participants appear to experience an improvement in mood, particularly with flotation REST. And, in the case of darkness therapy, "clients and therapists both report that the course and speed of therapeutic progress is facilitated by the experience of darkness" (Suedfeld, Rank, & Malůš, 2018, p. 567).

It has been thought by some that it is reduced rigidity of thinking and behaving that has been at the root of successful habit modification with REST. The idea is that sensory restriction provides an opportunity to develop flexibility of mind with regard to the "thoughts, emotions, motivations, and behaviors supporting [a] habit" (Suedfeld & Borrie, 1999, p. 552), thereby creating the possibility for new psychological patterns to emerge that are consistent with a participant's desire to change. In the treatment of smoking addiction, a 12- to 24-hour chamber REST session in complete darkness and silence has sometimes been combined with another proven smoking cessation method such as self-management training, hypnosis, or counseling, creating an additive effect of the benefits of either method used alone. What is particularly significant is that the addition of REST to the treatment program dramatically decreases the probability of relapse. In one study in which "hypnotherapy and counseling with an experienced clinician were combined with 1–3 very brief chamber REST sessions" (Suedfeld & Borrie, 1999, p. 552), 47% of participants were abstinent at a 19-month follow-up compared with 4% to 36% abstinence for hypnosis only or hypnosis combined with other methods, and 6% for an untreated control group (A. F. Barabasz, Baer, Sheehan, & Barabasz, 1986). It is possible that in this study, the results may have been due in part to the increased suggestibility and hypnotizability of participants found during and immediately following REST (cf. Suedfeld & Borrie, 1999).

A not unexpected effect of sensory restriction is *stimulus hunger*, the tendency after 24 or more hours in a dark, silent room to "respond positively to information or stimulation that breaks the sameness of the environment" (Suedfeld & Borrie, 1999, p. 550). For example, participants will request to hear boring materials and comply with "counter attitudinal behavior in order to obtain information" (Suedfeld & Borrie, 1999, p. 550), although unpredictable and cognitively challenging stimuli are preferred. The presence of stimulus hunger as a result of sensory restriction has been used for treating people with phobias. In one study, participants with a fear of snakes were placed in a REST chamber for 5 hours. At the end of this time, they could push a button that allowed them to view slides of snakes of varying degrees of realism. Subsequently, participants demonstrated diminished fear of snakes compared with a control group that had seen the slides but had not experienced REST. In keeping with the affinity for the unpredictability of sensory information during sensory restriction, it was found that random presentation of the slides of snakes with regard to their realism was more effective for diminishing fear than any other order, including a hierarchical order from least to most realistic that would be used in traditional therapeutic treatments of phobias.

Not only has REST been shown to be effective in a variety of clinically relevant situations (e.g., M. Barabasz, Barabasz, & Dyer, 1993; Harrison & Barabasz, 1991; Ruzyla-Smith & Barabasz, 1993), it has also been demonstrated to contribute to enhanced performance in other areas of life, such as athletic performance. Collegiate basketball playing, tennis playing, and rifle marksmanship have all improved subsequent to the use of REST (A. F. Barabasz, Barabasz, & Bauman, 1993; McAleney & Barabasz, 1993; McAleney, Barabasz, & Barabasz, 1990; Wagaman & Barabasz, 1993; Wagaman, Barabasz, & Barabasz, 1991). For example, in a study of 22 college basketball players, the participants who experienced flotation REST for six sessions in addition to imagery training had better game performance than players who experienced only imagery training (Wagaman et al., 1991).

Sensed Presences

Lilly (1978) became concerned about his exploits in the flotation tank when "he realized that there were apparent presences" of people "who he knew were at a distance from the facility" and "strange and alien presences with whom he had had no known previous experience" (p. 103). He subsequently came to believe that he had established contact with an alien civilization made up of solid-state beings.

A *sensed presence* is a feeling that another being is present when no other being is actually physically present. In addition to occurring deliberately induced sensory restriction, sensed presences have been known to occur in situations of social isolation, such as solitary sailing, polar exploration, and mountain climbing, as well as during religious rituals and traumatic events (cf. Suedfeld & Mocellin, 1987; Suedfeld et al., 2018). Charles Lindbergh sensed presences during his pioneering solo transatlantic flight from New York to Paris in 1927. Even though they seemed to be behind him, Lindbergh (1953) said that he could see them because his skull was "one great eye, seeing everywhere at once" (p. 389). The presences appeared and disappeared from the cockpit of his airplane and spoke to him above the engine's roar, encouraging him and advising him regarding his flight. In one study, sensed presences were evoked in participants by stereo-acoustic stimuli, suggesting to the researchers that transient brain activity may give rise to the phenomenon (Johnson & Persinger, 1994). However we may account for them, sensed presences can sometimes be productively utilized, as we have previously noted with regard to the wise being of the inner dialogue exercise and as Lindbergh apparently was able to do. As we shall see, alien presences and apparent discarnate entities show up in a number of alterations of consciousness often with their ontological status not quite as firmly established as we might suppose (cf. Suedfeld et al., 2018).

SUMMARY

We started this chapter by considering the history of the study of consciousness and the manner in which a person can come to know something of their subjective experience, namely, through various introspective activities. What, then, does introspection of some form or other appear to reveal about subjective experience? William James identified five characteristics of thought, which have stood the test of time, and Erik Klinger found three dimensions of thinking. Furthermore, one's inner life appears to be a mixture of perceptions, thoughts, images, self-talk, emotions, music, and other events that occur in one's experiential stream. As we explored the nature of the waking state, we shifted attention to the imaginative aspects of the stream and considered mind wandering and daydreaming, and the uses of the imagination both for psychological and physiological benefit within our own bodies as well as those of others. We ended with an examination of sensory restriction and its practical applications.

A number of thematic threads were woven through our survey, such as the application or abnegation of the will, the meaningfulness of interior events, the nature of an apparently transient self, the benefits of guided imagery and sensory restriction, the extent to which feelings of reality provide assurance of anything being actually real, and, at the end, a question about the veridicality of sensed presences.

Let us now cross the threshold from waking imaginal activity into the prototypical altered state of consciousness, sleep, and see what further we can learn about the characteristics of the human psyche.

3

Sleep

Although the ordinary waking state is the state against which all other states are compared, sleep is the prototype of an altered state. Clearly there are physiological, cognitive, and experiential changes associated with sleep. Indeed, the stages of sleep are defined by some of the physiological changes that occur during sleep, so we will pay more attention to the physiological perspective in this chapter than we have previously. But for all that it is familiar, just as with the ordinary waking state, the history of sleep research has revealed sleep to be a varied phenomenon. Although fundamental questions about the nature of consciousness and reality surface less often with the study of sleep than other alterations of consciousness, there are other provocative questions specific to the subject matter. What happens to the body during sleep? What happens to consciousness during sleep? How do different drugs affect sleep? Why do we sleep? What are some of the ways in which sleep becomes disordered? What happens during sleepwalking? Should we be held accountable for actions that we commit while asleep? The answers, to the extent that they are available, may surprise us, so that by the time we get to the end of this chapter and through most of the next one concerning dreams, we will see that some of the fundamental distinctions between wakefulness and sleep have disappeared.

http://dx.doi.org/10.1037/0000200-003
Alterations of Consciousness: An Empirical Analysis for Social Scientists, Second Edition,
by I. Baruš

SLEEP PHYSIOLOGY AND BEHAVIOR

Let us start at the beginning—not the historical beginning this time, as in Chapter 2, but the biological beginning, with the brain. That will allow us to describe the physiological changes that take place during sleep.

The Nervous System

The brain is made of two types of cells, nerve cells and glial cells, as well as open spaces that are filled with a fluid, called the *cerebrospinal fluid*. *Nerve cells* are the cells in the body that are usually associated with the processing of information. *Glial cells* are support cells of various types with specific functions, such as providing insulation for nerve cells, but which have also been found in the last several decades to be involved in information processing in the body (Fields, 2009; McGinty & Szymusiak, 2017). Extending from the brain is the *spinal cord*, which is made up of nerve cells inside the backbone. Or we can think of it the other way around. The spinal cord, on its way into the head, widens to become the *brainstem*, the top of which is a structure called the *thalamus*, located in the center of the head, which in turn opens up into the multiply folded *cerebral cortex*, which wraps around the lower parts of the brain (Netter, 1986).

This is how the system works. Your cat snuggles up against your hand, a message travels along peripheral nerve cells from your hand to the spinal cord, up the spinal cord, through the brainstem into the part of the cortex that maps the sensation of touch in your hand, then into the rest of the brain where higher levels of processing take place; you decide to pet your cat; the motor part of the cortex, called the *motor cortex*, sends a message back down through the brainstem, the spinal cord, and peripheral nerves to the arm and hand; then you stroke your cat. Simple, yes?

There are other aggregates of nerve cells attached to this corridor to which we will need to make reference. A structure called the *hypothalamus* hangs from the thalamus and is implicated in the regulation of bodily processes, such as temperature, food and water intake, and emotional behavior (Netter, 1986). The *hippocampus*, also within the middle of the brain, with some connections to the thalamus, is implicated in memory. The *prefrontal cortex* is a part of the cortex at the front of the brain, with important connections to the thalamus, and implicated in the deliberate management of one's own behavior. Both the hippocampus and central regions of the prefrontal cortex are part of the more extensive default mode network to which we have already alluded. So suppose that your mind starts to wander as you pet your cat, thereby resulting in *perceptual decoupling* from sensory input; that would further engage the default mode network even as you continue to pet your cat (Smallwood, Margulies, Bernhardt, & Jefferies, 2018, p. 77).

The brain is bilaterally symmetrical, in that structures horizontally away from the midline come in pairs. That applies also to the cerebral cortex, which has a *left hemisphere* and a *right hemisphere* connected by a number of bundles of nerve cells (Carlson, 1994; Netter, 1986).

Much is known about the higher levels of processing in the brain, but there is considerable controversy concerning the manner in which sensations become conscious perceptions, how perceptions can be conscious, how consciousness arises in the brain, how volition plays a role in cognitive processing, and whether, indeed, human experience can be explained entirely in terms of brain processes (Libet, Freeman, & Sutherland, 1999; Searle, 2000; Shear, 1996). Those are all themes that will continue to play out as we move forward in this book.

Messages travel from one nerve cell, or *neuron*, to the next. The neuron's *cell body*, along with branching projections called *dendrites*, is the receiving end of the neuron, while a branching projection from the cell body, called an *axon*, is the transmitting end. Messages along neurons are actually changes in the electrical potentials across the cells' walls created through electrochemical processes. Communication between nerve cells in human beings takes place through the release of chemicals called *neurotransmitters* into the intercellular fluid from various locations on the axon of one cell and the attachment of the chemicals to *receptor sites* on the dendrites or cell bodies of subsequent cells. Electrochemical processes are thereby activated that can inhibit or enhance a subsequent cell's ability to send a message. After binding to receptor sites for a while, neurotransmitters are taken up by the cell from which they came or broken down and flushed away in the intercellular fluid (Carlson, 1994).

Historically, it was thought that nothing happened in the brain unless it received stimulation through the senses so that sleep was the result of a dormant brain (Dement, 2000). In fact, this was a hypothesis that Lilly tested by climbing into the isolation tank. As he found out, removal of almost all sensory stimulation did not inevitably cause sleep (Lilly, 1978). Nor, as we shall see, is the brain dormant during sleep. A fair amount of spontaneous electrochemical activity goes on at all times. Not all of the activity is excitatory. Many neural circuits are inhibitory in that they attenuate the activity in other neural circuits, including those that bring sensory messages from the periphery. There are also groups of nerve cells known as *pacemakers* in various parts of the brain that synchronize the electrochemical activity of other groups of nerve cells (Steriade, 2000).

Polysomnography

If the electrochemical activity of groups of cells can become synchronized, is it possible to measure any resultant collective voltage changes? Yes, some voltage changes can be measured. Electrodes attached at various locations on the scalp can detect changes in electrical potential across the dendritic membranes primarily of layers of the cortex close to the skull (Aldrich, 1999; McGinty & Szymusiak, 2017). In other words, there is electrochemical activity throughout the brain, including the rhythmic activity of pacemakers that entrain whole groups of cells. If we stick electrodes on a person's scalp, we can pick up changes in electrical activity of groups of cells that are not too far from the electrodes. The observed changes of electrical potential over time look like waves, which can be recorded using an *electroencephalogram* (*EEG*). More sophisticated methods of imaging brain activity have been developed in recent years that allow for better spatial and temporal resolution of brain activity (Lester, Felder, & Lewis, 1997; Stevner et al., 2019), and we shall consider these as we go along. But the EEG is the primary instrument that has been used for defining the physiological changes associated with sleep (Keenan & Hirshkowitz, 2017; Rechtschaffen & Kales, 1968).

Some of the patterns of voltage changes over time that are seen with an EEG can be classified into frequency bands. Waves of frequency greater than 13 cycles per second (cps) are called *beta waves*, those 8 to 13 cps are *alpha waves*, those 4 to 7 cps are *theta waves*, and those less than 4 cps are *delta waves* (cf. Aldrich, 1999; Carskadon & Rechtschaffen, 2000; Keenan & Hirshkowitz, 2017; Walter & Dovey, 1944). In general, shorter, more rapid waves tend to be of lesser amplitude, whereas longer waves of lower frequency tend to be of greater amplitude. Delta waves, for example, can exceed amplitudes of 200 microvolts from trough to peak (e.g., Rechtschaffen & Kales, 1968). Other, more specific waveforms with regard to frequency and amplitude have also been identified, as we shall see.

In addition to an electroencephalogram, two other electrical devices have been used for defining the course of sleep. One of these is the *electrooculogram* (*EOG*), which is used for detecting eye movements through electrodes taped close to the eyes. The other is the *electromyogram* (*EMG*), which measures muscle tension through electrodes placed beneath the chin (Carskadon & Rechtschaffen, 2000; Keenan & Hirshkowitz, 2017). A number of other devices can be used to measure physiological events of interest such as heart rate, oxygen content of the blood, breathing difficulties (Kryger, 2000), penile circumference (Ware & Hirshkowitz, 2000), and motor movements (Spielman, Yang, & Glovinsky, 2000). The simultaneous recording of various physiological measures during sleep is called *polysomnography* (Aldrich, 1999; Keenan & Hirshkowitz, 2017).

Traditionally, polysomnography has been carried out in a sleep laboratory associated with a university or a clinic. A participant would spend one or more nights sleeping in a bed in a room in the sleep laboratory while being monitored. A digital copy of the sleep record would be obtained, which would be recorded, scored, and summarized on a computer. With increasing miniaturization of electronics, *portable computerized polysomnography* has become feasible so that sleep records can be obtained from people sleeping at home in their own beds. This has the advantage of collecting data in a naturalistic setting in which sleep cannot be disturbed by the strangeness of sleeping in a laboratory (cf. Carskadon & Dement, 2017). When the purpose is to look for sleep-disordered breathing, such portable monitoring is called *home sleep testing,* and has been found to be as accurate as testing done in a sleep laboratory (Penzel, 2017, p. 1610).

A more versatile and less expensive way of collecting information about sleep is to use *actigraphy*, the measurement of movement using *actigraphs*, devices that are usually worn on the wrist and that can detect movement (Ancoli-Israel et al., 2015; Stone & Ancoli-Israel, 2017). The idea is that when we sleep, we do not move around much, so measuring amount of movement could be used for detecting when we are asleep and if we are moving around too much during sleep. Actigraphy has been used in both clinical as well as research settings, and can be helpful for specific populations such as children or people in late adulthood with dementia, where polysomnography might not be tolerated (Stone & Ancoli-Israel, 2017).

Sleep Stages

Using the physiological measures of EEG, EOG, and EMG, we can investigate what happens when we sleep. At the most general level, what we find is that sleep can be divided into two main types: *rapid eye movement* (REM) sleep and nonrapid eye movement (NREM) sleep, which itself is further subdivided into four stages.

Note two things before we consider the details. First, in a manual published in 2007, the American Academy of Sleep Medicine grouped Stages 3 and 4 of NREM sleep into a single stage and renamed them so that NREM sleep Stages 1 to 4 became N1, N2, and N3. REM sleep was renamed "R" sleep. There were several other changes made to scoring sleep, but the changes have not been universally accepted (Carskadon & Dement, 2017), so we will continue to use the more established version. Second, given that there are variations in the physiology of sleep with age, it should be noted that the following description of sleep stages pertains to young adults.

While awake, in the ordinary waking state, the EEG reveals beta activity with some intermixed alpha activity and occasional theta. The EOG shows rapid eye movements and eye blinks, and the EMG indicates "high levels of muscle activity" (Aldrich, 1999, p. 10). For 85% to 90% of people, relaxing and closing their eyes results in the occurrence of alpha rhythm. The onset of sleep is indicated by the attenuation of alpha and the predominance of theta (Aldrich, 1999) so that the EEG pattern of NREM Stage 1 sleep has been described as "relatively low voltage, mixed frequency EEG" (Rechtschaffen & Kales, 1968, p. 5). "Slow, often asynchronous eye movements" (Carskadon & Dement, 2000, p. 16) occur during the transition from wakefulness to Stage 1 sleep; their onset usually preceding the beginning of sleep by 1 or 2 minutes, although the lead time can be as long as 15 minutes (Carskadon & Rechtschaffen, 2000). While there "generally is no discrete change in EMG amplitude in the wake-to-sleep transition . . . a gradual diminution of the EMG signal amplitude may occur within moments" (Carskadon & Rechtschaffen, 2000, p. 1203) of sleep onset. Although lack of behavioral reaction to sensory stimuli can be used as a criterion, there is some ambiguity regarding the exact point at which a person is to be regarded as having fallen asleep. For instance, in a study of sleep onset, participants sat at a desk and alternately tapped two switches at a steady pace. Their tapping behavior continued for "several seconds after the EEG changes to a stage 1 sleep pattern" (Carskadon & Dement, 2017, pp. 17–18) and "may explain how impaired, drowsy drivers are able to continue down the highway" (p. 18).

Stage 1 sleep lasts for 1 to 7 minutes before giving way to Stage 2 sleep (Carskadon & Dement, 2000) characterized by the presence of K complexes and sleep spindles against a "background of mixed frequencies predominantly in the theta range" (Aldrich, 1999, p. 11). A *K complex* is a waveform lasting for at least 0.5 second that consists of a sharp negative component "several hundred microvolts" in amplitude immediately followed by a "positive slow wave" (Aldrich, 1999, p. 12) of smaller amplitude (Aldrich, 1999). About one to three K complexes per minute would occur during Stage 2 in young adults (Carskadon & Rechtschaffen, 2000). A *sleep spindle* is a brain wave of about 12 to 14 cps in frequency (cf. Aldrich, 1999; Hirshkowitz, Moore, & Minhoto, 1997; Rechtschaffen & Kales, 1968), lasting 0.5 to 1.5 seconds, that often waxes and wanes in amplitude. About three to eight spindles per minute would occur during Stage 2 sleep in normal adults, and "spindle rate appears to be a fairly stable individual characteristic" (Carskadon & Rechtschaffen, 2000, p. 1203). Slow eye movements "may infrequently and only very briefly persist after the appearance of sleep spindles and K complexes" (Carskadon & Rechtschaffen, 2000, p. 1204). The EMG is "generally at a low amplitude relative to wakefulness" (Carskadon & Rechtschaffen, 2000, p. 1204).

As Stage 2 sleep deepens, high-amplitude delta waves become more frequent. When delta waves slower than 2 cps of at least 75 microvolts occupy more than 20% of the sleep record, the sleeper is said to be in Stage 3. If such slow, high-amplitude delta waves occupy more than 50% of the sleep record, then the sleeper is in Stage 4 sleep (Rechtschaffen & Kales, 1968). Both K complexes and sleep spindles can occur in Stages 3 and 4, although they may be difficult to differentiate from the predominant delta activity. Stages 3 and 4 of sleep are sometimes collectively referred to as *slow-wave sleep* (SWS), "delta sleep, or deep sleep, or N3" (Carskadon & Dement, 2017, p. 20). During slow-wave sleep there are no eye movements and, while muscle tension is still present, the levels are low (Carskadon & Rechtschaffen, 2000). In the course of its first occurrence after falling asleep, Stage 2 has a duration of about 10 to 25 minutes, Stage 3 usually lasts only a few minutes, and Stage 4 persists for 20 to 40 minutes (Carskadon & Dement, 2000).

About 80 minutes from sleep onset there is a change in the polysomnograph, indicating a transition to yet another sleep stage (Aldrich, 1999). The delta activity declines, there may be a few minutes of Stage 3, 2, or 1 (cf. Aldrich, 1999; Carskadon & Dement, 2000), and then a "low voltage, mixed-frequency" (Rechtschaffen & Kales, 1968, p. 7) rhythm occurs that resembles that of Stage 1. There may, however, be alpha activity that is about 1 to 2 cps slower than waking alpha and *sawtooth waves* of 2 to 6 cps occurring intermittently "usually in runs lasting 1 to 5 seconds" (Aldrich, 1999, p. 14). These changes in EEG are accompanied by changes in EOG and EMG. Sometimes the eyes move sporadically in a jerky manner during this stage, giving rise to the moniker REM, although the rapidity of eye movements is not greater than that during waking (Aserinsky, 1996; Aserinsky & Kleitman, 1953). The rapid eye movements "occur singly or in bursts" (Aldrich, 1999, p. 14), often accompanied by sawtooth waves and brief episodes of facial muscle activity (Aldrich, 1999). It is the presence of rapid eye movements during this sleep stage that led to the moniker REM sleep, with the previous stages being called non-REM sleep (Carskadon & Dement, 2017).

Within REM sleep, the periods of time when there is "muscle twitching with bursts of eye movements" have often been "referred to as *phasic REM sleep*," whereas periods of time during REM sleep when there are "few or no eye movements and muscle twitches" have been "referred to as *tonic REM sleep*" (Aldrich, 1999, p. 14). The muscle twitches during REM sleep are short-lived events against a background of muscle atonia, which consists of the "suppression of skeletal muscle tone and reflexes" (Carskadon & Rechtschaffen, 2000, p. 1205) to levels below those of the other sleep stages (Carskadon & Rechtschaffen, 2000). Characteristic also of REM sleep are penile erections in men and "changes in erectile tissue" in women that begin "within a few minutes of the onset of REM sleep and [persist] throughout the REM period" (Aldrich, 1999, p. 19). Whereas NREM sleep has been characterized as "a relatively inactive yet actively regulating brain in a movable body" (Carskadon & Dement, 2000, p. 15), REM sleep has been described as "a highly activated brain in a paralyzed body" (p. 16). Because of the presence during sleep of brain activity comparable to that of waking, REM sleep has also been known as *paradoxical sleep* (Jouvet, 1993/1999, p. 2). The first REM sleep period lasts from a few minutes to about 15 minutes (cf. Aldrich, 1999; Carskadon & Dement, 2000).

Patterns of Sleep Stages

The cycling of NREM and REM sleep is repeated throughout a night's sleep, with the average length of the first cycle about 70 to 100 minutes, increasing to about 90 to 120 minutes in the second and later cycles so that there would be a total of 4 to 6 NREM–REM sleep cycles a night. The amount of time spent in slow-wave sleep decreases in the second cycle, and slow-wave sleep "may disappear altogether from later cycles, as stage 2 sleep expands to occupy the NREM portion of the cycle" (Carskadon & Dement, 2000, p. 20). Meanwhile, "the duration of REM sleep periods tends to increase with each successive cycle" (Aldrich, 1999, p. 14) so that the average period of REM sleep ends up being about 22 minutes long (cf. Carskadon & Dement, 2000). Stage 1 sleep constitutes 2% to 5% of sleep, Stage 2 is 45% to 55%, Stage 3 is 3% to 8%, Stage 4 is 10% to 15%, and REM sleep constitutes 20% to 25% of a night's sleep (Carskadon & Dement, 2000). Brief arousals and awakenings can occur from any of the sleep stages (Aldrich, 1999) and are regarded as a "natural concomitant of sleep" (Parrino & Terzano, 2017, p. 1578).

The proportions of different sleep stages as a percentage of a night's sleep that have been given here are those for young adults. Whereas "no consistent male versus female distinctions have been found in the normal pattern of sleep in young adults" (Carskadon & Dement, 2000, p. 19), as mentioned at the outset, there are differences in the physiological patterns of sleep associated with age. Although the alteration of NREM sleep and REM sleep is present in newborn infants, it has a period of only 50 to 60 minutes (Carskadon & Dement, 2000). Infants often enter the cycle through REM sleep, which "constitutes approximately 50% of the sleep period" (Hirshkowitz et al., 1997, p. 22), and declines until adolescence, when it "stabilizes at adult levels" (pp. 22, 25), which are "maintained well into healthy old age" (Carskadon & Dement, 2000, p. 21). The EEG patterns of NREM sleep emerge "over the first 2 to 6 months of life" with slow-wave sleep being "maximal in young children" and decreasing "markedly with age" (Carskadon & Dement, 2000, p. 21). Indeed, slow-wave sleep may no longer be present by age 60, with women maintaining slow-wave sleep later into life than men (Carskadon & Dement, 2000). "Total sleep time declines throughout the life span, and after middle age, wakefulness intermixed with sleep . . . begins to increase in many individuals" (Hirshkowitz et al., 1997, p. 25). Variability in the characteristics of sleep increases in late adulthood so that it is difficult to "make generalizations such as those made for young adults" (Carskadon & Dement, 2000, p. 21).

Another factor plays a role in the length and timing of sleep stages—namely, the presence of biological rhythms. *Circadian rhythms* are approximately 24-hour cycles generated by an internal *circadian pacemaker system* that constrains a multiplicity of physiological and behavioral events including sleep and waking, "endocrine secretions, body temperature regulation, sensory processing, and cognitive performance" (Mistlberger & Rusak, 2000, p. 321). It has been proposed that sleep is regulated by both homeostatic and circadian processes. During the day and subsequently as long as waking continues, sleep need increases and with it the homeostatically regulated pressure for slow-wave sleep. The circadian process increases the propensity for sleep during the night and decreases it during the day. Thus, the circadian rhythm helps to maintain sleep during the night as sleep pressure from the homeostatic process declines, and it helps to maintain alertness during the day as sleep pressure escalates (Borbély & Achermann, 2000; see also Aldrich, 1999).

The distinction between REM and NREM sleep dates back to the 1950s (Pelayo & Dement, 2017) and the use of technology that was available at that time, namely, the EEG, EOG, and EMG. The brain is a complex organ, and these are crude measures. Furthermore, the standard technique for scoring sleep stages requires only a single EEG channel (Keenan & Hirshkowitz, 2017)! What happens if we investigate sleep using more sophisticated brain imaging techniques?

Angus Stevner and colleagues monitored 57 healthy volunteers using functional magnetic resonance imaging, which is a brain imaging technology capable of detecting physiological activity in the brain, as well as EEG, as they were falling asleep. Rather than just three or four NREM stages, the researchers found 19 whole-brain states, each of which could last from seconds to tens of seconds, indicating the complexity of the brain's activity during NREM sleep. For instance, "brain activity prior to sleep is significantly different from just after sleep" (Stevner et al., 2019, p. 12) so that if we wake up after having briefly fallen asleep, we are not in the same state that we had been in before falling asleep, even though both of those states would be regarded as being awake. A higher resolution picture of brain activity during sleep could be helpful for a more nuanced understanding of sleep physiology.

EFFECTS OF DRUGS ON SLEEP

One of the common ways in which the normal sleep pattern can be disturbed is through the ingestion of drugs. For instance, *adenosine* is a chemical in the brain whose concentrations increase during wakefulness, thereby creating pressure to sleep. Caffeine, however, blocks adenosine receptors so that adenosine cannot exercise its effects and sleep can be delayed (M. Walker, 2017). There is a variety of chemicals with various effects (e.g., Kilduff & Mendelson, 2017; Lydic, Keifer, Baghdoyan, Craft, & Angel, 2017; Schweitzer & Randazzo, 2017), but we will consider only one example here, for illustrative purposes.

There is a class of drugs known as *selective serotonin reuptake inhibitors* (*SSRIs*) used in the treatment of depression, whose primary effect is to block the reuptake of the neurotransmitter serotonin so that it cannot be taken back up into the cell from which it was released. The result is that serotonin remains in the synapses longer, continuing to stimulate the next cell in the communication sequence. Serotonin is associated with arousal; its levels need to decrease in order for the mechanisms associated with REM sleep to become activated. Since SSRIs keep levels of serotonin high, we would expect that SSRIs would interfere with sleep. And that is indeed what has been found, although the mechanism is not necessarily the obvious one. SSRIs worsen sleep, generally increase wakefulness, and decrease total sleep time (Schweitzer, 2000; Schweitzer & Randazzo, 2017; Wichniak, Wierzbicka, Walęcka, & Jernajczyk, 2017).

A number of detrimental effects on sleep have been attributed to an SSRI called *fluoxetine*. In one study 41 clinical outpatients with depression were evaluated for nocturnal eye movements and muscle tension in a sleep laboratory before and after 4 to 5 weeks of daily treatment with 20 milligrams of fluoxetine. "Every subject showed increased activity from baseline in at least one measure of oculomotor activity" (Armitage, Trivedi, & Rush, 1995, p. 161). Fourteen participants had increases in eye movements and muscle tone in all sleep stages, 29 had an increased number of eye movements, 30 had increased size of eye movements, and 33 had increased muscle tension. "The eye movements induced by fluoxetine are not classic, binocularly symmetrical, rapid eye movements" but "are better characterized as medium to fast eye movements" (Armitage et al., 1995, p. 163). Fluoxetine intoxication leads to increased eye movements even in sleep Stages 2 to 4 of NREM sleep (Armitage et al., 1995). In another study, the polysomnographic records of nine depressed hospital inpatients being treated with 10 to 80 milligrams of fluoxetine who were complaining of insomnia and fatigue were compared with six depressed inpatients not being treated with fluoxetine but also complaining of insomnia and fatigue. Those being treated with fluoxetine had worse sleep efficiency, a greater number of eye movements during Stages 2 to 4 of NREM sleep, and took longer to enter REM sleep (Dorsey, Lukas, & Cunningham, 1996).

The detrimental effects of fluoxetine extend to disturbing muscle activity. *Periodic limb movements* are "four or more" (Montplaisir, Nicolas, Godbout, & Walters, 2000, p. 744) movements of the legs and sometimes arms (Aldrich, 1999), each of which lasts from 0.5 to 5 seconds and is separated by an interval of 4 to 90 seconds from temporally adjacent ones (Montplaisir et al., 2000). Periodic limb movements are found most frequently during Stages 1 and 2 of NREM sleep, less frequently during slow-wave sleep, and are "generally absent" (Aldrich, 1999, p. 177) from REM sleep. *Periodic limb movement disorder* is diagnosed if there are more than five periodic limb movements an hour for each hour of sleep (cf. Montplaisir et al., 2000). In the study with depressed hospital inpatients, four of the nine participants being treated with fluoxetine had "clinically significant" (Dorsey et al., 1996, p. 440) periodic limb movement disorder. "Some aperiodic leg movements also were observed" in the fluoxetine group, and "elevation of overall muscle tone was apparent in all fluoxetine recordings" (Dorsey et al., 1996, p. 440).

Results somewhat similar to those just described were found in a study of six children and adolescents with an average age of 12 years tested before and after about 11 months of using 10 to 20 milligrams of fluoxetine daily. The percentage of Stage 1 sleep almost doubled, the number of arousals increased, the number of eye movements during REM sleep increased, and there were five times as many leg movements, with four of the six children meeting criteria for periodic leg movement disorder (Armitage, Emslie, & Rintelmann, 1997). Much as it looks as though that should be the case, it is not clear whether these effects of fluoxetine can be attributed directly to the potentiation of serotonin in neural pathways regulating sleep, or whether the effects are, in fact, more indirect, for example, through serotonergic effects on dopaminergic pathways (Armitage et al., 1995).

SLEEP MENTATION

We have opened this chapter from the physiological perspective. Let us turn for a bit to the experiential perspective. What is a person's experience while they sleep? An obliteration of consciousness? Thinking? Dreaming? Let us begin by considering arousal from sleep and then the various sorts of mental activity that could go on as we sleep, subject matter that we will take up more fully in the following chapter, "Dreams."

Arousal

The possibility of being aroused from sleep by external stimulation depends on the sleep stage and the meaningfulness of the stimulus. It is easiest to awaken someone from Stage 1, most difficult from Stage 4, with the difficulty of waking someone from REM sleep being variable (Aldrich, 1999). In particular, "it is nearly impossible" to awaken young children from the slow-wave sleep of the "night's first sleep cycle" (Carskadon & Dement, 2000, p. 21). In some studies, "using meaningless stimuli" (R. Broughton, 1986, p. 464), it has been found that the thresholds for awakening from REM sleep were higher than those for awakening from Stages 3 and 4 of NREM sleep. However, in other studies it has been shown that individuals can be easily awakened from REM sleep by stimuli that are significant to them. "An example of a particularly effective stimulus is the playing of a tape recording of her infant's crying to a sleeping mother" (R. Broughton, 1986, p. 464). In general, meaningful stimuli are more effective than meaningless stimuli in evoking K complexes (R. Broughton, 1986), thereby showing that the brain is processing stimuli while we sleep. There are other event-related waveforms corresponding to the automatic detection of changes in sound. Their presence has been used to infer that auditory stimuli are processed without awareness in REM sleep (Nashida et al., 2000). What these data collectively suggest is that we monitor at least some sensory stimuli while we sleep and wake up if they are too intense or of sufficient significance to us (R. Broughton, 1986).

Brief awakenings from sleep may not be remembered. In one study, participants monitored with a polysomnograph were presented with word pairs at 1-minute intervals through speakers located by the bed in which they were lying and "were requested to repeat each word pair aloud . . . after hearing it" (Wyatt, Bootzin, Anthony, & Stevenson, 1992, p. 113). In the course of this task, participants fell asleep and were subsequently awakened after either 30 seconds or 10 minutes of sleep. When asked to recall the word pairs, participants who had been awakened after 10 minutes of sleep showed impaired performance for the word pairs presented within 3 minutes before sleep onset. The same decrement in performance was not noted for those who were awakened after only 30 seconds of sleep (Wyatt et al., 1992). It may be that sleep interferes with the consolidation of short-term memory into long-term memory. Whatever the explanation, we are unlikely to remember what happened during the few minutes before falling asleep after having slept for about 10 minutes. This memory impairment includes the inability to remember the moment of falling asleep, forgetting conversations that occurred in the middle of the night, and having difficulty remembering dreams (Carskadon & Dement, 2000).

Dreaming

Of course, when we think of sleep, we usually think of dreaming, the experiences that go on for us as we sleep. In other words, even with diminished consciousness$_1$ and usually absent behavioral consciousness$_2$, subjective consciousness$_2$ and perhaps consciousness$_3$ go on, at least for some people some of the time. But how is dreaming related to the sleep stages? In Eugene Aserinsky's initial sleep laboratory studies, when participants were awakened from REM sleep, 20 of 27 times (74%) they reported "detailed dreams usually involving visual imagery" (Aserinsky & Kleitman, 1953, p. 273), whereas when they were awakened from NREM sleep only two of 23 (9%) reported such dreams, with two others reporting having had "'the feeling of having dreamed,' but with inability to recollect any detail of the dream" (pp. 273–274). So, historically for a while, dreaming became identified with REM sleep (Foulkes, 1996).

However, the situation is not nearly so simple. Considerable effort to try to characterize the differences between NREM and REM dreams has resulted in the conclusion that some NREM dreams can be indistinguishable from REM dreams (Cavallero, Cicogna, Natale, Occhionero, & Zito, 1992, p. 565; Nielsen, 2017). Why, then, have fewer dreams been reported from NREM sleep than REM sleep? In one study, even when participants could not recall a dream upon awakening from slow-wave sleep, participants would frequently make comments such as "definitely there was something going on, but now it is gone" (Cavallero et al., 1992, p. 565). The investigators have offered the suggestion that "mental activity is continuously present during sleep and that cortical activation (even if synchronized as in SWS) is a sufficient condition for dream production" (Cavallero et al., 1992, p. 565; see also Schredl, Brennecke, & Reinhard, 2013).

But what counts as dreaming? For some researchers, sleep mentation counts as a dream only if it meets specific criteria, such as the presence of a narrative involving oneself as the protagonist. In fact, borrowing concepts from virtual reality, there has been a trend to define dreams using simulation language, so that dreams are defined as immersive experiences of an embodied self engaged in a hallucinated world (Nielsen, 2017; Windt, Nielsen, & Thompson, 2016). But that leaves out a lot. We already saw that during the ordinary waking state thoughts can be degenerated, and that is also the case with mentation that occurs during sleep onset and sleep.

Jennifer Windt and her colleagues have proposed the following typology of *dreamless sleep experiences*. First, there can be "Non-Immersive Imagery and Sleep Thinking," such as static images in any sense modality, sensations of movement, or just thinking, without the "narrative complexity of dreams" that frequently occur during sleep onset or NREM sleep. Second, there can be "Perceptual Experiences and Bodily Sensations" that are sensory impressions intruding into a person's experience, such as pain, possibly intermixed with a hallucinatory setting. Third, there can be "'Selfless' States and Contentless Experiences" in which there is no imagery or thinking occurring, just consciousness$_3$ witnessing sleeping or wakefulness (Windt et al., 2016, p. 873). This reflects some of the variety of the phenomenology of sleep mentation with less preoccupation with its theoretical manageability. And that reminds us of our fourth thematic thread, that maybe, sometimes, something unusual is occurring.

THE BENEFITS OF SLEEP

> Scientists have discovered a revolutionary new treatment that makes you live longer. It enhances your memory and makes you more creative. It makes you look more attractive. It keeps you slim and lowers food cravings. It protects you from cancer and dementia. It wards off colds and the flu. It lowers your risk of heart attacks and stroke, not to mention diabetes. You'll even feel happier, less depressed, and less anxious. Are you interested? (M. Walker, 2017, p. 107)

Researchers used to wonder what the point was of sleep. No longer. So many benefits have been identified that questions regarding the need for sleep have pretty much disappeared. But could those benefits be available without the sort of mutated mentation that goes on during sleep? Could our bodies not sleep and still reap the benefits of sleep while we continue to actively engage with our environment with the full clarity of our ordinary waking state? Good question. But that gets us back to the mysterious presence of consciousness. Why is it there anyway? We will briefly consider sleep need before considering some of the benefits of sleep.

Sleep Need

If we completely deprive a person of sleep, the most obvious consequence is sleepiness (Bonnet, 2000) with marked decreases in cognitive performance being more insidious (Everson, 1997). Initially, poor task performance can be overcome by motivation, but after about 48 to 64 hours of total sleep deprivation "poor performance cannot be overcome by motivational forces" (Everson, 1997, p. 38). Longer periods of sleep loss have greater impacts on task performance than shorter periods, with "speed of performance" (Bonnet, 2000, p. 53) being more affected than accuracy. Tasks that are most affected by sleep loss are "long, monotonous, without feedback, externally paced, newly learned, and [contain] a memory component" (Bonnet, 2000, p. 58). Mood appears to be more strongly affected than cognitive ability, which, in turn, appears to be more strongly affected than motor activity (Bonnet, 2000). Mood changes can occur after a single night of sleep loss, "worsen as the sleep deprivation is prolonged" and result in "emotional instability" (Everson, 1997, p. 39) during the time of sleep loss. Misperceptions and hallucinations, "primarily visual and tactile" (Everson, 1997, p. 39), are commonly reported, sometimes after only 48 hours of total sleep deprivation, although they become more intense as sleep loss progresses. In one study, after 205 hours of total sleep deprivation, the participants experienced lapses, which were sometimes associated with transient periods of disorientation, confusion, forgetfulness, or reports of dreams (Everson, 1997). In studies of partial sleep loss, investigators have found rapid functional impairment with nightly sleep periods of 5 hours or less, and the possibility of measurable decrements following 6-hour sleep periods (Bonnet, 2000).

We live in a culture of sleep deprivation. In the United States, 35% to 40% of adults sleep less than 7 to 8 hours a night during the week, with 15% sleeping less than 6 hours a night (Banks, Dorrian, Basner, & Dinges, 2017). In a "large European study of almost 25,000 individuals" (M. Walker, 2017, p. 184), the investigators found that "sleeping six hours or less was associated with a 40 percent increased risk of developing cancer, relative to those sleeping seven hours a night or more" (pp. 184–185).

We make it difficult for ourselves to get adequate sleep. For instance, in one study, reading a book on an electronic tablet suppressed the release of melatonin, a sleep-promoting substance in the brain, by over 50% compared with reading a book made of paper, because of the light emitted by the electronic device, which alerts the brain to be awake (M. Walker, 2017). In another study, smartphone addiction by university students was related to depression, anxiety, and sleep quality (Demirci, Akgönül, & Akpinar, 2015). And nonprescription drug use among college students was associated with various sleep problems (Alamir et al., 2019). And that is just a taste of the behaviors that can lead to sleep impairment.

Physiological Benefits

At the most basic level, sleep seems to play a biologically restorative function. The brain seems to be resting, at least during SWS. The presence of delta waves corresponds to lowered brain activity as evidenced by cerebral metabolic rates and blood flow rates that, in Stage 4 sleep, are 75% of what they are during waking (Carlson, 1994). The activity of the *sympathetic division of the autonomic nervous system*, a subsystem of the nervous system that induces physiological activation in the body (cf. Carlson, 1994), is decreased by about 30% to 50% during slow-wave sleep compared with wakefulness (Aldrich, 1999). A restorative function for sleep has also been suggested by "increased rates of cerebral protein synthesis" (Schwartz, 1997, p. 5) during slow-wave sleep. Slow-wave sleep has also been associated with the secretion of growth hormone, which, because of its particular importance for stimulating children's growth, may explain why "SWS is high during children's peak developmental years and declines (or can even disappear) with advancing age" (Hirshkowitz et al., 1997, p. 31).

More recently, in studies with mice published in 2013, Maiken Nedergaard with colleagues uncovered a *glymphatic system* in the brain that clears out toxic materials surrounding neurons, such as the breakdown products of synaptic processes. What is striking is that, during NREM sleep, the glial cells in the brain shrink, thereby creating a 60% increase in the spaces between the cells, allowing cerebrospinal fluid to flow through the opened channels to efficiently flush waste material from the brain during this glymphatic process (Kanda et al., 2016; M. Walker, 2017; Xie et al., 2013). The researchers concluded that "the restorative function of sleep may be due to the switching of the brain into a functional state that facilitates the clearance of degradation products of neural activity that accumulate during wakefulness" (Xie et al., 2013, p. 377).

Some of the toxic chemicals that are cleared from the brain are beta-amyloid proteins and tau proteins, both of which have been implicated in the development of Alzheimer's disease. Put crudely, "wakefulness is low-level brain damage, while sleep is neurological sanitation" (M. Walker, 2017, p. 161). Other authors have showed the relationship between beta-amyloid accumulation and deterioration of sleep quality (Branger et al., 2016; B. M. Brown et al., 2016) and noted that sleep can ameliorate the accumulation of toxic proteins through the activity of the glymphatic system during sleep (Petit, Montplaisir, St. Louis, & Boeve, 2017). So, not surprisingly, insufficient sleep across the life span is associated with the development of Alzheimer's disease. And, conversely, there is some evidence that improving a person's sleep quality can slow the cognitive decline associated with Alzheimer's disease (M. Walker, 2017).

Cognitive Benefits

As I was reading the material for rewriting this chapter, such as the studies showing the different ways in which sleep increases learning and improves memory, I had great difficulty staying awake, so I ended up taking a nap in the morning! Then, another nap in the afternoon! Two naps in one day. And I reflected on the benefits of such somnolence as I practiced what I was reading.

Our ability to learn deteriorates during the day. In a study by Matthew Walker, at noon, young adults engaged in a task to learn 100 face–name pairs. Then, one group got to take a 90-minute nap while the remainder stayed awake. At 6:00 p.m. there was another set of 100 face–name pairs to memorize. Even though both groups retained their ability to concentrate, there was a "20 percent learning advantage for those who had slept" (M. Walker, 2017, p. 110). The replenished ability to learn was related to the number of sleep spindles that a person experienced during Stage 2 of NREM sleep. The more sleep spindles, the greater the replenished learning capacity. And these spindles were related to back-and-forth pulses between the hippocampus, implicated in short-term memory, and the cortex, associated with long-term memory, suggesting that sleep facilitated clearing out the hippocampus so that it could engage in new learning. In other studies, Walker also found the reverse effect with aging: "the fewer the number of spindles an elderly brain produced on a particular night, the lower the learning capacity of that older individual the next day" (M. Walker, 2017, p. 111).

Sleep after learning provides a benefit of 20% to 40% compared with remaining awake. For factual learning, again, it is NREM sleep that appears to shift the locus of memories from the hippocampus to the cortex, with the implication that the memories have thereby been consolidated into long-term memory (M. Walker, 2017). In a study with children by other researchers, a 90-minute nap after learning allowed for the reorganization of memories so that, after the nap, they were being retrieved from prefrontal areas, again, with the idea that they have thereby been assimilated with existing knowledge (Urbain et al., 2016). Not only does sleep assist with memory consolidation, but it can restore memories that have been forgotten since learning them. And it can selectively remember information that has been tagged as being important to remember and forget the information that has been tagged for forgetting, through the same interactive process of the hippocampus, specifically with the frontal lobe of the cortex. And it is not just factual memory that is improved by NREM sleep, but all forms of motor skills as well (M. Walker, 2017).

Whereas NREM sleep seems to facilitate tamping down what we know and what we can do, REM sleep appears to extend past learning toward comprehension by providing us with opportunities to combine what we know in unexpected ways leading to improved problem-solving abilities. In a study carried out by Walker, participants were given the task of unscrambling anagrams over a 90-second period while still awake and then after being awakened from NREM and REM sleep. Participants were able to solve 15% to 35% more puzzles after REM sleep than either after NREM sleep or while still awake. Furthermore, solutions were produced more quickly after REM and seemed to be more effortless than the more deliberate solutions following NREM or during presleep waking performance. The implication is that REM sleep facilitates abstract thinking that can lead to creative problem-solving. In other studies, it has been shown that problem-solving ability improves dramatically if a person dreams about elements of the problem that she is required to solve, suggesting that dream content can be linked to the improvements in comprehension taking place during REM sleep (M. Walker, 2017). So, in keeping with our eighth thematic thread, normal sleep is beneficial for well-being in a variety of specific ways.

SLEEP-WAKE DISORDERS

In the fifth edition of the *Diagnostic and Statistical Manual of Mental Disorders* (*DSM-5*; American Psychiatric Association, 2013), 11 sleep disorders are identified; of these, we will consider narcolepsy, a breathing-related sleep disorder, insomnia disorder, and some of the NREM sleep arousal disorders.

Narcolepsy

One of the oldest known sleep disorders is *narcolepsy* (Dement, 2000), a condition in which an individual experiences irresistible sleep attacks of "unintended sleep in inappropriate situations" (American Psychiatric Association, 2000, p. 610). For instance, one moment a person will be talking to someone; the next, she will fall over sound asleep (American Psychiatric Association, 2000). After a few minutes to possibly more than an hour, she wakes up relatively refreshed with "a refractory period of 1 to several hours before the next episode occurs" (Guilleminault & Anagnos, 2000, p. 677). Varying degrees of daytime sleepiness can also be present that cannot be entirely eradicated no matter how much sleep a person gets (Aldrich, 1999).

Cataplexy is a second symptom of narcolepsy. During a *cataplectic attack* there is bilateral muscle weakness that can range in severity from fleeting sensations of weakness throughout the body to "a slight buckling of the knees," stuttering, clumsiness, or "a complete loss of muscle tone" possibly leading to "total body collapse and the risk of serious injuries" (Guilleminault & Anagnos, 2000, p. 677). Cataplectic attacks can occur apparently spontaneously, or they can be brought on by emotions such as laughter or anger, "stress, fatigue, or heavy meals" (Guilleminault & Anagnos, 2000, p. 677), and they can last a few seconds to 30 minutes. Perhaps it is becoming clear what happens in narcolepsy. As a person falls asleep, not exclusively, but often, she goes directly into REM sleep rather than going through the NREM stages of sleep. Cataplexy occurs when the mechanisms for muscle atonia associated with REM sleep become activated without the person even having fallen asleep (cf. Carskadon & Dement, 2000).

A third possible symptom of narcolepsy that can result from a disconnection of REM sleep components is sleep paralysis. *Sleep paralysis* is "partial or total paralysis lasting a few seconds or minutes that occurs during transitions between sleep and wakefulness" (Aldrich, 1999, p. 155). What happens in sleep paralysis is similar to what happens in cataplexy except that it happens immediately before or after sleep. Sleep paralysis can also occur outside the context of narcolepsy, with 40% to 50% of individuals in the general population having experienced at least a single episode of sleep paralysis at some time in their lives (American Psychiatric Association, 2000).

Sometimes, associated with sleep paralysis in the context of narcolepsy while at other times occurring independently of it at the interface of sleep and waking (Aldrich, 1999), there can be vivid images that are called *hypnagogic* when they occur upon falling asleep and *hypnopompic* when they occur upon awakening. They are usually visual but can also be auditory or kinesthetic (American Psychiatric Association, 2000). There may be impressions of being rubbed or touched, "changes in location of body parts" (Guilleminault & Anagnos, 2000, p. 676), and *exosomatic* experiences—that is to say, experiences that appear to occur outside of one's body, including seeing one's body lying some distance below oneself (cf. Guilleminault & Anagnos, 2000). The prevalence rate of hypnagogic and hypnopompic images among the general population is approximately 10% to 15% (American Psychiatric Association, 2000). We shall return to a discussion about hypnagogic images in Chapter 4. In some cases of narcolepsy, sleep can be so disrupted that those with narcolepsy feel that "they spend the entire night drifting in and out of sleep with nightmares, intermittent hallucinations, and episodes of paralysis" (Aldrich, 1999, p. 156).

In some classification schemes, a distinction is made between *narcolepsy Type 1* (Na-1), in which cataplexy is present, and *narcolepsy Type 2* (Na-2), in which cataplexy is not present. The basis for this distinction is a recent observation that Na-1 appears to be an autoimmune disease of the brain in which hypocretin neurons originating in the hypothalamus are destroyed so that hypocretin peptides, also called *orexins*, cannot stimulate the brain systems that are required to sustain constant wakefulness (Cao & Guilleminault, 2017; Mignot, 2017). Hence NREM and REM breaks through into wakefulness. The same biological markers are not present for Na-2, which therefore appears to have a different etiology from Na-1.

Both behavioral and drug treatments have been used for narcolepsy. Behavioral treatment strategies consist of 15- to 20-minute naps every 4 hours during the day and good sleep hygiene, which is briefly characterized below in the section about insomnia. Drug treatments can include the use of stimulants such as amphetamines to offset daytime sleepiness and medications such as fluoxetine to counteract the muscle atonia associated with cataplexy (Cao & Guilleminault, 2017; Guilleminault & Anagnos, 2000). Indeed, such use of fluoxetine is an example of a drug whose side effects for one condition become the curative effects for another, highlighting the question of the relative dangers and benefits of drugs.

Sleep Apnea

Another long-standing sleep disorder is *obstructive sleep apnea hypopnea*, a form of breathing-related sleep disorder (American Psychiatric Association, 2013), in which a person experiences breathing disturbances resulting in a poor night's sleep and daytime sleepiness. What happens in obstructive sleep apnea is that a person falls asleep, their muscles relax, and the upper airway becomes blocked so that they cannot breathe (American Psychiatric Association, 2000). While they are not breathing, the level of carbon dioxide in the blood increases until the increase is registered by the nervous system, which wakes the person up enough to restore muscle tension, thereby opening the upper airway and allowing them to breathe (cf. Carlson, 1994). From what we have said previously regarding memory prior to sleep onset, such transient arousals are unlikely to be remembered by a person in the morning. However, someone present while the person is sleeping could hear "loud snores or brief gasps that alternate with episodes of silence that usually last 20–30 seconds" but can be "as long as 60–90 seconds" terminated by "snores, gasps, moans or mumbling, or whole-body movements" (American Psychiatric Association, 2000, p. 616). The throat does not always fall completely shut, causing apnea, but may close only partially, as evidenced by snoring, in which case we would call that *hypopnea*. Sometimes neither apnea nor hypopnea occur, nor does a drop in the oxygen content of the blood that usually accompanies them; it is just that upper airway resistance is increased, leading to "sleep fragmentation" (Sanders, 2000, p. 879).

Sleep apnea can have serious consequences. In one study, participants with severe sleep apnea had 13.0 motor vehicle accidents per million kilometers, whereas for those with milder sleep apnea that number was 1.1, and for those in a control group without sleep apnea it was 0.8 (Horstmann, Hess, Bassetti, Gugger, & Mathis, 2000). More generally, sleep apnea has been associated with decreased quality of life (Yang et al., 2000).

There is a noninvasive method of treating breathing-related sleep disorders, known as *continuous positive airway pressure*. If the problem is a collapse of the upper airway, increasing the pressure against the walls of the airway should open it. In using this treatment, a person with obstructive sleep apnea, hypopnea, or upper airway resistance would wear a mask over their nose, providing pressurized air to the upper airway, thereby keeping the airway open, which allows them to breathe. Indeed, this is often an effective form of therapy with increased slow-wave sleep and REM sleep being seen during the first week of use (Grunstein & Sullivan, 2000). Newer devices, using *autotitrating positive airway pressure* (APAP), optimize the air pressure in real time to compensate for variations in resistance. However, there are problems with compliance, as actual use of CPAP and APAP is around 40% to 83% (N. Freedman, 2017).

Insomnia Disorder

Insomnia refers to sleeplessness, difficulty falling asleep, nighttime awakenings, and early morning awakening (Partinen & Hublin, 2000). "Insomnia is the most common sleep-wake–related complaint, and sleeping pills are among the most commonly prescribed drugs in clinical practice at the primary health care level" (Partinen & Hublin, 2000, pp. 558–559) with the incidence of long-standing insomnia in middle-aged adults being about 10%, with women 1.5 times more likely to be affected than men (Partinen & Hublin, 2000). Although individual sleep needs differ (Carlson, 1994), insufficient sleep or sleep of insufficient quality leads to daytime sleepiness (Roehrs, Carskadon, Dement, & Roth, 2000), and can be accompanied by subjective feelings that one has slept poorly and wakened unrefreshed, deterioration of mood and attentional ability, and increased complaints of daytime fatigue (American Psychiatric Association, 2000).

Daytime sleepiness, in and of itself, need not be a sign of insomnia. In some cases, sleepiness is simply the result of chronically insufficient sleep, in which case there may be reports of sleeping about an additional 2 hours on weekend nights compared with weekday nights and polysomnographic evidence of unusually high sleep efficiency (Roehrs et al., 2000). There appears to have been a historical trend toward "voluntary curtailment of sleep" in that men in 1980, when compared with men in the 1930s, "were more likely to report fatigue and tiredness, although they were no more likely to report disturbed nocturnal sleep" (Bliwise, 1996, p. 462).

Sometimes subjective complaints of insomnia are not borne out by objective measures, in which case the condition is classified as *sleep state misperception*. In one study, participants with subjective complaints of insomnia without objective evidence for them were found to have a higher percentage of slow-wave sleep relative to participants with objectively verified insomnia and those without complaints, suggesting that the sleep of those with sleep state misperception is better rather than worse than that of others (Dorsey & Bootzin, 1997). In some cases, sleep state misperception may be the result of dreaming all night that one is awake, trying to fall asleep (Carlson, 1994), or simply witnessing sleep during NREM without oblivion but also without immersive, narrative dreams. However, in general, people underestimate the amount of sleep obtained when compared with polysomnographic recordings so that, in a sense, sleep state misperception is a matter of degree, with those identified as having sleep state misperception representing the extreme manifestation of this phenomenon (Hauri, 2000).

Smoking tobacco has been associated with "difficulty initiating and maintaining sleep, as well as having increased daytime sleepiness" (Sanders, 2000, p. 881). It has been found that "people who smoke on a regular basis sleep poorly, and when they abruptly stop smoking, their sleep improves moderately" (Kales & Kales, 1984, p. 149). In addition, it is possible that difficulty sleeping that is associated with smoking is breathing related. "Smokers have a four- to five-fold greater risk than those who never smoke of having at least moderate sleep-disordered breathing" (Sanders, 2000, p. 881). Cigarette smoking may irritate the walls of the throat, leading to "increased upper airway resistance" (Sanders, 2000, p. 881), thereby contributing to poor sleep. For those who imbibe caffeine, alcohol, and nicotine before going to sleep, there can be a synergistic arousing effect from all three once the initial sedation associated with alcohol has worn off (Zarcone, 2000).

Poor sleep hygiene can contribute to insomnia. Staying away from caffeine, alcohol, and nicotine before bedtime can improve sleep. It is also important to recognize the presence of a homeostatic drive and circadian rhythms so that, for example, regular bedtimes would contribute to better sleep. Potential sources of arousal in the sleep setting should be avoided. Thus, the sleep setting should be quiet and dark with minimum interruptions by people and pets. Clocks can be turned to face away from the sleeper so that they are less likely to worry about how little time is left in which to sleep. Ideally, the bedroom should be used only for sleeping. Engaging in other activities in the bedroom can lead to an association of the bed with arousal, so that when it is time to sleep, the arousing associations can keep one from falling asleep (Zarcone, 2000). In fact, lying in bed, trying to fall asleep can itself create sufficient stress about the inability to fall asleep so as to cause arousal.

In *psychophysiological insomnia* a person who sleeps "poorly during a period of stress" can become worried about their inability to sleep and come to associate going to bed with "frustration and arousal" (Hauri, 2000, p. 634). Paradoxically, the harder they try to sleep, the more they become tense, and the less they can sleep (Hauri, 2000). One strategy that is sometimes successful with insomnia is to get out of bed after 15 to 20 minutes of sleeplessness and to do something relaxing in order to break the association of worrying with being in bed (Aldrich, 1999). Often there is an inability to create psychological distance between daily concerns and sleep. "Any sort of bedtime ritual that breaks the connection between psychological stressors of the preceding day and the sleep period is to be encouraged" (Zarcone, 2000, p. 659). Such rituals can include various techniques of relaxation or stress management, such as making up a "list of the psychological stressors that have occurred during the preceding day, along with the plans to deal with each the next day" (Zarcone, 2000, p. 659).

Parasomnias

About 50% of adults have at least occasional nightmares. However, the repeated presence of nightmares, occurring usually in the second half of the night during REM sleep, from which a person awakes fully alert, would be classified as *nightmare disorder* provided that the nightmares cause "clinically significant distress" (American Psychiatric Association, 2013, p. 404) or occupational or social disruption (American Psychiatric Association, 2013). The NREM sleep version of nightmares are *sleep terrors*, which "consist of sitting up during sleep, emitting a piercing cry, and showing behavioral features of acute terror" (R. J. Broughton, 2000, p. 696) lasting about 30 seconds to 5 minutes (R. J. Broughton, 2000). Physiological arousal is present, although the person may be difficult if not impossible to awaken and may remember nothing upon awakening except perhaps single images (American Psychiatric Association, 2000) of "suffocation, burial, impending death, or monsters" (Aldrich, 1999, p. 262), for example. "The medieval interpretation was that something, usually the devil, was pressing on the chest of the sleeper, causing feelings of suffocation and terror" (R. J. Broughton, 2000, p. 697). Sleep terrors usually begin in slow-wave sleep and appear to occur as "incomplete cortical activation in response to an arousal stimulus" (Aldrich, 1999, p. 263).

Various degrees of behavioral activity are possible during incomplete arousal from slow-wave sleep. At one end of the spectrum are *confusional arousals* in which a person is markedly confused upon awakening from sleep "but without the occurrence of any expression of terror or of leaving the bed and walking away" (R. J. Broughton, 2000, p. 694). During sleep terrors, a person will sit up in bed and scream (American Psychiatric Association, 2013), possibly also try to "leave the bed or the room . . . jump from windows . . . [or] react violently to attempts to restrain them" (Aldrich, 1999, p. 262). Sometimes their behavior will progress to sleepwalking (R. J. Broughton, 2000).

Sleepwalking can begin with quiet motor activity such as sitting up in bed, looking around "with a relatively blank facial expression," and perhaps picking at the blankets or "rearranging the pillows" (R. J. Broughton, 2000, p. 701). A person may then leave their bed and walk around in a manner that is more clumsy than during waking. There may be vocalizations or even conversations and engagement in complex behaviors such as texting, cooking, or cleaning the house. Some sleepwalkers, usually women, "go to the kitchen and eat every night" (Arnulf, 2018, p. R1288). A person who is sleepwalking is relatively unresponsive to efforts at communication or awakening (R. J. Broughton, 2000). After several minutes to a half hour the sleepwalker wakes up or lies down in bed or elsewhere to continue their sleep (American Psychiatric Association, 2000).

Sleepwalking is "common in young children," with 15% to 30% "of healthy children" having had "at least one episode" and 3% to 4% of children having had "frequent episodes" (R. J. Broughton, 2000, p. 701). Sleepwalking is heritable in that "about 80% of sleepwalkers have an immediate family history of either sleepwalking or sleep terrors" (R. J. Broughton, 2000, p. 700). A number of treatment strategies have been used, including drugs, the avoidance of any known predisposing factors (R. J. Broughton, 2000), and waking the sleepwalker "about 15 to 30 minutes before the usual time" (Frank, Spirito, Stark, & Owens-Stively, 1997, p. 349) of their episodes for 1 month.

A criminal incident occurred just up the road from the university where I teach that resulted in a landmark decision of the Supreme Court of Canada concerning sleepwalking. Kenneth Parks, a "young married man" (McCall Smith & Shapiro, 1997, p. 41) experiencing a great deal of stress, was having difficulty sleeping. One night he fell asleep "on the couch of his living room" (McCall Smith & Shapiro, 1997, p. 41). In the "early hours of the morning" he "got up from the couch, put on shoes and a jacket," got in his car, and drove 23 kilometers "along a busy road" (McCall Smith & Shapiro, 1997, p. 41) until he got to "the home of his parents-in-law" (p. 42). He took a tire iron from the car, entered the house, got a knife from the kitchen, "went into the bedroom," and "inflicted a series of knife wounds on both the father-in-law and the mother-in-law" (McCall Smith & Shapiro, 1997, p. 42), killing his mother-in-law. His father-in-law survived. Parks maintained that he had been asleep and that, therefore, he was not responsible for his behavior. His actions were judged to be "non-insane automatism" (McCall Smith & Shapiro, 1997, p. 45), and he was completely acquitted. The court agreed with expert medical testimony presented at the trial that this was a case of somnambulistic homicide.

Cases of sleepwalking, such as that of Parks, raise questions about our ability to carry out complex behaviors without any apparent awareness of them. In other words, a disconnection occurs between consciousness$_1$ and consciousness$_2$, which is instructive to remember when we consider other alterations of consciousness in which aspects of the psyche appear to become disconnected from one another. What happens in such cases? Should a person be held accountable for behavior that appears to occur without any awareness on their part? One of our thematic threads recurs again as well, in that even though sleep is a naturally occurring altered state, in the form of sleepwalking it can be dangerous. In other words, it is not only contrived alterations of consciousness, such as drug-induced states, that can be dangerous.

SUMMARY

We started this chapter by considering the physiological activity of the brain and then using some of that information to identify the stages of sleep as measured with a polysomnograph. In particular, we distinguished between NREM and REM sleep, each of which is associated with somewhat different sleep mentation. We noted some of the benefits of sleep and the effects of drugs on sleep before concluding the chapter with a discussion of sleep–wake disorders. We engaged several of our thematic threads in this chapter, first, by considering the physiological perspective more thoroughly, by considering whether sleep mentation is mundane or extraordinary, and by considering both the beneficial and dangerous aspects of sleep.

So, now that we have established the physiological basis for sleep, let us turn to a more detailed consideration of sleep mentation. Yes, dreams. What do they reveal about the nature of our psyche?

4

Dreams

When we are asleep, we dream. Perhaps we dream all the time without later remembering that we have been dreaming; perhaps not. What we do know is that most of us dream some of the time that we are asleep by at least one of the definitions of sleep mentation that we considered in Chapter 3. Formally, the study of dreams is known as *oneirology* (Stevens, 1995), and sometimes dreamers are referred to as *oneironauts* (e.g., Kalas, 2018), but I rarely see that nomenclature used. Do dreams mean anything? If so, what do they mean? That is one of the thematic threads that runs through the disparate material in this chapter. But is that even a meaningful question? Suppose we were to ask the question "Is waking experience meaningful?" How would we answer that? Why is dreaming not just more life happening for a person? Why must dreams be just about one thing? Or nothing (cf. Barrett, 2017)?

Let us start by considering dream theories. Then I will bring in some of the empirical evidence that bears on dream content, which we started sampling in Chapter 3. Then I want to consider the imagery that occurs as we fall asleep, as an introduction to practical dream interpretation. After that we will consider three specific types of dreams: lucid, precognitive, and shared dreams. That will take us out of the ordinary into some anomalous material. And, well, that material raises some questions about the nature of reality.

http://dx.doi.org/10.1037/0000200-004
Alterations of Consciousness: An Empirical Analysis for Social Scientists, Second Edition,
by I. Barušs

DREAM THEORIES

Perhaps the place to start is to bring in the taxonomy of beliefs about consciousness and reality from materialist beliefs to transcendent beliefs and apply it to our examination of dreams. From a materialist perspective, dreams are meaningless. Or they can be regarded in an instrumental manner. By *instrumental*, I mean that dreams serve some specific purpose in the neuro-cognitive economy of the psyche. For example, in Chapter 3 we noted that problem-solving ability improves dramatically if a person dreams about elements of the problem that they are required to solve, suggesting that dream content can be linked to the improvements in comprehension taking place during REM sleep. In this case, specific dream content, dreaming about elements of a puzzle that is to be solved, improves a person's ability to solve the puzzle compared to not dreaming about the elements of a puzzle. If we approach dreaming from a conservatively transcendent position, then meaning becomes important and we are interested not just in the utility of some specific dream content but also in meaningful interpretations of our dream lives. And for the extraordinarily transcendent, consciousness is nonlocal in nature, and altered states, such as sleep, give us an opportunity to explore dimensions of reality that are unavailable to us in the ordinary waking state. And so dreams could be conceptualized as journeys in other realms of existence. With that structure in mind, let us proceed.

Physiological and Cognitive Theories

Throughout history, people have been fascinated with dreams and have attributed various meanings to them. For example, in classical Greece, people would come to the "temples sacred to Asklepios, the Greek god of healing" (Stevens, 1995, p. 24), undergo purification rituals, be given a sleeping potion to drink, and then be left to sleep. The idea was that Asklepios would appear in their dreams with messages of healing. Against the context of a rich variety of ways of thinking about dreams (Stevens, 1995) in the 18th and 19th centuries, "the rise of rationalism led to a new theory that dreams were merely meaning-less random expressions of physiologic activity during sleep" (Aldrich, 1999, p. 83). So for the enlightened mind dreams do not mean anything.

Perhaps the most famous theory that dreams do not mean anything is the *activation–synthesis hypothesis* proposed by J. Allan Hobson and Robert W. McCarley (1977). According to Hobson and McCarley, there are two components to the dream process. The first of these is *activation,* whereby, as a result of the activity of brainstem mechanisms during REM sleep, the brain becomes acti-vated, sensory impressions are reduced, and motor movements inhibited. But the brain, activated without sensory input or feedback from motor movements, does the best that it can to inject meaning into random signals by construct-ing dreams from images retrieved from memory. This is the second component of the dream process, *synthesis* (Hobson, 1990; Hobson & McCarley, 1977;

Hock, 1999; see also Hobson, Pace-Schott, & Stickgold, 2000). In other words, we create fictional simulations of living in a reality that resembles our waking state reality (Domhoff, 2018b). This theory hinges on a clear disconnection between waking experience, nonrapid eye movement (NREM) dreams, and rapid eye movement (REM) dreams. In fact, the argument is that the neurological substrate of REM dreaming is not the same as it is when awake or during NREM dreaming (Mutz & Javadi, 2017), so that dreaming is its own unique activity (Lee, 2015).

Another way to talk about such simulation is in the context of emergence. An emergent property of a system arises from the confluence of its constituent elements, but it cannot be predicted beforehand from the properties of those elements. So it is with dreaming. In the absence of adequate executive control, as revealed by inactivity of the prefrontal regions of the brain, the remaining areas of the brain are engaged collectively to produce a dream narrative. Such a narrative can have unexpected themes that arise from bringing together disparate content, but they need not mean anything (Kahn, 2016; see also Kahn, Krippner, & Combs, 2000).

Of course, we also now know that sleep stages are not neatly parsed into big chunks, so that REM sleep mentation could intrude whenever there is an "adequate level of brain activation in the absence of external distractions" (Domhoff, 2018a, p. 355). Also, there is considerable overlap of the parts of the brain that are activated during REM sleep and the default mode network, or just "default network," (Mutz & Javadi, 2017), so that we could say that "it is unlikely that dreaming is more than the accidental activation of an augmented portion of the default network" (Domhoff, 2018a, p. 366).

An analogy that comes to mind when thinking about these theories is that of a symphony orchestra on the evening of a concert. Prior to the entrance of the concertmaster, members of the orchestra take the opportunity to individually warm up their instruments and practice difficult passages. The result is a cacophony of sound that reveals the acoustic qualities of the various instruments as they fade in and out of the random playing, which creates some sort of emergent nonsensical musical landscape. However, once the concert begins under the baton of a conductor, the musicians follow a score that is musically meaningful. The suggestion in these theories is that, while awake, the orchestra plays whatever music is handed to it but, while asleep, it is forever warming up. Is it possible that there is also music to be played while asleep?

Psychodynamic Theories

There have been cognitive theories whereby dreams have been conceptualized as cognitive events that are understood as perhaps revealing something about the structure of the psyche (e.g., Foulkes, 1966, 1985, 1990) or its dynamics, so that dream interpretation can be useful (e.g., Hill, 1996; Hill & Rochlen, 1999). Also, we have already noted an empirically based instrumental approach.

Which dreams, when dreamt, make a difference relative to not having been dreamt, on some behavioral measure (e.g., M. Walker, 2017)? But I want to say a little bit about psychoanalysis and some of its offshoots.

Psychoanalysis begins with the Viennese physician Sigmund Freud and, arguably, with the publication of his book *The Interpretation of Dreams* (1900/1950) in 1900. I want to acknowledge at the outset that Freud is a polarizing figure. Some of my students complain that I say anything at all about him in class. However, I have kept him in this book because surveys of psychotherapists have shown that psychoanalytically oriented therapists tend to do dream work in therapy, so these ideas about dreams continue to persist practically, whether we like them or not (Leonard & Dawson, 2018).

Perhaps the first thing to understand is that Freud's theory is a psychodynamic theory. What does this mean? The 19th century saw the coming-of-age of hydraulic machinery, which functions on the basis of fluid pressure. When you press on the brake pedal of your car, you push the brake fluid in the master cylinder, which then creates pressure along the tubes running to the slave cylinders at the wheels, which activate the brakes. The psyche is modeled after hydraulic systems, so that if you push on it in one place, that pressure is going to have to be released somewhere, even if the release point has nothing to do with the source of the pressure. If I am frustrated about the pace at which I am writing the second edition of this book, that frustration might not get directed toward the written page but perhaps displaced onto the people around me in the form of curt behavior. That is the idea, and, in talking to psychotherapists, I have found that one reason psychoanalysis has survived is because therapists feel that they see such dynamics in their practice. Notice that this is a different conception of the psyche from the one that we have been considering thus far, namely, that the psyche is a computing machine.

For Freud, "dreams do really possess a meaning" (Freud, 1900/1950, p. 32), namely, that all dreams are instances of wish fulfillment. Well, that is clearly false. We have not wished for nightmares, confusing concatenations of images, reflective sleep thinking, and a variety of forms of sleep mentation without narrative structure, in any reasonable meaning of *wished*. But that issue gets obscured, because, for Freud, dreams are not direct productions of the unconscious. For Freud, every dream has not only a *manifest content*, which is just the apparent content of a dream, but also a *latent content*, which is what a dream is really about (Freud, 1900/1950). What a dream is really about, according to Freud, is our repressed wishes that he believed to be "infantile in origin and usually sexual in nature" (Stevens, 1995, p. 46). Unknown to us, these disturbing feelings are repressed from entering our dreams during sleep by a part of our psyche that Freud called the *censor*. But that is not the end of the forbidden impulses. This is where the psychodynamic machinery kicks in. The forbidden impulses cleverly disguise themselves through a process "which Freud called the *dream work*" (Stevens, 1995, p. 38) in order to sneak by the censor and appear in symbolic form as manifest content. Indeed, the purpose of dreams is to protect us from disturbing impulses so that we can sleep (Stevens, 1995). The task of *dream interpretation* is to proceed backward to identify the symbols of the manifest content and translate them into the latent content of the actual dream thoughts (Freud, 1900/1950). And when we do that, according to Freud, we find repressed infantile wishes.

Carl Jung was a Swiss psychiatrist who maintained a 6-year relationship with Freud until Freud's refusal to tolerate Jung's criticisms of his theory led to Jung's going his own way. Jung had dreams that contributed to his understanding of dreaming. In one of his dreams Jung found himself "in a mountainous region on the Swiss-Austrian border" (Jung, 1965, p. 163) at evening time. A stooped, elderly man with a peevish expression dressed "in the uniform of an Imperial Austrian customs official" (Jung, 1965, p. 163) walked by. Someone present in the dream said that it was "the ghost of a customs official who had died years ago" (Jung, 1965, p. 163). Then Jung found himself around midday in a city "bathed in an intense light" (Jung, 1965, p. 164). In the midst of a crowd of people streaming home for dinner "walked a knight in full armor" (Jung, 1965, p. 164) wearing a "white tunic into which was woven, front and back, a large red cross" (p. 165). Jung asked himself in the dream the meaning of the apparition and was told that "the knight always passes by here between twelve and one o'clock, and has been doing so for a very long time and everyone knows about it" (Jung, 1965, p. 165).

In Jungian dream interpretation, dream images are *symbolic*. They are symbolic not in the Freudian sense of admitting a direct translation of one meaning into another, such as the CN tower in Toronto being a penis and the Chauvet Cave in France being a vagina (cf. Hall, 1977), but as meaningful images compounded of the unconscious and conscious (Stevens, 1995) that are the best possible formulations of "relatively unknown [facts]" (Jung, 1921/1971, p. 474). Dream interpretation depends upon the ability to find meaningful parallel ideas to the symbols found in dreams. In his dream, Jung interpreted the dead customs inspector to be Freud, and the knight, which he associated with the beginning of alchemy and the quest for the Holy Grail, suggested "something still unknown which might confer meaning upon the banality of life" (Jung, 1965, p. 165). For Jung, dreams arise from the unconscious in order to compensate the conscious attitude of a person for the sake of providing balance to the personality (Hall, 1977). In this case, the dream's message for Jung was to correct his "conscious high opinion and admiration" (Jung, 1965, p. 164) of Freud and "to go on like the knight supported only by his own inner light and the few congenial souls he was able to collect at his own Round Table" (Stevens, 1995, p. 62).

When Jung worked at the Burghölzli Hospital in Zürich he was struck by the similarities that the "delusions and hallucinations" (Stevens, 1995, p. 51) of schizophrenic patients had, not only to one another, but also to the "myths and fairy tales derived from peoples all over the world" (pp. 51–52). These observations led him to believe that there was a "universal substratum" of the mind underlying "human experience and behaviour" (Stevens, 1995, p. 52) which he called the *collective unconscious*. The "essential psychic characteristics" of the collective unconscious "that distinguish us as human beings" he called *archetypes*; he said that they could give rise "to similar thoughts, images, and feelings in people, irrespective of their class, creed, race, geographical location, or historical epoch" (Stevens, 1995, p. 52). Manifestations of archetypes include variations on the relationship between male and female, the conflict between good and evil, the course of the human life cycle, and the ordeals encountered in life. For example, life's tribulations could be represented by "negotiating a maze or a labyrinth" (Stevens, 1995, p. 182). Archetypes surface as symbols in culturally shaped forms in myths, legends, and fairy tales (Stevens, 1995, p. 183) as well as in dreams. In Jung's dream, the Christian knight was an archetypal figure of the warrior following "a destiny which he has no choice but to fulfil" (Stevens, 1995, p. 60) just as Jung was to feel compelled to pursue his ideas about the human psyche.

For the Italian psychiatrist Roberto Assagioli, who developed his own psychodynamic theory, psychosynthesis, there are "many kinds of dreams." And while some dreams "do give access to the unconscious of the subject, we have often found that they give access only to one part of it . . . [which] is able or cares to express itself through dreams" (Assagioli, 1965, p. 94). This does not diminish the importance of symbols for working with the psyche, as we have already seen with the guided imagery exercise in Chapter 2.

DREAM CONTENT

Are we getting anywhere? Are any of these theories helpful for understanding dreams? Are dreams compensations of waking experiences? Where does dream content originate? Is it just a continuation of a day's events, according to the so-called continuity hypothesis (Schredl, 2017, p. 555)? How would we know, anyway? We have considered some of the research concerning dreams in Chapter 3 in the context of sleep, so let us return to an explicitly empirical approach.

A number of methods have been used for gathering dream data. Dreams have been collected from participants awakened in a sleep laboratory, from clients receiving psychotherapy who have reported their dreams in the context of a psychotherapeutic relationship, from studies of dream journals, and from participants anonymously completing forms in group settings (Domhoff, 2000) or online (e.g., Schredl, Stumbrys, & Erlacher, 2016). Recently, as we saw in Chapter 3, home dreams have been gathered while participants have been monitored using portable computerized polysomnography. In addition, as we have seen in the case of Jung, and as was true also of Freud (1900/1950) and Hobson (1988), data about one's own dreams have been used by dream researchers for understanding their nature.

Let us begin a discussion of dream content by reviewing some of the research concerning the incorporation of stimuli in dreams before returning to a discussion of hypnagogic and hypnopompic imagery, which, it seems to me, can serve as a transition to dream interpretation, which we will consider afterward.

Stimulus Incorporation in Dreams

In dreams collected in a sleep laboratory, not surprisingly perhaps, the sleep laboratory itself has showed up in the dreams of participants. In one study, 112 REM sleep dreams obtained from 20 participants, each spending two nights in a sleep laboratory, were analyzed. It was found that 52% of those dreams had at least some incorporation of the laboratory in them. Most frequently, the experimental situation showed up "in individual dream scenes; next came dreams which used the dream experiment as a major theme; about every 10th dream contained only isolated elements of the experiment, scattered among dream events" (Strauch & Meier, 1992/1996, p. 172). Realistic inclusion of "actual experiences from the preceding evening" was rare, so that, "for the most part, the laboratory situation was transformed in an alienated fashion" (Strauch & Meier, 1992/1996, p. 172). A dreamer in another study found herself in the sleep laboratory in her dreams. She dreamt that she was unable to fall asleep, so she "went outside to go sledding" (Strauch & Meier, 1992/1996, p. 171) with her boyfriend, intending to come back in time to be awakened. She "suddenly had a small motorbike" but got lost, "and it simply got too late" (Strauch & Meier, 1992/1996, p. 171).

Deliberate efforts to introduce stimuli into dreams in many cases have been less successful than the natural incorporation of activities in the sleep laboratory itself (De Koninck, 2000). Early studies demonstrating that presleep thoughts about desired personality characteristics would show up in dreams could not be replicated in some subsequent similar studies. As well, having independent judges identify the incorporation of an "increasing and decreasing sound of a jet fighter or the weepy sobbing of a person," played to participants "five minutes after the onset of REM sleep" (Strauch & Meier, 1992/1996, p. 177) led to inconclusive results. Participants shown films prior to sleep could incorporate the emotional tone of the films into their dreams, but rarely the content. In one study, thinking about a personal problem prior to sleep increased the frequency of dreaming about it from 20% to 40%. However, presleep stimuli that are irrelevant to a person's own concerns are unlikely to make it into a person's dreams, so that "the closer the topic is related to the personal issues of the dreamer, the higher the chance of an effect of presleep manipulation on dreams" (Schredl, 2017, p. 558).

What about the incorporation of waking events other than the sleep laboratory into dreams? Well, the things we do while awake frequently become contents in our dreams. So, for instance, consistent with what we just saw with presleep stimuli, emotions from social interactions during the day can carry over into dreams. Talking to friends is common in dreams. In one study, cognitive activities such as reading or working on a computer took up 42% of a person's waking life but only 19% of their dreams. Driving a car, on the other hand, is "significantly overrepresented in dreams" (Schredl, 2017, p. 559). And, of course, we can also dream about events that have never occurred in our waking lives, such as flying for any of us or walking by congenital paraplegics. There seems to be good agreement among researchers that, with one exception that we will address next, dreams are not a replay of episodic memories. There is no clean one-to-one correspondence between waking events and dream events (Schredl, 2017). "Dreams are not simply a replay of waking activity and concerns but draw on these experiences in ways that are complex and little understood" (De Koninck, 2000, p. 504). A dream "keeps its own counsel on whether to respond to a suggestion or signal, and if it does take them into account, it remodels them in unpredictable ways and places them into a different frame of reference" (Strauch & Meier, 1992/1996, p. 239).

Traumatic Dreams

Unlike everyday events, whose dream incorporation is inconsistent, are events that occur in the course of traumas such as natural disasters, automobile accidents, criminal violence, and war. One third to more than one half of individuals who have experienced "rape, military combat and captivity, and ethnically or politically motivated internment and genocide" end up with posttraumatic stress disorder (PTSD; American Psychiatric Association, 2013, p. 276). Among the common symptoms of posttraumatic stress disorder are nightmares and recurrent dreams. At first, the "dreams are fairly close to a literal reenactment of the trauma, sometimes with the twist that an additional horror, averted in real life, is added to the dream reenactment" (Barrett, 1996c, p. 3). Eventually the trauma is portrayed more symbolically and interwoven "with concerns from the dreamer's daily life" (Barrett, 1996c, p. 3). According to Deirdre Barrett, in one long-term study of women "with a documented history of childhood hospital visits for sexual abuse" (Barrett, 1996c, pp. 3–4) it was found that "a significant proportion of them repressed and then later remembered the abuse," with dreams being "one of the modes in which these memories first returned" (p. 4).

From what researchers have learned about the consolidation of memories during dreams, rehearsing traumatic material repeatedly while asleep would just reinforce the trauma. However, the brain mechanism mediating the memories of emotionally arousing stimuli uses the neurotransmitter noradrenalin (Pigeon & Mellman, 2017), whose levels are usually low during REM sleep, thereby creating an emotionally calm environment in which to process emotionally disturbing memories so that they lose their emotional charge. However, for people with PTSD, levels of noradrenalin are higher than normal and may remain high during REM sleep, so that they are unable to disconnect the dysphoric emotional tone from the traumatic content (M. Walker, 2017). In fact, in some studies treatment with prazosin, which blocks the activity of noradrenalin, decreased the occurrence of nightmares in PTSD (Pigeon & Mellman, 2017), although other studies have found no effect of the drug (Mellman, 2018).

Hypnagogic Imagery

In order to help us to understand the content of dreams, let us return to a consideration of hypnagogic imagery, the imagery that occurs upon falling asleep. There is a variety and richness of hypnagogic imagery from the "faintly perceptible to concrete hallucinations" (Mavromatis, 1987a, p. 14), which can include formless images made up of colors and clouds, geometric designs including spirals, "faces, figures, animals, objects, nature scenes" (p. 25; emphases removed), people, and printing and writing. Faces seem to be particularly prevalent among adults, often taking shape out of "misty stuff" (Mavromatis, 1987a, p. 25). For example, in one case, faces would "come up out of the darkness, as a mist, and rapidly develop into sharp delineation, assuming roundness, vividness, and living reality" (Mavromatis, 1987a, p. 17). Then they would fade, making way for others. At first these faces had been diabolical in appearance, but over the years they had become "exquisitely beautiful" (Mavromatis, 1987a, p. 17). Most visual hypnagogic images appear to be external to the viewer, vivid, sharp, and detailed. The capacity for detail has been characterized by one person as the ability to "see *into* the material without its being made coarser as it would appear through a magnifying glass" (Mavromatis, 1987a, p. 29). Indeed, for some people hypnagogic images have evoked "feelings of *heightened reality*" (Mavromatis, 1987a, p. 30). This touches on our fourth thematic thread: encountering something apparently extraordinary. Whereas visual images appear to predominate in hypnagogic states, auditory phenomena can also occur, such as hearing "one's name being called" (Mavromatis, 1987a, p. 34) or hearing the ringing of a doorbell. There can also be olfactory, gustatory, or somatic sensations such as a sense of falling (Mavromatis, 1987a).

This is a short list of possible imagery. We saw in Chapter 3 that the wake–sleep transition could be broken down into 19 different states. More manageably, perhaps, it has also been broken down into nine stages using the electroencephalogram (EEG). Not surprisingly, sleep mentation can differ between such stages, progressing from a sense of immersion in the usual physical manifestation to a hallucinatory dream world, so that a broad range of types of sleep mentation can occur as one is falling asleep (Nielsen, 2017).

What I want to consider, however, is an observation that has been made regarding hypnagogic imagery, namely, that it can be *autosymbolic* in the sense that the images that occur during the hypnagogic state may be symbolic representations of preceding events, such as the contents of thoughts, the attributes of one's mental activity, and sensations, including those that are produced by external stimuli (Nielsen, 2017). Mavromatis described one of his autosymbolic experiences. He was "lying in bed with eyes shut, half asleep, thinking of the difficulties of trying to remain awake" while experiencing a hypnagogic state, when he had a visual image of a man "rolling a stone bigger than [himself] up a small conically shaped hill and trying to place it on its tip" (Mavromatis, 1987a, p. 59). If he could make it to the top, then he could see all around. But the best that the man could do was to "get to just below [the tip] and then keep going round the tip trying to stop [the stone] from rolling away" (Mavromatis, 1987a, p. 59). Mavromatis interpreted this image as a symbolic depiction of his "thoughts about the difficulties of maintaining waking awareness" (Mavromatis, 1987a, p. 59) as one is going into the hypnagogic state.

Here is the point of this discussion: there is a symbol production mechanism in the psyche that can take ordinary cognition, metacognition, sensory impressions, and so on, and convert them into symbolic images of those mental events (Mavromatis, 1987a; Nielsen, 2017). It is in this sense that I think that hypnagogic imagery can serve as a transition to dream interpretation. Our psyches have the capacity for symbolic expression, so it is hardly surprising that dreams could, in fact, be symbolic expressions of what is going on for us. With that, let us turn to the matter of dream interpretation.

DREAM INTERPRETATION

We have been discussing dreams as though they were fixed programs that run in our heads while we are falling asleep or actually asleep. Many years ago, as a graduate student, I was struck by Frances Vaughan's (1979) statement that "it is common knowledge that people in Jungian analysis have Jungian dreams, while those in Freudian analysis have Freudian dreams" (p. 104). That is clearly silly, I thought. Of course, the same dream would be interpreted differently by a Freudian therapist than a Jungian therapist. But that is not what she was saying. What she was saying was that people will dream the dreams that are appropriate for their therapists. And now, with another 35 years of experience, it is clear to me that not only was Vaughan correct, but that she massively understated the plasticity of dreams. When we dream, analyze our dreams, and seek to influence our dreams, we are not interacting with a rigid program but rather an intelligence, sometimes called the *dream architect*, that can be surprisingly responsive, in its own idiosyncratic ways, to the manner in which we approach it (Baruš, 2007c). So, with that in mind, let us turn to meaningfulness in dreams, practical dream interpretation, encountering the shadow in dreams, and, finally, dream incubation.

Meaningfulness of Dreams

Are dreams meaningful? Within Western cultures, particularly science and academia, meaningfulness in general has largely been defined in terms of rationally coherent statements, in particular, statements that can be explicitly written using words on paper. Furthermore, there is an assumption, usually made without explicit acknowledgment, that anything that is meaningful must follow from using the rules of classical formal logic. Indeed, computer analogue computational theories of mind are based on such logical systems. In such theories, the assumption is made that all mental events, including perception, emotions, and consciousness, are by-products of formal classical logical processes (cf. Hofstadter, 1979). But classical logic is not the only kind of logic that exists (e.g., Goldblatt, 1979; Mac Lane & Moerdijk, 1992), nor is it likely to be the correct logic of the mind (Barwise, 1986). Nor, as we have already suggested in Chapter 1 by referencing modes of understanding superior to rational thought, is it likely to be the only way in which meaning can be established. In other words, meaning could be available to us in forms other than those in which it is usually recognized. And symbolic representation could play a significant role for those alternate modes of knowledge.

From a psychodynamic point of view represented by Freud, Jung, and Assagioli, unconscious material can become conscious whenever we relax our rational grip on our experiences. Such irruption could occur through accidental occurrences such as inadvertently saying something we had not planned to say, responding to ambiguous stimulus situations such as inkblots, free drawing whereby we draw whatever inspires us, mind wandering, and dreaming (Ferrucci, 1982). It is as though there were a communications device that allowed the unconscious to become conscious. The problem is that unconscious material frequently presents itself in symbolic form. In dreams, for Freud, such symbols were to be translated into unconscious wishes; for Jung, symbols had depth of meaning that revealed what it was that we needed in order to become whole; and for Assagioli, symbols were tools that allowed us to understand and work with psychological realities, including the superconscious, which may initially be inaccessible to us otherwise (Assagioli, 1965).

It has been suggested that by being concerned with the differences between waking and dreaming, we have drawn the line in the wrong place. Where we need to draw the line is "between symbolic consciousness manifested as such in emergent, creative imagination versus consciousness subordinated to the pragmatic demands of constructing and maintaining the everyday common sense world, a distinction cutting across both dreaming and wakefulness" (Hunt, 1986, pp. 216–217). Dreaming provides an opportunity for the emergence of another, more intuitive, mode of knowing; one that functions through the use of symbols. And, once understood, perhaps, rather than being obscure, "dreams may express the truth even more bluntly" (Stevens, 1995, p. 75) than we may encounter it in waking life. Montague Ullman has maintained that just as a camera aperture opens in the dark, so our psyches have an "ethical aperture" (Ullman, 1999, p. 101) that opens wider when we are asleep, so that we can better see the circumstances of our lives, allowing us to be in a better situation to make moral judgments.

And what it is that becomes visible to us? Pretty much anything, I think. Psychological junk: our wishes and fears, entertainment, solutions to personal or professional problems arising from wise parts of our psyche, the world around us, the past, the future, interactions with others, both living and dead. Okay, I might have lost some readers with that last sentence. For Assagioli, our psyches are permeable, so that we access material not only from our own preconscious, subconscious, and superconscious, but also from the world around us. And we can do this through anomalous processes. And these can be facilitated when we are asleep (cf. Laughlin & Rock, 2014). In fact, sleep is not the only alteration of consciousness in which we can shift toward a more expanded awareness of reality. Sensory restriction, mind wandering, trance, psychedelic states, transcendent experiences, and experiences associated with death could all be more conducive to the availability of such knowledge.

Practical Dream Interpretation

If dreams are potentially meaningful, from a practical point of view, how could a person go about interpreting them? Let me answer this question from the literature as well as my own experience of working with my dreams and helping others to work with theirs. A word of caution, though: it is advisable to find an "experienced helper," since working with dreams on one's own is a precarious business (Stevens, 1995, p. 233).

At the outset, a person needs to record and keep track of their dreams. For someone interested in knowing about themself, it is helpful to keep a journal that functions both as a record of significant psychological events and as a workbook. Dreams can be written into the journal while lying in bed upon awakening or at the first opportunity after arising. It is helpful to review dreams immediately on awakening, before moving, to be better able to remember them. One can also record dreams on an audio recorder or cellphone and write them out later, although one has to be careful not to leave the writing so long that the details become forgotten. In recording a dream, its different dimensions can be described, such as settings, characters, events, and mood (cf. Stevens, 1995).

After having written out a dream, the dreamer can ask themself what associations are called forth, not just from the dream as a whole but from the various elements in the dream. Yes, we frequently dream about events that have occurred in our lives. I think of those events as the furniture in the dream. Recall that the incorporation of life events is idiosyncratic, so I think of the meanings of a dream as being given by the ways in which that furniture has been arranged. In other words, how have these events been changed and reassembled in the dream?

As a dreamer investigates possible associations, meanings may suggest themselves. In Jungian dream analysis, two levels of associations have been identified. One of these is personal, the other cultural. For example, I play ice hockey regularly throughout the year, and playing some version of hockey occasionally shows up in my dreams. I have come to associate academic publication with scoring goals and the manner in which they are scored while playing hockey in my dreams. Playing hockey is a personal symbol. For most people, neither hockey nor academic publication has anything to do with their lives.

On the other hand, we share cultural symbols. We already noted that driving cars is overrepresented in our dreams. Cars could symbolize the personality. Another common symbol for the personality is a house whose basement can be related to the lower unconscious, the main floor with the conscious, and upper floors and attic to the higher unconscious and spiritual dimensions of one's being. Events that occur in the house could symbolize the occurrence of psychological events (e.g., D. Baker & Hansen, 1977).

An additional way of working with dreams while awake is to use the imagination to interact with dream images. For example, one can engage a dream character in dialogue in order to help to ascertain the meaning that that character had in a dream (Stevens, 1995). The process can also be turned around. Rather than just seeking to determine the meaning of a dream, one can use the images in the dream as a way of creating changes in oneself. In keeping with ideas presented in Chapter 2, symbols may have some ability to restructure a person's psyche when those symbols representing desired changes are visualized (Ferrucci, 1982).

Although dreams can sometimes be quite directed, they need not have a single meaning, but they can be layered so as to be concerned with various issues in one's life. Sometimes dreams are about one's psychological life, sometimes about a situation in which one finds oneself, sometimes about planetary events, and sometimes perhaps about all of those at once. Sometimes dreams can be overly dramatic and exaggerate reality in order to draw attention to something that needs to be rectified. One of the benefits of keeping track of dreams over time is to learn which dreams are meaningful, if they are meaningful, what it is that they are concerned about, and what the meanings are of different dream images.

The Shadow

Apparently in Western cultures, before the widespread availability of electric lighting, when it got dark out, people went to bed. They would sleep a "first sleep," then lie awake for several hours before having a "second sleep" (Warren, 2007). When Thomas Wehr confined seven participants to 14 hours of darkness a night, he found the same pattern emerge after 4 weeks, suggesting that human sleep is biphasic at night, as it is for other animals (Wehr, 1992). During the periods of wakefulness, there are elevated levels of the hormone prolactin, which is associated with deep rest (Naiman, 2014). The conventional understanding, however, continues to be that human sleep is monophasic at night (M. Walker, 2017). At any rate, what is clear is that through the use of electricity, we have artificially extended our daytime while shrinking the time that we spend in darkness.

The consequence of such extended lighting, according to Rubin Naiman, is that we could be suffering from "darkness deficiency" (Naiman, 2014, p. 61) and *psychospiritual night blindness*, failing to understand the importance of night-time in our lives. In parallel with the ideas of Ullman, Naiman has advocated developing *nocturnal lucidity*, which allows us to extend "our awareness into arenas we believe lie outside of our awareness," thereby learning to see in the dark (Naiman, 2014, p. 22). As day dissolves into night, through a parallel process, our "waking consciousness dissolves into our deeper self" (Naiman, 2014, p. 48). And as it does so, "cognitive popcorn" (Naiman, 2014, p. 58)—incessant, spontaneous thoughts—might go through our minds. But we can also come in contact with "suppressed psychological material" (Naiman, 2014, p. 37, emphasis removed). This brings us to the shadow.

The *shadow* can be defined as "the negative side of a person's personality, comprising all personal and collective elements that do not fit in with the person's self-perception" (Colman, 2015, p. 693) or simply as the "thing one has no wish to be" (Naiman, 2014, p. 169). This is a part of ourselves that we do not like and from which we frequently try to distance ourselves. We wish that the trauma had never occurred. We wish that we were not so afraid. We wish that we were not so old, or ill, or poor, or neurotic. From an instrumental approach, our effort is to get rid of distressing material, including nightmares. On the other hand, if we engage in self-transformation, we could enter into a dialogue with our shadows, redacting and transforming them so as to integrate what is worthwhile into an effective economy of the psyche.

Dream Incubation

Whatever one's theoretical disposition with regard to the meaningfulness of dreams, as we have seen already, sleep and dreaming can facilitate creative problem-solving (Krippner, 1981; Krippner & Dillard, 1988; Laughlin & Rock, 2014; Sio, Monaghan, & Ormerod, 2013; M. Walker, 2017). But rather than just relying on incidental solutions to problems, can we turn around the process and request an answer from the dream architect? A person could deliberately seek answers to questions in dreams by writing the questions in their diary and posing them to themself in their mind as they fall asleep. They can then pay attention to their dreams, on that and subsequent nights, particularly dreams that occur just prior to awakening. The idea is that an answer to their questions can occur in dreams, if not on the first, then possibly on subsequent nights upon repetition of the process. That would be *dream incubation* (Barušs, 2007c, p. 77; cf. D. Baker, 1977; D. Baker & Hansen, 1977).

Dream incubation experiments usually involve giving a participant a brain teaser and then seeing if the person can dream the solution. For instance, Morton Schatzman asked a medical colleague to dream about which two words in the English language begin and end with the letters *h-e*. In a dream, the colleague gets pain in his chest and is rushed to the hospital. A physician insists that he tell him in "plain language" what his problem is, to which the dreamer replies, "You could call it anything, even heartache," at which point the dreamer is told that he can go home. But there is still pain, and the physician tells him that he needs to see a "word specialist." Morton Schatzman appears in the dream and reminds the dreamer that he had told him that there had been two things wrong with him, and that he "must learn to juggle words and pains." "Riddles give me headaches" says the dreamer, and, with that, his pain is gone completely. The two words are *heartache* and *headache* (Schatzman, 1983, p. 693). When I give this brain teaser to my students to try, I have noticed that about one out of 100 will dream one of the words, with most students not even trying to do so.

Of course, the point of dream incubation is not to solve brain teasers but to find solutions for personal or professional problems. And that certainly seems to occur (Barrett, 1993, 2017). I myself have used dream incubation on a number of occasions for a range of issues. For instance, both spontaneous and incubated dreams have helped me with academic publication, by showing me, for example, who will publish my work and who will not (Barušs, 2013).

LUCID DREAMING

In Chapter 1, I indicated that a number of different aspects of subjective experience have been proposed along which alterations of consciousness can occur. There are three such dimensions that are particularly relevant when considering dream experiences. The first is that of *discrimination*, the degree to which a person recognizes the state in which they find themself, which is related to the degree to which a person is aware of themself as a subject (cf. Sparrow, Hurd, Carlson, & Molina, 2018). The second is that of *control*, the degree to which a person has apparent control over the events occurring within their experience. The third is that of *feelings of reality*, the degree to which experiences that are occurring for a person feel real, which we already introduced in Chapter 2. This last is not the ability to discriminate between events that are objectively real in the normal sense and those that are subjective, that ability being included in the first dimension, but rather the sense of how real one's experiences feel, irrespective of their objectively determined ontological status. In that sense, the third dimension is related to consciousness$_3$.

Characteristics of Lucid Dreams

A number of differences between waking and dreaming have been noted, including, usually, the lack of critical reflection while dreaming, so that the dreamer fails to realize that they are dreaming in spite of various absurdities that could be present in their dreams (Aldrich, 1999). In some cases, however, the dreamer is aware of their actual situation—namely, that they are dreaming. They may also be more likely to act deliberately (LaBerge & Gackenbach, 2000) and to feel that what is happening feels as real as waking experience (LaBerge & Rheingold, 1990). Dreams with such qualities are known as *lucid dreams* (e.g., van Eeden, 1913), although, in keeping with contemporary scientific usage, we shall adopt a broad definition of a lucid dream as any dream in which one knows that one is dreaming (LaBerge & Gackenbach, 1986).

In the tradition of dream researchers, let me give some examples of my own dreams for illustrative purposes, the first of which is a lucid dream.

> In the continuation of a nonlucid dream that I was having, I floated out of a building through the front door and was looking for my car. As I was going through a parking garage, I realized that I was dreaming. I do not know why that realization occurred to me; perhaps I subconsciously had noticed that I was floating. At any rate, the contents of my dream imagery became more solid. In fact, I went over to a wall and tested it. It was solid. Even though I knew that I could do anything I wanted to do because it was a dream, that did not appear to be true. With some effort, I eventually managed to penetrate through the ceiling. That had an odd effect, as though everything, including myself, were made of some sort of rubbery liquid, so that I experienced a pleasing satisfaction as I scrunched through the ceiling and came up out of the floor of the level above. I decided to visit my girlfriend, thinking that my intentions would be enough to make that occur, but nothing happened. I was stuck by myself inside the empty rooms in some sort of building. Eventually I was able to rise until I ended up in a tower that was open to the night sky. There was an angel with me, a chubby sort of fellow, who turned out to be Cupid. Then I lost my lucidity.

How are lucid dreams different from nonlucid dreams? That depends on the amount of experience with lucid dreaming that the dreamer has had. Lucid dreaming is a skill that can be learned with a variety of techniques available for inducing lucidity. Among those inexperienced with them, lucid dreams "are more similar than dissimilar to nonlucid dreams" (LaBerge & Gackenbach, 2000, p. 155). This was the conclusion reached in a study of the differences in content between nonlucid and lucid dreams collected mostly "from dream diaries [and] from questionnaires" (LaBerge & Gackenbach, 2000, p. 155). There were, nonetheless, "more auditory and kinesthetic sensations" as well as a greater "sense of control" (LaBerge & Gackenbach, 2000, p. 155) in lucid dreams than in nonlucid dreams. Greater differences between lucid and nonlucid dreams were found in a study of members of an organization devoted to lucid dreaming, who would have been "more likely to use specialized techniques for lucid dream induction, control, and stabilization" (LaBerge & Gackenbach, 2000, p. 156). For the experienced lucid dreamers, "compared with nonlucid dreams, lucid dreams had significantly higher levels of control, more positive emotions, and higher levels of visual vividness, clarity of thinking, physical activity, and changes of scene" (LaBerge & Gackenbach, 2000, p. 156). It would appear that the development of lucid dreaming leads to enriched dream experiences.

Stephen LaBerge, a pioneer in lucid dream research, along with his colleagues, found that some dreamers, while asleep, can indicate the onset of lucidity with "eye movements and fist clenches" (LaBerge, 1990a, p. 110) that could be observed on a polysomnograph in a sleep laboratory. This led them to a series of experiments concerning lucid dreaming. In one study, they found that "76 signal-verified lucid dreams" from 13 participants all occurred during REM sleep with 5 to 490 seconds "of uninterrupted REM sleep" (LaBerge, 1990a, p. 112) following the lucid dream signals. A comparison of physiological data for 5 minutes before and 5 minutes following "the initiation of lucidity" (LaBerge, 1990a, p. 112) revealed "highly significant increases in physiological activation during the 30 [seconds] before and after lucidity onset," indicating that the onset of lucid dreaming occurs during phasic REM sleep. In other studies, they have shown that lucid dreaming is more likely to occur during later rather than earlier REM sleep periods. They have also found that "time estimates during . . . lucid dreams [are] very close to the actual time" (LaBerge, 1990a, p. 119) and "that there is a very direct and reliable relation between the gaze shift reported in lucid dreams and the direction of [polysomnographically] recorded eye movements" (p. 199). Results such as these suggest that, contrary to the assumptions of some sleep theorists, cognitive activity during lucid dreaming is comparable to waking cognitive activity, at least in those dreamers who are capable of signaling while asleep.

Lucid Dream Induction

There are two ways that a person can try to induce lucid dreams: They can try to add dreaming while they are awake or they can add wakefulness while they are dreaming. In other words, they can seek to retain continuity of consciousness while falling asleep, or they can seek to become aware while dreaming that they are dreaming. The problem with trying to retain lucidity upon going to sleep is that it means that, for most people, lucidity will need to be carried through NREM sleep, although there have been cases of lucidity in NREM Stages 1 and 2 (Baird, Mota-Rolim, & Dresler, 2019). This would work better if a person were to sleep for 5 or 6 hours, then wake up and become active for 10 minutes to more than 1 hour, and then fall asleep, because they are more likely to go directly into REM sleep. That technique is known as *wake back to bed* (Aspy, Delfabbro, Proeve, & Mohr, 2017).

Dream-initiated lucid dreams are more frequent than wake-initiated lucid dreams (LaBerge & Rheingold, 1990) and can be brought about by a variety of methods. One technique is to try to remember to notice events in dreams that could not occur during the waking state and then make the critical judgment that such inconsistencies indicate that one is dreaming (LaBerge & Gackenbach, 1986). A person can, in fact, keep track of events in their dreams that are contrary to ordinary physical reality, what LaBerge has called *dream-signs*, and then look for them in subsequent dreams (Laberge & Rheingold). Floating or flying, such as in the example of my dream given above, is a dreamsign. In some cases, a dreamer may simply note that occurrent events are "dreamlike" and hence that they must be dreaming (LaBerge & Gackenbach, 1986). However, a person can try to develop a critical faculty that can alert them when they are dreaming. This critical faculty can be exercised while awake by asking oneself some five to 10 times a day: "Is this a dream?" It is important at that point not to reflexively assume that one is awake but to scrutinize one's experience "for any oddities or inconsistencies that might indicate . . . dreaming" (LaBerge & Rheingold, 1990, p. 62). The point is to have access to such a critical faculty while dreaming so as to be able to notice unusual dream events when they occur.

Because presleep thoughts and stimuli can carry over into dreams, appropriate presleep mentation should increase the probability of lucid dreaming. When training himself to have lucid dreams, LaBerge developed a mnemonic method for the induction of lucid dreams (LaBerge, 1990b; LaBerge & Gackenbach, 1986; LaBerge & Rheingold, 1990). The *mnemonic method for the induction of lucid dreams* involves two activities to be done as one is falling asleep. First, a person is to "concentrate singlemindedly on [their] intention to remember to recognize that [they are] dreaming" (LaBerge & Rheingold, 1990, p. 78) and to try to feel that they really mean it. If their thoughts stray from this intention, they are to be returned to it. Second, they are to imagine themselves back in a recent dream, with the difference being that they imagine themselves recognizing that it is a dream. The recalled dream is to be examined critically for dreamsigns, identified as a dream, and continued in fantasy with whatever actions they would like to perform while lucid dreaming. These two activities are to be repeated in such a way "that the last thing in [their] mind before falling asleep is [their] intention to remember to recognize the next time [they] are dreaming" (LaBerge & Rheingold, 1990, p. 79). Two requirements for learning this technique are high motivation and the ability to recall at least two or three dreams per night (LaBerge & Gackenbach, 1986; see also Aspy et al., 2017).

Nightmares can induce lucidity. Events in dreams can be so terrifying that the only way for a person to deal with them is to realize that they are dreaming. Once lucid, they may be able to exercise some degree of control, although less control has been reported in nightmare-induced lucid dreams than in lucid dreams induced by the dreamlikeness of a dream (LaBerge & Gackenbach, 1986). Lucid dreaming can also be cultivated as a treatment for nightmares. In addition to learning to induce dream lucidity, a person can practice, while awake, replacing thoughts of being a victim of their dreams with thoughts of empowerment over them. Then, just as in the method for the induction of lucid dreams, they can imagine themself in a previous nightmare confronting rather than avoiding that of which they are afraid and "creating a better outcome" (Levitan & LaBerge, 1990, p. 11).

Even though the threshold for perceiving external stimuli is increased in sleep, stimuli can sometimes still be detected and incorporated, often in modified form, in one's dreams. On this basis, LaBerge has developed devices that can present cues to the sleeper while they are dreaming. One such device, called the DreamLight, is a mask containing miniaturized electronic equipment with an attached computer that can detect the wearer's eye movements and turn on flashing lights directed at their eyes while they are in REM sleep.

Upon going to sleep at night, a person would put on the mask and intend to be on the lookout for light in their dreams. In one study, those using a mnemonic method for the induction of lucid dreams together with a DreamLight had "five times as many lucid dreams as those not using any lucid dream induction technique" (LaBerge & Rheingold, 1990, p. 89). Sometimes the light has the same appearance in a person's dreams as it does during waking. "However, 80 percent of the time the light takes on aspects of the dream world, becoming . . . seamlessly woven into the fabric of the dream" (LaBerge & Rheingold, 1990, p. 89).

The transformation of light in dreams is illustrated by a dream that I had one night when I was wearing a NovaDreamer, a device that is essentially the same as the DreamLight. In my dream I was walking along a somewhat darkened city street when suddenly a nuclear bomb went off some four or five blocks in front of me. I was terrified. I had forgotten all about the NovaDreamer and did not realize that the nuclear bomb was my cue that I was dreaming. At other times, the light can be recognized, but our penchant "to rationalize rather than think logically" (LaBerge & Rheingold, 1990, p. 89) can result in the conclusion that we are awake.

If a dreamer wonders whether or not they are awake, the NovaDreamer has a *reality test button* mounted in the center of the mask that can be used to check if they are dreaming. When the button is physically pushed, the lights flash once, indicating to the person that they are awake. If a person tries to push the button during a dream, on the other hand, all sorts of interesting things can happen. Thus, if the lights do not flash when the button is pushed, a person can conclude that they are dreaming. One night while I was asleep, I saw the lights flash in my dreams and recognized them for what they were. I was certain that they had awakened me. I pushed the reality test button anyway and nothing happened. "Darn," I thought, "I can't believe that the batteries are already dead." In the morning, when I was really awake, to my surprise, there was nothing wrong with the batteries and the NovaDreamer worked just fine.

There is a drug, *galantamine,* which has been shown to have an impact on awareness of oneself as an agent and on self-determination in dreams, as well as increasing the frequency of lucid dreaming (Sparrow, Hurd, Carlson, & Molina, 2018). For instance, LaBerge and colleagues gave 121 participants 4-milligram and 8-milligram doses of galantamine in conjunction with having them practice the mnemonic method for the induction of lucid dreams within a wake back to bed protocol. The result was a 27% and 42% increase, respectively, in the frequency of lucid dreams compared with an active placebo condition, showing a dose dependence. Furthermore, "dream recall, cognitive clarity, control, positive emotion, vividness and self-reflection were increased during lucid compared to non-lucid dreams," leading one to draw the conclusion that "the integrated method of taking galantamine in the last third of the night with at least 30 minutes of sleep interruption and with an appropriately focused mental set is one of the most effective methods for inducing lucid dreams available today" (LaBerge, LaMarca, & Baird, 2018, p. 1).

ANOMALOUS DREAMING

As we have seen, dreams turn out to be more interesting than they at first appear to be when we take some time to look at them. They can be sources of symbolic meaning at least for some people, solutions to problems, and venues for fantastic adventures in full awareness. But what about one of the most basic assumptions of most dream theories, that dream content is basically a mixture of material dredged up from memory, even if recast in meaningful form? What about the future? Could some of the stuff of dreams be from the future? From a materialist viewpoint, that is not even a question that we are supposed to ask. "Yet stubbornly, persistently, exasperatingly, people have reported dreaming about the future in all ages and cultures that we know" (Ullman & Krippner, 1973, p. 175). Another assumption of most dream theories is that dreams are confined to the inside of the skull of the dreamer. What about the outside? Could some dreams occur in some sort of objective domain? Is the psyche open or closed? Again, from a materialist perspective, we are not even supposed to ask that question. Yet shared dreams have shown up again and again in the historical record (Magallón, 1997). Let us have a look at these phenomena. And as we do so, we can contemplate several of our thematic threads: Are dream events mundane or extraordinary? Is reality material or transcendent in nature? Is the mind open or closed?

Examples of Precognitive Dreams

Let us define *precognitive dreams* as dreams in which there are "meaningful coincidences" (Houran & Lange, 1998, p. 1411) between dream contents and actual future events whatever explanation there may end up being for such coincidences. I had the following dream in the middle of the night on April 9, 2019, which I wrote down upon awakening in the morning:

> I was driving in a van with mother beside me. I came toward an intersection where I needed to turn left. I noticed that there seemed to be something wrong with the automatic transmission. This was unexpected. And there was already something that was going on with the van. I turned the corner and then pulled well up on the side of the road, which segued into a field, although I could not get the van quite straight by the time it died on me completely. I was partially awake at that point, and realized that I needed to call the [Canadian Automobile Association] to tow me to the garage to have the transmission fixed.

I usually interpret cars and my mother in my dreams as my body or my personality. And I am used to my dreams showing me future events, so I interpreted this dream as an unexpected health issue.

Two weeks later, on April 24, 2019, I was driving my car, making a left turn, pulling out of a parking lot when the axle snapped so that the transmission became disconnected from the wheels. I had just enough momentum to drift into the center lane of a busy five-lane street before coming to a stop. That center lane is used only for making left turns. I could not quite get the car lined up straight as I came to a stop, so that the angle of my car ended up being the same as the angle of the van in the dream. I called the Canadian Automobile Association and got towed to the garage. On May 25, 2019, I was driving to Toronto to give a keynote talk at a conference, when my car stalled several blocks from the venue. I managed to limp my way to the talk and back home by starting the car every time it stalled. So there had already been something that had been wrong with the car.

There are differences between the dream imagery and the corresponding event. In the dream, I am driving a van. I used to drive a van, but now I drive a car. In the dream my mother is with me, but in the corresponding event I am by myself. In the dream, I come to a stop at the right side of the road in a lane that is paved and slightly raised, but not a normal driving lane. In the corresponding event, I come to a stop in the middle of the road in a lane that is level with the surface of the roadway and that is not a normal driving lane. The striking similarities between the dream and corresponding event are the fact that this event was unexpected, that I am making a left turn, that I cannot drive farther and am forced to drift to a stop, that the problem seems to be with the transmission, the angle at which the car comes to a stop, and the fact that there was already something wrong.

I have written about my precognitive dreams in another book, called *The Impossible Happens* (Baruss, 2013). In that book I describe how it took me several decades to figure out that some of my dreams really are precognitive. This is not a conclusion I reached frivolously. But having come to that realization, the first interpretation that I usually try on a dream is to wonder whether the dream is a symbolic representation, or perhaps a not-so-symbolic actual event, of something that is going to happen in the future. Had I not had a history of precognitive dreaming, I would have noted the curious coincidences between the dream and actual events in this case, and perhaps just dismissed them as curious coincidences.

Here is another example. On the night of November 16, 1995, astronomer Paul Kalas had a dream about a star with a dust belt surrounding it in such a way that the star was offset from the geometrical center of the dust belt. On waking, he drew a sketch and wrote out his dream. Nine years later, on November 1, 2004, Kalas sent an email to two colleagues, along with images from the Hubble Space Telescope, showing the star Fomalhaut with an offset dust belt. Kalas found "four striking similarities between [his] drawing and the eventual scientific images" (Kalas, 2018, p. 55). For instance, the belt is "tilted downward to the lower left" by about 27 degrees in the drawing and 21 degrees in the Hubble image, and, in both cases, the star is "'displaced' to the upper right relative to the geometric center of the belt" (Kalas, 2018, p. 55). Not everything matched; there was a sentence in the dream report that does not make sense. The fact that the dust belt is offset suggests the presence of a planet, and, indeed, subsequently, after taking further images with the Hubble telescope, Kalas has been credited with the first-ever photograph of a planet outside of our solar system (Kalas, 2018).

Is this a case of precognition? Kalas's precognitive dream is similar to mine in that some of the dream elements strikingly match later events in physical reality, but others do not. However, just as my history of precognitive dreaming allowed me to conclude that the dream was likely precognitive, so, too, Kalas's history of precognitive dreaming led him to interpret the dream about an offset dust belt around a star as meaningfully precognitive. However, for those of us reading his account, that seems possible, but perhaps not particularly convincing. What does systematic research reveal?

Empirical Studies of Precognitive Dreams

Two famous studies to test precognition in dreams were carried out at the Maimonides Medical Center in Brooklyn, New York, where Montague Ullman was the director of the Maimonides Community Mental Health Center and Stanley Krippner was the director of the Dream Laboratory. The participant in both studies was Malcolm Bessent, who appeared to have had previous precognitive experiences (R. S. Broughton, 1991). In the first study, the idea was to provide Bessent with a multisensory experience in the morning upon awakening and to see whether his dreams of the previous night could anticipate the contents of that experience. On eight nonconsecutive nights Bessent slept in the sleep laboratory, where he was awakened during the night for dream reports. In the morning, after the tape of Bessent's dreams had been mailed out to be transcribed, a target was selected using a random number system and a multisensory experience prepared for Bessent (R. S. Broughton, 1991). "Three outside judges would compare each night's [dream reports] to each of the eight target experiences on a 100-point scale" (Ullman & Krippner, 1973, p. 177).

For the first session, the target that ended up being randomly selected was the word *corridor* (Ullman & Krippner, 1973, p. 178). Krippner, who had had "no contact with Bessent or his dreams" (Ullman & Krippner, 1973, p 177) and whose task it was to make up the multisensory experience, chose as the theme a painting by van Gogh, which they identified as *Hospital Corridor at St. Rémy*, in which a lone figure can be seen "in the corridor of a mental institution" (p. 179). In the morning, Bessent was addressed as "Mr. Van Gogh," was "led through a darkened corridor of the lab," was "given a pill . . . and a glass of water," was "'disinfected' with acetone daubed on a cotton swab," was shown slides of "paintings by mental patients" (Ullman & Krippner, 1973, p. 179), and got to listen to eerie music and hysterical laughter. Bessent's dreams of the previous night had included the presence of "doctors and medical people" who had expressed hostility toward him, a "large concrete building" (Ullman & Krippner, 1973, p. 177), a "concrete wall," and a patient who was escaping (p. 178). Subsequently the judges matched the previous night's dreams with the target "corridor," so this session was considered to be a direct hit. Altogether, there were five of eight direct hits, and the probability of the overall results occurring by chance was calculated to be 1 in 5,000 (Krippner, 1993; Ullman & Krippner, 1973).

It could be argued that the direct hit of the first night was not surprising given what we know about the incorporation of presleep stimuli in dreams. However, the relative influence of presleep stimuli was tested in the second experiment in which a comparison was made of the incorporation of the target in dreams before and after the participant had been exposed to it.

Bessent was the participant again in the second experiment. This time he was presented with a slide show that had "an accompanying sound track" (R. S. Broughton, 1991, p. 97) on the evening after having reported his dreams in the sleep laboratory. Then he would try to dream about the slide show on the following night. In this way a comparison could be made between the incorporation of the stimulus in dreams that occurred before and after its presentation (R. S. Broughton, 1991). Again, there were eight targets, but this time there were 16 nights of dream reports. EEG technicians from outside who knew nothing about the design of the experiment were brought in to ensure that those gathering the dream reports would not favor either the precognitive or post-experience dreams. Again, the dream reports were scored by three outside judges on a 100-point scale for similarity to the eight targets without knowing the order in which the dreams had occurred (Ullman & Krippner, 1973).

The highest score for a dream report and target pair was 98. This was for a precognitive night on which Bessent dreamed repeatedly of the color blue, water, and themes concerning birds. He said, in fact, "'I just have a feeling that the next target material will be about birds'" (Ullman & Krippner, 1973, p. 184). And it was. The target was a slideshow about birds. The following night he dreamed about a secretary going for dinner to a restaurant at the top of a high building but not about birds. The correspondence between the bird target and the following night received a rating of 18 out of 100 by the judges. Overall, for "seven of the eight pairs of nights the precognition night had greater correspondence to the experience than the post-experience nights" (Ullman & Krippner, 1973, p. 184). The probability that the results had occurred by chance was about one in 1,000 (Ullman & Krippner, 1973).

Efforts to replicate these studies have had patchy results. Caroline Watt was able to successfully replicate them in one of two studies (Watt, 2014) but not the other (Watt & Vuillaume, 2015). There have been two other unsuccessful replications. However, these studies had a methodological problem in that after having registered their dreams, participants were shown all four of the potential targets rather than just the actual target. Participants cannot be exposed to the nontargets because those could end up in a participant's dreams instead of the target designated as such by the investigators (Baruš & Mossbridge, 2017). Furthermore, as with all apparently anomalous skills, some people are simply better at them than others. Malcolm Bessent was flown in from England for the Maimonides studies because of his demonstrated ability to correctly predict future events (Ullman & Krippner, 1973). To demonstrate the existence of a phenomenon, it is necessary to solicit participants who have already demonstrated an ability to produce the phenomenon.

Unfortunately, studies concerning anomalous psychological phenomena have sometimes been misrepresented and falsified in secondary descriptions of them in the psychological literature. For example, some critics have described the multisensory experience associated with the target "corridor" as having occurred before Bessent reported his dreams rather than after he had reported them, as was actually the case (Krippner, 1993). Those reading such descriptions would be likely to reach the conclusion that "the researchers were completely incompetent" (Child, 1985, p. 1228) instead of appreciating the possibility of the occurrence of an interesting psychological phenomenon.

What if we were to take the results of the Maimonides dream experiments seriously in the same way that we would take the results of other scientific experiments seriously, particularly considering that these results are consistent with other studies of anomalous precognitive perception during the waking state (Jahn & Dunne, 1987)? Is it possible that, in addition to being fanciful productions of an experience generating system, dreams can sometimes be meaningful? That not only can they sometimes be meaningful, but that they can provide us with knowledge about ourselves and the world around us. What if dreams sometimes facilitate access to a level of reality from which we are usually excluded in our ordinary waking state? What if alterations of consciousness as such can sometimes let us see underneath the surface of life?

Shared Dreaming

At this point, I have been teaching university students for 40 years, and during that time I think that at least about a half-dozen times students have told me about dreams that they appear to have shared with someone else. What I mean by *shared* here, is that they interacted with someone in a dream and that that person with whom they interacted recalls some of the same elements of the dream. I have chosen the expression *shared dreams* to match up with the expression *shared near-death experiences* to be consistent with material in later chapters. There is no standardized terminology for this subject matter. To be more precise, we could use the expression *meeting dream* to refer to a dream in which at least two people in a dream both report, when awake, having seen each other in the same dream and agree about some of the elements in the dream (McNamara, Dietrich-Egensteiner, & Teed, 2017; Waggoner, 2009). And a *mutual dream* is a dream in which at least two dreamers report dreams with similar content without necessarily meeting one another in the dream (McNamara et al., 2017). There have been descriptions of such dreams collected in the past (Magallón, 1997; cf. Krippner & Faith, 2001), but almost no academic investigation of the subject matter (cf. McNamara et al., 2017).

Let me give an example of mutual dreaming by Dale Graff, one of the military remote viewers to which we alluded in Chapter 1. A remote viewer with whom he was working was given a target by a third person. She was unable to carry out a remote viewing session at the designated time. However, that night at 3:00 a.m. she had a lucid dream. In the dream she was falling through the sky toward the earth, where she could see a "huge mountain" (Graff, 2000, p. 27). Looking back up, she saw something that looked like a multicolored parachute, but she was not attached to it. And she said that "someone else is nearby, but I cannot see who it is" (Graff, 2000, p. 27). The same night at 4:00 a.m. Graff had a lucid dream in which he was also falling toward the earth where he could see a mountain. Looking up, he could see a "large multicolored shape that [looked] like a parachute" (Graff, 2000, p. 25). And he said that "someone is nearby, also falling, but I do not recognize the person" (Graff, 2000, p. 25). The target turned out to be a photo of a hot-air balloon race near Sleeping Giant Mountain in Colorado. Graff noted the correspondences between the two dreams as well as between the dreams and the target. And he noted that the deep subconscious psyche seemed to have a sense of humor as well as a lesson that "we all have a *Sleeping Giant* within us, and our inner giants are there for us to welcome, unafraid" (Graff, 2000, p. 31).

Graff's account of apparent lucid mutual dreaming does, however, suggest a research protocol for studying them. Two researchers who are proficient at lucid dreaming could agree to meet in each other's lucid dreams. Robert Waggoner (2009) has attempted such experiments, in which each dreamer is to "pass on a preselected secret word and special gesture" (p. 218) to the other dreamer in the lucid dream. This is about as difficult as it sounds, not least because of the difficulty of initiating lucid dreams in the first place (cf. Waggoner, 2009), so it remains to be seen how such experiments play out.

What if people really are meeting up with each other in shared dreams? The idea is simple: we each have a subtle body, sometimes called the *double* (Guiley, 1991, p. 154; Muldoon & Carrington, 1929, p. xv), that can leave the physical body and interact with other subtle bodies in a nonphysical domain of reality. When asleep, or dead, the double leaves the physical body and operates in an objectively real, alternate reality (Barušs, 1996; Barušs & Mossbridge, 2017). There has certainly been considerable writing about this outside the academic literature (e.g., O. Fox, 1975; Monroe, 1972/1975; Phillips, 2005; Yram, 1967) but almost nothing within. The assumption is that the psyche is closed. But what if it were to be open? We will consider out-of-body experiences in more detail in Chapter 9, but the idea does fit that of shared dreams. But this does bring us full circle in this chapter, back to classical Greece. Can we actually meet Asklepios in our dreams? And if so, can he heal us? Note that this is congruent with reports of healing in cases of sensed presences during sensory restriction. The psyche may yet be open to more than we currently imagine.

SUMMARY

We started this chapter by considering dream theories from the perspectives that we established in Chapter 1, our first thematic thread. These brought out our fifth thematic thread: are dreams meaningless or meaningful? The answer to that question clearly appears to be yes, at least in some cases such as lucid and precognitive dreaming, bringing out our 11th thematic thread: the degree to which we can control our dreams or the events in our lives. Dreams are meaningful also in that they can reveal useful information about a person or the world, which touches on our eighth thematic thread concerning the benefits of altered states.

What do the empirical data reveal about dream content? Dream content sometimes appears to come from past or future experienced events, but it is frequently representational in nature and reorganized in unexpected ways. And shared dreaming calls into question some of our basic assumptions about the nature of reality, along several of our thematic threads: our 10th thread, is the psyche open or closed? and our second thread, is reality material or transcendent in nature? Our investigation of altered states of consciousness continues to open up dimensions of reality that we had perhaps previously not suspected of existing. Let us proceed to have a look at hypnosis to see what further we can learn about the nature of consciousness and our psyches.

5

Hypnosis

A s I was preparing to write this chapter, I had a dream. In my dream I was looking at my face in a mirror and realized that my face looked dramatically different from the way that it normally does. It was somehow rounder, softer. Odd, I thought, that I should look like that. I assumed that my facial appearance had somehow changed. It did not occur to me to recognize this improbable circumstance as a sign that I was dreaming.

Shortly before going to bed the night before my dream, I had read an article about a study in which the researchers had suggested to participants a change of sexual identity following a hypnotic induction. Eighteen participants who were "hypnotic virtuosos" (Register & Kihlstrom, 1986, p. 84)—that is, those extremely susceptible to hypnosis—all "responded positively to the sex change suggestion" (Noble & McConkey, 1995, p. 71). The researchers later confronted the participants by requesting them to look at a video image of themselves and asking them to tell the researchers what they were experiencing as they looked at themselves on the screen. Eleven of the 18 virtuosos "continued to maintain their positive response to the suggestion" (Noble & McConkey, 1995, p. 72). During a postexperimental inquiry, 7 of the 18 virtuosos "said that the image on the screen was not them," and six others said that they were "confused because what they were feeling conflicted with what they were seeing" (Noble & McConkey, 1995, p. 72).

In my dream, I had looked at a distorted image of myself and assumed it to be real even though it did not coincide with what I knew to be my appearance,

http://dx.doi.org/10.1037/0000200-005

Alterations of Consciousness: An Empirical Analysis for Social Scientists, Second Edition, by I. Baruš whereas in the hypnotic sex-change study some virtuosos looked at a true image of themselves and assumed it to be incorrect because they were convinced that they were the opposite of their actual sex. In both cases, there was an inability to properly reconcile perception of oneself with one's self-identity. These cases also have in common the assumption that the experiences in the altered condition were real. This brings us back to our notion of feelings of reality. In a hypnotized state, a person can be convinced that what they are experiencing is real, even though it is not real by objective evaluation (Jensen et al., 2017; Terhune, Cleeremans, Raz, & Lynn, 2017).

Historically, similarities have been noted between sleep and hypnosis (Hilgard, 1987), with hypnotists frequently using the terminology of sleep in the context of hypnosis (H. Spiegel & Spiegel, 1978). Indeed, the word *hypnosis* itself has apparently been derived from the word *Hypnos*, the Greek god of sleep (K. Barber, 2004; Braid, 1883/1960). However, we have to be careful not to overstate the similarities to sleep (H. Spiegel & Spiegel, 1978), which just raises the question of what, really, is hypnosis. Is hypnosis an altered state of consciousness? Or is there anything altered about it at all? In fact, one of our thematic threads runs throughout much of this chapter, namely, is there anything extraordinary about hypnosis, or is it just a mundane phenomenon?

Questions concerning the nature of hypnosis are more difficult to answer than it seems that they should be. And something with which we have quickly become familiar in this book, there is little agreement among researchers concerning the phenomena and theories of hypnosis. Since the beginning of its modern history with the study of animal magnetism by Franz Anton Mesmer in the 18th century (Hilgard, 1987), hypnosis has been both enigmatic and controversial. In Chapter 1 we considered various psychological dimensions that could be used for defining altered states of consciousness, including dimensions of changes to body image and personal identity. Hence, from the earlier example of the hypnotically suggested sex change we can see that at least in some cases hypnosis can be considered to be an alteration of consciousness. Of course, to say that hypnosis is an alteration or an altered state of consciousness is to classify rather than explain it (Kirsch & Lynn, 1995). But is even that minimal classification undue glorification of what may be nothing more than the expression of thoughts and behaviors appropriate to a social situation that is defined as hypnosis (Spanos, 1982, 1986, 1991; cf. Kauders, 2017)?

Indeed, the hypnosis research community appears to be bifurcated with regard to whether hypnosis is an altered state of consciousness or just a particular instance of ordinary sociocognitive processes. Or, to put the bifurcation in its simplest terms, whether hypnosis is a special process or just ordinary psychological functioning. Such a split is not new. It already existed in the 18th century (Jensen et al., 2017, p. 9). Note that this is consonant with our fourth thematic thread. Is hypnosis ordinary, or is there something extraordinary about it? But how to proceed? Rather than taking sides, perhaps we can see that this bifurcation is an unproductive way of framing hypnosis research. "The resolution of this question, namely whether hypnosis is or is not an altered state of consciousness, is unlikely to lead to any significant theoretical advances" (Terhune et al., 2017, p. 68). And more collaborative research efforts are "unlikely to proceed in a context dominated by individual research agendas committed to waging a divisive state versus nonstate conflict" (Jensen et al., 2017).

So, in a spirit of cooperation, making neither camp happy, let us proceed with a discussion of hypnosis, first by defining it and describing the phenomena that are labeled as hypnosis, and then considering hypnotic susceptibility, a person's ability to express hypnotic behavior. Having established the phenomena, let us look a little bit at the neurophysiology of hypnosis, and then plunge back into the explanations to see if we can reconcile the entrenched theoretical positions. Finally, we will consider some applications of hypnosis. And, as we proceed, well, the reader should not be surprised if some anomalous phenomena surface here and there.

HYPNOTIC PHENOMENA

The phenomena associated with hypnosis are elusive. "Hypnosis, like a chameleon, seems to take on the beliefs and characteristics of the particular experimenter or laboratory in which it is being studied" (Watkins & Watkins, 1986, p. 135). Furthermore, not only is there a variety of hypnotic experiences (Krippner, 1999), but they appear to blend into other psychological experiences, as we shall see later in this chapter as well as in Chapter 6. So, that is where we will start, with some definitions and then descriptions of the phenomena of interest to us.

Defining Hypnosis

I am never quite sure what to say about hypnosis when I teach students in my Altered States of Consciousness class. It is difficult to talk about something that cannot be adequately defined. And the problem with the definitions is that they mirror the theoretical positions taken by hypnosis researchers, so that there is little agreement as to what a definition should look like. For instance, the Hypnosis Definition Committee of Division 30 of the American Psychological Association defined *hypnosis* as a "state of consciousness involving focused attention and reduced peripheral awareness characterized by an enhanced capacity for response to suggestion" (Lynn et al., 2015, p. 390). So, by this definition, a student who is mesmerized by their phone and responsive to its deliberately addictive "pings" (C. Thompson, 2019) is hypnotized (cf. Woody & Sadler, 2016). The definition has also been criticized for promoting an altered states view of hypnosis (Lynn et al., 2015; cf. Facco, 2017).

What do ordinary people say? In a meta-analysis of 31 studies polling people's ideas about hypnosis, the authors found that

> most people believe that: hypnosis is an altered state which requires collaboration to enter; once hypnotized perception changes; hypnotherapy is beneficial for psychological issues and is supportive of medical interventions; hypnosis can also enhance abilities especially memory. (Krouwel, Jolly, & Greenfield, 2017, p. 75)

Okay. Nonspecialists in the study of hypnosis think of hypnosis as an altered state of consciousness that requires induction by a hypnotist. Just one more: "'Hypnotic' responding is a neurobiologically rooted . . . , genetically inherited . . . ability of the human brain to shift, knowingly or unknowingly, to *a motivated mode of neural functioning that enables most humans to alter, to varying degrees, their experience of body, self, actions, and world*" (Dell, 2017, p. 162; italics in original). This appears to be another definition of *altered state*. However, this time the hypnotist is missing as part of the definition, thereby including the irruption of spontaneous alterations of consciousness within the scope of hypnotic phenomena (Dell, 2017). We might want to rule out people with heritable mental disorders who are hallucinating. Or perhaps not, given that there has also been investigation of the overlap between hypnosis and mental disorders (cf. Dell, 2019; Rosen et al., 2017; D. Spiegel, 2003).

Perhaps a practical way to proceed is to give up on a definition of *hypnosis* and, instead, to define a *domain of hypnosis* (Hilgard, 1973a, p. 972; Terhune et al., 2017, p. 62) consisting of the topics that are studied in hypnosis research. In other words, we can delimit the range of psychological phenomena that are to be considered as being hypnosis. Of course, whatever hypnosis is could apply also to phenomena that fall outside the corpus of what has been already studied. Nonetheless, let us look at the traditional hypnotic phenomena.

Hypnotic Induction

When there is an effort to produce it deliberately, hypnosis starts with an *induction*, which could proceed as follows. A *hypnotist* speaks while a person being hypnotized listens. The hypnotist begins by telling the person to close their eyes, to pay attention to the hypnotist's voice, and to relax. The hypnotist assures them that hypnosis is safe. Then the hypnotist may tell them that they are sleepy and that they will go into a deep sleep in which they will be able to do what the hypnotist tells them to do. The hypnotist counts from 1 to 10, telling the individual that, with each count, they are going into a deep sleep. After having counted to 10 the hypnotist tells them that they will respond to suggestions to be made by the hypnotist. At that point, various suggestions may be made. A hypnotic session ends with the hypnotist indicating to the individual that the session is over, for example, by counting backward from 5 to 1, telling the person that they will be more fully awake with each count (cf. Spanos, Radtke, Hodgins, Bertrand, et al., 1983; Spanos, Radtke, Hodgins, Stam, & Bertrand, 1983).

There are many variations of the hypnotic induction. An induction can last from a few seconds to an hour or more (A. F. Barabasz & Barabasz, 2016; Jensen et al., 2017). People can be hypnotized individually or in groups (Shor & Orne, 1962). The induction may be done in person or previously recorded and played on a sound system. *Self-hypnosis* is possible in which a person listens to a recorded induction, or actively plays the role of both hypnotist and the person being hypnotized (S. F. Kelly & Kelly, 1995). Individuals may be asked to close their eyes, as in the example above, or to look at a target such as a button or tack (Weitzenhoffer & Hilgard, 1962). One induction technique includes having individuals roll their eyes upward and then close their eyelids. An induction can be leisurely or abrupt. One hypnotist, in the middle of a tussle with a man who was trying to kill him, claims to have hypnotized his adversary by telling him to "look at that ink bottle and keep looking at it!" (H. Spiegel & D. Spiegel, 1978, p. 24).

An induction does not need to be characterized in terms of sleep. In one study, suggestions of alertness were substituted for suggestions of drowsiness, and increased effort substituted for relaxation in the usual induction protocol. Participants pedaling a stationary bicycle "received suggestions that the pedaling would not seem difficult and would be without discomfort, that the room would seem bright, and that alertness would be increased as the pedaling went on" (Hilgard, 1979, p. 148). That also worked. This is an example of *active-alert hypnosis*, of which there have been also other variations (Alarcón, Capafons, Bayot, & Cardeña, 1999).

There does not seem to be anything particularly compelling about a hypnotic induction. Indeed, it appears to be simply a guided imagery exercise that is used in a situation that has been labeled as hypnosis. Why should we suppose that that would be enough to cause a person's consciousness to change in a fundamental way? And, indeed, often a person's consciousness does not change in any significant way.

Let us use the expression *hypnotic trance* or just *trance* to refer to whatever the condition is in which a person finds themself who actually is responsive to suggestions after an induction. We will reassign the word *trance* a slightly different meaning in Chapter 6, but in this chapter, *trance* just refers to hypnotic trance. So one way to conceptualize what is happening in hypnosis is to think that a person is entering a trance. The point of an induction, therefore, is to do whatever it takes to try to get a person into the state of trance. Some people may be able to enter trance spontaneously, some may be manipulated into it, whereas others may be impervious to efforts to change them. Once an induction has been completed, there should be a check to see if the induction succeeded and the person really is in a state of trance. Yet, in practice, such a check appears to be frequently missing, for instance, after having a person listen to an audio-recorded induction (A. F. Barabasz & Barabasz, 2016).

Is an induction even necessary? "The available evidence tends to indicate that use of a hypnotic induction, compared to no induction at all, has surprisingly modest effects on subsequent responsiveness to suggestions, increasing it by no more than 10%–20%" (Woody & Sadler, 2016, pp. 138–139). So the type of induction and how conscientiously it has been conducted might have little effect on responsiveness to suggestions.

Hypnotic Suggestions

Following an induction, a person who has been hypnotized would usually be given *suggestions*. Suggestions can be *direct* or *indirect*—for instance, "your arm is getting heavier" versus "I wonder if you might be starting to notice a change in your arm" (Jensen et al., 2017, p. 6). Indirect suggestions are worded in such a way as to convey the impression to a person that their responses to them are involuntary (Terhune et al., 2017). There are four types of suggestions: motor, challenge, cognitive, and posthypnotic. Let us consider each of these in turn.

Motor suggestions involve making or not making appropriate motor movements in response to imagined situations. For example, a person may be asked to extend their arm in front of them at shoulder height and told that it is being filled with helium like a balloon, that it feels lighter and lighter. The arm may rise noticeably.

Challenge suggestions entail requesting individuals to breach a previous suggestion and then seeing whether the response to the prior suggestion continues to be maintained. For instance, a person might first be told that their arm is rigid and then asked to try to bend it (cf. Spanos, Radtke, Hodgins, Bertrand, et al., 1983; Spanos, Radtke, Hodgins, Stam, & Bertrand, 1983).

Cognitive suggestions, consisting of suggestions involving changes in perception, thought, and memory, are usually more difficult for people to execute (Weitzenhoffer & Hilgard, 1962). For example, in a *hallucination suggestion*, a person could be told that a cat has crawled on their lap and asked to look at the cat and to pet it. An *amnesia suggestion* could be given whereby a person would be told they would forget the previous suggestions that had been given and then subsequently challenged to write them down (cf. Spanos, Radtke, Hodgins, Bertrand, et al., 1983; Spanos, Radtke, Hodgins, Stam, & Bertrand, 1983). The sex-change suggestion mentioned at the beginning of this chapter is also a cognitive suggestion.

Posthypnotic suggestions are given during hypnosis with the intention that they take effect after the hypnosis session has been terminated. For example, in one study, during hypnosis, it was suggested that for the subsequent 48 hours every time a participant heard the word *experiment* they would touch their forehead with their right hand (Bowers, 1976).

Suggesting to a person the presence of something that is not objectively real, such as the hallucinated cat mentioned previously, is known as a *positive hallucination* (Bowers, 1976). Let us consider the following study by Martin Orne (1959) in which a positive hallucination was suggested. A collaborator of the experimenter sat within eyesight of a participant who had been hypnotized in a room together with the experimenter and the participant. Once the person's eyes were closed, the collaborator got up quietly and stood behind them. Subsequently, they were told to open their eyes, and a positive hallucination of the collaborator sitting in the chair was suggested to them. Then the participant was told to turn around and asked who that was standing behind them. In such a case, a person will typically look back and forth between the collaborator and the empty chair and say that they were "perceiving two images of the same person" (Orne, 1959, p. 296). The "ability . . . to mix freely . . . perceptions derived from reality with those that stem from . . . imagination" (Orne, 1959, p. 295) was called *trance logic* by Orne and considered by him to be one of the "principal features of the hypnotic state" (p. 297).

Not only could a hypnotist suggest a positive hallucination, they could also suggest a *negative hallucination*, the absence of something that is objectively real. For example, it could be suggested to a hypnotized individual that they will not see a "chair that is in the middle of the room" (Bowers, 1976, p. 103). However, if then asked to walk around the room with eyes open, the person "will not bump into the chair" (Bowers, 1976, p. 104; emphasis removed). This is again an example of "the ability to tolerate logical inconsistencies" (Orne, 1959, p. 297) during hypnosis.

On rare occasions, a person who has been hypnotized spontaneously cannot remember what happened during hypnosis. It is also possible to give a posthypnotic suggestion to a person to the effect that they will forget everything that transpired during hypnosis until they are given a cue from the hypnotist to remember it. Upon receiving the cue, an awakened individual "suddenly remembers—often with apparent amazement—what he had forgotten up to that moment" (Bowers, 1976, p. 41). But in what sense has information been forgotten in cases of hypnotic amnesia?

Ironic processes are cognitive processes whereby efforts to suppress thoughts have the opposite effect of occupying a person's attention. A study was done in which participants "were asked to name a favorite automobile that they would really like to own but could only afford to fantasize about" (Bowers & Woody, 1996, p. 382). Then they "were instructed to prevent any thoughts or mental pictures of their favorite automobile from coming to mind by keeping their mind completely blank" (Bowers & Woody, 1996, p. 382) for 2 minutes. However, if during that time they did have intrusions of their favorite automobile, they were to push a button for the length of time that those intrusions were present. Participants were then hypnotized and the thought suppression procedure repeated. Then, while participants were still hypnotized, a suggestion was given to them that they would forget about their favorite automobile, and they were again asked to press the button if any intrusions occurred. What happened? Highly hypnotizable participants pushed the button an average of almost five times in the waking condition, an average of only twice in the hypnotic blank mind condition, and an average of once in the hypnotic amnesia condition. These results suggest that hypnotic amnesia is not just a matter of thought suppression (Bowers & Woody, 1996). We need to be careful interpreting these results because of the demand characteristics of the experiment. A person is told not to do something and then to confess when they are doing what they are not supposed to be doing. That could override the intended experimental manipulations.

HYPNOTIC SUSCEPTIBILITY

One of the core features of hypnotic phenomena is the suggestibility of individuals who have been hypnotized as gauged by their responsiveness to hypnotic suggestions. As we have already seen, the presence of increased suggestibility following hypnotic induction has sometimes been used as part of a definition of *hypnosis*. This implies, of course, that suggestibility is already present (cf. Cialdini, 1988), just augmented by hypnosis. That raises the question of whether or not the augmented suggestibility is the same as a person's baseline suggestibility.

Hypnotic Susceptibility Scales

The predominant line of contemporary research concerning hypnosis has been defined by the measurement of hypnotic susceptibility based on the use of a small number of similar scales (Woody, 1997). In fact, there has been recent criticism that these scales are outdated (Terhune et al., 2017) and that they lack construct validity because they fail to distinguish between voluntary and involuntary responses (Jensen et al., 2017). So, what do they look like?

One of the commonly used hypnotic susceptibility scales is the Stanford Hypnotic Susceptibility Scale (SHSS) developed by Ernest Hilgard and André Weitzenhoffer (Bowers, 1976; Hilgard, 1987). While the SHSS was designed for individual administration, the Harvard Group Scale of Hypnotic Susceptibility was adapted from one of the forms of the SHSS for group administration (Bowers, 1976; Shor & Orne, 1962). Participants in studies of hypnosis would first be given a standardized induction and then a series of suggestions. The induction and suggestions of arm levitation, arm rigidity, hallucinated cat, and amnesia, described previously, are similar to the protocol of the Carleton University Responsiveness to Suggestion Scale (CURSS) in which a total of seven suggestions is used (Spanos, Radtke, Hodgins, Stam, et al., 1983). If a person responds as suggested, then they are said to have passed that item. The total number of items passed results in a score of hypnotic susceptibility.

Using these types of scales, most people end up being moderately hypnotizable since they would "pass most of the easier items and few of the really difficult ones" (Bowers, 1976, p. 63). Subjects who are particularly unresponsive would be classified as *low* on hypnotic susceptibility, those particularly responsive would be classified as *high* (Bowers, 1976), and those who score perfect or almost perfect on susceptibility scales would be classified as *virtuosos* (cf. Register & Kihlstrom, 1986), a term that we have already used to designate the extremely susceptible. By one estimate, 86% of the population would be medium or high (T. Thompson et al., 2019).

Is hypnotic susceptibility really the sort of psychological characteristic of which there can be more or less? That is to say, is hypnotic susceptibility a dimension or a type? Scales used previous to the SHSS had resulted in the observation that "most people have little or no hypnotic ability" (Woody, 1997, p. 233), so Weitzenhoffer and Hilgard had added easy items to their scales to get a healthy number of midrange scores. In that regard, it is notable that four of the seven items on the CURSS involve making or inhibiting motor movements, whereas only three are cognitive (Spanos, Radtke, Hodgins, Stam, et al., 1983). In favor of the notion that hypnotic susceptibility is categorical are the results of analyses from hypnosis scale data indicating that there are two types of people: those who are responsive to hypnosis and those who are not. It appears that hypnosis is a type rather than a dimension in spite of the use of susceptibility scales in which it is treated as a dimension (Woody, 1997).

Although the question of whether hypnotic susceptibility is dimensional or typological is theoretically significant, it has had less importance methodologically because often only those scoring high and low on susceptibility scales have been chosen to participate in research (Woody, 1997). Indeed, a common protocol in hypnosis research, suggested by Orne (1959), has been to compare the behavior of hypnotized participants to that of nonhypnotized participants who have been instructed to pretend that they are hypnotized. Orne's idea behind such a strategy was to determine how much of what happened during hypnosis was due to hypnosis rather than to the implicit demands placed on a participant in a hypnotic situation. Differences in behavior between real and simulating participants could be attributed to hypnosis, whereas the status of behavior that was similar would remain indeterminate since such behavior could be the result of hypnosis by the hypnotized participants and successful faking by the simulators. When Orne tried this method, he was surprised to find that the behavior of the simulators was not different from that of those who were "in deep trance" (Orne, 1959, p. 294). The problem is that simulators could end up being inadvertently hypnotized unless they are low in hypnotizability and impervious to the hypnotic induction. For that reason, high hypnotizable individuals are usually used as reals and low hypnotizable individuals as simulators (Bowers, 1976). This paradigm is not a foolproof method of determining the characteristics of hypnosis since those who are really supposed to be hypnotized could also be faking, with differences in performance between reals and simulators resulting from differences in task demands.

Differences in Hypnotic Responding

To see the effects of the real versus simulator protocol let us consider some of the previously mentioned studies. In the sex change study at the beginning of the chapter, 100% of simulators, 89% of high hypnotizable participants, and 100% of the virtuosos "responded positively to the sex change suggestion" (Noble & McConkey, 1995, p. 71). When confronted with an image of their actual appearance, 41% of simulators, 0% of highs, and 73% of virtuosos "continued to maintain their positive response to the suggestion" (Noble & McConkey, 1995, p. 72).

A group of simulators was used in the study in which participants were given a posthypnotic suggestion to touch their foreheads with their right hands every time they heard the word *experiment* within the following 48 hours. To remove the influence of participants' expectations of being evaluated, a laboratory secretary included the word *experiment* three times in her dialogues with participants "in circumstances that permitted the recording of the subjects' responses to the cue word" (Bowers, 1976, p. 19). Under these conditions, participants who were simulators responded to the cue 8% of the time, those who were reals responded 30% of the time, and a subgroup of those who were reals who had passed all of the items on a hypnotic susceptibility scale touched their foreheads 70% of the time (Bowers, 1976).

In Orne's (1959) study, the concurrent appearance of a positive hallucination of the experimenter's collaborator and the collaborator's actual presence was apparently accepted by those who were really hypnotized. Participants who were simulating hypnosis, on the other hand, after having had a positive hallucination induced and then having been asked to turn around to look at the collaborator, "in most cases, either refused to see anyone behind them, or claimed that they could not recognize the person" (Orne, 1959, p. 296). What we see in each case is the persistence of suggested behaviors on the part of those who are high or very high on hypnotic susceptibility in a manner that is not matched by those who are simulating hypnotic behavior.

Subjective Experience of Hypnosis

Perhaps the most characteristic subjective feature of hypnosis is the *classic suggestion effect*, whereby "hypnotic responses are experienced as occurring involuntarily" (Kihlstrom, 1985, p. 388). Those who experience hypnosis for the first time are typically "surprised because they do not experience themselves as making the behavior happen; instead, they experience the behavior as happening to them" (Bowers, 1976, p. 116). In keeping with language that we have already been using for other phenomena, we could define *feelings of agency* as the subjective feelings associated with self-determination. Or, to say this somewhat differently, feelings of agency are the sense that we cause our own behavior (cf. Terhune et al., 2017). Feelings of agency are frequently missing for those who have been hypnotized. Or, to use the language of Chapter 1, it is frequently the case that a hypnotized individual does not consciously$_2$ decide to respond to hypnotic suggestions that appear to proceed consciously$_1$. And our 11th thematic thread surfaces about the degree to which we can exercise our volition in any given situation.

The absence of feelings of agency has sometimes been taken as the core experiential characteristic of hypnosis (Terhune et al., 2017; Woody & Sadler, 2016). So, for instance, if we are checking after an induction to see whether or not a person is hypnotized, we could ask to see if the person experiences suggested behaviors as occurring voluntarily or involuntarily. If they are occurring voluntarily, then the person is simply complying with the task demands of a social situation in which they find themself as described by social–cognitive theories of hypnosis. If a person perceives their actions as occurring involuntarily, then we could say that they are hypnotized (cf. Woody & Sadler, 2016).

To see how the subjective experience of hypnotized individuals can differ depending upon their degree of hypnotic susceptibility, let us consider a study in which participants were required to rate the extent to which they were experiencing what the hypnotist was asking them to experience. The rating was done by having each participant turn a dial to indicate their experience, with the leftmost position corresponding to "not at all experiencing the suggestion" (McConkey, Wende, & Barnier, 1999, pp. 27–28) and the rightmost position corresponding to completely experiencing the suggestion (p. 28). The participants were 33 high, 47 medium, and 28 low hypnotizable undergraduate students, none of whom was asked to simulate hypnosis. Participants were tested for three suggestions: arm levitation, arm rigidity, and *anosmia*, which is the inability to smell something that is actually present. The anosmia suggestion was tested by placing oil of wintergreen under a participant's nose and asking them to indicate what they could smell. The investigators found "a strong concordance between subjects' behavioral responses and their subjective responses (as indexed by the dial method)" (McConkey et al., 1999, p. 29).

There were also some interesting differences between groups in the subjective rating study. Only seven of the 28 low hypnotizable participants passed arm rigidity, but those who did "made very low ratings of their experience" (McConkey et al., 1999, p. 31) in contrast to the medium and high hypnotizable participants. In other words, low hypnotizable participants behaved as though their arms were rigid without feeling that they were, whereas medium and high hypnotizable participants behaved as though their arms were rigid and indicated that they felt that they were. High hypnotizable participants who failed the anosmia item had the same subjective ratings as high hypnotizable participants who passed this item until the response was tested, at which point the ratings of the highs who failed the test decreased while the ratings of the highs who passed the test increased and did not diminish when the hypnotist gave an explicit instruction to cancel the suggestion. This pattern was not found for the medium hypnotizable participants who failed or passed the anosmia item. What these results suggest is that the positive experience of the high hypnotizable participants "during the test of anosmia enhanced and encouraged the intensity of their experiential involvement, and this intensity was not diminished by an explicit instruction from the hypnotist that was intended to cancel their experience" (McConkey et al., 1999, p. 34). Moreover, "across the items, the offset of the experience progressed relatively slowly" (McConkey et al., 1999, p. 34), making it inappropriate to assume "that the cancellation of a hypnotic experience is easy and instantaneous" (p. 35).

Overall, what this study shows is that the subjective experience of respond-ing to suggestions is more complex than tallies of passed behavioral items on hypnotic susceptibility scales would indicate. In fact, "future measures will need to more optimally integrate behavioral and experiential measures, rather than focusing solely on the former" (Jensen et al., 2017, p. 6) if hypnosis is to be properly measured. Furthermore, the omission of medium susceptibility participants in many hypnosis studies, and, more recently, the additional omission of low-susceptibility participants in brain-imaging studies of hypnosis, calls into question not only the validity but also the generalizability of the results of these studies, given that most people would score low to midrange on hypnotic susceptibility (cf. Jensen et al., 2017).

EXPLANATIONS OF HYPNOSIS

We have now considered some of the phenomena, behavioral and subjective, to which the term *hypnosis* has been applied and the nature of hypnotic susceptibility, so we have some feeling for what we are talking about. But are we any further in our understanding of hypnosis than we were when we started? I think so. Throughout the history of the study of hypnosis, researchers have tried to find neurophysiological markers of hypnosis and have had frus-tratingly little success (Terhune et al., 2017). That has slowly been changing. So let us start there. Then I will introduce a tripartite theory of hypnosis, which I think sheds light on some of the mystery surrounding hypnosis. Dissociation comes up in the tripartite theory, so we will conclude this section by saying a little bit about dissociation before returning to it in Chapter 6.

A Physiological Marker of Hypnotic Responding

Event-related potentials (ERPs) are electroencephalogram (EEG) waveforms that follow on the presentation of a series of stimuli. The amplitudes of waveforms occurring 200 to 500 milliseconds after stimulus presentation are thought to be affected by cognitive factors so that, "for example, stimuli that are rare, that require a response, or that demand conscious attention tend to produce larger positive amplitudes" (D. Spiegel, Bierre, & Rootenberg, 1989, p. 749).

In a study by Arreed F. Barabasz (2000), five high susceptible and five low susceptible participants were selected based on earlier screening of hypnotic susceptibility. An EEG was used to measure ERPs in two conditions while participants listened to series of "25 tone pips presented at 1 second intervals" (A. F. Barabasz, 2000, p. 166). In the first condition, both low and high suscep-tible participants were told to imagine foam earplugs in their ears that would reduce the volume of the sound. Following the first condition, low hypnotiz-able participants were instructed to simulate hypnosis and both low and high susceptible participants were exposed to an alert hypnotic induction. The same suggestion was then given in the second condition as had been given in the first condition followed by the series of 25 tone pips "while EEG data were collected" (A. F. Barabasz, 2000, p. 167). Subsequently the suggestion was reversed and "an independent post experimental inquiry was conducted to determine strategies employed by participants in response to the alternative conditions" (A. F. Barabasz, 2000, p. 167). The question is whether there are physiological differences between just imagining having earplugs and imagining having earplugs while hypnotized. What did Barabasz find?

In his study, Arreed F. Barabasz (2000) found that there were no differences in the amplitudes of ERPs between the nonhypnotic and hypnotic conditions for those who were low in hypnotic susceptibility. However, there was a significant decrease in the average amplitude of ERPs from the nonhypnotic to the hypnotic condition for the high susceptible participants, which suggests that the hallucination of the presence of earplugs while hypnotized was associated with altered perception of the auditory stimulus. Four of the five high hypnotizable participants "showed attenuation of their average ERPs in the hypnosis condition of at least 50% in contrast to the suggestion only condition" (A. F. Barabasz, 2000, p. 167). One of the high hypnotizable participants "demonstrated virtually identical ERPs between the two conditions" (A. F. Barabasz, 2000, p. 167). During the postexperimental inquiry, this participant said that when he had been spanked by his father as a child, he "could turn off the pain like just going to another place" (A. F. Barabasz, 2000, p. 168) and that he had done what he had learned to do as a child upon being given the initial suggestion to place earplugs in his ears and then again when given the same suggestion in the hypnosis condition. "This response appears to be a classic example of spontaneous hypnosis with apparent dissociation" (A. F. Barabasz, 2000, p. 168). The results of this study appear to show that there are physiological differences in perception associated with hypnosis, although it is not clear exactly what cognitive processes are subserved by the ERP changes.

Neurophysiology of Hypnosis

The results of brain imaging studies are less clear. "The current body of findings concerning the neural correlates of hypnosis is marked by inconsistency" (Landry, Lifshitz, & Raz, 2017, p. 76). For instance, some authors have stated that hypnosis is not primarily a matter of imagination (Jensen et al., 2017; Woody & Sadler, 2016), whereas others have found that the area of the brain robustly correlated with hypnotic responding is "likely indexing mental imagery" (Landry et al., 2017, p. 92). Part of the problem is trying to separate out the neural processes that can be attributed to hypnosis specifically from the production of behaviors more generally (Terhune et al., 2017). Another problem goes back to that of using different definitions of hypnosis, in that across studies there is the inclusion of a diverse range of responses, for instance, conflating voluntary and involuntary responses (Jensen et al., 2017). So can we learn anything at all about hypnosis from brain imaging studies?

I think that perhaps the greatest contribution of a cognitive neuroscience approach to hypnosis is the precision that it brings to identifying different psychological processes that could be implicated in hypnosis and then checking to see if they are involved or not. One result has been that "neuroimaging research has consistently demonstrated that subjective changes in response to suggestion are associated with corresponding changes in brain regions related to the specific psychological function in question" (Jensen et al., 2017, pp. 2–3). In other words, the brain regions that are recruited through suggestion, such as a reduction of pain, correspond to the brain regions that would be associated with the actual change in perception of the suggested response. Such a finding is consistent with the attenuation of ERPs in Arreed F. Barabasz's study. In other words, we can believe what hypnotized individuals tell us about their experiences, provided that they really are "hypnotized," of course. "Hypnotic subjects are not merely pretending when they report profound changes in their experience due to hypnosis" (Jensen et al., 2017, p. 3).

The loss of feelings of agency associated with the classic suggestion effect could be due to relinquishment of metacognition, so that a person is not aware of having directed their own behavior. Individuals who are high in hypnotic susceptibility have less activation in parts of the prefrontal cortex that are part of the default mode network. The default mode network, as we have already discussed, is associated with cognition relevant to a person's self. Such cognition includes "metacognitive judgments pertaining to the sense of agency" (Terhune et al., 2017, p. 66). Although still speculative, the loss of the sense of agency during hypnosis may not be due to an actual loss of control, as it would seem, but may be the result of losing introspective access to having exercised control. As neurophysiological research continues, these are the kinds of psychological processes that could become clarified.

A Tripartite Theory of Hypnosis

Let us consider a contention proposed by Theodore Barber (1999) that "hypnosis continues to baffle investigators because it has three separate dimensions" (p. 21). One of these dimensions, consistent with a social–cognitive approach, is embodied by the *positively set person*. Responsiveness to suggestions of a positively set person is not the result of any extraordinary personal characteristics but a "favorable collocation of 'ordinary' social psychological variables such as attitudes, motivations, and expectancies toward the situation; relationship with the hypnotist; and readiness to think with and not contradict the hypnotist's suggestions" (T. X. Barber, 1999, p. 27). Such individuals have a positive attitude toward the hypnotic situation, are motivated to follow the suggestions that are made, and expect to be hypnotized and to "experience the suggested effects" (T. X. Barber, 1999, p. 28). They apparently succeed by devising various cognitive strategies that allow them to respond appropriately to hypnotic suggestions.

Another type of excellent hypnotic subject is a *fantasy-prone person* (T. X. Barber, 1999; Lynn, Pintar, & Rhue, 1997; Lynn & Rhue, 1988). This is some-one with "an overriding extreme involvement in *fantasizing per se*" who is "able to 'hallucinate' at will" (Wilson & Barber, 1981, p. 134) in all of their sensory modalities. For such a person, "fantasy appears to be as vivid as reality" (Wilson & Barber, 1981, p. 134), and what is fantasized appears to be experienced in the same way as reality (Wilson & Barber, 1981) even though the nature of the imagery of such individuals has not been shown to be different from that of other people (Council, Chambers, Jundt, & Good, 1991). During childhood, the fantasy-prone person "typically lived in a make-believe world" (T. X. Barber, 1999, p. 22) that included their dolls, imaginary companions, angels, and other beings. As an adult they retain vivid memories of their life, including apparent memories of events before age three. Almost all fantasy-prone people are convinced that they have had paranormal experiences such as "premonitions; telepathic impressions; pre-cognitive dreams; out-of-body experiences; and contact with spirits, ghosts, or apparitions," and some have reported having had "intense religious expe-riences or exceptional abilities as healers" (T. X. Barber, 1999, p. 23). There is an evident connection between mental and bodily events. For example, 75% of women who are fantasy-prone can reach orgasm without tactile stimulation during sexual fantasies. A fantasy-prone person is often highly susceptible to hypnosis, not needing a hypnotic induction in order to respond to hypnotic suggestions (T. X. Barber, 1999). Some studies have found only a modest correspondence between fantasy-proneness and hypnotic susceptibility, perhaps because of the need for a positive set toward hypnosis, even for those who are fantasy-prone (T. X. Barber, 1999; Lynn & Rhue, 1988).

There is also a third dimension of hypnosis. Deirdre Barrett (1996b) conducted a study with 34 participants who scored perfect or almost perfect on two scales of hypnotic susceptibility. They were split into two groups on the basis of those who could enter hypnosis quickly without a formal induction and those who could not. On investigation, 19 participants who could enter hypnosis quickly turned out to be characterized by "vividness of fantasy processes" (Barrett, 1996b, p. 124) and hence were identified as *fantasizers*—that is to say, as being fantasy-prone. The other 15 participants tended to be amnesic and dissociative and were referred to as *dissociaters* (Barrett, 1996b).

Barrett (1996b) found that dissociaters had difficulty remembering the content of fantasies, and what content they did remember was mundane compared with that of the fantasizers. "Dissociaters experienced dramatic psychophysiological reactions even more extreme than those of fantasizers" (Barrett, 1996b, p. 127); for example, some of them were able to feel pain experienced by other people who had been traumatized. However, none of the dissociaters could achieve an orgasm simply on the basis of fantasy as the fantasizers could. In fact, some of the dissociaters "knew that they had sexual fantasies but usually couldn't remember them afterward" (Barrett, 1996b, p. 127). Fewer dissociaters than fantasizers believed that they had

had psychic experiences, and for many of those who had such beliefs, those experiences "were confined solely to altered states of consciousness" such as "dreams . . . , automatic writing and trance-like seance phenomena" (Barrett, 1996b, p. 127). Whereas fantasizers tended to have difficulty with amnesia suggestions during hypnosis, "amnesia was consistent and total for [dissociaters] whenever it was suggested, and it sometimes persisted even once removal cues had been given" (Barrett, 1996b, p. 129). Dissociaters had more difficulty than fantasizers in distinguishing suggested hallucinations from reality. For example, one dissociater "remained convinced" that, by coincidence, when a hallucination of a fly was suggested, "a real fly happened to begin to buzz around him" (Barrett, 1996b, p. 129). Whereas fantasizers were immediately alert upon awaking from hypnosis, dissociaters "looked confused at first" (Barrett, 1996b, p. 129), and in some cases they appeared to be disoriented (Barrett, 1996b). Theodore Barber used the term *amnesia-prone* (T. X. Barber, 1999, p. 25) to refer to highly suggestible individuals who are dissociaters.

Dissociation

The concept of *dissociation* has had a troubled history that goes back to the late 19th century when the terms *disaggregation* and later, *dissociation*, were introduced to refer to the fragmentation of personality elements, which was believed to be the cause of hysteria. The idea was that the psychological integrity of a healthy individual was maintained by associative mechanisms. However, in some individuals, those who are so predisposed, there is insufficient energy to bind the ingredients of the personality so that those parts of the personality that have resulted from the occurrence of trauma could remain outside of consciousness (Hurley, 1985e; Woody & Bowers, 1994). By the turn of the 20th century, "the concept of dissociation was so familiar that it was a term of the common vocabulary" (Hilgard, 1987, p. 308). However, with a decline in "interest in the kinds of problems that dissociation was designed to explain" (Hilgard, 1987, p. 309), the term *dissociation* fell into relative disuse.

The notion of dissociation was revived in the 1970s by Ernest Hilgard (1973b), who proposed a *neodissociation theory* of hypnotic phenomena. He found that some hypnotized individuals who responded positively to a suggestion for the attenuation of pain, could nonetheless "reveal that some pain had actually been felt" (Hilgard, 1987, p. 309) when it was suggested to them during hypnosis that there was a hidden part of themselves that knew what was happening to their bodies (Bowers, 1976). According to the neo-dissociation interpretation, there is a *hidden observer* present within a person when they are hypnotized, experiencing pain in a dispassionate manner when they are subjected to painful procedures, in spite of the analgesia experienced consciously during hypnosis (Hilgard, 1973b). The idea was that hypnosis introduces an *amnesic barrier* between a person's higher level cognitive functions from which reports of subjective experiences are normally made and sensory subsystems in which painful stimuli are processed (cf. Hilgard, 1973b). In cognitive terms, we could say that, with hypnosis, metacognitive monitoring has become disconnected from the interoception of pain, and that, somehow, suggesting the existence of a hidden observer reestablishes some sort of monitoring.

In contrast to using the notion of dissociation for explanatory purposes, it may be more prudent for us to use the term *dissociation* in a descriptive sense to refer to any functional disconnection between elements of a person's psyche (cf. MacMartin & Yarmey, 1999) irrespective of what the psychological or physiological mechanism of that disconnection may turn out to be. In that way, we can talk freely about dissociation being a third dimension of hypnosis alongside positivity and fantasy proneness.

When the Phenomenology of Consciousness Inventory (PCI; Pekala, 1991) has been given to hypnotized individuals, a number of individual differences in hypnotic experiences have been distinguished. In particular, it has been found that there are two types of highly susceptible individuals. One type has been "characterized by moderate alterations in consciousness and experience, a great deal of vivid imagery, moderate positive affect, but only mild-to-moderate losses in rationality and memory," whereas the second type has had "large alterations in state of consciousness and moderate altered experiences; a loss of volitional control, self-awareness, rationality, and memory; and little vivid imagery" (Pekala & Kumar, 2000, p. 116). These appear to be the differences between fantasizers and dissociaters consistent with Theodore Barber's tripartite theory. However, the PCI has also revealed complexities that do not fit a simplistic version of the theory. For instance, low but not midrange scores on hypnotic susceptibility accompanied by a subjective experience of being hypnotized have been associated with a high degree of dissociation (Pekala & Kumar, 2000). That suggests that some individuals may enter a trance but dissociate to such an extent that they cannot generate the necessary behavior to be measured on the hypnotic susceptibility scales, or that they have become altogether disconnected from the hypnotic relationship with no predilection to comply with a hypnotist's suggestions.

Clearly, much remains to be done in order to understand hypnosis. Nonetheless, the tripartite theory helps us to make sense of the variety of hypnotic phenomena that we have considered. It allows us to see that in many cases responses to suggestions could result primarily from the engagement of cognitive processes in response to the context in which hypnosis takes place. But for a small number of individuals, there may be a discrete shift into a trance whose features vary depending upon whether there is a tendency toward fantasy or dissociation. Is it possible, in some cases, that trance may turn out to be more interesting then we think? Could it be that trance is a gateway to a range of phenomena that are usually not accessible to us? We will take up that train of thought in Chapter 6.

APPLICATIONS OF HYPNOSIS

Let us turn away from the theoretical to the practical aspects of hypnosis for the remainder of this chapter by considering the use of hypnosis for memory enhancement, the clinical applications of hypnosis, and problems that could arise from its use.

Hypnotically Recalled Memories

We have seen that some highly hypnotizable individuals are amnesia-prone. But it is the opposite, *hypermnesia*, the enhanced recall of previous events, that is perhaps one of the most controversial phenomena associated with hypnosis, one that turns out to have wide-ranging practical consequences. One of the items that is found on some hypnotic susceptibility scales is that of age regression. An individual would be asked to write their name on a pad of paper. Then it would be suggested to them that they are getting younger until they are back in a fifth-grade class. They would again be asked to write their name on the paper. Then it would be suggested that they are back in a second-grade class and again, they would be asked to write their name. An individual would be said to pass the item if the handwriting changes for either of the regressed ages (Weitzenhoffer & Hilgard, 1962).

In some cases of hypnotic age regression, individuals can apparently recall traumatic childhood events of which they were unaware in the ordinary waking state, such as the example of a medical student who recalled that as a child he had seriously injured another boy with a pitchfork, for which he was subsequently severely punished (Erickson, 1979). But are these real childhood memories, or are they imagined? Are these delusional or veridical experiences? During a criminal investigation a police officer may hypnotize witnesses or victims in order to try to gain additional information about a crime (Hibler, 1995). Although there have been some dramatic successes, such as, in one case, the hypnotic recall of all but one digit of a license plate number (Giannelli, 1995), there have also been "cases in which the hypnotically recalled information was clearly incorrect, despite vows of confidence from those who had been hypnotized" (Hibler, 1995, p. 320).

Perhaps the most problematic are "cases in which adults undergoing psychotherapy claim to have recovered long-repressed memories of sexual abuse at the hands of parents or other family members" (Schacter, 1995, p. 2). In such cases, we have childhood memories with criminal implications. In fact, such purported memories led to the "memory wars" of the 1990s about what was remembered and what was fabricated in cases of childhood sexual abuse (Patihis & Younes Burton, 2015, p. 153). Clearly, if independent corroboration of hypnotically retrieved memories is possible, then a determination of the accuracy of such memories does not need to depend on factors intrinsic to the process of remembering itself. But what if it is not possible to find any independent evidence? How is one to assess the remembered experiences?

In general, so-called hypnotically refreshed (Giannelli, 1995, p. 212) memories are not reliable. The evidence concerning hypnotic hypermnesia indicates that individuals who have been hypnotized tend to recall more information but that much of the additionally recalled information is incorrect (Frankel & Covino, 1997), as illustrated in the following study. Fifty-four participants were presented with "60 slides of simple black-and-white line drawings of common objects" (Dywan & Bowers, 1983, p. 184). They were then required to do a forced recall task by being asked "to write the name of a line drawing in each of the 60 blank spaces provided for [that] purpose" on a sheet of paper, indicating which of the names "represented memories and which were just guesses" (Dywan & Bowers, 1983, p. 184). This task was repeated twice after 3-minute rest periods and then once each day for the following 6 days. The average number of items recalled rose from an average of 30 on the first trial to 38 by the ninth trial, but so did the number of errors "from an average of less than one error on the first trial to an average of four errors by the ninth" (Dywan & Bowers, 1983, p. 184).

Participants in the hypnosis hypermnesia study were then divided into experimental and control groups, with participants in the experimental group being hypnotized and those in the control group not being hypnotized. Participants in both groups "were told to relax and focus all their attention on the slides they had seen the week before" (Dywan & Bowers, 1983, p. 184). Participants in the hypnosis group reported an average of about five additional remembered items, whereas those in the nonhypnosis group only reported an average of about two additional remembered items. However, most of the additionally recalled items were incorrect, with an average of less than one in every five additional items being correct for either group. The most correct additional items that any of the participants could recall was five, whereas many could not produce any correct new information at all. Perhaps not surprisingly, the increased output for the hypnotized group was due almost entirely to the efforts of those who were high in hypnotic susceptibility. However, the hypnotized highly susceptible participants also made "almost three times as many errors" as were made by the hypnotized low susceptible participants and those in the control group (Dywan & Bowers, 1983, p. 185).

Considerable research has shown that personal memory is usually reconstructive in nature. Memory recall does not involve the replaying of a sequence of events as it actually occurred but rather the reconstruction of experiences colored by general knowledge, subsequent events, and environmental factors at the time of retrieval. "Retrospective bias appears to be most pronounced when people attempt to remember specific episodes and least pronounced when they reflect on the general features of their autobiography" (Schacter, 1995, p. 17). The construction of erroneous memories is known as *confabulation*, and the erroneous memories themselves are called *false memories* (cf. Schacter, 1995).

In the so-called Deese–Roediger–McDermott (DRM) paradigm, the production of false memories can be demonstrated by reading a list of associated words to a person and then asking them if an associated word that had not been read to them, called a *critical lure*, had been on the list. Studies with variations on this sort of protocol have shown that people will acknowledge recognition of associated material that has never been presented to them. In one study, participants falsely remembered 65% of critical lures, which is consistent with previous research (Patihis, Frenda, & Loftus, 2018). Furthermore, some of the neurophysiological correlates of the DRM task have been identified, apparently allowing for the ability to predict some memory errors (Chadwick et al., 2016). However, there does not appear to be a confabulation personality type so that no single false memory task can determine whether a person will form false memories when presented with different types of tasks or form them in real-world situations (Patihis et al., 2018).

An additional problem with hypnotically refreshed memories is that hypnotized individuals tend to think that erroneous information is correct (Schacter, 1995). This appears to be particularly true when individuals can imagine information vividly, or when it is accompanied by strong emotional attachment. "Emotional intensity, rather than a real experience, . . . invites confidence in the truth of what is remembered" (Frankel & Covino, 1997, p. 356). In other words, individuals may be using the feelings associated with prior events, rather than actual recall of those events, to make judgments about their veridicality. We have to be careful, not just in the case of memory recall, but in alterations of consciousness more generally, to determine as much as possible the criteria that a person uses for making judgments that something is actually true. This is, of course, also relevant to judgments about what is and is not real, colored by feelings of reality, which gets us back to our third thematic thread concerning veridicality.

However, there are those who have argued that traumatic memories, precisely because of the emotional intensity that is associated with them, are not susceptible to the kinds of memory distortions that occur with ordinary biographical memories. The idea is that traumatic events, at the time that they occur, are actively repressed in the unconscious or dissociated from consciousness, in order to protect a person against the distress that they cause. While repression and dissociation do not refer to the same purported psychological processes, their effects are the same—namely, to isolate traumatic experiences from explicit awareness (MacMartin & Yarmey, 1999). Thus, it is thought that memories of traumatic events can remain unchanged (Schacter, 1995) somewhere in a person's psyche until they are reawakened in psychotherapy, perhaps with the assistance of hypnosis (Frankel & Covino, 1997). Although there is growing evidence that "emotional arousal typically enhances the accuracy of memory for the central aspects of an [emotionally arousing] event and impairs memory for more peripheral details" (Schacter, 1995, p. 18), there is no good evidence that "people can forget and then recover years of repeated, horrific abuse" (p. 28). On the other hand, there is also "no hard scientific evidence" that "people can falsely create an entire history of traumatic sexual abuse when none occurred" (Schacter, 1995, p. 28).

What is needed is research that can extend the determination of the conditions under which events are likely to be remembered and the conditions under which they are likely to be distorted so that better judgments can be made about the possible accuracy of reported memories. We will return to this discussion in Chapter 6 in the context of trauma that has been associated with dissociation.

Hypnotic Analgesia

One of the early uses of hypnosis, during the 19th century, before the invention of chemical anaesthetics, was to use *mesmerism*, as it was then called, to suggest a negative hallucination of the absence of pain during major surgery (Hilgard, 1987). Since then, in spite of continuous controversy about the nature of hypnosis, analgesic effects of hypnosis have been demonstrated in both clinical and laboratory settings (J. Barber, 1998a; Dinges et al., 1997; Facco, Pasquali, Zanette, & Casiglia, 2013; Jensen et al., 2017; Knox, Morgan, & Hilgard, 1974; Lambert, 1996; Mauer, Burnett, Ouellette, Ironson, & Dandes, 1999; M. F. Miller, Barabasz, & Barabasz, 1991; Montgomery, DuHamel, & Redd, 2000; J. T. Smith, Barabasz, & Barabasz, 1996). Hypnotic analgesia has been shown to be effective, not just for the elimination of acute pain, but for the reduction of recurrent pain in chronic conditions (e.g., Dinges et al., 1997). It has been found that hypnotic suggestions relieved pain for three quarters of participants over a number of studies and different types of pain (Lynn, Kirsch, Barabasz, Cardeña, & Patterson, 2000). Also, an analysis of 85 experiments of evoked pain in healthy participants revealed that a direct analgesia suggestion reduced pain by 42% for highly susceptible participants and 29% for medium susceptible participants (T. Thompson et al., 2019).

Although not particularly representative, the following study of hypnotic analgesia serves an illustrative purpose. A surgeon hypnotized himself prior to performing "liposuction surgery of his upper and lower abdomen and flank areas" (Botta, 1999, p. 299). Being uncertain of what to expect, the surgeon used a number of techniques to suggest analgesia. For example, "the areas of the abdomen and flanks were dissociated as if they were another patient's body parts and not the surgeon's own" (Botta, 1999, p. 300). The surgical procedure was performed in a standing position over the course of 4 hours. This case illustrates hypnotic analgesia particularly well "given the fact that the skin is inundated with cutaneous nerve endings," which would ordinarily result in "a continual bombardment of nerve stimulation" (Botta, 1999, p. 301) during liposuction. This case also illustrates the ability to carry out highly skilled cognitive and manual tasks while in a sufficiently deep trance so as to experience analgesia (Botta, 1999). Usually, attempting to do something else during self-induced hypnotic anaesthesia would "likely cause loss of the anesthesia" (Ewin, Levitan, & Lynch, 1999, p. 302). In this case, the surgeon has been able to dissociate what should have been his experience of pain from his ability to perform the surgery. It is also interesting to consider the extent to which dissociation that occurs in a case such as this is similar to dissociation during sleepwalking as discussed in Chapter 3. Indeed, apparently "some early forms of hypnosis resembled sleepwalking" (Bowers, 1976, p. 41).

Clinical Applications of Hypnosis

We have seen already a number of practical applications of hypnosis, such as its use to induce analgesia and to attempt to recall previously forgotten information. Hypnosis has been used, not just in forensic settings to find information about a crime and in clinical settings to recover purported traumatic memories but also in clinical settings as an adjunct to psychotherapy more generally (e.g., Meyerson, 2010; H. Spiegel & Spiegel, 1978). In general, the use of hypnosis in addition to more traditional cognitive behavioral treatments for a number of disorders such as "obesity, insomnia, anxiety, pain, and hypertension" (Lynn, Kirsch, et al., 2000, p. 244) has been shown to be more effective than the use of the cognitive–behavioral treatments alone. Hypnosis has also been shown to be more effective than no intervention for smoking cessation (Lynn, Kirsch, et al., 2000). In fact, hypnosis has been used in a wide range of situations in clinical practice (Kihlstrom, 2018; Walling & Baker, 1996) although clinicians tend to disregard whether or not their clients can be hypnotized (Kihlstrom, 2018). In one study, for example, it was found that "although virtually all the academics regarded hypnotic susceptibility as being relevant to therapeutic outcome, only half of the clinicians did so and few measured it in clients" (West, Fellows, & Easton, 1995, p. 143). This is perhaps justified in that in clinical settings therapeutic outcomes would be the result not only of hypnosis specifically but also of nonspecific factors that contribute to psychological well-being (cf. Kihlstrom, 2018; Zilbergeld, 1983).

A variation on clinical applications of hypnosis is to have people apply hypnosis by themselves to themselves. "Self-hypnosis can be defined as self-induction into the hypnotic process produced by self-generated suggestions" (Eason & Parris, 2019, p. 262). There is a wide range of techniques that have been used for that purpose (Eason & Parris, 2019), including combinations with other self-development modalities such as mindfulness practice (Elkins, Roberts, & Simicich, 2018). In a review of 22 controlled, randomized, clinical trials involving self-hypnosis, it was found that "self-hypnosis was an effective treatment" in 18 of them, "with 14 studies outperforming active controls" (Eason & Parris, 2019, p. 272) for conditions such as pain, childbirth, "stress, anxiety, and hypertension" (p. 271).

Hypnosis has applications outside forensic and clinical settings. Dissociation has been used by captured military personnel, for example, as a way of preparing to be tortured. With the potential for assisting captives with "effective dissociation, ego enhancing, stress coping, and anxiety and pain reduction" (Wood & Sexton, 1997, p. 208), instruction in self-hypnosis has been advocated as part of military training programs. In a somewhat different venue, students for whom it was suggested during hypnosis that they would "be relaxed and have excellent concentration and complete recall for their coursework" (Schreiber, 1997, p. 637) performed better on the final examination than students who were given "motivational talks" (p. 637). From these examples, it can be seen that there could be a broad range of applications of hypnosis for helping a person to solve problems with living (e.g., S. F. Kelly & Kelly, 1995).

Problems With Hypnosis

Let us end this chapter with a word of caution. The claim has been made by some hypnotists that hypnotized individuals cannot be harmed because they are protected by unconscious mechanisms from harmful suggestions (J. Barber, 1998b). However, in one study, one third of practitioners using hypnosis reported having experienced "unexpected complications" (West et al., 1995, p. 146) in the course of their work. One clinician, for instance, gave examples of inappropriate emotional arousal, unexpected hostility, amnesia, obedience, disorientation, paralysis, and memory contamination as problematical effects of hypnosis during psychotherapy (J. Barber, 1998b). Another problem is that in some cases hypnotized individuals fail to awaken from hypnosis at the end of a session (Gravitz, 1995). While rare, failure to dehypnotize is not surprising given the results of the study we considered previously in which cancellation suggestions appeared to be less effective than they have normally been assumed to have been. And there is greater awareness now of the need to ensure that hypnotized individuals have returned to their prehypnotic ordinary waking state at the termination of a hypnotic session (Howard, 2017).

Sometimes there are problems with *stage hypnosis*. In one case, a young man experienced a psychotic breakdown after performing as a volunteer for a stage hypnotist (Allen, 1995), and in another case, a healthy young woman who was frightened of electricity died following her participation in a stage hypnosis performance in which it was suggested to her that she would experience an electrical shock of 10,000 volts. Indeed, there have been complaints from people participating, or even just sitting in the audience, of adverse effects from stage hypnosis shows (Heap, 1995). Thus, we see that while its applications appear to be largely benign, sometimes hypnosis can cause problems.

SUMMARY

In the end, then, what are we to make of hypnosis? What is it? Is it mundane or extraordinary? We began this chapter by considering various definitions of hypnosis and the phenomena that fall within the domain of hypnosis. This information was supplemented by considering individual differences in hypnotic susceptibility and some of the academic research concerning hypnosis. There is evidence that there is more to hypnosis than deliberate enactment of appropriate behavior—that hypnosis may, indeed, be better conceptualized as a special state of trance. These indications include changes in neural processing evidenced during responses to hypnotic suggestions; behaviors in natural settings, such as pain relief during surgery, in which there appear to be actual psychological or physiological changes associated with those behaviors; and the fantasy proneness and dissociative tendencies of hypnotic virtuosos. These characteristics of hypnotic behavior suggest that something extraordinary may be going on at least some of the time during hypnosis. The tripartite theory consisting of positively set, fantasy-prone, and amnesia-prone dimensions fits the evidence but needs to be further tested empirically. In fact, considerable research is required to clarify not only the characteristics of phenomena associated with hypnosis but also the details of the psychological and physiological mechanisms through which these phenomena occur. Whether it is considered to be mundane or extraordinary, hypnosis has been widely used for practical effects such as memory enhancement and therapy. Indeed, controversies surrounding some of these practical applications will surface again in the following chapters.

A number of our thematic threads surfaced in this chapter. The most obvious was our fourth thread, the question of whether hypnosis was mundane or extraordinary. But, through the classic suggestion effect, we also saw the emergence of questions regarding the degree to which we can exercise volitional control when experiencing hypnotic phenomena and that, indeed, this could be a defining characteristic of this alteration of consciousness. But we also touched on the third, eighth, and seventh threads concerned, respectively, with the ways in which we can become deluded and the ways in which hypnosis can be beneficial and enhance well-being.

To some extent hypnosis serves as a gateway to the more dramatic alterations of consciousness that we will look at next. In fact, we will need much of the material from this and the previous chapters to try to understand the phenomena considered in Chapter 6.

6

Trance

We have considered a number of alterations of consciousness—such as mind wandering, sensory restriction, dreaming, hypnosis, fantasy proneness, and dissociation—in which we are removed from our everyday ways of thinking about the world. And here and there, such as the Ganzfeld studies, sensed presences, and the Maimonides studies, we have come across intimations that alterations of consciousness may be a gateway that allows us to encounter other aspects of reality. Is that true? Materialists believe that mental events are necessarily skullbound, whereas transcendentalists believe that they are not. But what does the evidence tell us? Is the psyche open or closed? Here and there, in dreams and hypnosis, we have come across alterations of self-identity. Who are we? Are we single or multiple entities? Are we always ourselves, or are we sometimes somebody else? Combining these two lines of questioning, we can ask whether there are entities in alternate aspects of reality that can intrude into our psyches so as to change our self-identity. And if we believe that we have had strange encounters of some sort, are we crazy? And even if we are suffering from some form of psychopathology, is what is happening nonetheless real? Are experiences of intrusion delusional or veridical? Are such alterations of consciousness dangerous? Almost all of our thematic threads surface in this chapter as we consider shamanism, mediumship, dissociative identity disorder, and alien abduction experiences. We may not be able to answer our questions by the end of this chapter, but perhaps we will understand the questions better.

http://dx.doi.org/10.1037/0000200-006
Alterations of Consciousness: An Empirical Analysis for Social Scientists, Second Edition,
by I. Barušs

In contradistinction to the definition of *hypnotic trance* in Chapter 5, henceforth let us use the word *trance* to refer to states of consciousness in which the appearance of awareness is present but that are actually sleeplike states characterized by involuntary behavior and decreased environmental responsiveness (Pekala & Kumar, 2000). That definition applies sometimes to the alterations of consciousness that we are considering in this chapter, but at other times there are fundamental questions about what awareness a person may be experiencing and to what degree self-determination may or may not be present. In that sense, the title *trance* only loosely fits the subject matter discussed in this chapter.

SHAMANISM

We briefly considered shamanism in Chapter 1 in the context of noting the tendency to pathologize alterations of consciousness. We return to a discussion of shamanism first by describing its characteristics, then by comparing it with schizophrenia, and, finally, by looking at its relationship to hypnosis.

Characteristics of Shamanism

The word *shaman* originated from native Siberian languages (Laughlin & Rock, 2014; Winkelman, 2011) but has been generalized to denote individuals in aboriginal societies with the same functional role as Siberian shamans; it has also been appropriated by some Western spiritual groups involved with healing, spiritual practices, and altered states of consciousness (Laughlin & Rock, 2014). In order to rule out the last of those meanings, let us define *shamanism* as a practice in which an individual deliberately alters their consciousness for the purpose of interacting with spirits in order to serve the community in which they find themself (cf. Ripinsky-Naxon, 1993). The following are the core characteristics of a shaman.

A *shaman* is a charismatic individual, usually male, whose training includes a "vision quest interaction with the spirit world" and a "death-and-rebirth experience." They participate in "communal chanting, music, drumming, and dancing," and are involved in "healing, diagnosis, divination, and assistance in hunting," believing that illness is caused by soul loss or intrusions by objects or entities. They deliberately alter their consciousness, engage in soul journeying, control animal spirits, and believe that they can change into animals and to harm others through sorcery (Winkelman, 2011, p. 162). *Soul journeying* involves travels to otherworldly realms in which spirits are encountered. More specifically, in soul journeying a shaman may experience themself flying or falling though an opening in the earth, arriving at another level of reality that is experienced as being as real as ordinary reality, having imaginal adventures and encountering various spiritual entities in that realm, and then, upon returning, being able to remember the events that transpired

(Cardeña, 1996). Changing into other animals includes not only empathically experiencing what animals experience and mimicking their behavior but, ostensibly, the "physical transformation of a shaman into an animal," which is known as *shape-shifting* (Saniotis, 2019, p. 81). From a materialist perspective, these are imaginary spirits, since real spirits do not exist, and shape-shifting is a delusion since a human being cannot physically change into anything else.

The label *shamanism* has sometimes been restricted to these core features (e.g., Walsh, 1989; Winkelman, 2011), but let us open it up a little bit to include not only soul journeying as a means of interacting with spirits but also *possession*, whereby spirits work through the shaman's body. In possession experiences, there is not much imagery, "but rather a sense of dizziness, alterations in body image and a not infrequent experience of weight or pressure on the shoulders or neck, frequently explained as being 'mounted' by a spirit" (Cardeña, 1996, p. 92). With possession, often there is loss of self-awareness and an inability to recall the events that occurred during the time of spirit incorporation (Cardeña, 1996).

The distinction is sometimes made between *ecstasy*, whereby a shaman leaves their body, and *trance*, allowing the spirits to use the body. The former originates from older hunter–gatherer societies, whereas the latter is a more recent variation found in sedentary communities (Cardeña & Krippner, 2018). In a study of 42 societies, shamans in 10 societies engaged in journeying, those in 18 societies used "spirit incorporation," 11 societies had both, and 3 had some other "different altered state" (Krippner, 1999, p. 158). The various forms of shamanism seem to have arisen in different cultures directly from the experiences of their people (Ripinsky-Naxon, 1993). Given that soul journeying appears to involve fantasy, whereas possession is characterized by dissociation, we thereby set up a parallel with the distinction for highly hypnotic individuals between fantasizers and dissociaters (Cardeña, 1996).

Shamans may, although not always (Krippner & Combs, 2002), become who they are through a process of initiation in response to a call (Ripinsky-Naxon, 1993). The Nepalese Tamang shaman Bhirendra's calling was described by him as a "frightening encounter with fiendish ghosts in a cemetery who picked at him with spears and pulled flesh from his body until he was 'saved by a white light' that appeared once he had surrendered to his impending death" (Peters, 1989, pp. 123–124). Initiation is marked by ordeals of death and rebirth whereby neophytes are often isolated from society, subjected to deprivation, and experience exhaustion, suffering, and symbolic death, resulting apparently in access to another realm of existence. The neophyte is reconstituted, sometimes with a change of identity, including sexual identity, and sometimes with purportedly changed body parts such as having intestines made of quartz. Psychedelic drugs are often used to induce experiences of the other world, including soul journeys. A second stage of the learning process consists of the shaman receiving instructions from a mentor concerning such matters as the preparation of herbal medicines and the "oral traditions and myths" (Ripinsky-Naxon, 1993, 87) of their people. The ordeals of initiation can be dramatically visceral, as in Bhirendra's case, or "barren and uneventful" (Ripinsky-Naxon, 1993, p. 89) in other cases that appear to be largely symbolic.

Shamanism and Schizophrenia

Altered states of consciousness have been a prime candidate for *pathomorphism*, the tendency to label psychological phenomena that we do not understand using pathological categories (Barušs, 2000b). In particular, comparisons have been drawn between shamanism and schizophrenia (Fotiou, 2016; cf. R. M. Ross & McKay, 2018), as we already noted in Chapter 1. This brings to the surface our seventh thematic thread: Are shamanic states pathological?

Schizophrenia is a psychological condition usually characterized by disorganized speech and behavior as well as the presence of psychotic symptoms such as hallucinations and delusions. *Delusions* are beliefs that are contrary to reality, such as the belief that one is being tormented; that one's internal organs have been replaced with those of another person; or that one's body, thoughts, or actions are being controlled by an outside force. Such psychological distortions are sometimes labeled as *positive symptoms*, whereas ordinary psychological functions that are attenuated, such as lost emotional expression or motivation, are called *negative symptoms*. In order to diagnose a person with schizophrenia, at least some of these symptoms need to be present to such a degree that they impair self-care or social or occupational functioning (American Psychiatric Association, 2013).

Is shamanism schizophrenia? The shamanic initiation resembles schizophrenia to the extent that initiatic crises involve perceived dismemberment, disintegration of self-identity, the presence of visions, and the adoption of a world view in which the initiate believes that they are interacting with spirits. However, while there may be such similarities between the experiences of a person with schizophrenia and a neophyte shaman, the shaman's disintegration makes possible their reconstruction as a healer and social reintegration. whereas a person with schizophrenia often remains disorganized and becomes a social outcast (Halifax, 1990). In fact, the causal direction has sometimes been reversed, so that it has been argued that an individual experiencing a psychotic episode could reconceptualize their experiences as an expansion of consciousness that can be restructured into a state of exceptional well-being (Halifax, 1990; Lukoff, 1985; Lukoff & Everest, 1985; Shaffer, 1978; cf. Barušs, 1996). In other words, if there are similarities between the shamanic initiation and schizophrenia, particularly in the case of positive symptoms (R. M. Ross & McKay, 2018), can we use the successful reintegration of shamans into their society as a template for the treatment of a mental disorder?

Whereas shamanic initiation can resemble schizophrenia, this is not true of a shaman's experiences more generally. Roger Walsh (1995) proposed a method of *phenomenological mapping* whereby experiences in different states of consciousness can be compared along a number of dimensions. The following are some of the differences along Walsh's dimensions between soul journeying and schizophrenic states. To begin with, shamans have good *control* over entering and leaving an altered state and some control over the contents of that state, whereas there is a "dramatic reduction of control" (Walsh, 1995, p. 42) for those with schizophrenia. Whereas *concentration* is increased during soul journeying, with the shaman's attention moving "freely from object to object" (Walsh, 1995, p. 35), one of the characteristics of schizophrenia is the disorganization of thought as demonstrated by disorganized speech that can include jumping from one loosely associated topic to another (American Psychiatric Association, 2013). A shaman's *sense of self* is that of a spirit or soul that has been "freed from the body" (Walsh, 1995, p. 36) in what resembles an *out-of-body experience*, whereas a person with schizophrenia can have a disintegrated sense of self and rarely have out-of-body experiences (Walsh, 1995), although the prevalence of out-of-body experiences is higher among those with schizophrenia than in the general population (Alvarado, 2000). Whereas a shaman can experience positive or negative *affect* during soul journeying, the emotional expression of a person with schizophrenia is often negative, inappropriate, or absent. The *content* of experience for the shaman is coherent and determined by the cultural cosmology and purpose of the journey, whereas for a person with schizophrenia the content is "often disorganized and fragmented" (Walsh, 1995, p. 42).

There are similarities between shamanism and schizophrenia along some of Walsh's dimensions. In the case of both shamanism and schizophrenia, *arousal* can be high, *awareness of the environment* low, and the *ability to communicate* with surrounding people limited. However, overall, phenomenological mapping reveals that soul journeying is not the same as schizophrenia (Walsh, 1995).

Shamanism and Hypnosis

Direct comparisons have been made between hypnosis and shamanism. In one study, Etzel Cardeña requested 12 hypnotic virtuosos "to go into as deep a state of hypnosis as they could" (Cardeña, 1996, p. 92) and then asked them about every 5 minutes what they were experiencing. Cardeña found significant differences compared with a condition of no hypnosis. During light levels of hypnosis there were alterations in body image followed by imaginal experiences. There was frequent "mention of floating or flying sensations . . . sinking, falling down . . . or going through tunnels" (Cardeña, 1996, p. 92), separation of the self from the physical body, and "journeys to unusual worlds" such as "being in a dark world [or] encountering a limitless sea" (p. 93). During deeper levels of hypnosis, participants heard music, saw colors, and "reported synesthesia" (Cardeña, 1996, p. 93), which is the experience of a stimulus in sensory modalities other than the one in which it is received. All of the participants saw a "very bright light or, in some cases [became] one with it"; some had "transcendent experiences such as being in a timeless/spaceless realm"; and "intense positive emotions" (Cardeña, 1996, p. 93) were associated with these various events. "At follow-ups immediately after completing the project and at four months, every experient reported positive effects from the experiment, from mild ones such as better concentration, to a sense of profound contact with the self" (Cardeña, 1996, p. 93). To use the terminology of one of our thematic threads, it is interesting to note not only the lateral meaningfulness but an indication of vertical meaningfulness in some of the participants' accounts.

Even without phenomenological mapping, it is not difficult to see that the experiences of the hypnotic virtuosos in Cardeña's study share many similarities with the experiences of shamans. There were also differences, such as the absence among Cardeña's participants of plant and animal imagery typically found in shamanic adventures, as well as their lack of the shaman's cosmology. Nonetheless, according to Cardeña, what these data suggest is that "the alterations in consciousness found in shamanism and deep hypnosis are likely the product of innate biological/cognitive dispositions rather than the mere byproduct of a particular culture" (Cardeña, 1996, p. 94).

A defining symbol of shamanism is the shaman's drum; ritual drumming can produce a rhythm-induced trance. In one brain-imaging study, rhythmically induced trance states were associated with activation of both the default mode network as well as the control network, a brain network associated with cognitive control. In a follow-up EEG study, researchers found that trance was associated with lower than normal event-related potentials to sounds among shamanic practitioners. Taken together, these results suggest that shamans maintain a meaningful subjective stream of experience while disconnected from the environment (Hove & Stelzer, 2018). We see commonalities here with sensory restriction, dreaming, and hypnosis.

MEDIUMSHIP

We have considered the soul-journeying aspect of shamanism, but what about possession? Let us briefly consider possession and then channeling, a phenomenon that may or may not include possession. This discussion will take us outside the context of shamanism into a more general consideration of the possibility of interaction with discarnate entities.

Characteristics of Possession

Possession can be defined as a "condition in which a person has been taken over by an external entity" (Barušs, 1996, p. 158). Well, we need to be a little bit careful with this definition. A person can be said to have been possessed, in the sense of having been invaded by a spirit, without exhibiting any unusual alterations of consciousness, such as in cases of illness attributed to evil spirits. To be more precise, the term *possession trance* can be used for possession in which alterations of consciousness are evident (Bourguignon, 1979; C. A. Ross, Somer, & Goode, 2018). Varieties of possession experiences can also include "voluntary and involuntary possession" (Krippner, 1997, p. 344), possession that proceeds in distinct phases, differences in reactions to being possessed by different entities (Krippner, 1997), and the malevolence or benevolence of possessing entities (cf. Krippner, 1994). In Western cultures, sometimes the notion of a *possession syndrome* is used for characterizing these types of experiences (Ferracuti, Sacco, & Lazzari, 1996; Grosso, 2014; Isaacs, 1987; McNamara, 2011; Trethowan, 1976).

As part of a field study, the anthropologist Larry Peters undertook to become a shaman under the tutelage of the Tamang shaman Bhirendra, mentioned previously. Peters was invited to a "purification ritual" to "see whether or not the gods would come to possess [him]," handed a drum, and told "to play along" (Peters, 1981, p. 10). However, nothing happened to Peters "while Bhirendra and his disciples shook furiously" (Peters, 1981, p. 10). Finally, Peters "started to shake consciously," gradually letting go so that "the shaking in [his] legs became more automatic," and he "began to shake" and bounce "all over the room" (Peters, 1981, p. 10). When they saw Peters start shaking, Bhirendra and his other disciples became certain that Peters "had been chosen by a god to become a shaman" (Peters, 1981, p. 11). However, in spite of losing control of his movements and becoming frightened, Peters did not feel the presence of an "alien power" (Peters, 1981, p. 11).

During a subsequent ritual, again while drumming, Peters felt his "mind split off from [his] body" so that he was watching his "body shaking and jumping into the air as if [his] consciousness was separated from it" (Peters, 1981, p. 14). Then suddenly he found himself "flying over a quiet valley towards a green glow" as though he were dreaming (Peters, 1981, p. 14). There was light before him and "the upper torso of a green figure" (Peters, 1981, p. 14) visible through the open windows of the upper floor of a three-story house. It was from what appeared to be an eye in the figure that the green light was emanating. Peters realized that he was dreaming as he "felt water being poured on [his] head" by Bhirendra (Peters, 1981, p. 14). Here we have various elements that we have already encountered, such as a positive set toward possibly anomalous experiences, automaticity associated with actions during hypnosis, dissociation, and what appears to have been hypnagogic imagery, but no possession, even though that had been the intention of the rituals.

There is certainly no shortage of accounts of people believed to have been possessed (Coons, 1993). During Peters's purification ritual, another of Bhirendra's disciples "shook furiously" and "became possessed by his grandfather" (Peters, 1981, p. 10). Bhirendra himself would become possessed, sometimes by a "tiger spirit," at which times he would run around "on all fours, growling and pounding on windows and doors" (Peters, 1981, p. 8). There have been cases of possession in religious contexts. For example, in some Christian movements such as Pentacostalism, some practitioners engage in the practice of *glossolalia*, "speaking in tongues" (Hood, Spilka, Hunsberger, & Gorsuch, 1996, p. 201), whereby they conceptualize themselves as having been visited by "the Spirit" (Beauregard, 2011, p. 71) and speaking an incomprehensible language over which they claim to have no control. Our 11th thematic thread surfaces in that practitioners appear to be surrendering to an automatic process. So does our fourth thematic thread: Is there anything unusual about this phenomenon? Analyses of the utterances reveal that they are unlike natural languages and have "no systematic grammatical structure" (Colman, 2015, p. 316). In one brain imaging study with five practitioners, lowered activity in the prefrontal cortex was found during glossolalia compared with singing, "consistent with the participants' description of a lack of volitional control over the performance of glossolalia" (Beauregard, 2011, p. 71).

There have been cases of apparent possession outside the context of shamanism and religion. Sumitra, a woman who lived in India, after seemingly having died and been revived, believed that she was Shiva, a woman who had died violently about 2 months previously in a village about 100 kilometers away. Sumitra recognized 23 people known to Shiva and "showed in several respects new behavior that accorded with Shiva's personality and attainments" (Stevenson, Pasricha, & McClean-Rice, 1989, p. 81). For example, Sumitra insisted on being called Shiva, changed her style of dress so that it was more in the manner of Shiva's, and showed increased fluency and interest in reading and writing. There appeared to have been no ordinary means whereby Sumitra could have obtained "knowledge of the people and events in Shiva's life" (Stevenson et al., 1989, p. 81). The investigators concluded that possession or reincarnation was the most plausible explanation (Stevenson et al., 1989). This raises our second thematic thread: Can we explain these events in material terms, or do we need postmaterialist ideas to understand them?

Channeling

Channeling, or *mediumship*, can be defined as the communication of information or energy from apparently nonphysical sources, such as spirits (cf. Baruš, 1996; M. F. Brown, 1997; Hastings, 1988, 1991; Klimo, 1987). There are various degrees to which a person has been presumably taken over by an entity during channeling (Baruš, 1996), from *trance channeling*, in which possession occurs, to *conscious channeling*, in which it does not (see also Sudduth, 2016). There has been a range of entities channeled, with some, such as biblical figures or beings identified by late 19th-century Theosophists, having reached "the status of public-domain spirits" (M. F. Brown, 1997, p. 156). Perhaps the most popular entity to be channeled has been Jesus (Baruš, 1996). Jane Roberts, known for having channeled an entity called Seth (M. F. Brown, 1997), has also channeled William James. The James channeled by Roberts has purportedly communicated his ideas regarding his view from the balcony of life, world developments since his time, and the nature of life after death, and has expressed regret that, during his lifetime, while he had "evidence of the soul's existence" from his own experience, he had "dismissed this as beside the point since in no way could [he] produce the scientific proof that could demonstrate to others the actuality of such a hypothesis" (J. Roberts, 1978, p. 138). It is difficult to know how many people are involved with channeling, although it is known that some channeled books have sales of a half-million copies or more (M. F. Brown, 1997).

The following is an example of contemporary North American channeling that was brought to my attention:

> Basically what happened is that a strong, cold wind moved into the centre of my body, and information began to pour through my brain and mouth that was not my own—though I was clearly aware of what I was saying and often made or added my own comments to the information I heard and spoke. I spoke to each person in the circle about her role in the spiritual work she had undertaken, basically clarifying issues or addressing hidden questions she had. I seemed to know their thoughts and spoke to them directly. I saw things (the questions in the minds of the participants and the answers to their queries) in images and words. As this process unfolded, the "entity" when asked, named itself. There was a point after the channelling started when others could feel a cold wind moving through the room, circling, settling, and moving around. The whole thing lasted perhaps one hour or so, and at the end of it I was quite tired. In fact, over the next two days I felt feverish, alternately cold and very hot and had to rest. I felt very energized during the experience but extremely done in afterwards, including the exhaustion lasting several days.

In this report we can see dissociation, the occurrence of events perceived to be anomalous, identification of an external entity, and some subsequent somatic effects. There was a spiritual context in which an apparently meaningful interchange occurred between the channeled entity and those present. What happened?

The quality of the information produced during channeling varies from the banal to the profound (Barušs, 1996; Hastings, 1991). Is any of it correct? Perhaps surprisingly, the answer is yes. Good mediums, those who do the channeling, sometimes produce correct information that they could not reasonably have obtained through ordinary means. This has been empirically demonstrated, most notably by Julie Beischel and her colleagues. They start by pretesting mediums to see which ones can produce correct information in research settings and which ones cannot. Then they bring in a sitter, the person for whom the medium is trying to produce correct information. An experimenter who does not know the identity of the sitter asks the medium for information about the sitter's deceased relatives and friends, such as their appearances, personalities, hobbies and interests, and causes of death. Then the sitter is given the transcript of the information provided by the medium along with a transcript created for another sitter without being told which is theirs, and asked which of the two transcripts is a better match for her (Beischel, 2007, 2013). In one study using such a protocol, 66% of the sitters chose the transcript intended for them (Beischel, Boccuzzi, Biuso, & Rock, 2015), and in a separate study the sitters chose 81% of their transcripts (Beischel & Schwartz, 2007). These results do not surprise me, given that

I used to bring a medium to my classes, and she would regularly produce specific, correct information for students without knowing anything about them (Barušs, 2013; Barušs & Mossbridge, 2017).

So, good mediums can produce correct information. But does any of that information originate from the deceased? Or are mediums just really good at anomalous information transfer? Are there discarnate entities out there to be channeled and to possess us? Well, for a materialist, there are no nonphysical domains from which to obtain information, nor can there be actual soul journeys or possession by external entities. Shamanism, possession, and channeling are products of fantasy, dissociation, and delusions. In Western cultures, the notion of possession, in particular, has been replaced with a mental disorder known as dissociative identity disorder (C. A. Ross, 1996). So let us take a look at this disorder.

DISSOCIATIVE IDENTITY DISORDER

In this section I define *dissociative identity disorder*, note the presence of trauma as an etiological factor, describe its psychodynamics, and then bring the discussion back to the question of possession. Our ninth thematic thread is acutely raised in this section: What is the nature of the self?

Definition of Dissociative Identity Disorder

Dissociative identity disorder (DID) is a mental condition whose primary characteristic is the presence of "two or more distinct personality states or an experience of possession" (American Psychiatric Association, 2013, p. 292). Different prevalence rates for DID in the general population have been given by different sources: 1.5% (American Psychiatric Association, 2013), 1% (Şar, Dorahy, & Krüger, 2017), and 0.5% to 5% (Parry, Lloyd, & Simpson, 2018). Gender differences are about evenly distributed between males and females, although the disorder presents differently, with females exhibiting dissociative symptoms and males expressing antisocial behavior. In fact, men with DID may end up in prison given that "a high incidence of dissociative disorders [has been found] among convicted sex offenders" (Kluft, 1996, p. 351).

We need to be careful not to confuse DID with schizophrenia. In schizophrenia, there is a breakdown of thinking, emotions, and behavior at the microscopic level, so to speak, so that an individual's sentences, succession of emotional states, and motor behavior are demonstrably impaired. The breakdown in DID is more macroscopic, in that the basic functions of the psyche continue to be operative, but there is a fragmentation of self-identity, or there is the sense of being possessed (cf. Kluft, 1996). It is important to get a correct diagnosis given that DID "does not undergo spontaneous remission and rarely resolves in a treatment that fails to address it directly" as found in a longitudinal study of 210 people with DID (Kluft, 1996, p. 348). One form of treatment consists of establishing communication among the alternate personality states, called *alters*, and their integration into a homogeneous self (cf. Wilbur & Kluft, 1989). Given that successful treatments for DID have been developed, an early and proper diagnosis could circumvent years of suffering for those for whom it occurs (Brand et al., 2016; C. A. Ross, Norton, & Wozney, 1989; see also Gentile, Dillon, & Gillig, 2013; Gillig, 2009).

Trauma as an Etiological Factor

Here is one way to think about what happens. A child is subjected to physical or sexual abuse and dissociates as a means of escaping from an intolerable situation. Individuals with DID are capable of dissociation, which appears to be related to the dissociation dimension of hypnotizability, in that "DID patients, when stable and cooperative enough for such testing, are highly hypnotizable on standard instruments" (Kluft, 1996, p. 356). So another way of thinking about what happens is to say that these individuals use their ability to escape abuse "via autohypnotic maneuvers such as 'going away' into trance, getting 'out of body' and going up to the ceiling, going into a safe or pleasant fantasy world, forgetting intolerable events via amnesia, creating an alter personality, and so on" (Dell, 2019, p. 53).

Richard Kluft (1996) proposed a *four-factor theory* of DID. The first factor is a biological potential for dissociation. The second factor is the presence of *overwhelming experiences*. The third factor is that of *shaping influences*, both intrapsychic and environmental, that lead to the particular alter personalities that develop. For example, alters can develop that are based on television characters. The fourth factor is *absence of restorative experiences* following traumatization so that there are no opportunities for healing (Hurley, 1985a; Kluft, 1996). What appears to happen is that children who are unremittently traumatized and have the capacity for dissociation will enlist intrapsychic and environmental resources to create alternate identities as a way of coping with the trauma.

Are these just false memories of abuse? Across a number of studies the rates of reported abuse have ranged from 89% to 98%, with at least some corroboration of abuse having been found for 73% to 95% of people with DID (Kluft, 1996). One way to think about what is happening is to note that frequent trauma changes the neurobiological development of the brain during childhood (Bailey & Brand, 2017) so that a child simply cannot develop the phenomenological experience of a unified self across a range of different behaviors. In an EEG study, neurophysiological differences were found between alters for individuals with DID that were not found for individuals who did not have the disorder (Şar, Dorahy, & Krüger, 2017), suggesting that there are neurophysiological markers associated with DID.

In Chapter 5, we considered the argument that memory for traumatic events is encoded differently from memory for everyday events. Indeed, there is evidence "that traumatic experiences are processed by the brain differently from normal experiences" (D. Brown, Scheflin, & Hammond, 1998) so that "traumatic experiences are initially imprinted as sensations or feeling states" (van der Kolk, 1996, p. 296) rather than being integrated into a personal narrative as part of autobiographical memory. At some later point in time these sensations and emotions may resurface as flashbacks (Krystal, Bennett, Bremner, Southwick, & Charney, 1996) "with the same vividness as if the subject were having the experience all over again . . . frequently leaving victims in a state of speechless terror, in which they may be unable to articulate precisely what they are feeling and thinking" (McFarlane & van der Kolk, 1996, p. 565). Once these images and emotions have resurfaced, the person for whom they have occurred seeks to make some sense of them (van der Kolk, 1996) through "inferential narrative smoothing" by knitting together fragments of memories into a "plausible autobiographical episode" (Nadel & Jacobs, 1998, p. 156). Confabulation enters the process at the point of creating an autobiographical narrative. Thus, whereas the memories of traumatic events may be essentially correct, caution is needed with regard to the interpretation of the "precise details" (Kluft, 1996, p. 353) of abuse given by adults.

Dynamics of Alternate Personalities

Once the capacity to establish alternate personalities has been exercised, we can consider their psychodynamics. According to Richard Kluft (1996), "at the time of diagnosis . . . approximately two to four personalities are in evidence" (p. 344) with more manifesting in the course of treatment. Less elaborated alters, known as *fragments*, may also be present. According to Kluft, about 15% to 25% of people with DID are complex cases with at least 26 alters (Kluft, 1996), as in the case of Cassandra, who claimed to have had "more than 180 personalities or fragments" (Hurley, 1985c, p. 4). With an apparently unlimited possibility of splitting, the alters can better be thought of as reconfigurations of the organization of the mind rather than as segments of a unit (Kluft, 1996). The purpose of the splitting is ostensibly to "create alternative self-structures and psychological realities within which or by virtue of which emotional survival is facilitated" (Kluft, 1996, p. 344). One way to appreciate the extent of fragmentation of self-identity that can occur in DID is to note that in one study 26% of 23 psychotherapy clients treated for DID "had had personalities experience the same dream from different perspectives" (Barrett, 1996a, p. 74) so that "two or more personalities reported dreaming at the same time and experiencing each other as characters" (p. 75) in their shared dreams.

The *host personality* is regarded as "the personality who is in control of the body for the greatest percentage of time during a given period" (Hurley, 1985b, p. 22) and is apparently usually "depressed, anxious, . . . compulsively good, . . . conscience-stricken, . . . and suffers both psychophysiological symptoms and time loss and/or time distortion" (Kluft, 1996, p. 345). But then there appears to be a variety of alters. There could be *childlike personalities* who can recall the traumas, *anesthetic personalities* whose purpose is to block out pain, *guardians of memories and secrets, expressers of forbidden pleasurable or antisocial impulses, inner persecutors* that are "often based on identification with the aggressor" (Kluft, 1996, p. 345), and *inner self-helpers* whose purpose is to try to reintegrate the personality (Damgaard, 1987).

Alters apparently seek to affect one another so that whoever has control of the body may be subjected to the influences of other alters. In one study, 82% of 28 participants with DID experienced "recurrent command hallucinations," and 100% experienced strong emotions "that were associated with alters that were not ostensibly in control . . . at the time, but which were . . . flooding the alter that was 'out' with their subjective experiences" (Kluft, 1996, p. 347). In the same study of dreams in DID already cited, it was found that 26% of 23 people with DID appeared to have "had at least one personality able to design dreams to be experienced by other personalities" (Barrett, 1996a, p. 77). Inner persecutors in particular apparently try to make an impact on which-ever personality is present in the body without emerging by "urging it toward self-harm or suicide" or by seizing motor control in order, for example, to fling the body "down the stairs" or "steer an automobile toward an embankment" (Kluft, 1996, p. 347), much to the horror of the personality that is out. In one study it was found that 72% of 236 people with DID had attempted suicide and that 2% had succeeded (C. A. Ross et al., 1989).

Amnesia for important personal information is one of the defining symptoms of DID (American Psychiatric Association, 2013). However, amnesia need not always be present, and when it is, it can be selective, so that there can be awareness by one personality of the "thoughts, feelings or actions of other alters" (Hurley, 1985c, p. 5). Such awareness is known as *coconsciousness.* In general, there will be a complex constellation of relationships among alters that often recapitulates the alleged abuse relationships between the person with DID and their abusers. The greater the degree of coconsciousness and cooperation among alters the less likely it is that changing between alters would be noticed (cf. Kluft, 1996). In fact, according to Kluft (1996), "many alter systems are organized in such a way as to keep themselves secret and may become very skilled in covering over their DID phenomena" (p. 348).

"The process by which control of the body passes from one personality to another is called *switching*" (Hurley, 1985c, p. 3) and usually occurs in 1 or 2 seconds. Switching can be voluntary or involuntary and can occur in response to a person's physiological or psychological condition or envi-ronmental situation (Hurley, 1985c). Switching can also occur in dreams, "usually nightmares" (Barrett, 1996a, p. 71). Switching can sometimes happen at inopportune times. For example, Brenda, a woman with DID, found her-self "in a strange place with a strange man" (Reich, 1989b, p. A6) after one of her alters, Janice, had picked him up. In another case, "during surgery in a London hospital, a frightened personality emerged wide awake on the operating room table while the host was under anesthesia" (Reich, 1989a, p. A6). Apparently this "caused no end of grief" (Reich, 1989a, p. A6) for the surprised surgeons.

Physiological changes can accompany switching between personalities, with apparent insensitivity to anesthesia being among the most dramatic. There can be "differences in visual acuity, pain tolerance, symptoms of asthma, sensitivity to allergens, and response of blood glucose to insulin" (American Psychiatric Association, 2000, p. 527). For example, allergies to animals such as cats can disappear with a change to a personality that is apparently not allergic to them (Hurley, 1985d, p. 20). In one study, more than one third of clinicians reported having seen changes of preference for which hand is being used, half of their clients "were reported to have alternate personalities who responded differently to the same medications," three quarters of the clients "had alternate personalities with different physical symptoms, and one quarter had alternate-personality specific allergies" (Putnam, 1984, p. 32). Sometimes there are dermatological reactions that are specific to alternate personalities. For example, a woman who had apparently had lighted cigarettes put out on her skin would manifest burn marks that would last for 6 to 10 hours when "the personality that received burns took over during therapy sessions" (Hurley, 1985d, p. 20). Given the rapid changes in physiology that sometimes accompany changes of personality, it is not surprising that people with DID sometimes apparently "heal more quickly than other people" (Hurley, 1985d, p. 20). Just as in Chapter 2 we saw that changes to the immune system can sometimes correspond to imagined changes, with DID we see that physiological changes follow upon changes of self-identity. It would be instructive to learn how such changes are brought about, both to understand the role of personality factors in disease (cf. Putnam, 1984) and to seek to duplicate beneficial effects in people who do not have DID (Hurley, 1985d).

Dissociative Identity Disorder and Possession

Are channeling and possession just instances of DID? Is the mind closed? It is perhaps interesting to note that, as a group, individuals with DID "are likely to believe in psychic experiences and phenomena such as extrasensory perception" (Kluft, 1996, p. 360). What do the data reveal?

In one study, "ten trance channels" were interviewed "to determine the degree of overlap between the complex of symptoms that characterizes [DID], and the phenomenological experience of the trance channels" (Hughes, 1992, p. 182). Although "three of the ten channels" (Hughes, 1992, p. 187) could have met diagnostic criteria for what is now called DID, none of them had the relevant secondary features, such as "handwriting changes, . . . periods of missing time, . . . flashbacks, . . . auditory hallucinations, [or] speaking of oneself in the plural tense" (p. 186). There were numerous other differences, not the least of which was the fact that DID usually has a traumatic origin, whereas trance channeling is often a learned behavior acquired by using visualization techniques in a meditative context (Hughes, 1992). Channeling is not DID, but that does not mean that the mind is not closed.

A better case could be made that possession trance is just DID, particularly since possession counts as a diagnostic criterion of DID. "Possession-form identities in dissociative identity disorder typically manifest as behaviors that appear as if a 'spirit,' supernatural being, or outside person has taken control, such that the individual begins speaking or acting in a distinctly different manner" (American Psychiatric Association, 2013, p. 293). In one study it was found that 29% of 236 people with DID had a personality that was "identified as a demon," while 21% had a "personality identified as a dead relative" (C. A. Ross et al., 1989, p. 415).

But relabeling possession as DID does not close the mind. All it does is raise the question of whether the mind is open and the alters in DID are entity intrusions. Are the demon and dead relative alter personalities really demons and dead relatives? Perhaps severe childhood trauma functions as an initiatic crisis breaking down the boundaries of the psyche so that the intrusion of spirits becomes possible. Stanley Krippner (1994) observed that in Brazil some healers who have been aware of DID have given dual diagnoses of DID and "involuntary spirit possession" (p. 354). There could be both. There can be fragmentation of self-identity, as we see with the characteristics of alters in DID; there could be actual spirit intrusion; and, in some cases, there could be a mixture of both. In addition to our ninth thematic thread concerning the nature of the self, our fourth thematic thread is prominent in these discussions: Is there something extraordinary occurring?

ALIEN ABDUCTION EXPERIENCES

Among the most enigmatic contemporary phenomena are alien abduction experiences, which are characterized by the belief that one has been taken "against one's will by apparently non-human entities, usually to a location interpreted as an alien spacecraft" where one has been subjected to various "physical and psychological procedures" (Appelle, Lynn, & Newman, 2000, p. 254). "Alien spacecraft" could be *unidentified flying objects* (UFOs), also sometimes called *unidentified aerial phenomena* (UAP). It seems ridiculous to think that these experiences could be what they appear to be, nor is there evidence acceptable to skeptics that aliens are actually abducting people (Mack, 1999), yet there currently are not any alternative compelling explanations for the abduction phenomenon (Appelle, Lynn, Newman, & Malaktaris, 2014).

The incidence of alien abduction experiences has been difficult to determine, but estimates have ranged from about 0.04% to 2% of the population. When one physician queried 266 colleagues and patients, 43 of them said that they had seen a UFO, and four of those were considered to be probable abduction cases resulting in an incidence figure of 1.5% (J. G. Miller, 1994). In a survey of 1,564 adults in the United States in the year 2000, 43% believed that UFOs were real, whereas 42% believed that UFOs were imaginary, with 15%

volunteering the response that they were not sure. Furthermore, 1% maintained that they had "had an encounter with beings from another planet" (C. Fox, 2000, p. 56). From a survey of 1,114 Americans in 2012, it was estimated that 36% of the population believe that UFOs are alien spacecraft (Appelle et al., 2014, p. 215).

Alien or not, something is happening. According to Hal Puthoff, there is a program, Advanced Aerospace Threat Identification Program, that was initiated by the Defense Intelligence Agency in the United States and continued by the Department of Defense, to address concerns about "continuing engagements between U.S. military platforms and UAP of seeming technological superiority over anything in the U.S. inventory" (Puthoff, 2018, p. 32). In other words, according to Puthoff, there have been encounters between the U.S. military and UFOs that exceed the capabilities of U.S. military hardware (see also Greer, 2001).

Let us start by describing some of the characteristics of alien abduction experiences and by giving an example. Then we will consider some of the explanations for them as well as some of the critical features of alien abduction experiences that make them enigmatic. We will conclude by putting these experiences in the context of self-transformation. Our thematic threads get a good exercise in this section. Second: Is there anything transcendent about alien abduction experiences? Third and fourth: Is there anything veridical or extraordinary about these experiences? Fifth: Are these experiences meaningful? Seventh and eighth: Are they pathological or dangerous? Ninth: Who are we, anyway? Tenth: Are these direct intrusions into our psyche from other dimensions of reality? Eleventh: How much control do we have over what happens to us?

Characteristics of Alien Abduction Experiences

In general, initial contact in an abduction case may occur while a person is in their home or driving an automobile. There may be unexplained lights or buzzing sounds and perception of the presence of humanoid beings or a strange craft. "After the initial contact, the abductee is commonly 'floated' (the word most commonly used) down the hall, through the wall or windows of the house, or through the roof of the car" (Mack, 1994a, pp. 18–19) and into a spacecraft of some sort. An experiencer may realize that they have been paralyzed by one of the beings and feel terrorized by their strange circumstances and sense of helplessness. During the time of their abduction, family members may claim that the experiencer has been missing. The experiencer may find themself in a brightly lit room with curved, white walls and ceilings in which there are "body-conforming chairs and tables" (Mack, 1994a, p. 22) and computerlike equipment. The most commonly described alien beings are the *grays*, "humanoid beings three to four feet in height" with large heads, "long arms with three or four long fingers" (Mack, 1994a, p. 22), thin torsos, spindly legs, and large, black, compelling eyes.

During an abduction, an experiencer may be subjected to various procedures in which "instruments are used to penetrate virtually every part" (Mack, 1994a, p. 23) of their body, including the head and, most commonly, reproductive system. Male experiencers have reported having sperm samples taken, and females have reported having been impregnated and the subsequent possibly human–alien fetuses removed and placed "into containers on the ships" (Mack, 1994a, p. 24). An experiencer may be shown images of the destruction of the earth through nuclear holocaust, pollution, or natural disasters and informed of human responsibility for the fate of the planet. An experiencer is returned, usually to the place from which they were abducted, and generally feels tired afterward as though they had "been through some sort of stressful experience" (Mack, 1994a, p. 26; see also Jacobs, 1998).

The following are several facts about alien abduction experiences. Experiencers have histories of the occurrence of anomalous events, and, sometimes the abduction experiences appear to increase the frequency of such events (Appelle et al., 2014). Experiencers frequently have *scoop marks* on their bodies, which are small, round depressions on the skin, and which experiencers attribute to abduction experiences (Chalker, 2005). There have been frequent reports of various physical conditions having been healed as a result of the abduction experience (Burkes & Dennett, 2018; Hernandez, Davis, Scalpone, & Schild, 2018). And, particularly disturbingly, whereas the rate of attempted suicide is about 1% in the general population, in one study it was found that 57% of experiencers had reported having attempted suicide (Appelle et al., 2014, p. 215).

An Example of an Alien Abduction Experience

A person who has apparently been abducted will often have periods of missing time for which they cannot remember what happened, and it is during these periods of missing time when the abduction ostensibly occurs. For example, Carol was staying at a state park in the United States when she found herself walking alone down a hill to her log cabin with no idea what time it was. She realized that it was getting dark and wondered what she had done all day. She had some hot dogs, baked beans, and coffee for dinner and then threw up. The next morning "she was surprised to see her car in the middle of the road" (Bryan, 1995, p. 311). As soon as she touched the door handle of the car she remembered the events of the previous day.

Carol remembered that she had been sitting on the porch of her cabin when she had noticed fog drifting "slowly down the hill toward her" (Bryan, 1995, p. 298). She was alarmed by the fog and panicked when she saw "two thin, short gray legs" (Bryan, 1995, p. 298) at the bottom of it. She ran into the cabin, realized that she could not lock out the beings, grabbed her car keys, and ran toward her car. Three small, gray beings were "floating down the hill . . . like skiers . . . [with their] knees and ankles locked" (Bryan, 1995, p. 299). Carol slid into the car and started the motor. The three small grays were now only a few feet in front of her. She put the car in reverse and backed out onto the road. One of the grays "had raised his arm and was pointing at the front end of Carol's car" (Bryan, 1995, p. 299). The car went out of gear. Carol tried to put the car back in reverse but the "shift lever slid through the gears as if through butter" (Bryan, 1995, p. 299). At that point she said out loud that she would go with the beings since she did not want them to further damage her car. She found herself floating up the hill and "then, suddenly, she was inside their ship" (Bryan, 1995, p. 299). The room in which she found herself had a "white, curved interior wall [that] was rounded and seamless" (Bryan, 1995, p. 299). She was floated to a reclining chair that "molded itself to her form" (Bryan, 1995, p. 300).

The three small grays who had brought her had moved out of Carol's line of sight, but eventually three tall grays appeared. Carol heard in her head one of the tall beings telling her that she would be changed and that the things that were being done to her were important. Carol asked why they were important and was told that she did not need to know, leading her to feel that the grays were arrogant and using her as they would use a tool. The grays then proceeded to inject her with various colored fluids and draw blood from her arm. When Carol tried to find out why her blood was being taken, the tall gray said that she had to be tested "to see if everything's okay" (Bryan, 1995, p. 304; emphasis removed) and reiterated again that she would be changed. Then the gray told her that she must "only eat cow things" (Bryan, 1995, p. 304; emphasis removed). Carol protested saying that "human beings cannot eat just cow" (Bryan, 1995, p. 304; emphasis removed), to which the being replied that she could because she was changed. She asked about horses with pads in place of hooves which she had seen previously in a dream and was shown pictures of horses milling about on a screen whose feet she could not see. When she protested that she could not see the horses' feet, the screen with the horses was replaced with one with cows that had tubes sticking out from their sides. She was told that "cows are changed. Horses are changed. People are changed" (Bryan, 1995, p. 307; emphasis removed). And she was also told not to act crazy. Then she was allowed to get dressed, was led down a corridor, told to look at one of a number of "square boxes aligned along the corridor's left-hand wall" (Bryan, 1995, p. 309), and found herself walking down the hill toward the log cabin in the state park.

A week later Carol awoke "in pain with two more fresh punctures just below her belly button" (Bryan, 1995, p. 311) which was one of the sites on her body where she had previously received injections. "A clear fluid was leaking from the holes" (Bryan, 1995, p. 311). A week after that she had blood on her arm and blood coming from the same holes in her stomach. "Furthermore, every time she accidentally ate something that was not a beef or dairy product, she broke out in a rash and suffered severe stomach cramps" (Bryan, 1995, p. 311).

Explanations of Alien Abduction Experiences

What are we to make of alien abduction experiences such as this? Perhaps the first thing that comes to mind is that those who report such accounts are afflicted with a mental disorder. However, despite efforts to find it, there is little evidence of psychopathology among experiencers (Appelle et al., 2014; Donderi, 2013; but see McNally, 2012). This is not to say that there are no psychological disturbances among experiencers who appear to be suffering from stress consistent with that induced by trauma (Appelle et al., 2000) and "accompanying psychiatric conditions" (Mack, 1994b, p. 373). However, the point is that any emotional disorders that are present are insufficient to account for the alleged abduction experiences (Mack, 1994b).

It has been suggested that alien abduction experiences are somehow related to dissociation (Bryan, 1995). The idea is that some sort of trauma occurs that leads to dissociation and false memories about alien abduction. The obvious candidate is childhood sexual abuse, although fewer than one quarter of experiencers have reported sexual abuse (McLeod, Corbisier, & Mack, 1996). Nonetheless, given that there is a correlation between reported childhood abuse and reported alien abduction experiences, it has been suggested that the alien abduction scenarios are screen memories of actual sexual abuse. The idea is that remembering the actual sexual abuse is too traumatic, so an abduction scenario is made up in its stead (Appelle et al., 2000). However, when asked to rate how upset they were at the time of abduction on a scale from 0 to 10 with "10 = *as upset as they could possibly imagine*" (McLeod et al., 1996, p. 164) "experiencers rated their distress 10 to 100" (p. 164). In another study, "recollection of alien encounter memories produced reactions statistically indistinguishable from recollection of extremely stressful memories" (McNally, 2012, p. 7). In fact, one of the characteristic features of the abduction phenomenon is the degree to which experiencers feel abject terror in association with their experiences (Bryan, 1995). In one case, in a direct comparison, abduction experiences were perceived to be much more painful and fearful than being raped (Mack, 1999). It is not clear why a traumatic event would be covered up with an apparently even more traumatic one. It is also not clear how reports of sexual abuse could become reports of alien abductions (Appelle, 1996) or indeed, how a highly articulated narrative could be produced that has nothing to do with "*any* of the actual experiences that led to the dissociation" (Mack, quoted in Bryan, 1995, p. 268).

Nonetheless, it could be argued that these experiences must somehow be delusions (Banaji & Kihlstrom, 1996), false memories (McNally, 2012; Newman, 1997), fantasies (Appelle et al., 2000), hallucinations, poor reality monitoring, or some combination of all of those (French, Santomauro, Hamilton, Fox, & Thalbourne, 2008). A recently popular explanation has been to ascribe alien abduction experiences to false memories created through elaborations of phenomena that occur during sleep paralysis. An individual who believes in paranormal phenomena experiences sleep paralysis along with hypnopompic hallucinations of aliens in their bedroom and goes to a hypnotist who encourages them to confabulate an alien abduction scenario based on narratives available in the media that then becomes a false memory (cf. French et al., 2008; McNally, 2012). Perhaps, in some cases.

It is noteworthy that hypnosis has been used in 71% to 90% of cases to recover these purported memories (Newman & Baumeister, 1996), and in

Chapter 5 we saw the unreliability of hypnotic hypermnesia. However, some abduction researchers have argued that in some sense experiencers' memories are switched off during their experiences and that hypnosis "seems uniquely capable of undoing the amnesia that occurs in the abductions" (Mack, quoted in Bryan, 1995, p. 318; see also Donderi, 2013). While this may seem to be an overly facile rationale for the use of hypnosis, from a practical point of view, whether or not hypnosis has been used seems to make little difference since "hypnotically recovered material does not differ in basic structure from material reported by individuals with a clear waking memory of abduction events" (McLeod et al., 1996, p. 166). Certainly, Carol's consciously recalled experiences are as lurid as many of the accounts in the abduction literature that have been obtained with the use of hypnosis.

Critical Features of Alien Abduction Experiences

According to John Mack, who has been approached by over 3,000 individuals concerning their abduction experiences (McLeod et al., 1996), there are a number of features of the abduction phenomenon that must be taken into account in any explanation for it. The first is the *sincerity* of the people who report such experiences. Based on his background in forensic psychiatry, Mack cannot find any reason to suppose that experiencers are motivated "to distort their experience or to lie or to self-aggrandize" (Mack, quoted in Bryan, 1995, p. 258). Nor is it "uncommon for an experiencer to prefer to be diagnosed with a mental illness rather than believe that the experience happened in a physical sense" (McLeod et al., 1996, p. 159). The second feature is the *intensity of emotion*, particularly fear, displayed by experiencers when they recall abduction experiences. Something has traumatized these people (Bryan, 1995). That is something that we have already noted. However, dysphoric alien abduction experiences may only be a small part of alien contact phenomena, with some researchers finding their respondents' experiences to have been positive overall (Hernandez et al., 2018).

The third feature of abduction experiences that needs to be explained is the *narrative consistency* of the accounts of abduction experiences (Mack, 1994b). Critics, however, have pointed out the similarities between alien abduction accounts and the fictional portrayal of aliens in the media, so that the consistency of fantasized accounts could be a result of the prevalence of stories about aliens in our culture (Appelle, 1996). On the other hand, some of the investigators who have documented these narratives have argued that there is consistency among abduction reports with regard to details that have never been published. For example, there are apparently strong resemblances between notational systems attributed to aliens that have been recalled by experiencers (Hopkins, 2000). And there are elements of alien abductions that are popular in the media that are missing from experiencers' accounts, such as the use of weapons by the aliens. The fourth feature, which we have already mentioned, is the absence of any mental illness that is sufficient to account for the behavior of experiencers (Bryan, 1995; Mack, 1994b). The fifth feature is the presence of *corroborative physical evidence* that is enough to "win over those who are prepared to believe in the phenomenon but not enough to convince the skeptic" (Mack, 1999, p. 10). Corroborative physical evidence has included UFO sightings, missing people, body lesions, and apparent implants (Mack, 1999). For example, Carol's oozing and bleeding puncture wounds following purported abductions could be considered as corroborative physical evidence. So would the presence of scoop marks or unexpected healing. The sixth feature is the association of abduction experiences with *UFO sightings by other witnesses* at the time of abduction (Bryan, 1995). This can extend to multiple experiencers "describing their participation in the same abduction event" (Appelle et al., 2014, p. 215) similar to shared dreaming.

The seventh feature of abduction experiences that needs to be explained, according to Mack, is their *presence in children*. Children as young as 2 years of age have talked about being taken up into the sky or having things stuck into them. Finding abduction accounts in young children argues to some extent against the contention that these accounts reflect the influence of the media, since such an influence would be expected to be somewhat less in young children (Bryan, 1995; Mack, 1994b). Not only have children apparently been involved, but some of the phenomena associated with abduction experiences appear to be transgenerational. Carol's father had experienced missing time twice in the 1930s and could not be found by others looking for him during those periods of missing time. Her grandfather had got up in the middle of dinner one day in a daze, walked out of the house, and was never seen again. There could, of course, be mundane explanations for both of these cases. Carol's 4-year-old granddaughter had drawn a picture of a flying machine and a gray being who, she had said, sometimes took her up in the flying machine. Her granddaughter also played with an imaginary ball that she said had been given to her by the gray being's friends and that she acknowledged was "sort of" (Bryan, 1995, p. 296) invisible.

But there are also problems with the *ET hypothesis* (Appelle, 1996). Just as there have been cases in which people appear to have been missing during abduction experiences, there have been others in which they clearly were not missing. For example, an Australian woman lapsed into unconsciousness in the presence of two UFO investigators and described to them being abducted into a round room in which she observed the presence of an entity (Basterfield, 1994). In fact, in a large online study of alleged experiencers, out-of-body experiences were common, with alien encounters ostensibly occurring in dimensions of reality other than the physical (Hernandez et al., 2018).

Even if abduction experiences have actually been associated with UFOs, and one third of investigated UFOs do not have prosaic explanations (Appelle, 1996), that does not mean that experiencers are being taken aboard spacecraft being flown by extraterrestrials (Vallée, 1990). It is also interesting to note "that the piloters of UFOs have been taking on aspects of our own most disturbing behavior" (Grossinger, 1989, p. 46) by "treating sentient beings with precisely the kind of scientific contempt we now exhibit epidemically, carrying out clandestine operations complete with cover stories" (pp. 46–47). There have been suggestions that some abduction experiences are clandestine government experiments (e.g., Vallée, 1991). Alternatively, we could be somehow projecting our own disturbing behavior in a way that becomes objectively visible (Grossinger, 1989).

Transformational Aspects of Alien Abduction Experiences

In some respects at least, alien abduction accounts resemble shamanic initiations. To begin with, the experiencer appears to be "somehow entranced" (Ring, 1989, p. 17) during the time of the abduction and goes on a journey to another level of being where they are terrorized and have to face the possibility of their own death. They meet with spirits in the form of alien beings and are dismembered to varying degrees in a round chamber symbolic of "a womb or a place of new beginnings" (Ring, 1989, p. 17). They telepathically receive some sort of important information and then they are mysteriously returned to the normal world within which they may end up taking on a new role as a healer. Indeed, many experiencers move past the stage of terror and come to view their abduction experiences as an awakening that can include the awakening of "powerful psychic gifts" (Mack, 1999, p. 253). They may come to develop meaningful connections to the alien beings including feelings "of love so profound as to be felt to be incompatible with earthly love" (Mack, 1999, p. 19). They may also become aware of the precarious plight of the earth and seek to do what they can to help. In other words, alien abduction experiences can trigger a process of self-transformation much as shamanic initiatic crises can. The question is whether such transformation "derives simply from a kind of stretching of the psychic sinews that can occur with any sort of trauma and recovery process" (Mack, 1999, p. 229), or whether there is something about the abduction phenomenon itself that promotes this.

Some shamans themselves have claimed to have encountered aliens, including grays, as part of the panoply of spirits with whom they purportedly interact and, in some cases, have had the same degrading experiences as other experiencers. The alien entities encountered by shamans are characterized by the shaman's inability to manage them using their skills, by the intense energies that may be transmitted to the shaman, by a "transtribal universalism that they represent" and by a direct link to "divine intelligence" (Mack, 1999, p. 165) that these beings seem to possess. Alien entities are more progressive and have more to do with the future than other beings the shaman may encounter who have more to do with the traditions of the past (Mack, 1999).

But now we are back to the question of whether the psyche is open or closed. If spirits are real for the shaman at another level of reality, is it possible that aliens are also real but nonphysical? Perhaps aliens are not squishy things in tin cans from another solar system but entities in other dimensions that have figured out how to insert themselves into our physical and psychological dimensions of existence. In my discussing this with John Mack, I know that this was the conclusion reached by him. And from my hearing French scientist Jacques Vallée talk about it, I know also that that was the conclusion reached by him. So this places alien abduction experiences within the spectrum of anomalous phenomena associated with alterations of consciousness more generally (see also Hernandez et al., 2018).

One final point. According to Mack, the transformation that occurs for experiencers is not just generic transformation resulting from an effort to heal trauma, it also depends, in part, on the *ontological shock* that occurs when the boundaries between the normal physical world and the world of the aliens are shattered (Mack, 1999). McKenna (1989) has argued that "science has begun to threaten the existence of the human species as well as the ecosystem of the planet" (p. 24), what Steven Greer has called *planeticide* (Greer, 2001, p. 15), so that "a shock is necessary for the culture" (T. McKenna, 1989, p. 24)—a shock that is sufficient to stop the "materialist juggernaut" by producing a "radical change in consciousness" (Mack, 1999, p. 296), or, as one experiencer has said, the abduction phenomenon is one part of "a spiritual emergence" (p. 256) of humanity.

SUMMARY

So where does this leave us? What are we to think of alterations of consciousness such as shamanic journeying, mediumship, DID, and alien abduction experiences? To begin with, we have come across surprisingly little psychopathology, our seventh thematic thread. Even DID, which is regarded as a mental disorder, can be viewed as a healthy way of dealing with an unhealthy situation, namely trauma. These alterations of consciousness certainly raise questions about our identity, our ninth thematic thread. What does it mean to be someone other than who we ordinarily think we are? Or to believe that we are spirits, freed from our bodies, and able to interact with other spirits in a nonphysical realm? In fact, is there a nonphysical realm in which spirits and aliens can be encountered, our second thematic thread? Are these experiences delusional or real, our third thematic thread? Is the psyche open or closed, our ninth? And do we really need to wake up, back to the second and third? As usual, I will leave it up to the reader to make up their own mind.

7

Psychedelics

We started out in this book examining the ordinary waking state and then considered some naturally occurring and behaviorally evoked alterations of consciousness. As we have proceeded, the alterations have become increasingly dramatic, some with sinister aspects. In this chapter, we consider chemically induced alterations. Chemicals that have psychological effects are known as *psychoactive drugs*, and those that are illegal are called *illicit drugs* (Levinthal, 1996). Although there is a range of interesting alterations of consciousness that psychoactive drugs can induce, I will not try to survey all of them. Rather, I emphasize the so-called *classical psychedelics* (Pollan, 2018), whose prototype is *d-lysergic acid diethylamide* (Grinspoon & Bakalar, 1979), which I abbreviate as *LSD*, and only briefly consider several other drugs that are sometimes discussed in the context of the psychedelics. The possession and use of most of these drugs are illegal in North America (Grinspoon & Bakalar, 1979; Pollan, 2018).

Let us start right off by considering drug dangerousness. Then go back in time a bit and look at the modern history of psychedelic drugs. After that we will briefly consider some specific psychoactive drugs, then examine their adverse and potentially therapeutic effects, and finally end with a couple of experiments to induce mystical experiences using psychedelics. The seventh and eighth thematic threads in particular run through this chapter: Do psychedelic drugs create a pathological condition, or do they enhance well-being? And are psychedelic drugs dangerous or beneficial? Other threads are also

http://dx.doi.org/10.1037/0000200-007
Alterations of Consciousness: An Empirical Analysis for Social Scientists, Second Edition,
by I. Barušs

present, often just below the surface, as in the case of the first thematic thread, concerning the physiological perspective, but at other times brought explicitly into the discussion, such as the third, concerning veridicality.

DRUG DANGEROUSNESS

I want to make it clear that, whatever I say about them in this chapter, in no way am I advocating the use of illicit drugs. In addition to the moral imperative not to engage in illegal activities is the undesirability of supporting criminal organizations that produce and distribute illegal drugs and the danger of ingesting substances whose composition is unknown (Levinthal, 1996; Sferios, 1999; Tart, 1972a; Weil & Rosen, 1993). In fact, I have refrained from using information about drugs that has been obtained from illicit use, such as research concerning *microdosing*, which refers to taking fractional amounts of drugs. My only exception is this discussion of drug dangerousness.

There is a news story that will not go away as I write the second edition of this book, and that is the escalating number of deaths attributed to opioid overdose (Andrew & Duval, 2017; Butler & Batalis, 2017; Creppage et al., 2018). *Opium* is a chemical compound extracted from the seed pods of opium poppy plants. *Opioids* are substances that contain opium or its psychoactive constituents or chemically similar drugs (cf. Colman, 2015). *Synthetic opioids* are synthetically produced drugs chemically similar to naturally occurring opioids. For instance, *fentanyl* is a synthetic opioid used as an analgesic and anaesthetic (Gilson, Shannon, & Freiburger, 2017; Lenz & Dunlap, 1998). The problem is that these drugs are frequently abused, leading to opioid-related disorders (American Psychiatric Association, 2013). Such is the case with heroin, which is derived from morphine, itself a constituent of opium (Colman, 2015). An additional problem is that heroin has been cut with increasingly larger amounts of the more powerful fentanyl until medical examiners were seeing overdose cases in the United States in which only fentanyl had been used. Then, in mid-2016, carfentanil, the "most potent commercially available opioid" began to show up on the illicit drug market and in death investigations in the United States (Schueler, 2017, p. 36). Furthermore, overdose deaths from opioids may be underreported in the United States given that, in one study, it was found that no drugs had been specified on 25% of death certificates for overdose deaths (Slavova et al., 2015).

David Nutt, together with his colleagues, has made comprehensive evaluations of drug dangerousness based on acute reactions to a drug, long-term dependence, and its social and health care impacts (Nutt, King, & Phillips, 2010; Nutt, King, Saulsbury, & Blakemore, 2007). Perhaps the first thing to note about the relative dangerousness of drugs is that psychedelic drugs are not regarded as more dangerous than some other legal and illegal drugs. Not surprisingly, heroin is more dangerous than psychedelics. But also, Nutt has said that he was asked on a television show "You're not seriously telling us that LSD is less harmful than alcohol, are you?" to which he says that he replied, "Of course I am!" (Pollan, 2018, p. 300). However, there is something else to keep in mind. When I show my students the charts of relative drug dangerousness published in the papers by Nutt et al., I point out that none of them is zero! All psychoactive drugs come with risks associated with their use, whether they are legal or illegal.

A MODERN HISTORY OF PSYCHEDELICS

In the mid-1980s, as a doctoral student at the University of Regina, in the province of Saskatchewan on the Canadian prairies, I took a reading course about consciousness with Duncan Blewett. I was the only student taking the course, so our classes consisted of freewheeling discussions about consciousness. As I recall, every time, partway into our tête-à-têtes, Professor Blewett would say something like, "You know, we wouldn't even be talking about any of this had it not been for psychedelic drugs in the 1960s" (cf. Blewett, 1969). And then he would proceed to tell me about the research that he and his colleagues had carried out to look at the effects of psychedelics and their potential therapeutic benefits, such as for the treatment of alcohol addiction. And because the psychedelics mimicked psychoses, the researchers themselves would take the drugs to understand the experiences of psychotic patients. It is noteworthy that the British-born psychiatrist Humphry Osmond, who coined the neologism *psychedelic* in 1956 to mean mind-manifesting or soul revealing (Grob & Harman, 1995; Mangini, 1998), had been the director of the Weyburn Mental Hospital, about 115 kilometers southeast of the university. And Osmond's director of research was a Canadian psychiatrist, Abram Hoffer. Who would have suspected that a mental hospital in the middle of the Canadian prairies would "become the world's most important hub of research into psychedelics" (Pollan, 2018, p. 147)? So let us start with the invention of LSD, its early promise, the ensuing government suppression, and subsequent renaissance.

The Invention of LSD

In 1938, Albert Hofmann was looking for new medicines at the Sandoz company in Basel, Switzerland, when he produced a new chemical, the 25th in a series of lysergic acid compounds that he designated as "LSD-25" (Hofmann, 1979/1980, p. 12). Testing with animals proved uninteresting, and so his research with the drug was discontinued. However, Hofmann had "a peculiar presentiment" that LSD "could possess properties other than those established in the first investigations" (Hofmann, 1979/1980, p. 14), and so he produced some once again. On April 16, 1943, during the last stage of the synthesis, he was interrupted in his work by feelings of restlessness and slight dizziness, forcing him to go home. At home he lay down and closed his eyes. He found that his imagination was so stimulated that for 2 hours he "perceived an uninterrupted stream of fantastic pictures, extraordinary shapes with intense, kaleidoscopic play of colors" (Hofmann, 1979/1980, p. 15). Hofmann reasoned that some of the LSD must have been absorbed through his fingertips during the crystallization process.

Three days after his first experience, Hofmann took what he assumed to be a conservative dose of 250 micrograms of LSD, unaware of the potency of the drug that he had created. Again, he had to get on his bicycle and go home. That day, April 19, is now commemorated as "Bicycle Day" by LSD aficionados (Pollan, 2018).

This time, "the dizziness and sensation of fainting" (Hofmann, 1979/1980, p. 17) were so pronounced that he could no longer stand and was forced to lie down. "Everything in the room spun around, and the familiar objects and pieces of furniture assumed grotesque, threatening forms" (Hofmann, 1979/1980, p. 17). The worlds outside and inside of him disintegrated, and he felt as though a demon had invaded him, against which his will was impotent. He was "seized by the dreadful fear of going insane" (Hofmann, 1979/1980, p. 18), believed himself to be outside his body, and wondered if he were dying. Gradually his terror subsided, and Hofmann began to enjoy "the fantastic images" that "surged" toward him, "alternating, variegated, opening and then closing themselves in circles and spirals"(Hofmann, 1979/1980, p. 19). Sounds became changing, vivid images, each "with its own consistent form and color" (Hofmann, 1979/1980, p. 19). The following morning he felt refreshed and found sensory experiences to be extraordinarily pleasurable.

Hofmann believed that the new compound could be particularly useful in psychiatry, so that, after other employees at Sandoz had confirmed the effects of LSD, samples of the drug were sent to various research institutions. By 1960, more than 500 papers about LSD had been published (Grinspoon & Bakalar, 1979).

John Lilly "obtained some LSD-25 from the Sandoz Company" (Lilly, 1978, p. 123) and injected himself with 100 micrograms before climbing into an isolation tank. He was terrified, having received warnings that it was dangerous to take LSD without supervision. But then he reasoned with himself that he could control his brain circuits and neutralize the fear. He relaxed as the LSD effects began with sensations of electrical excitation coursing through his body. "The darkness, the silence, the wetness, and the warmth disappeared. The external reality of the tank disappeared" (Lilly, 1978, p. 127). His awareness of his body and his brain disappeared. All that was left was "a small point of consciousness in a vast domain" (Lilly, 1978, p. 128). He felt that light was being formed into atoms and atoms into light directed by "a vast consciousness" (Lilly, 1978, p. 128). Time had ceased to exist, so that he was in "an eternal place, with eternal processes generated by beings far greater than [himself]" (Lilly, 1978, p. 128). Eventually, he reentered his body, got out of the tank, and wrote up his notes (Lilly, 1978, p. 129).

A number of names have been proposed for the classification of drugs such as LSD in order to appropriately characterize them. We have already been using the term *psychedelic*, but I think that it is instructive to consider some of the other ones. In the first article concerning LSD in 1947, LSD was called a *phantasticum* (Grinspoon & Bakalar, 1979). Particularly in the context of drug laws and medical research (Grinspoon & Bakalar, 1979), psychedelics have often been classified as *hallucinogens*, drugs that produce hallucinations (Levinthal, 1996). However, that is not an altogether accurate term, given that it is rare during intoxication with psychedelics to mistake imaginary events as being physically real (Grinspoon & Bakalar, 1979), if that is to be taken as the meaning of *hallucination* (cf. Aggernæs, 1972). Rather, what occur are distortions of ordinary perceptions of the environment, so that the word *illusionogenic* has been proposed as an alternative to hallucinogenic (Levinthal, 1996).

Psychedelics are *psychotropic* in the sense of being mind-altering (Grob & Harman, 1995), although the term has also been used to refer to moving a person "closer to a normal state of mind" (Levinthal, 1996, p. 377). A term with pejorative connotations is *psycholytic*, meaning mind-dissolving (Levinthal, 1996), although *psycholytic* has also been used to mean just mind-freeing or mind-loosening, referring to the release of "emotional and cognitive inhibitions" (Grob & Harman, 1995, p. 8). These drugs have also been called *psychotomimetic*, meaning "mimicking or inducing psychosis" (Grob & Harman, 1995, p. 8). For all that the Saskatchewan researchers were initially interested in those properties of psychedelics, that meaning has been contested, for example, by pointing out that it was not surprising that participants in early studies acted in a psychotic manner given that they were carried out in sterile hospital settings by psychiatrists in white coats (Tart, 1972a). On the other hand, because these drugs sometimes appear to "awaken or generate mystical experiences" (Forte, 1997, p. 1), as we have already seen, psychedelics have also been referred to as *entheogens*. And, finally, psychedelic drugs that appear to provide extrasensory empowerment have been called *telepathines* (Grinspoon & Bakalar, 1979; Schultes, 1982).

The Psychedelic Sixties

Psychedelic drug use received a substantial impetus during the 1960s from Timothy Leary, an academic psychologist at Harvard University (Grinspoon & Bakalar, 1979), whose "advice to people in America" was to "turn on, tune in, and drop out" (T. Leary, 1965/1970, p. 287). Upon taking psychedelic drugs for the first time, Leary had "the deepest religious experience of [his] life," convincing him that he "had awakened from a long ontological sleep," a process which he characterized as "turning on" (T. Leary, 1965/1970, p. 13). This is the same ontological awakening that sometimes occurs for those who have had alien abduction experiences, as I noted in Chapter 6, and that is typical of those tending toward the extraordinarily transcendent position of the material–transcendent dimension of beliefs about consciousness and reality. "Tuning in" referred to harnessing one's "internal revelations to the external world" (T. Leary, 1965/1970, p. 287), as, for example, in the form of artistic expression (p. 288), and "dropping out" meant to "gracefully detach [oneself] from the social commitments to which [one was] addicted" so as to be able to pursue an authentic spiritual quest (p. 291).

After hundreds of psychedelic drug trips, Leary maintained that he and his colleague Richard Alpert had moved beyond the usual concerns of academic psychologists. They came to believe that careful scientific evaluation of psychedelics was pointless and instead held group sessions that resembled "a cross between religious convocations and wild parties" (Grinspoon & Bakalar, 1979, p. 65). In terms of our thematic threads, it is possible that this change of strategy represented an attempted vertical shift in meaningfulness. Leary and Alpert gained considerable media attention as a result of their connection with Harvard University, from which they ended up being dismissed in 1963. Leary believed that people's lives consisted of playing games of which they were unconscious but from which they could be liberated by the psychedelics. He was the most charismatic proponent of a mixture of social commentary, hedonism, and Eastern religions, which "became, mostly in diffuse and vulgarized versions, the founding philosophy of the hippie movement" (Grinspoon & Bakalar, 1979, p. 65).

By the late 1960s, psychedelic drugs had spawned a counterculture with characteristic lifestyles, leaders, and "status distinctions and internal rivalries" (Grinspoon & Bakalar, 1979, p. 68), which could be found in enclaves in cities around the world. Some of the participants had a sense of being present in the midst of significant events that were somehow right. They believed that the energy of the counterculture would prevail against the established medical and legal norms of society. Those who used LSD were charged by the authorities with being "sick and dangerous," to which drug advocates replied "that it was they, the established powers, who were sick and dangerous" (Grinspoon & Bakalar, 1979, p. 68) because they were afraid to see the emptiness of their own lives and desperately tried to prevent others from becoming liberated from repressive social control. Medical personnel and lawmakers were accused of approving enslaving drugs such as alcohol and nicotine and prohibiting the liberating psychedelics. LSD had apparently become the sacrament that provided anyone who wanted them with visionary experiences that had previously "been the property of solitary mystics" (Grinspoon & Bakalar, 1979, p. 71) and esoteric collectives. This direct experience was at the heart of what appeared to be "a transformation in consciousness that would sweep the world" (Grinspoon & Bakalar, 1979, p. 68).

Whereas Timothy Leary was the most visible proponent of a psychedelic revolution, these drugs had significant impact elsewhere as well. James Fadiman, who had been introduced to psychedelics by Richard Alpert, was one of a group of researchers giving psychedelics to "artists, engineers, architects, and scientists" (Pollan, 2018, p. 179) in the San Francisco Bay area to see whether the drugs could enhance creativity. The participants ostensibly reported greater mental fluidity and an increased ability to visualize and recontextualize problems. Some of the engineers have gone so far as to credit LSD for contributing to the birth of the computer revolution in Silicon Valley, where "interest in psychedelics as a tool for creativity and innovation" has apparently continued to the present (Pollan, 2018, p. 175).

But there was trouble brewing. Osmond and Hoffer traveled to meet with Leary to try to dial him back a bit, pointing out that he cannot treat these "powerful chemicals [as] harmless toys" (Pollan, 2018, pp. 198–199). Osmond tried renaming the psychedelics a second time by introducing the neologism *psychodelytic* as a way of trying to distance legitimate research from the drugs more frivolous use, but that did not work (Pollan, 2018, p. 199). In the United States, psychedelic drugs such as LSD were freely available to physicians until 1963, at which time restrictions were placed on their availability. In 1966, laws against the manufacture and sale of psychedelics came into effect, and in some states laws against possession were enacted. In 1968, possession became illegal throughout the United States. Then, in the Comprehensive Drug Abuse Prevention and Control Act of 1970 (Grinspoon & Bakalar, 1979, p. 310) many psychedelic drugs "became Schedule I Controlled Drugs, a designation that indicates lack of safety even in medically supervised use, high abuse potential, and no current accepted medical use" (Mangini, 1998, p. 396). The rest of the world followed the lead of the United States, and legitimate research using psychedelic drugs virtually ground to a halt (Grinspoon & Bakalar, 1979), although some previously sanctioned research continued into the mid-1970s (Pollan, 2018; cf. Richards, 2016).

Although the psychedelic movement did not survive or create a promised revolution, "many of the several million people who used LSD never abandoned the idea that in some sense they had achieved expanded awareness" (Grinspoon & Bakalar, 1979, p. 86). One psychiatrist who studied psychedelics during the 1950s and 1960s has said subsequently that "not a single person believes that LSD represents a folly of our youth" (quoted in Rayl, 1989, p. 30). People's LSD experiences prompted interest in spiritual practices, particularly those of the East, as a way of exploring consciousness without the use of drugs (Grinspoon & Bakalar, 1979). For example, after leaving Harvard University, Alpert traveled to India in 1967, where he settled down to study with a guru, Neem Karoli Baba, who, Alpert has claimed, showed no effects of intoxication after having swallowed 900 micrograms of LSD and again, 3 years later, 1,200 micrograms (Dass, 1979). In a 1990 questionnaire survey of Tibetan Buddhist practitioners, Tart (1991) found that 77% of 64 respondents "reported previous experience with major psychedelics" (p. 148), whereas 32% claimed that major psychedelics had contributed at least somewhat to attracting them to Tibetan Buddhism.

Renaissance

A quarter-century after being banned, some government-sanctioned research with psychedelics quietly resumed "in the early 1990s" (Grob & Harman,

1995, p. 7). Previously, the emphasis on the unique ability to powerfully alter "experience, perception, understanding, and belief in the nature of reality" had backfired precisely because these drugs undermined the "conventional structures of authority"(Grob & Harman, 1995, p. 7). In the 1990s, however, the strategy was to consider these drugs as any other drugs to be investigated, not for their phenomenological but "for their physiological and neurological . . . effects" (Grob & Harman, 1995, p. 7), with possible eventual uses, for example, in the treatment of "severe substance abuse" and "pain and depression" (p. 6) associated with terminal illnesses.

Of course, such restrictive use of the psychedelics misses harnessing their unique ability for ontological awakening and the intensification of existential and spiritual well-being. However, three events occurred in 2006 that appeared to create a shift in attitudes toward the potential benefits of psychedelics. The first was the celebration of Albert Hofmann's 100th birthday, with an accompanying symposium, which drew 200 journalists and over 1,000 participants with various backgrounds. The second was a decision by the U.S. Supreme Court to allow the religious sect União do Vegetal to import the psychedelic brew ayahuasca into the United States for its ceremonies. The third was the publication of an academic paper reporting the results of an experiment at Johns Hopkins University in Baltimore, in which volunteers were given the psychedelic mushroom psilocybin (Griffiths, Richards, McCann, & Jesse, 2006; Pollan, 2018). And so, more than a decade later, "there are more clinical trials in psychedelics happening today, both for basic effects and therapeutic purposes, than at any time in history" (Doblin, Christiansen, Jerome, & Burge, 2019, p. 93). The psychedelics are back.

VARIETIES OF PSYCHEDELICS

Let us survey the effects of some specific psychedelics and then briefly consider the brain mechanisms through which they work. Here we are bringing out our first thematic thread, in that we are engaging all three of our perspectives on consciousness at once . . . and the fourth thematic thread, since a question recurs of the extent to which, in spite of the apparently delusional nature of psychedelic drug intoxication, could there nonetheless be veridical elements present?

LSD

"LSD is one of the most potent drugs known" (Weil & Rosen, 1993, p. 95), with doses as small as 10 micrograms producing "some mild euphoria, loosening of inhibitions, and empathic feeling" (Grinspoon & Bakalar, 1979, p. 11). Psychedelic effects begin at around 50 to 100 micrograms and "increase up to about 400 or 500 micrograms" (Grinspoon & Bakalar, 1979, p. 11). A typical dose is 50 to 150 micrograms, with effects beginning within 45 to 60 minutes after ingestion (Levinthal, 1996). It becomes clear now that at 250 micrograms, Hoffman's altered state of consciousness was a serious psychedelic trip. The physiological effects of LSD are variable and appear to follow from the psychological effects, although "increased heart rate, blood pressure, and body temperature," dilated pupils, and "mild dizziness" (Grinspoon & Bakalar, 1979, p. 11) are common.

The psychological effects of psychoactive drugs in general (Weil & Rosen, 1993), and LSD in particular (Levinthal, 1996), depend, to some extent, on set and setting. The term *set* refers to the expectations that a person has at the time of taking a drug. We have already seen the importance of expectations in other alterations of consciousness such as sensory restriction and hypnosis. *Setting* refers to the "physical, social, and cultural" (Weil & Rosen, 1993, p. 226) environment in which a drug is taken. In general, as we saw in the examples given earlier, LSD produces an "intensification of mental processes" (Grinspoon & Bakalar, 1979, p. 12) with vivid perceptions, magnified feelings, and profound introspective thoughts. Perceptual changes can include the intensification and distortion of sensory impressions, synesthesia, and, with eyes closed, the presence of geometric patterns, fantastic landscapes, and symbols (Grinspoon & Bakalar, 1979; see also Siegel, 1977; Siegel & Jarvik, 1975). There can be dramatic mood swings from happiness to sadness and back again (Levinthal, 1996), as well as the simultaneous presence of disparate emotions (Grinspoon & Bakalar, 1979). A person may visualize themselves as a participant in an imaginary drama, believe themselves to be encountering mythical beings, or experience a "boundless, timeless, and ineffable" (Grinspoon & Bakalar, 1979, p. 13) domain that transcends everyday life.

An anthropologist with an interest in "animal metamorphosis rites" (Masters & Houston, 1966, p. 75) took about 500 micrograms of LSD with an expectation that a metamorphosis would take place. He abandoned himself to some "appropriate ritual music" and found himself yielding to "a wild, animalistic sensuality and emotional outpouring" (Masters & Houston, 1966, p. 76). After some period of time, he found himself on his hands and knees in front of a "full-length mirror . . . confronted by a huge, magnificent specimen of a tiger" (Masters & Houston, 1966, p. 76). He felt himself having a tiger's body in a way that he had never felt his own body (Masters & Houston, 1966, p. 76). Reacting to the image in the mirror, "partly anyhow," as if it were another tiger that he had unexpectedly encountered, the anthropologist made "spitting and snarling noises" (Masters & Houston, 1966, p. 77) and prepared for combat. Eventually he turned away from the mirror and "padded restlessly around the apartment, still making those sounds that somehow indicated to [him] bafflement and rage" (Masters & Houston, 1966, p. 77). He returned to "human consciousness . . . by gradations," realizing that he had not been "very happy as a tiger," yet feeling "that the tiger represented some valid and essential aspect of what or who [he was]" (Masters & Houston, 1966, p. 77). This account raises the issue of shape-shifting and the question whether the Tamang shaman Bhirendra experienced himself in a manner that was similar to that of the anthropologist under the influence of LSD.

Psilocybin

Terence McKenna was walking across a meadow in Colombia with some friends when one of them "pointed out a single large specimen" (T. McKenna, 1993, p. 2) of the mushroom *Stropharia cubensis*. McKenna ate the whole thing and kept walking. A while later, he "paused and stretched," sat "heavily on the ground," and felt a "silent thunder . . . shake the air" (T. McKenna, 1993, p. 2). For McKenna, "things stood out with a new presence and significance" (T. McKenna, 1993, p. 2).

Stropharia cubensis is one of about 90 mushroom species that contain *psilocybin* or *psilocin* (Grinspoon & Bakalar, 1979), which were identified and named by Hofmann in 1958 after examining *Psilocybe mexicana* mushrooms (Hofmann, 1979/1980). Psilocybin, the more stable of the two compounds (Hofmann, 1979/1980), gets converted to psilocin when ingested.

Fifteen milligrams or more of psilocybin results in a trip that "generally lasts from two to five hours" (Levinthal, 1996, p. 189). The physiological effects of psilocybin are "like LSD but gentler," and the psychological effects are similar to those of LSD except that they tend to be "more visual, less intense" (Grinspoon & Bakalar, 1979, p. 17), and less dysphoric (see also Schultes & Winkelman, 1996). We shall see other examples of psilocybin experiences toward the end of this chapter.

Mescaline

The *peyote cactus*, containing more than 30 psychoactive substances, including *mescaline*, is one of a number of cacti with psychedelic effects that has been used by native people from northern Mexico and the southwestern United States from at least as early as 100 BCE (Grinspoon & Bakalar, 1979). One way of ingesting peyote is to cut and dry the tops of the cactus to form *buttons* that can then be eaten. The buttons have a bitter taste and "can cause vomiting, headaches, and . . . nausea" (Levinthal, 1996, p. 191). An effective dose of mescaline is about 200 milligrams or about three to five buttons, with effects lasting from 8 to 12 hours. The drug is said to produce more intense physiological arousal and to result in a more sensual, perceptual, and stable trip than LSD (Grinspoon & Bakalar, 1979). In general, however, LSD, psilocybin, and mescaline produce similar effects (Hollister & Sjoberg, 1964).

Huston Smith (2000), upon taking mescaline at one of Leary's parties, was struck by the apparent fact that the drug "acted as a psychological prism" (p. 10) revealing multiple layers of the mind among which he could move at will by shifting his attention. Although these layers were all real, they ranged in importance from "the clear, unbroken Light of the Void" to levels with "multiple forms" and lower intensities, leading him to conclude that descriptions of the "brain as a reducing valve" (H. Smith, 2000, p. 11) were accurate. Furthermore, seeing the structure of these layers of reality had the "force of the sun" against which "everyday experience reveals only flickering shadows in the dim cavern" (H. Smith, 2000, p. 11). For Smith, ideas about the nature of reality that had previously been merely conceptual were now verified through direct perception.

DMT

The chemical compound *N,N-dimethyltryptamine* (*DMT*) has been found throughout the living natural world, including the human body and brain, and has also been synthesized (Strassman, 2001). When 50 milligrams or more of DMT are smoked or injected, effects similar to those of LSD—except of greater intensity—begin almost immediately and end after about a half hour (Grinspoon & Bakalar, 1979).

In one case, a young woman was told that she would see God and injected with DMT. Everything happened much too quickly. Where there had previously been "doors and cabinets," now there were "parallel lines falling away into absurdities" (Masters & Houston, 1966, p. 162). She had been promised that she would see God, so she closed her eyes. There was something there, all right. It started as a pinpoint and grew into a formless shape until it became a "cosmic diamond cat" (Masters & Houston, 1966, p. 163) that filled all of space. It was all that existed. The cat "moved in rhythmic spasms" accompanied by a shrill voice telling her that she was "a wretched, pulpy, flaccid thing; a squishy-squashy worm," and she knew that "this was the only reality [she] had ever known" (Masters & Houston, 1966, p. 163).

One of the seminal events that propelled the psychedelic renaissance was a study conducted by Rick Strassman at the University of New Mexico, where he injected participants with various doses of DMT. One of the striking results was the finding that with a sufficiently high dose, an individual would report the experience of having been propelled into a world that appears to exist independently of the individual's mind. Furthermore, as one participant said, "You return not to where you left off, but to where things have gone since you left. It's not a hallucination, but an observation. When I'm there, I'm not intoxicated. I'm lucid and sober" (Strassman, 2001, p. 195). And those landscapes are not empty. They are populated by beings such as "clowns, reptiles, mantises, bees, spiders, cacti, and stick figures" (Strassman, 2001, p. 185). Furthermore, "contact with 'aliens,' being experimented on in highly technological settings, implantation of devices, and transmission of information" (Strassman, 1997, p. 158) have been found with DMT intoxication, leading one to wonder whether a surge of DMT in the brain could account for alien abduction experiences. In particular, it has been suggested that the pineal gland, a tiny gland in the middle of the brain that produces melatonin, could be the source of a DMT surge (cf. I. Miller, 2013). The answer is no, the pineal gland does not appear to have the capacity to do so. Nor are there any other likely candidates in the brain for the production of the amount of DMT that would be required to create otherworldly experiences (Nichols, 2018).

Ayahuasca

In the region of the upper Amazon in South America, indigenous people, including many shamans (Shanon, 2001, 2002), drink a psychedelic cocktail for which they have over 70 names, including *ayahuasca*, the one that we are using (Domínguez-Clavé et al., 2016). Ayahuasca is made by pounding and cooking in water the woody (Weil & Rosen, 1993) *Banisteriopsis* vines (Schultes, 1982), such as *Banisteriopsis caapi* and usually adding any of 90 additional different plants to "lengthen and heighten the intoxication" (Schultes & Winkelman, 1996, p. 218), such as *Psychotria viridis* (Schultes, 1982; D. J. McKenna, 2004). *Banisteriopsis* itself contains a number of psychoactive ingredients such as the *beta-carbolines*, including "harmine, harmaline and tetrahydroharmine" (Schultes, 1982, p. 212). There are differing accounts of the effective doses of the beta-carbolines, with probably about 200 milligrams of harmine or harmaline being needed for a 4- to 8-hour trip (Grinspoon & Bakalar, 1979). The inclusion of *Psychotria viridis* adds DMT to ayahuasca. Normally DMT is broken down in the stomach by monoamine oxydase (MAO; Weil & Rosen, 1993). However, the beta-carbolines inhibit the action of MAO so that DMT remains active (D. J. McKenna, 2004; Schultes & Winkelman, 1996). The addition of DMT to ayahuasca is said to make for "better and brighter visions" (Weil & Rosen, 1993, p. 105).

Ayahuasca is known as a purgative in part because it induces vomiting and severe diarrhea (Schultes & Winkelman, 1996). Other physiological effects include "increases in blood pressure and cardiac rate, profuse sweating, tremors, pricking feeling in the skin, and a buzzing sound in the ears" (Schultes & Winkelman, 1996, p. 219). Psychologically there can be "a sense of flying"; images of "coloured lights"; "geometric patterns" (Schultes & Winkelman, 1996, p. 218); and animals such as "jaguars, birds, and reptiles" (Grinspoon & Bakalar, 1979, p. 15); as well as "visions of spirit helpers, demons, deities, and distant events" (Schultes & Winkelman, 1996, p. 15). "The dreamlike sequences are sometimes said to be longer, more vivid, and more realistic than those produced by mescaline or LSD" (Schultes & Winkelman, 1996, p. 15). Some indigenous people have attributed a number of purportedly paranormal abilities to the ingestion of ayahuasca, such as "acquiring protective spirits," determining "the causes and cures of diseases," prophesying the future, "contacting distant relatives," and "gaining direction and guidance throughout life" (Schultes & Winkelman, 1996, p. 220). Indeed, at one time the psychoactive ingredients of *Banisteriopsis* were named *telepathines* (Schultes, 1982), presumably to reflect the alleged extrasensory empowerment that they provided (Grinspoon & Bakalar, 1979).

In Western cultures, there has been a surge of interest in alternative forms of spirituality and healing that have included travel to the Amazonian jungle to look for them by legally drinking ayahuasca (Bauer, 2018; Holman, 2011). Since the 1990s, ecotourism operators started offering ayahuasca ceremonies as part of their packages, with the highest concentration of retreat centers being found around Iquitos in Peru (Fotiou, 2016). And *ayahuasca tourism*, as travel for the purpose of consuming ayahuasca has come to be called (Callicott, 2016; D. J. McKenna, 2004), now involves tens of thousands of travelers (Bauer, 2018). Ayahuasca has been touted as a panacea that can cure pretty much anything (Callicott, 2016) with some apparent successes (e.g., Tafur, 2017). However, aside from the obvious risks of being assaulted or killed (Callicott, 2016; Trichter, 2010), there are other problems. For instance, there has been a tendency to romanticize indigenous people as living in some sort of fictitious harmony with nature rather than individuals facing complex challenges "not the least of which is the recent commercialization of indigenous spirituality" (Fotiou, 2016, p. 151). And in our fascination with ayahuasca shamanism we tend to highlight its potential life-changing benefits as a possible cure for posttraumatic stress disorder, for example, but downplay its darker elements, such as sorcery (Fotiou, 2016). I think that the message is that naive psychedelic enthusiasm needs to be tempered with knowledge about the reality of ayahuasca tourism (cf. Fotiou, 2016; Trichter, 2010; Tupper, 2009). This discussion highlights our eighth thematic thread: Are these alterations of consciousness in this context dangerous or beneficial?

Neuropharmacology of Psychedelics

In the context of drug use, the term *tolerance* refers to the need for increased amounts of a substance in order to achieve a desired effect or "a markedly diminished effect with continued use of the same amount of the substance" (American Psychiatric Association, 2000, p. 192). Tolerance for LSD develops "within two or three days" (Grinspoon & Bakalar, 1979, p. 11) and then disappears just as quickly. The pattern of tolerance is similar for psilocybin, mescaline, and DMT. Furthermore, there is *cross-tolerance* between many of the psychedelics, including LSD, psilocybin, and mescaline (Grinspoon & Bakalar, 1979), meaning that intoxication with one of them will inhibit the effectiveness of a second one if it is taken shortly after the first. Cross-tolerance suggests that these drugs may have common effects in the brain.

Because the LSD molecule is structurally similar to the neurotransmitter serotonin, as indeed are also psilocybin, DMT, and the beta-carbolines (cf. Grinspoon & Bakalar, 1979), investigators reasoned that psychedelic effects result from the mediation of serotonergic neural pathways in the brain (Jacobs, 1987). In fact, it has been demonstrated that many psychedelic drugs, such as LSD, DMT, and psilocybin increase activity in serotonergic pathways by stimulating the 5-HT$_2$ subtype of serotonergic receptors (Sadzot et al., 1989;

Strassman, 1996; Vollenweider et al., 1997). However, the neuropharmaco-
logical action of psychedelics turns out to be extremely complex, so that, for
instance, a psychedelic can both excite and inhibit by attaching to different
receptors on the same neuron (Nichols & Chemel, 2011).

What we can say is that under the influence of psychedelics, the brain
appears to degrade incoming sensory information, allowing internally generated signals to play a greater role in one's experience. Ordinarily, the brain
anticipates sensory information in order to construct our ordinary waking
reality (Hoffman, 1998). But when the incoming stream becomes patchy and
the brain does not receive the information it needs, it fills out our perceptions
using internally generated signals (Nichols & Chemel, 2011), thereby creating
the semi-hallucinations characteristic of psychedelic intoxication. Also, perhaps
paradoxically, activity of the DMN is attenuated (Speth et al., 2016), which
could account for transformations of self-identity, including death and rebirth
experiences. Finally, even though the brain's usual neural networks, such
as the DMN, become disintegrated, there is overall greater integration across
brain structures, which could explain perceptual phenomena such as synesthesia, as well as the apparent creativity attributed to the use of psychedelics
(Pollan, 2018). There is also some evidence that, in some cases, with regular
use, some of the brain changes could become permanent (Domínguez-Clavé
et al., 2016). Taken together, these neurological modifications could shift
a person out of their usual ways of perceiving and conceptualizing themself
and the world into others, which may be more meaningful or less meaningful
than the previous ones.

LONG-TERM EFFECTS OF PSYCHEDELICS

We have seen in the previous examples some of the dramatic changes of
perception, emotions, and thoughts that can occur during intoxication with
psychedelics, including the presence of acute anxiety. The worst situation
is one in which there is a "fixed intense emotion or distorted thought" such
as "remorse, suspicion, delusions of persecution or of being irreversibly
insane" (Grinspoon & Bakalar, 1979, p. 158). An extension of this situation
is the "metaphysical bad trip" in which "the drug taker's . . . wretched feelings
are seen as revelations of the ultimate nature of the universe" (Grinspoon
& Bakalar, 1979, p. 158), such as the woman's encounter with a cosmic cat
given previously. In general, however, "painful or frightening feelings"
(Grinspoon & Bakalar, 1979, p. 158) are an expected part of psychedelic
experiences and may prove to be valuable sources of information about
oneself.

Sometimes the disorganization of the mind induced by psychedelics does
not end with the end of a drug trip but persists for months (Grinspoon &
Bakalar, 1979) or years (H. D. Abraham & Aldridge, 1993) after the termination
of psychedelic drug use. For example, there can be an increase in hypnagogic

imagery, and dreams may "take on the vividness, intensity, and perceptual peculiarities of drug trips" (Grinspoon & Bakalar, 1979, p. 160). In fact, there is a broad range of health effects of naturally occurring, as well as a continuously increasing number of synthetic psychoactive compounds, both legal and illegal (Schifano, Orsolini, Duccio Papanti, & Corkery, 2015). Here we just briefly consider two long-term adverse consequences of psychedelic drug use—namely, perceptual and psychotic effects—and then some of the potentially beneficial therapeutic uses of psychedelics. In this way we are returning again to our eighth thematic thread concerned with the dangers and benefits of particular alterations of consciousness.

Perceptual Effects

Perhaps the most common adverse effect is the occurrence of *flashbacks*, "the transitory recurrence of emotions and perceptions originally experienced while under the influence of a psychedelic drug" that can last for just "seconds or hours" (Grinspoon & Bakalar, 1979, p. 159) and can include any of the features of the drug experience itself. Usually, they are only somewhat disturbing, although occasionally they can "turn into repeated frightening images or thoughts" (Grinspoon & Bakalar, 1979, p. 159). Flashbacks can sometimes be triggered by intoxication with drugs such as marijuana and selective serotonin reuptake inhibitors (SSRIs). Indeed, there is a "psychopharmacological resemblance" (Grinspoon & Bakalar, 1979/1997, p. xviii) between psychedelics and SSRIs with not only reports of SSRIs triggering flashbacks but an apparent heightening of SSRI activity by psychedelics (Grinspoon & Bakalar, 1979/1997; cf. Picker, Lerman, & Hajal, 1992). Hence there are warnings against mixing psychedelic drug use with SSRIs (e.g., Bauer, 2018).

With the accumulation of more research, the perceptual aspects of flashbacks have been subsumed in a broad category of postpsychedelic perceptual disturbances called *hallucinogen persisting perception disorder* (American Psychiatric Association, 2013). These long-term alterations of perception can last from seconds to years and can include, among other distortions, intensification of color, changes in size, images of geometric forms, images in the peripheral visual fields, afterimages, and stationary images of moving objects (H. D. Abraham & Aldridge, 1993; American Psychiatric Association, 2013). This disorder has been considered to possibly arise from as little as a single dose of LSD and to be "slowly reversible or irreversible" (H. D. Abraham & Aldridge, 1993, p. 1331).

One way to think about this is to note that the brain appears to function in a manner that maintains *synaptic homeostasis* so that flooding receptor sites with chemical agents that can activate them leads to a compensatory attenuated response. In one study, "repeated administration of LSD to rats was found to decrease the availability of the 5-HT$_2$ receptor subtype" (Jacobs, 1987, p. 389). In another study, "chronic administration of LSD over a period of seven days was found to result in alterations in behavior of rats that were detectable more than thirty days after the drug treatment" (King & Ellison, 1989, p. 72). Some investigators have thought it possible that hallucinogen persisting perception disorder may result from long-term changes to the structure of serotonergic neurons (H. D. Abraham & Aldridge, 1993), while others have considered it to be "chiefly a post-traumatic reaction, or the effect of a lower threshold for the involuntary production of imagery and fantasy" (Grinspoon & Bakalar, 1979/1997, p. xviii).

Psychotic Effects

To what extent do psychedelic drugs not just mimic but actually cause psychosis? There has been a great deal of confusion with regard to this question. Given that changes to serotonin receptor binding have been noted in those with schizophrenia, that some medication used in the treatment of schizophrenia blocks $5\text{-}HT_2$ receptors, and that some psychedelics "can elicit schizophrenia-like symptoms in humans" (Vollenweider, Vollenweider-Scherpenhuyzen, Bäbler, Vogel, & Hell, 1998, p. 3897), it has been hypothesized "that excessive $[5\text{-}HT_2]$ receptor activation may be a critical factor in psychotic symptom formation and cognitive deficits in schizophrenia" (p. 3902), at least in some cases. If that is true, then psychedelics could precipitate schizophrenia. Others have argued that the similarities between psychedelic intoxication and schizophrenia are superficial rather than substantive (Bravo & Grob, 1996; Levinthal, 1996), in which case the question becomes that of whether psychedelics can cause some form of psychosis resembling schizophrenia that persists after the termination of a drug trip. Certainly, there have been those who have experienced "mood swings, visual hallucinations, mania, grandiosity, and religiosity" (H. D. Abraham & Aldridge, 1993, p. 1329) following the use of LSD. In older clinical and experimental studies with LSD, incidence figures for psychosis following use of psychedelics have ranged from 0.08% to 4.6% (H. D. Abraham & Aldridge, 1993).

It turns out that many of those with psychedelic psychoses have had "prior histories of psychosis" (H. D. Abraham & Aldridge, 1993, p. 1330). For example, in a summary of three studies, it was found that 37% to 49% of those hospitalized for LSD psychosis had received "previous psychiatric treatment" (H. D. Abraham & Aldridge, 1993, p. 1330). In a direct comparison of people with schizophrenia with and without previous drug use and a control group of people without schizophrenia, it was found that those using drugs had had better psychological adjustment before the onset of schizophrenia than those not using drugs but worse psychological adjustment than the non-schizophrenic individuals (Breakey, Goodell, Lorenz, & McHugh, 1974). This raises the question of whether the drugs precipitated a psychosis or instead had an ameliorative effect on a disorder that would have manifested anyway.

A problem with the previous drug use study was the conflation of the effects of psychedelics with those of other drugs, given that hallucinogens were not the only drugs previously used by the participants (Breakey et al.,

1974). In fact, among those with schizophrenia who had used drugs, multiple drug use was common, making it difficult to implicate any single drug "as a causative agent for chronic psychosis" (Boutros & Bowers, 1996, p. 268), not only because of the confounding effects of the other drugs but also because "the psychotomimetic effect of different drugs of abuse can be additive" (p. 266).

Nonetheless, differences have been found between acute psychoses that developed 2 to 7 days after using LSD and psychoses in which no drugs had been used, suggesting that some people may be vulnerable to psychoses induced by psychedelics (H. D. Abraham & Aldridge, 1993). This should not surprise us considering the complex constellation of psychedelic effects in the brain that can lead to a profound shift in a person's experience, possibly to a more disorganized state.

Psychedelic Treatment of Alcoholism

One night in 1953, as they were brainstorming in an Ottawa hotel room, Hoffer and Osmond noted the similarities between delirium tremens, the hallucinations reported by people in the throes of alcoholism, and psychotomimetic experiences under the influence of LSD. Recovered alcoholics have pointed to the awakening that their experiences of delirium tremens hallucinations precipitated that had allowed them to remain sober. Why not, Hoffer and Osmond speculated, give alcoholics a high dose LSD session to mimic delirium tremens before they sink to that stage? And they did, with apparently good results, although they came to reconceptualize the LSD experiences as instances of mystical transcendence rather than psychosis (Pollan, 2018). Have there been studies with proper controls?

Arnold Ludwig and his colleagues randomly assigned 176 alcoholic hospital inpatients into four groups of 44 each. All of the participants received milieu therapy (Ludwig, Levine, & Stark, 1970, p. 5), a form of humane institutionalized care (Carson, Butcher, & Mineka, 1996). Participants in one group received only the milieu therapy; those in a second group received, in addition, a single LSD session; those in a third group received psychotherapy as well as LSD; and those in a fourth group received LSD, psychotherapy, and hypnosis. The researchers' rationale for the last of these combinations was that the use of hypnosis would allow the LSD sessions to be more structured and hence of greater therapeutic benefit. Participants in this group would receive a high dose of LSD and then be hypnotized while the LSD took effect. Once the drug effects began, participants would be led in discussions of their major problems and then "given posthypnotic suggestions to continue working on [their] problems and to make a greater effort in accepting responsibility and leading a more productive life" (Ludwig et al., 1970, p. 48). Then hypnotized participants were awakened from trance and all participants in LSD sessions were left alone in a room with paper and a pencil in case they desired to write about their experiences (Ludwig et al., 1970, p. 48).

In Ludwig's study, despite the fact that the "dramatic accounts" (Ludwig et al., 1970, p. 127) written by participants in the latter part of their sessions "were all that could have been hoped for" (p. 241), there was no evidence that any of the LSD sessions made a difference in therapeutic outcome at follow-up intervals of up to 1 year. Furthermore, there was no measurable relationship between the "degree of alteration in consciousness" that had been achieved during the LSD sessions and "therapeutic or personality change" (Ludwig et al., 1970, p. 183).

The results of this study were consistent with the results of a number of other studies done around the same time in which there were either no differences in outcome with the use of LSD or the differences disappeared by the time of 6-month follow-ups (Ludwig et al., 1970). While there have been some criticisms of Ludwig's study, it has been acknowledged to be "the most methodologically elaborate and rigorously constructed study of LSD therapy for treatment of alcoholism" (Mangini, 1998, p. 401) prior to the cessation of psychedelic research. However, given the serious social burden posed by alcoholism and the fact that individuals seeking treatment have had 3.5 previous treatment attempts, illustrative of the failure rate of conventional forms of treatment, psychedelic treatment is being reexamined to see if there are ways of harnessing it as an effective treatment for alcohol use disorders (Eischens & Atherton, 2019).

Psychedelics in Palliative Care

Stanislav Grof has done extensive research concerning the administration of psychedelic drugs to those who were dying of cancer (Grof, 1987). The purpose of the psychedelic therapy was "not treatment of cancer, but relief from emotional and physical pain and change of the attitude toward death through deep mystical experiences induced by psychedelics" (Grof, 1987, p. 136). Indeed, among the benefits of psychedelics has been relief from pain "on occasion even in individuals who did not respond to high dosages of powerful narcotics" (Grof & Halifax, 1978, p. 118). Moreover, the analgesic effects of psychedelics have sometimes persisted for weeks after their acute effects have worn off (Nichols, 1999). In some cases pain has been attenuated, or it has simply disappeared entirely. In other cases, pain has still been present, but it has no longer monopolized a person's attention and emotional resources.

Psychedelics have also changed people's attitudes toward death. Those who had transcendent experiences during their psychedelic sessions "developed a deep belief in the ultimate unity of all creation," so that death appeared to be but "a transition into a different type of existence" (Grof & Halifax, 1978, p. 127). Similar results were found more recently at Johns Hopkins University, where patients have been given psilocybin on an experimental basis. Erica Rex (2013), a participant in the study, said that

> I have come to realize the universe consists of more than what readily meets the
> eye. An abiding sense of the inexplicable vastness of what is real and what is

possible has affected my worldview. I no longer define myself by what has happened to my body, or even my emotional life, since my cancer diagnosis. (p. 66)

The ontological awakening that sometimes accompanies psychedelic experiences appears to reconcile some people to their impending death (Dyck, 2019). This gets at our second thematic thread: the possible transcendent nature of reality. Let us consider the transcendental effects of psychedelics more carefully.

TRANSCENDENTAL EFFECTS OF PSYCHEDELICS

The transcendental effects of psychedelics were the focus of attention in the most controversial study in the psychology of religion, the Good Friday experiment (Hood, Spilka, Hunsberger, & Gorsuch, 1996, p. 257), in which divinity students were given psilocybin before participating in a Good Friday service on April 20, 1962 (Malmgren, 1994). Let us consider this experiment and then a follow-up experiment in 2006 that has been credited with the renaissance of psychedelic research.

The Good Friday Experiment

Walter Pahnke, a doctoral student in Religion and Society at Harvard University (Pahnke, 1963), conducted the Good Friday experiment "with Timothy Leary as his principal academic advisor" (Doblin, 1991, p. 1) to determine the extent to which "experiences described by mystics" (Pahnke, 1963, p. 2) were similar to those induced by psychedelics. Because of their importance in psychedelic experiences, "the effects of set and setting were planned to maximize the possibility that mystical phenomena would occur" (Pahnke, 1963, p. 87).

   The 20 primary participants in the Good Friday experiment, mostly theological students (Pahnke, 1963; H. Smith, 2000), were prepared for the experiment in a manner that was "meant to maximize positive expectation, trust, confidence, and reduction of fear" (Pahnke, 1963, p. 87). Participants were divided into five groups of four with, in addition, two leaders familiar with the effects of psilocybin, assigned to each group. "The chief purpose of these leaders was to aid in creating a friendly and trust-filled set and setting" (Pahnke, 1963, p. 94). On the basis of random assignment, two of the student participants in each group received 30 milligrams of psilocybin and one leader received 15 milligrams of psilocybin, while the other two students and the other leader each received 200 milligrams of nicotinic acid. The effects of nicotinic acid are to cause relaxation and flushing of the skin. The purpose of giving nicotinic acid to the students in the control group was to encourage the suggestion that it was they who had received the psilocybin because all of the students "knew that psilocybin produced various somatic effects, but none of [them] had ever had psilocybin or any related substance before the experiment" (Pahnke, 1963, p. 89). The point was that this was to have been a double-blind study, so that those in the experimental and control groups could not identify who was in which group.

Eighty minutes after swallowing their capsules, the participants in the Good Friday experiment moved into a "small prayer chapel" (Pahnke, 1963, p. 98) in Marsh Chapel in Boston into which was piped a live Good Friday service led by Rev. Howard Thurman, the chaplain of Boston University (Malmgren, 1994). Disorder ensued as the half of the participants who had received the psilocybin "were in a condition where social decorum meant nothing, and the other half were more interested in the spectacle that was unfolding before them than in the service proper" (H. Smith, 2000, p. 101). After the 2-hour service, the participants remained in the chapel and nearby rooms until the effects of the drug had worn off, at which time they left. Data concerning their experiences were collected from student participants immediately following the service, within days, and at 6 months (Pahnke, 1963). In addition, Rick Doblin (1991) did a long-term follow-up 24 to 27 years later with nine of the participants from the control group and seven from the experimental group.

On the basis of written descriptions and responses to a 147-item questionnaire designed to assess the presence of the characteristics of mystical consciousness, participants "who received psilocybin experienced phenomena that were apparently indistinguishable from, if not identical with, certain categories defined by the typology of mystical consciousness" (Pahnke & Richards, 1972, p. 426). Numerical analyses revealed statistically significant differences in scores between the experimental and control groups on all of the characteristics of mystical experiences except sacredness (Pahnke & Richards, 1972). These differences were still present at the time of the long-term follow-up (Doblin, 1991). The following are some of the comments made by participants who received psilocybin. One said that he "lapsed into a period of complete lostness of self," and another said that "the more [he] let go, the greater sense of oneness [he] received" (Pahnke, 1963, p. 131), illustrating a loss of self associated with transcendence. A participant commented that he "was living in the most beautiful reality [he] had ever known, and it was eternal" (Pahnke, 1963, p. 144), indicating the experience of having transcended time. Deeply felt positive mood was found in the comment of a participant who said that he "had a brief but violently intense feeling of joy" (Pahnke, 1963, p. 150). Alleged ineffability associated with mystical experiences is found in the comment by a participant who said that he "cannot describe the sense of the Divine" (Pahnke, 1963, p. 184). In general, Pahnke's research supported the notion that with the right set and setting, the use of psychedelic drugs can lead to experiences with characteristics that are similar to mystical experiences.

Varieties of Psychedelic Experiences

Mike Young was one of the student participants in the Good Friday experiment who happened to get psilocybin. His psychedelic experience began gently, with the intensification of colors, etching of geometric figures around objects, and the presence of afterimages trailing people who moved. Upon closing his eyes, Young was greeted with "an incredible kaleidoscope of visual wonderment" (Malmgren, 1994, p. 1F). Subsequently, he had difficulty keeping track of what was happening inside and what was happening outside his head. Eventually, swirling bands of color resolved themselves into a "radial design, like a mandala" (Malmgren, 1994, p. 1F), with different colors leading out from the center, each representing a different path in life that he could take. Young felt that he himself was at the center of the circle immobilized "for what felt like an eternity" (Malmgren, 1994, p. 1F) by agonizing indecision. He has said that then he died, and, in dying, realized the freedom of becoming who he could be. Years later, Young understood this vision to be about "his struggle to make a career choice" (Malmgren, 1994, p. 1F). The visions went on intermittently for another 3 hours, but they were pleasant, and then the drug trip "tapered off" and "he started to notice what was going on around him" (Malmgren, 1994, p. 1F). Young has said of his experiences that "religious ideas that [had been] interesting intellectually before now were connected to something much deeper than belief and theory" (Malmgren, 1994, p. 1F).

Psychedelic experiences, no matter the preparation, are not necessarily uniformly pleasant. In that regard, they can be likened to the experiences that can occur during shamanic initiation. While immobilized with indecision in the center of his mandala, Young had the "incredibly painful" sensation that "his insides [were] being clawed out" (Malmgren, 1994, p. 1F). Of the seven psilocybin participants interviewed by Doblin, only two reported having had Good Friday experiences that were "completely positive without significant psychic struggles" (Doblin, 1991, p. 21). The remainder of the participants had experienced difficult moments that had been "resolved during the course of the Good Friday service and according to the subjects contributed to their learning and growth" (Doblin, 1991, p. 21).

Although Pahnke did not mention the incident in his thesis, one of the students who had received psilocybin had had a particularly unpleasant experience. Huston Smith, one of the group leaders, recalled that that participant had gone to the front of the chapel, where he had given "an incoherent homily, blessed the congregation with the sign of the cross" (H. Smith, 2000, p. 102), left the chapel, found an open door, left the building, and taken off down the street. Smith had pursued the man and tried to convince him to come back into the church. Unable to do so, Smith had run back to get help, and eventually, with the assistance of Pahnke and another helper, the three men had been able to walk the participant back into the church, where he had been injected with the antipsychotic drug thorazine. It appeared that the man had believed that "God had chosen him to announce to the world the dawning of the Messianic Age, a millennium of universal peace" (H. Smith, 2000, p. 103) and was suiting his actions to his new beliefs. Needless to say, this participant's evaluation of his experiences has been "heavily negative" (H. Smith, 2000, p. 104), and he has refused to participate in Doblin's follow-up study.

The Johns Hopkins University Experiment

There was a follow-up study at Johns Hopkins University some 40 years after the Good Friday experiment in which 36 participants received either 30 milligrams of psilocybin or 40 milligrams of methylphenidate hydrochloride, one participant at a time, using a double-blind protocol. Again, there was an effort to maximize set and setting so as to facilitate the occurrence of mystical experiences during the psilocybin sessions. Participants arrived at the laboratory for two separate sessions without knowing whether they would be receiving the psychedelic or the active placebo. Six individuals ended up with two placebo sessions and were given a third session in which they knew that they would be receiving the psychedelic (Griffiths, Richards, McCann, & Jesse, 2006).

As in the Good Friday experiment, again, there were elevated scores on mysticism scales for the psilocybin sessions but not the placebo sessions, at a 2-month follow-up and a 14-month follow-up. There were no significant differences in ratings between the 2-month and 14-month follow-ups. Eleven percent of participants rated the psychedelic experience as the "single most meaningful experience" of their lives, whereas 58% rated it as "being among the five most personally meaningful experiences of their lives" (Griffiths, Richards, Johnson, McCann, & Jesse, 2008, p. 630). Sixty-four percent felt that the psilocybin session had increased their "sense of well-being or life satisfaction" (Griffiths et al., 2008, p. 630), and none rated the experience as having decreased them.

Again, as we have learned with the psychedelics, there were dysphoric experiences. Eleven of the participants indicated that they had experienced "strong" or "extreme" fear at some point during their sessions. Four of them reported that a "significant portion of their session was characterized by anxiety/dysphoria" and an additional four reported that the entire session had been like that (Griffiths et al., 2006, p. 278). Three participants said that they never wanted to have "an experience like that again" (Griffiths et al., 2006, p. 279). Overall, however, 61% of participants had a "'complete' mystical experience" compared with 30% to 40% of participants in the Good Friday experiment (Griffiths et al., 2006, p. 281).

SUMMARY

Where does this leave us? What have we learned about psychedelics? What is most salient, perhaps, is the degree to which psychedelics can force alterations of consciousness and the frequently disruptive manner in which that can happen. There is potential for disorganization but also potential for reorganization and an opportunity to think about reality in a different way from that of the ordinary waking state of consciousness. Most impressive, perhaps, are the transcendent insights that can ensue during intoxication, although their veracity cannot be established by observers in the ordinary waking state. But the disruptions associated with psychedelics in some cases can be long-lasting, such as perceptual distortions and psychoses that can persist after the period of actual intoxication. On balance then, do psychedelics bring about pathology or well-being, our seventh thematic thread? Are they dangerous or beneficial, our eighth thematic thread? As usual, I will let the reader decide for themself.

Political situations can vary both geographically and temporally with regard to the sanctioned use of psychedelics so that their possible potential uses cannot always be explored and exploited. But the transcendent aspects of psychedelic experiences in which deepening of meaning appears to take place are similar to some of the characteristics of mystical experiences. What then, about the occurrence of such experiences without a little help from external chemical agents? Let us pay a bit more attention to our sixth thematic thread, the occurrence of the deepening of meaning, and turn next to a more comprehensive discussion of transcendence.

8

Transcendence

In the last chapter, we considered Pahnke's Good Friday experiment in which participants who were given the psychedelic psilocybin ostensibly had mystical experiences. Mystical experiences are a type of *transcendence* in that a person is in a state of being that is in some sense superior to ordinary existence. But that calls forth a number of fundamental questions associated with our thematic threads. Is there any sense in which transcendence is other than imaginary? Is a materialist account of transcendent experiences adequate? Are transcendent events meaningless or meaningful? Are they mundane or extraordinary? Are the insights that arise in transcendent states delusions, or are they true? Are the meanings of such insights lateral or vertical; which is to say, do they entail a deepening of meaning? And, perhaps most germane, what happens to the self? Do such experiences require effort or surrender? Our discussion will lead through a consideration of exceptional well-being, spontaneous transcendent experiences, meditation, persistent transcendent experiences, and, finally, efforts to explain what is happening.

VARIETY OF TRANSCENDENT EXPERIENCES

Perhaps we can start by asking what makes a person happy. Well, we have to be a little bit careful because what we really want to talk about is human well-being, which is more variegated than simple hedonic pleasure (Ryff, 1995).

http://dx.doi.org/10.1037/0000200-008
Alterations of Consciousness: An Empirical Analysis for Social Scientists, Second Edition,
by I. Baruš

Indeed, some of the greatest achievements of transcendence have occurred in the context of human suffering (e.g., Frankl, 1946/1984, 1948/1997a, 1995/1997b). However, even entering the discussion on the felicitous side of well-being, there is a variety of ways in which exceptional human functioning has been characterized. Let us consider three of those characterizations: flow, peak experiences, and mystical experiences.

Flow

Contrary to what we may naively suppose, Mihaly Csikszentmihalyi (1988) found that one of the things that can improve the quality of a person's experience is to be faced with challenges that are more demanding than everyday living. When a person's skills match the difficulties of the challenges, a state of consciousness that Csikszentmihalyi called *flow* can occur in which there is joyous and creative "total involvement with life" (Csikszentmihalyi, 1990, p. xi). I often enter such a state of consciousness when I am teaching. I become absorbed in drawing on my knowledge of the subject matter and organizing it into a narrative structure. The usual concerns of everyday life disappear into the background, and I lose track of time. Although it requires considerable effort, paradoxically this creative activity proceeds spontaneously and is accompanied by a sense of enjoyment.

More formally, Csikszentmihalyi (1990) identified five components of flow when participants in a study were asked "to describe how it felt when their lives were at their fullest, when what they did was most enjoyable" (p. 48). The first component is a *narrowing of attention* to the stimuli that are relevant for the ongoing activity to take place in such a way that there is complete but effortless focus. Second, *action and awareness can merge* so that only those events that are relevant to the ongoing activity remain in subjective consciousness$_2$. Third, a person may lose track of *time*. Fourth, there can be a *loss of self-consciousness*, in the sense of losing a reflective stance toward one's actions and potentially feeling that one has merged with the environment or other participants with whom one is engaged in the activity. Fifth, an individual has a *sense of control*. In addition, there are three conditions that are necessary for the occurrence of flow. The first of those, which we have already addressed, is the proper balance *between the challenge one faces and the skills necessary to succeed*. The second is the setting of *clear, proximal goals*. And the third is the presence of *feedback* that allows a person to know how well they are doing as the activity proceeds. What is important to note with flow is that this state of being is not an escape from one's engagement in the world but, rather, optimally functioning within it (Csikszentmihalyi & Nakamura, 2018).

Peak Experiences

Using a strategy similar to Csikszentmihalyi's, Abraham Maslow asked people to list and describe the most wonderful experiences of their lives. On the basis of their responses, Maslow characterized the changes to cognition and self-identity that can occur during these *peak experiences*. He found, for example, that sometimes peak experiences were felt to be perfect, complete, self-sufficient, self-validating, intrinsically valuable, and a source of justification for one's life. As such, they have been experienced as being "good and desirable" (Maslow, 1968, p. 81; emphasis removed) and never as "evil or undesirable" (Maslow, 1968, p. 81; emphasis removed) with the word *sacred* sometimes used to characterize them. Loss of self-awareness and temporary fusion with that which is not oneself can occur in peak experiences to the point of complete absorption in the object of one's attention so that it appears as if it were all there was in the universe, "as if it were all of Being, synonymous with the universe" (Maslow, 1968, p. 74).

In other peak experiences, particularly those identified as mystical, religious, or philosophical, "the whole of the world is seen as unity, as a single rich live entity" (Maslow, 1968, p. 88; emphases removed). Related to absorption, there can also be "disorientation in time and space" (Maslow, 1968, p. 80; emphasis removed) so that, for example, time may seem to be simultaneously both moving rapidly and standing still. Affect can change, with a loss of fear and hesitation and an expression of greater love, compassion, and acceptance of the world. Many of the features of peak experiences described by Maslow mirror those found by Csikszentmihalyi, including flow itself, which Maslow characterized as effortless, graceful, and decisive functioning.

Mystical Experiences

Note that the definition of *peak experience* is relative to the experiences that a person has actually had and is not given in terms of specific features. In some cases, peak experiences could be mystical experiences. So we need a definition of mystical experiences. Let us use the one developed by Walter Pahnke in which nine core elements have been identified.

The first characteristic of a *mystical experience* is that of *unity*, which can be either *internal*, if the subject–object dichotomy is transcended within a person, or *external*, if transcendence occurs "between the usual self and the external world of sense impressions" (Pahnke & Richards, 1972, p. 411). Internal unity occurs when "normal sense impressions" and "the usual sense of individuality" fall away so that one is left with "pure consciousness" (Pahnke & Richards, 1972, p. 411), whereas external unity involves increased awareness of particular sense impressions until one's identity merges with the sensory world in the recognition of an underlying oneness.

The second characteristic identified by Pahnke is that of *noetic quality*, whereby one has direct insight into the nature of being that is accompanied by the certainty that such knowledge is truly real and not a "subjective delusion" (Pahnke & Richards, 1972, p. 412). Third is the *transcendence of space and time*, although spatial transcendence may be only partial in external unity (Pahnke, 1963). Fourth is a *sense of sacredness*, "defined as a nonrational, intuitive, hushed, palpitant response in the presence of inspiring realities" (Pahnke & Richards, 1972, p. 414). Fifth is a *deeply felt positive mood* that can include "feelings of joy, love, blessedness, and peace" (Pahnke & Richards, 1972, p. 414). Sixth is *paradoxicality,* the characteristic that "significant aspects of mystical consciousness are felt by the experiencer to be true in spite of [violating normal logical principles]" (Pahnke & Richards, 1972, p. 415). An example of paradoxicality would be the claim that one has "experienced an empty unity that at the same time contains all reality" (Pahnke & Richards, 1972, p. 415). Seventh is the alleged *ineffability* of mystical experiences, the inability to adequately express transcendent events in words. Eighth is *transiency* (Pahnke & Richards, 1972, p. 416), the transient nature of mystical experiences relative to the permanence of everyday consciousness. The ninth characteristic of mystical experiences is the *positive change in attitude or behavior* that they can engender, at least insofar as self-reports of such changes are accurate (Pahnke & Richards, 1972). William Richards (2016) has a slightly shorter list as the defining elements of mystical consciousness, leaving out paradoxicality, transiency, and positive change in attitude or behavior, possibly because these are secondary to the core features of the experience itself.

Efforts have been made to determine the frequency of mystical experiences in the general population by conducting surveys in which questions have been asked about having had such experiences. The content of these questions has differed widely, as have the number of affirmative responses, resulting in a range of about 20% to 74% of the population claiming to have had some sort of significant mystical experience. A prudent approach to these figures has suggested that about "35% of persons sampled affirm some intense spiritual experience" (Hood, Spilka, Hunsberger, & Gorsuch, 1996, p. 247). In the consciousness survey of academics and professionals conducted by Robert Moore and myself in 1986, we found that 47% of respondents claimed to "have had an experience [that] could best be described as a transcendent or mystical experience" (Baruš, 1990, p. 169). However, in one study in which 34% of 305 participants agreed that they had been "close to a powerful spiritual force that seemed to lift [them] outside of [themselves]" (Thomas & Cooper, 1980, p. 78), analysis of the participants' more detailed reports indicated that only 1% actually met the criteria for having had mystical experiences.

When people are asked about transcending the normal human condition, at least along the dimension of having enjoyable and wonderful experiences, reports of flow, peak experiences, and mystical experiences have been obtained. These types of experiences have sometimes been conceptualized as lying on a continuum of consciousness, with those tending toward the mystical being properly regarded as transcendent (Waldron, 1998). While it is overly facile to align transcendent experiences in this way (cf. Maxwell & Tschudin, 1990; Privette, 1983), we shall focus on those psychological events that meet at least some of the criteria for mystical experiences. Let us begin with some examples.

EXAMPLES OF TRANSCENDENT EXPERIENCES

I have chosen three well-known examples of transcendent experiences that occurred under quite different circumstances: from observing the earth from space to being poisoned and coming close to death, and from having transient transcendent experiences to the occurrence of persistent transcendent states. Indeed, we need to be a bit careful here, in that persistent transcendent states are not necessarily the same as transient transcendent states, but persistent transcendent states can be transient in their own way as well, as we shall see toward the end of this chapter, so that we will not be overly concerned about the distinctions between transient and persistent states. There is something that all three of these individuals share, though, and that is a background in pure and applied mathematical sciences, which, I think, carries over to the clarity with which they have conceptualized their transcendent experiences.

Edgar Mitchell

On his way back from the moon, with the spacecraft functioning perfectly and not requiring his attention, Apollo 14 astronaut Edgar Mitchell had a chance to reflect on his journey. He fell into a quiet reverie as he looked out the window at the earth and the heavens from the vantage point of space. As he looked beyond Earth to the larger universe, he experienced a profound shift in his understanding of reality. He felt a sense of harmony and "interconnectedness with the celestial bodies surrounding [the] spacecraft" (E. Mitchell, 1996, p. 58). He was shaken "to the very core" by the silent authority of his feeling of connectedness to an intelligent "natural process" (E. Mitchell, 1996, p. 58). Even though he has found ways of characterizing it, Mitchell has been convinced that what he felt "always will be an ineffable experience" (E. Mitchell, 1996, p. 59).

However, Mitchell's peaceful reflection was broken by the knowledge that, in spite of its peaceful appearance, the earth was torn by discord and war. As his journey continued, he found himself moving between the euphoric transcendent state and dysphoric realization of human misery (S. Mitchell, 2006). Upon returning to earth Mitchell changed the course of his career and "became a full-time student of . . . the totality of consciousness" (E. Mitchell, 1996, p. 71), founding the Institute of Noetic Sciences for its multidisciplinary study. In Mitchell's epiphany we can see the characteristics of external unity—noetic quality, alleged ineffability, transiency, and positive changes in behavior—associated with mystical experiences.

John Wren-Lewis

John Wren-Lewis, when he was 60 years of age in 1983, was traveling by bus with his wife in Thailand, when he was poisoned after eating candy, apparently laced with morphine, which had been given to him by a thief.

He had unknowingly ingested a potentially fatal dose, as judged by the subsequent coma. It was some hours after awakening in a hospital room and
orienting himself to all that had occurred that Wren-Lewis began to wonder
why it was that the "rather shoddy hospital room seemed transcendentally
beautiful" (Wren-Lewis, 1988, p. 110). At first he wondered whether his
changed perception was the result of the morphine with which he had been
told he had probably been poisoned, but then he thought that the drug effects
should have worn off. Then he wondered if he had had a near-death experience
of the sort that we shall describe in Chapter 9, so he relaxed and tried to take
himself back in his imagination to a point in time just before he had awakened
from the coma (Wren-Lewis, 1988). What came to mind was that he had
emerged from "a deep but dazzling darkness" (Wren-Lewis, 1994, p. 109) that
was still there behind his ordinary consciousness.

Once recognized, the darkness that Wren-Lewis experienced was not a
vague impression but so palpable that he kept checking the back of his skull
as it seemed to have been sawn off, exposing his "brain to the dark infinity of
space" (Wren-Lewis, 1994, p. 109). Wren-Lewis (1994) felt as though he
were looking through the wrong end of a telescope "perceiving everything
very sharply from an immense distance yet at the same time [he] had the
uncanny sense that [he] actually *was* each thing perceiving itself" (p. 110).
In fact, he was the "timeless, spaceless void which in some indescribable
way was total aliveness" and which "budded out into manifestation" as
"everything-that-is, experiencing itself through the bodymind called John"
(Wren-Lewis, 1991, p. 5). Unlike his "personal consciousness," the darkness
was an "impersonal consciousness" that *seemed to know everything from the
inside* (Wren-Lewis, 1994, p. 110) and from which everything around him
arose anew at each moment. The presence of the darkness was accompanied by a sense of "surprised satisfaction" (Wren-Lewis, 1994, p. 110), peace
(Wren-Lewis, 1988), love (Wren-Lewis, 1994), bliss, and "joy beyond joy"
(Wren-Lewis, 1988, p. 113). Again, we see the characteristics of a mystical
experience, in this case one of internal unity.

One of the differences between mystical experiences as characterized by
Pahnke and that of Wren-Lewis is that Wren-Lewis's mystical state of consciousness persisted indefinitely. However, once in a while, every day, Wren-
Lewis would find that he would slip out of the mystical state "for minutes
or even hours at a stretch *without even noticing*" (Wren-Lewis, 1994, p. 110;
emphasis in original). Eventually he would realize that something was
wrong, whereupon the shining dark would come "flooding back" (Wren-
Lewis, 1988, p. 117) as if its presence in his consciousness had become his
"baseline" (p. 110). Wren-Lewis argued that it would be a "complete mis-
nomer" to regard his endarkened state as an "*altered* state of consciousness" (1991, p. 6; emphasis in original) because his state of being was not
a "high from which [he] can come down" (p. 5) but rather a normal state
in which things are truly just what they are. His previous state of ordinary
consciousness, however, was a "real alteration" in that it was an "artificially

blinkered or clouded condition wherein the bodymind has the absurd illusion that it is somehow a separate individual entity over against everything else" (Wren-Lewis, 1991, p. 6). Whose conception of reality is correct—our interpretation that Wren-Lewis's endarkenment is an altered state of consciousness, or his realization that our ordinary constricted condition is an altered state of consciousness? Just as our ordinary consciousness seems self-evidently real to us, so his ordinary consciousness seemed self-evidently real to him.

What is it that allows a person to have an ongoing sense of exceptional well-being such as that enjoyed by Wren-Lewis? Huston Smith (2000) was disappointed that 20 years of meditation failed to provide him with the mystical experiences that occurred, as we saw in Chapter 7, the first time that he took mescaline. Wren-Lewis has also been pessimistic about the effectiveness of strategies typically used to try to attain transcendent states (Wren-Lewis, 1994), but he has realized that, much as he would like to do so, he has no advice to give regarding the attainment of mystical states since he "could scarcely recommend taking a potentially fatal dose of poison" (Wren-Lewis, 1991, p. 7). Wren-Lewis (1994) proposed the hypothesis that transcendent consciousness is blocked by hyperactivity of a psychological survival mechanism within each of us. A person gets so locked into trying to secure the future of their "individual consciousness" that they shut out the "underlying universal consciousness, with its every-present-moment happiness, peace and wonder" (Wren-Lewis, 1994, p. 113). Coming close to death breaks the "spell *because the survival-mechanism gives up at this point*," sometimes giving a person access to knowledge of "what consciousness really is" (Wren-Lewis, 1994, p. 113). The result is that, upon coming back from the brink of death, sometimes the functioning of the survival mechanism gets restored without the previous hyperactivity.

Franklin Wolff

While studying philosophy as a graduate student at Harvard University, after having completed an undergraduate degree in mathematics at Stanford University, Franklin Wolff "became convinced of the probable existence of a transcendent mode of consciousness that could not be comprehended within the limits of our ordinary forms of knowledge" (Merrell-Wolff, 1994, pp. 251–252). According to Wolff, our ordinary forms of knowledge consist of sensory impressions and rational thinking, which do not allow us to know anything other than the "appearance of things" (Merrell-Wolff, 1995a, p. 32). In 1936, after 24 years of effort (Barušs, 1996), Wolff realized that he did not need to silence his thinking as he had been attempting to do in meditation, but simply to isolate "the subjective pole of consciousness" (Merrell-Wolff, 1994, p. 263). He conceptualized consciousness metaphorically as primarily streaming from the subject to the object, thereby creating the phenomenal world of one's experience. What Wolff claimed to have been able to do has been to create "a separation in the flow of consciousness"

(Merrell-Wolff, 1995b, p. 147) and to redirect part of the stream back toward the subject. When that has happened, the objects of consciousness have become dimmed and lost much of their relevance, while "the reverse flow toward the subject [has been] like a Light highly intensified" (Merrell-Wolff, 1995b, p. 147). Wolff likened the resultant intensification of consciousness "to the rising of another Sun so bright as to dull forever thereafter the light of the physical sun" (Merrell-Wolff, 1995b, p. 147). For Wolff, turning the outgoing stream of consciousness through 180 degrees led to a transcendent state of consciousness in which the subject–object duality characteristic of ordinary thinking was replaced by *consciousness-without-an-object-and-without-a-subject* (Merrell-Wolff, 1994, p. 421). *Appearance* in the ordinary waking state of consciousness had given way to *reality* in the transcendent state.

Wolff conceptualized a continuous relationship between the everyday and mystical states. In particular, for Wolff, "Reality is inversely proportional to Appearance" (Merrell-Wolff, 1995a, p. 61), so that the more that something can be conceptually grasped, the less it is real, whereas the more something is tenuous, the closer it is to reality. The turning of the light of consciousness upon itself revealed that which is real using a third way of knowing, which Wolff named *introception* (Merrell-Wolff, 1995b, p. 144), whereby knowledge results from identity with that which is known. This is reminiscent of Wren-Lewis's sense of knowing from the inside. From the outside, which is to say, from the perspective of everyday consciousness, such knowledge is so abstract and universal that it is "barely discernible as being of noetic character" (Merrell-Wolff, 1994, p. 265). Such is the noetic quality of introception.

In a like manner, by examining the events that occurred for him, Wolff has elaborated on some of the other characteristics of mystical experiences that we enumerated previously. For example, Wolff has discussed both the nature of unity as well as the sense in which it was permanent. He has said that transcendence brought with it a change of self-identity so that he felt as though "the roots of [his] consciousness" had been "forcibly removed" from the domain of everyday existence and "instantaneously transplanted into a supernal region" (Merrell-Wolff, 1994, p. 264) in which he was identified with "THAT which supports this universe" (p. 51). Just as in the case of Wren-Lewis, Wolff has maintained that the change of self-identity has not only been permanent but seemed to be "a much more normal state of emplacement than ever the old rooting had been" (Merrell-Wolff, 1994, p. 264). However, he did not continuously remain in a transcendent state of consciousness but moved in and out of it, noting each time a discontinuity so that "one consciousness blacks out and immediately another consciousness takes over" (Merrell-Wolff, 1995a, p. 51). In fact, Wolff said that he has "deliberately passed up and down, trying to maintain continuity of consciousness" during the transition but that "it could not be done" (Merrell-Wolff, 1995a, p. 51). He has used the term *escalating self* to refer to the identity of the self that can move between the two states of consciousness.

Wolff has tried to characterize the positive valence of the transcendent events that occurred for him. For example, he compared the feelings during transcendent events to inebriation "with that other wine of which the Persian mystics sing" (Merrell-Wolff, 1995a, p. 23). However, even drug metaphors fell short. "The mystics will write in terms that seem like impossible exaggeration, but the fact is that there is no language whatsoever that is not an understatement in the expressing of the value" (Merrell-Wolff, 1995a, p. 50). In fact, "to suggest the Value of this transcendental state of consciousness requires concepts of the most intensive possible connotation and the modes of expression that indicate the most superlative value art can devise" (Merrell-Wolff, 1994, p. 263; see also Baruš, 2007b, 2007c). Using our sixth thematic thread, we would characterize this as deepening of meaning or vertical meaningfulness.

MEDITATION

Meditation refers to mental strategies whose purpose is to effect transcendent states of consciousness (cf. Baruš, 1996; Gifford-May & Thompson, 1994), although the word is frequently restricted to those strategies that have been practiced in Asia and to their reformulations in Western cultures (E. Taylor, 1997). Well, even such a broad definition gives perhaps undue coherence to the variety of practices with different aims and methods that have been subsumed under the rubric of meditation. Nonetheless, one way to think about meditation is to conceptualize the mind as the gateway to transcendent states of consciousness. The ordinary functioning of the mind blocks transcendent states from occurring, so we need some mental techniques to remove the obstructive aspects of the mind. *Meditation* is the name given to those techniques (cf. Eifring, 2018). Let us start this discussion by looking at the history of meditation research and the way in which that has transformed the nature of meditation, then identify three different styles of meditation, and then look at a particular program of self-transformation in which a number of different techniques are used.

A Very Brief History of Meditation Research

Early published studies about meditation were concerned mainly with *transcendental meditation* (*TM*; E. Taylor, 1997), a type of meditation that was introduced by Maharishi Mahesh Yogi upon his arrival in North America in 1959 after having "spent almost his entire life in India" (Mason, 1994, p 4). The basic technique, as I understand it, consists of repeating a word that appears to have no meaning over and over again silently to oneself while sitting with eyes closed for about 20 minutes. Whenever one finds oneself thinking about anything other than that word, one redirects attention to the word and resumes its repetition. The word, called a *mantra*, is one of a number of words derived from "standard Sanskrit sources" (Goleman, 1977/1988, p. 67) that have been assigned in the past to a person by TM instructors on the basis of their age group (Morris, 1984; Persinger, 1980; Scott, 1978).

Charles Tart (1971) reported his "personal experience of doing TM for one year" (p. 135). He found that he became a more relaxed person with an increased ability to still his mind. He found initially that both recent and remote memories of unprocessed psychological material would occur during meditation tapering off and giving way to "current-events material" (Tart, 1971, p. 137) over the course of the year. Contrary to claims of its benefits by members of the TM organization, Tart did not experience "a joyful, oceanic feeling" and loss of "all sense of self" (Tart, 1971, p. 136). There were some apparent physiological changes in that he found that, while meditating, he had increased resistance to cold, and his enjoyment of alcohol decreased, in part because he began to get headaches after drinking more than small amounts of alcohol (Tart, 1971). Individuals' experiences in meditation can be quite different from one another, and it is not clear from case studies to what extent any changes are the result of meditation, the result of nonspecific factors associated with meditation (such as motivation to meditate), or independent of meditation altogether. I practiced TM as best I could for 2 years but could not identify any benefits from it.

In the early 1970s, Herbert Benson and his colleagues began to report the results of physiological studies of TM practitioners. What they found was a pattern of decreased bodily arousal during the time of meditation that Benson called the *relaxation response* (Benson, 1975). Furthermore, investigators found that the relaxation response could be induced in various ways other than TM, including a technique devised by Benson in which the word *one* played a role similar to that of the mantra in TM. However it has been induced, the relaxation response has been associated with lowered heart rates (Benson, 1983), reduced blood pressure (Andresen, 2000), lowered respiratory rates, and decreased oxygen consumption (Benson, 1983). The relaxation response and some forms of meditation have been beneficial in the treatment of hypertension, cardiovascular diseases, headaches, pain, premenstrual syndrome, insomnia, infertility, anxiety, depression, hostility, and stress. Because of the demonstrated effectiveness of meditation for alleviating these various disorders, it has become part of the therapeutic repertoire of many health professionals (Andresen, 2000). A national survey in 2012 in the United States led to the estimate that 18 million people were using meditation "as a complementary health approach" (Hasenkamp, 2018, p. 539).

We should note, though, that not all forms of meditation are designed to result in relaxation. And, even when they are, they can sometimes lead to increased levels of stress for some individuals, in some cases because meditation appears to facilitate recall of traumatic childhood memories (J. J. Miller, 1993). Nor is relaxation itself a homogeneous state but rather a diverse array of mental states and behaviors associated in various ways with the relaxation response (cf. J. C. Smith, Amutio, Anderson, & Aria, 1996). It is also noteworthy that the appropriation of meditation by Western cultures has fundamentally changed its context. Whereas the intention of meditation in Asia has been the cultivation of radical transformations of consciousness to resolve existential issues, it has found a place in the West as a tool for the enhancement of physical and psychological well-being, with a particular emphasis on the reduction of blood pressure and stress. The validity of isolating these techniques from their cultural contexts has been questioned (Eifring, 2018; Kirmayer, 2015).

But even in the West, meditation is not just about relaxation. In a recent online survey by Cassandra Vieten and her colleagues (2018), of 1,120 meditation practitioners solicited through online resources, aspects of mystical experiences, such as positive mood, ineffability, and transcendence, were frequently endorsed. The majority of respondents claimed to have also had unusual experiences. For instance, 30% of respondents reported having experienced clairvoyance or telepathy "many times or always," and 31% reported having had the experience "of objects moving or changing without apparent physical cause" (Vieten et al., 2018, p. 8). As we have seen throughout this book, whenever we pass from the ordinary waking state into altered states of consciousness, the frequency of occurrence of anomalous phenomena increases. This resonates with our fourth thematic thread, concerning the extent to which experiences in meditation are extraordinary.

Styles of Meditation

What are we doing when we meditate? Upon examining a range of meditation practices, I have found that most of them have two structural components: support and content. *Support* refers to the psychological processes that are required to maintain the meditation, whereas *content* is what the meditation is about. Support itself has at least three components: attention, monitoring, and volition. *Attention* refers to the act of attending to specific contents; *monitoring* refers to introspective tracking of what is happening during meditation; and *volition* is the ability to change what is happening, including redirecting attention. Content has at least three mental tracks to which we can attend: thoughts, words, and images. *Thoughts* refer to concepts that we can have in our minds, *words* refers to silent self-talk, and *images* refers to pictures that we can have in our minds that are separate from actual sensory perceptions. There are three main patterns of deployment of these psychological processes, which we will label as concentrative, witnessing, and reflexive *styles of meditation*.

In *concentrative meditation*, sometimes also called *focused attention meditation* (e.g., Eifring, 2018), one seeks to confine attention to a single object of thought, sometimes called a *seed* (Baruss, 1996). There is a great variety of ways in which that is done, even within specific traditions. As we have seen already, in TM meditation, purportedly derived from Hindu sources (Mason, 1994), a meditator focuses on the repetition of a word. Buddhist meditators may seek to imagine a visual representation of the Buddha (Wallace, 1998). Western forms of concentrative meditation can include keeping one's mind on a particular theme, such as love for one's fellow human beings (Ferrucci, 1982). What typically happens, not surprisingly given what we know about thinking, is that spontaneous thoughts arise that are unrelated to the chosen topic. When that happens, as done in TM, one can simply return one's attention to the object of meditation. However, controlling one's thoughts means that one needs to introspect so as to monitor their contents and to exercise one's will in order to redirect the stream of consciousness back to the object of meditation as well as to persist in one's task (cf. Wallace, 1998). From a cognitive point of view, concentrative meditation can be regarded as a vigilance task in which we are waiting to detect the occurrence of mind wandering, at which time we respond by returning the stream of thinking to the seed.

As one succeeds in resting one's thoughts on the seed of meditation, boredom can ensue. The idea is that it is precisely at that point that persistence is necessary to break the hold of the mind on one's consciousness. And when that is done, the mind might release into a silent space behind the thoughts. Or deeper meanings associated with the seed might be precipitated into one's consciousness. Or the subject merges with the object of meditation so that only the object remains. Or merging with the object leads to the collapse of intentionality, the subject–object structure of the mind, resulting in *nonduality*. More prosaically perhaps, such meditation practice has been associated with improved attention, less mind wandering, and greater introspective accuracy (Hasenkamp, 2018).

A second style of meditation is *witnessing meditation*, sometimes also called *open monitoring meditation* (Eifring, 2018), in which the idea is not to control the objects of attention but to simply watch the mind wander in an effort to understand its nature. When I lived for a while in the Canadian Atlantic province of Nova Scotia, sometimes on Sunday mornings I made my way to a drafty farmhouse hidden away from the main roads in the highlands along the province's northwestern shore. A small group of us, sometimes just two or three, would gather to practice witnessing meditation led by an elderly Buddhist meditation practitioner. A fire would often be burning in a fireplace in the meditation room as we sat on cushions on the floor facing a low altar furnished with burning candles and other religious paraphernalia. In the witnessing meditation that we practiced, the idea was to sit with open eyes and a straight back and to pay attention to whatever sensations, feelings, and thoughts occurred for us. As mental events took place, we were to label and dismiss them without judgment. If judgments occurred, they were to be regarded as just more mental events and perfunctorily labeled and dismissed. If our minds wandered, upon realizing that they had wandered, we were to label and dismiss that realization as well. The point was to witness what had transpired in the mind rather than try to suppress or change it. The process of attending to, labeling, and dismissing mental events is known as *mindfulness*. Sustained mindfulness is said to eventually develop into *insight* into the nature of the mind (Barušs, 1996; see also Cebolla et al., 2017).

Not used to sitting on a cushion with my legs tucked underneath me, within minutes of the beginning of witnessing meditation, I would find that my legs would begin to ache. As time went by, the aching in my legs would become so painful that I could barely contain myself. Thus, my meditation practice consisted of noticing and labeling the pain in my legs. After a half hour or so, we would stop the sitting meditation and practice walking meditation for a while. In walking meditation, the idea was to pay particular attention to the kinesthetic sensations that were present as we walked. In fact, restricting the locus of attention constitutes one of the variations of witnessing meditation (Tart, 1988). As another example, during sitting meditation, one could pay attention only to sensations in the left half of the body. Another variation is not to label mental events but just to register them (Baruš, 1996). After walking we would practice more sitting meditation. As another change of pace, some-one would read aloud for a while from a Buddhist text. Then we would go back to sitting meditation practice.

In a structural sense, in witnessing meditation, attention is directed to the objects of consciousness, that is to say, to the thoughts themselves. In my case, I was thinking about my aching legs. However, the focus of the meditation is really on the introspective process whereby one recognizes which thoughts one is having, with the will being used to sustain that mindfulness. In psychol-ogy, mindfulness itself has been lifted from the context of meditation practice and regarded as a potential ongoing feature of one's experience, with various associated cognitive benefits (Colman, 2015; Langer, 1989).

In concentrative meditation, the point is to attend to a chosen object of consciousness. In witnessing meditation, the focus is on monitoring the contents of the experiential stream. In contrast to both concentrative and witnessing meditation, when *reflexive meditation* is practiced, attention is placed on the subject of consciousness, the one who does the monitoring and willing and for whom there are objects of consciousness. Wait, you say—that is impossible given the intentional structure of consciousness. If we think of a continuum between identification with the subject and identification with the object, then we can imagine the possibility of isolating and becoming absorbed in the experience of consciousness, just as we could imagine becoming identified with the seed in concentrative meditation. In fact, when Franklin Wolff carried out the reflexive exercise of turning consciousness back on itself, he ended up momentarily identified with the pure self, without objects (Merrell-Wolff, 1994, 1995a, 1995b). So in meditation we can stretch the intentional structure of the mind to identify with the self or to identify with the objects. But to actually turn one's attention so as to perceive the subject as an object . . . nope.

And yet, for Buddhist meditation teacher Alan Wallace (2017), the point is to try anyway and just see what happens. And what happens, sometimes, is that the intentional structure of the mind starts the creak and groan. For Dudjom Lingpa (2016),

> at times it seemed as if that which appeared and that which was aware nondually
> dispersed outward . . . and then converged inward again. On other occasions,

that which appeared and that which was aware were nondually and spontaneously objectified and then naturally disappeared. At other times appearances
and awareness were nondually self-emergent and self-dissolving, such that
I understood that they were not projected out from within the body. (p. 149)

Eventually, the intentional structure of the mind breaks, so that the subject–
object distinction disappears and a person is left in a state of nonduality.
Another way of saying this is that a person's consciousness is usually psychologically trapped in such a way that all experience is structured by subject–
object duality until that structure collapses. This can happen not only through
the practice of reflexive meditation but also with other forms of meditation
in which the effort is to realize nonduality directly (Josipovic, 2014), or even
through some types of life experiences, such as trauma (Ataria, 2018). For
Wolff, his identification with the self was momentary, before it opened up
into the occurrence of a nondual state of consciousness.

Mathematical Yoga

According to Franklin Wolff, the strength of Western cultures has been
the development of theoretical thinking, which can be used in the effort
to attain transcendent states of consciousness. Following upon ideas suggested by Northrop (1946/1966), Wolff has maintained that there is a theoretic continuum ranging from a determinate pole, represented by science
and mathematics, to an indeterminate pole, the "transcendent ground of
knowledge" (Barušs, 1996, p. 155). Concepts that are concerned with physical
objects can be said to be *perceptually thick* but *introceptually thin*. Such concepts
belong toward the determinate pole of the theoretic continuum. On the other
hand, abstract concepts, such as mathematical constructions, lie closer to the
indeterminate pole and can be said to be *perceptually thin* but *introceptually
thick*. That is to say, concepts lying toward the indeterminate pole have something of the nature of transcendent knowledge about them (Merrell-Wolff,
1995b). At the borderline of the relative and transcendent lie concepts that
are determinate–indeterminate. "Insofar as they are determinate, they can be
used for communication" (Barušs, 1996, p. 90), whereas their indeterminate
aspect means that they are metaphorically "filled with something from above"
(Merrell-Wolff, 1995a, p. 36). In fact, for Wolff, determinate-indeterminate
concepts are not important of themselves. Rather, their value lies in their
use as vessels for the transcendent.

For Wolff, because mathematical constructions are perhaps the "most
abstract concepts in Western cultures, mathematics is the most faithful representation of introceptual knowledge and thus becomes the route by which we
can approach transcendent states of consciousness most directly, most freely"
(Merrell-Wolff, 1995a, p. 27). According to Wolff, there are three aspects to
mathematical yoga, the use of mathematics as an approach to transcendent
states of consciousness. The first is engagement with mathematics so that
one's thinking tends toward determinate-indeterminate concepts. The second

is the cultivation of meaning so that mathematical constructions are not regarded as vacuous arrays of symbols but embraced within one's meaningful understanding of reality. And since movement toward the indeterminate pole of the theoretic continuum appears to the personality as movement toward nothingness resulting in self-annihilation, the third aspect of a mathematical approach to transcendent consciousness is complete emptying of oneself; in other words, surrender. This is Wolff's reorientation toward meditation based on the strengths of Western cultures (Baruš, 2018b).

Finders Course

I spent 2 years practicing meditation and nothing interesting happened. Huston Smith spent 20 years practicing meditation and nothing interesting happened. We did consider the recent survey finding that individuals who meditate do have some interesting experiences. But is there a way of optimizing the occurrence of substantial shifts toward transcendence? Perhaps.

Jeffrey Martin sought out, interviewed, and gathered quantitative data from about 60 people from around the world who appeared to be living in an ongoing transcendent state of consciousness, which he called *persistent nonsymbolic experience*. Upon examination of his data, he found that he could place people into one of a number of *locations*, namely, Location 1, Location 2, and so on, with increasing numbers indicating greater degrees of subjective well-being. According to Martin, the primary characteristic associated with increasing locations and the sense of well-being is the attenuation of the *narrative self*, a part of the psyche that constructs stories about who one is, what is happening, and so on. Less mind wandering perhaps. Along with greater mental quiet, an individual's emotions become increasingly skewed toward positive emotions so that, by Location 3, negative emotions such as anger, sadness, and anxiety, including existential anxiety, are gone, and a single positive emotion remains that is a blend of love, joy, and peace. By Location 4, the positive emotions along with the negative ones have disappeared. And there are locations beyond Location 4 (Martin, 2019). Martin asked his participants what they had done that they thought had allowed them to shift into persistent non-symbolic experience. There were about a half-dozen techniques that they had used. So Martin created an 18-week online course, the Finders Course, starting with positive psychology exercises to create a positive tone followed by variations on the different meditation techniques that had been reported to him. Throughout, he collected self-report psychological data to determine what changes were taking place. And after running the course nine times, Martin claimed that 73% to 74% of participants who complete it transition to one of the locations on the continuum (Martin, 2017). Given the historical failure rates associated with meditation, if true, that is a striking level of achievement.

One of my students, Kelsey Thomas, and I surveyed the Finders Course alumni to try to determine for ourselves what was happening. We created an online questionnaire and invited the alumni to take part. Once we had received informed consent, we asked participants to sit quietly with eyes open for 1 minute, after which time we asked that they fill out the Phenomenology of Consciousness Inventory (PCI). Fifty-five participants completed the entire survey. They were spread across locations, including six who had not transitioned to a location and nine who were beyond Location 4. The score on a cluster of items that included life satisfaction, joy, and the experience of nonduality increased overall with location. Anger, sadness, and fear, as measured by the PCI, flattened to zero by Location 2 and remained at zero for all higher locations. Love and joy peaked at Location 3 and dropped for higher locations. We found similar patterns for the PCI scores a year later in a second survey with 16 participants. Overall, subject to the limitations of self-report data from our limited samples, our data confirm the psychological profile of Finders Course alumni found by Martin.

EXPLANATIONS OF TRANSCENDENCE

How are we to understand what is happening to a person in the course of having a transcendent experience? What kinds of explanations could account for them? Are transcendent experiences what they appear to be? In particular, do they really have the noetic features attributed to them, for example, by Franklin Wolff? Are transcendent states delusions or signs of psychopathology? Are they dangerous or beneficial? Here we return to our thematic threads, in particular our perspectives concerning consciousness, beliefs about consciousness and reality, and the distinction between lateral and vertical meaningfulness. Let us begin by looking at the neurophysiological correlates of some forms of meditation, then reductionist theories, and, finally postmaterialist theories.

Neurophysiology of Meditation

We have considered the activity of the brain's default mode network. There has been a tendency within the last decade or so of moving away from attributing cognitive functions to specific anatomical structures, the so-called *modular approach*, to assigning them to networks of anatomical structures, a *network approach* (Bressler & Menon, 2010). So, whereas some of the nodes of the DMN are more active in some situations than others, the DMN, overall, is an "integrated system for autobiographical, self-monitoring and social cognitive functions" (Bressler & Menon, 2010, p. 285). Let us consider two additional networks: the central executive network and the salience network. The *central executive network* (CEN) is considered to be engaged in cognitive regulation, including attention, working memory (Bressler & Menon, 2010, p. 277), and self-control (G. E. Miller et al., 2018). The *salience network* (SN), is associated with assigning meaning to incoming stimuli (G. E. Miller et al., 2018) and regulating the balance of DMN and CEN (Bressler & Menon, 2010).

With these networks in mind, let us go back to the cycle that we defined for concentrative meditation: focused attention on the seed, followed by mind wandering, followed by becoming aware of mind wandering, and then returning the brain to focused attention on the seed. In a brain-imaging study in which participants pushed a button when they found that their thoughts had strayed, those cognitive activities were found to map onto the expected neural networks. In particular, initial focused awareness corresponds to activation of CEN, mind wandering was associated with the DMN, awareness of mind wandering coincided with SN, and shifting back to focused attention engaged the CEN (Hasenkamp, 2018). As a different example, states of nonduality have been associated with an increase in the simultaneous activation of DMN and extrinsic networks that respond to external stimuli, matching the phenomenal experience of losing the distinction between self and object (Josipovic, 2014).

Reductionist Theories

Perhaps the simplest explanation for transcendent states of consciousness is to disregard any meaning that they might have and simply point to the corresponding neural substrates as an explanation for their occurrence, such as the ones that we considered in the previous section. As an additional example, activity in the DMN is lower during flow states (Josipovic, 2014), so we could say that that shift in brain activity is the cause of the phenomenal experience of absorption in one's task. And there have been other neurophysiological explanations of transcendence (e.g., Cook & Persinger, 1997; Mandell, 1980; Persinger, 1987, 2001).

Suppose for a moment that eventually the specific brain activity associated with transcendence were to have been correctly identified. Would its identification suffice as an explanation of transcendent states of consciousness? The answer to that question depends upon one's beliefs about the nature of consciousness and reality. If reality is thought to be physical, in a naive sense, and consciousness is assumed to be a by-product of brain activity, then identification of the brain processes that produce specific alterations of consciousness would be all that one could hope to achieve by way of an explanation. However, if one were to have transcendentalist leanings, whereby consciousness would be considered to exist apart from the brain, then knowledge of brain activity during transcendence would not be an explanation but just the identification of neurological correlates of events occurring in transcendent states of consciousness.

The analogy of a television program can be used to illustrate the difference between physicalist and transcendentalist beliefs. All I can see when I watch a hockey game on television are images moving across a screen. If I did not know any better, I would be misled into believing that the hockey game was taking place inside the television set. I could erroneously prove to myself that the television was the source of the hockey game by playing a digital file of another hockey game and seeing the same sorts of images on the screen. Analogously, the fact that I can identify the neural networks corresponding to various versions of transcendence, and can induce activity in the appropriate networks perhaps by using psychedelic drugs, does not mean that there cannot be actual transcendent phenomenological events that are being reflected by that activation (cf. Beauregard, 2012; d'Aquili & Newberg, 1999, 2000a, 2000b; Richards, 2016; Rosch, 1999; Saver & Rabin, 1997).

Inherent in efforts to reduce mystical experiences to underlying physiological activity is the assumption that religious attributions by those having the experiences are actually misattributions, in that neurophysiological activity gets misinterpreted in noetic terms. There are many variations on the explanation of mysticism as *erroneous attribution* (Hood et al., 1996, p. 228). Sigmund Freud, for example, postulated that feelings of unity are recollections from one's infancy of unity, perhaps with one's mother, to which religious beliefs get attached. According to this view, two errors are involved in mystical experiences: "an erroneous belief in the existence of a God, and the erroneous interpretation of regressive experiences as evidence of union with God" (Hood et al., 1996, p. 229). Other psychoanalysts have gone even further by "declaring mystical experience to be a sign of severe regression and a loss of reality orientation" (Wulff, 2000, p. 419). Certainly, if mystical experiences are conceptualized as misattributions, then those who have them risk being labeled as deluded or mentally ill (Hood et al., 1996).

One of the observations often made regarding mystical experiences is that they have common characteristics, be they physiological or phenomenological, that are independent of one's interpretation of them. We have been using a list of characteristics derived from Walter Pahnke although there are others (e.g., A. L. Smith & Tart, 1998; Stace, 1960). However, those who advocate a *contextual* (Wulff, 2000) or *constructivist* explanation maintain that the contents of mystical experiences, as for all experiences, are a product of one's culture, which would explain why there are cultural differences in religious experiences (Barušs, 1996). For example, "the Jewish mystic rarely, if ever" experiences "loss of self in unity with God" (Katz, 1978, p. 34). Rather, the Jewish mystics' experiences are ones of "loving intimacy" (Katz, 1978, p. 35) with a God that remains other than oneself. It has been argued, furthermore that reports of such experiences are not just the result of cultural overlays on what are inherently unitive experiences (Katz, 1978).

Transcendence as Exceptional Functioning

One of the problems with a contextual approach to mystical experiences is that some such experiences appear to have had unexpected features that had not been predicted within the experiencer's frame of reference. Such has been the case, for example, with the Christian contemplative Bernadette Roberts (1993), who said that she "had fallen outside [her] own, as well as the traditional frame of reference, when [she] came upon a path that seemed to begin where the writers on the contemplative life had left off" (pp. 10–11). In the 1986 consciousness survey by Robert Moore and myself, the claim that one's "ideas about life have changed dramatically in the past" (Barušs, 1990, p. 123) was correlated with claims of having had transcendent or mystical experiences. While such a correlation does not establish causality, it is consistent with the reports of epiphanies in transcendent states of consciousness. The antithesis of the contextual position is that of the *perennial philosophy* (Huxley, 1945), whereby mystical experiences are conceptualized as transcultural events interpreted according to the "categories, beliefs, and language that are brought to them" (Barušs, 1996, p. 75).

Sometimes transcendent experiences are explained as a further stage in the evolution of consciousness (Hood et al., 1996). That mysticism is a form of *evolved consciousness* (Hood et al., 1996, p. 228) was the position taken by Richard Maurice Bucke (1901/1991), who said that "Cosmic Consciousness . . . is a higher form of consciousness than that possessed by the ordinary man" (p. 1). Bucke has spent considerable effort describing the purported historical development of the capacity to discriminate colors as an analogy for the evolutionary development of cosmic consciousness. According to Bucke, while the capacity for seeing in color has become widespread, the relative frequency of color-blindness attests to its evolutionary recency. Analogously, cosmic consciousness, Bucke believed, was a relatively new faculty that had been seen in only a handful of the "best specimens of the race" (Bucke, 1901/1991, p. 65). Other investigators, however, who have conceptualized transcendent events in naturalistic terms have "assumed that mystical states are common" (Hood et al., 1996, p. 231) and have solicited and classified reports of their occurrence (Hood et al., 1996; see also Maxwell & Tschudin, 1990; S. Taylor, 2017). And, as we continue to understand transcendent states and create practices and technologies to shift people into them, as Martin (2019) has done, will transcendent states become the ordinary waking state for most of humanity as they already are for many of the individuals who have completed the Finders Course?

Perhaps, consistent with the perennial philosophy and evolutionary theory, transcendent states of consciousness are what they appear to be, a form of *heightened awareness* (Hood et al., 1996, p. 228) in which a person encounters the ground of being, however such an encounter is conceptualized. The key to this explanation is the recurrence of a noetic quality in reports of mystical experiences. Those who have awakened to a mystical state are convinced that what they encounter is real (Yaden et al., 2017). But is it? With hypnosis, we saw that individuals can have enhanced confidence about their mistaken knowledge of verifiable aspects of reality. In fact, it could be that the sorts of brain changes associated with transcendence, such as the loss of self-awareness, could also erode the ability to make good metacognitive judgments (cf. Mandell, 1980).

When I asked this question of Allan Smith, who has experienced a profound spontaneous transcendent state (A. L. Smith & Tart, 1998), he said that the difference between ordinary consciousness and cosmic consciousness was like the difference between seeing in black and white and seeing in color. A person who sees in color sees the same things as the person who sees in black and white except that what they see has an added dimension to it. In the same way knowledge during cosmic consciousness is synthetic, in that it consists of adding to one's knowledge rather than replacing that knowledge with something else. Furthermore, just as it is impossible to convince someone who is color-blind of the existence of color, so it is not possible to prove to those who have never experienced it, that transcendent knowledge is true knowledge.

Another way in which Allan Smith has conceptualized knowledge resulting from cosmic consciousness has been to liken it to seeing a new color while in a nonordinary state of consciousness and subsequently being able to visualize the new color at will in an ordinary state of consciousness. Whether or not the new color is a hallucination or delusion is beside the point, since its existence through whatever means becomes a fact about the real world. Allan Smith told me is that "what one learns about the nature of reality from cosmic consciousness is self validating in the same way" (see also Josipovic, 2014).

SUMMARY

Once again, in this chapter, alterations of consciousness have pushed the boundaries of our ordinary understanding of reality, this time by looking at transcendent experiences. Unlike the phenomena of Chapter 6, the question of psychopathology barely arises with regard to transcendent states, our seventh thematic thread. On the contrary, we seek to cultivate flow and to meditate for the sake of physical and psychological health, our eighth thematic thread. But meditation and spiritual strategies more generally are aimed at more than well-being. We can try to free ourselves from the constraints of our everyday ways of thinking about the world and seek states of consciousness in which the ground of being is revealed, bringing us back to the question of the third thematic thread of the extent to which our experiences are delusional or veridical. Suppose we succeed unexpectedly, as in the case of Wren-Lewis, or as the culmination of years of effort, as in the case of Wolff, or within the course of several weeks such as for some of the Finders Course alumni. What do such mystical experiences mean, our fifth thematic thread? What do they tell us? In what ways do they expand our understanding of reality, our second thematic thread concerning transcendence? I leave it to the reader to answer these questions.

There is one last class of alterations of consciousness left to consider, perhaps the most controversial of all: that associated with death. Let us see if we can push the boundaries of our knowledge even further. Let us turn to the final topic.

9

Death

What happens when we die? Does consciousness get extinguished, or does it survive in some form? Is the altered state of death a state of oblivion, or is it one of seemingly normal or perhaps even enhanced functioning? On the one hand, within scientism, these are questions that are not supposed to be asked. We are supposed to believe that consciousness is a by-product of the brain so that when the brain ceases to function, so does consciousness. Popular opinion, on the other hand, holds that life does continue after death. In a 1982 Gallup poll, 67% of respondents from the general population claimed that they believed in life after death, whereas the figures were only 32% for doctors and 16% for scientists (Fenwick & Fenwick, 1995). Moore and I found that 26% of our 1986 sample of 334 academics and professionals (Barušs, 1990) and 27% of our 1996 sample of 212 consciousness researchers agreed that "personal consciousness continues after physical death" (Barušs & Moore, 1998, p. 487). Within authentic science, questions about life after death are not a matter of belief but a matter of examining whatever relevant evidence bears on them. What, then, does the evidence reveal? Let us leave that question for the end of this chapter. In the meantime, there are alterations of consciousness associated with death that are intrinsically interesting.

It is important to note that in the following discussion I am describing people's experiences. I also posit theories as to what these experiences may mean, but the occurrence of the experiences themselves is not an issue. What is an issue are the meanings that these experiences often have for those for

http://dx.doi.org/10.1037/0000200-009
Alterations of Consciousness: An Empirical Analysis for Social Scientists, Second Edition,
by I. Barušs

whom they occur. Not surprisingly, in dealing with fundamental questions concerning our existence, all of our thematic threads arise in this chapter, although some of them are more dominant than others. Is materialism the correct explanation of reality, our second thematic thread? Are experiences associated with death delusional or veridical, our third thematic thread? Are they mundane or extraordinary, our fourth thematic thread? And, of course, is the psyche open or closed, our 10th thread?

OUT-OF-BODY EXPERIENCES

We have already encountered out-of-body experiences throughout this book, when examining sensory restriction, dreaming, hypnosis, trance, drug-induced states, and transcendent states. Let us now directly consider their characteristics, the possibility of veridical perception during out-of-body experiences, and a cognitive theory to account for them.

Characteristics of Out-of-Body Experiences

An *out-of-body experience* (OBE) is an experience in which a person has a "somaesthetic sense of being located outside" (Alvarado, 2000, p. 184) of their physical body, even though sometimes they may otherwise feel as though they were in their ordinary state of consciousness (Tart, 1998). The prevalence of OBEs is about 10% in the general population, 25% among college students, 42% for people with schizophrenia, 44% among marijuana users, 48% for those belonging to parapsychology groups, and 88% among fantasy-prone individuals (Alvarado, 2000). Moore and I found figures of 23% and 31% in our 1986 and 1996 surveys, respectively (Baruš, 1990; Baruš & Moore, 1998). Furthermore, there is a tendency for those reporting having had OBEs to report having had more than one (Alvarado, 2000).

The following example is a report of an OBE that was written by one of my students.

> There have been a few incidents in the past in which I have awoken in the middle of the night and been unable to move. It is as though my mind is wide awake, perhaps more so than usual, and yet my body is in a coma. This can be very scary and yet exhilarating at the same time. One time in particular stands out. One I will never forget.
>
> I awoke in this state one night, only I wasn't in my bedroom. I was looking down at my sleeping boyfriend in his apartment. I could see everything clearly and knew without a doubt that I was not dreaming. I saw his dog in the corner and the pile of clothes next to the bed. I knew I was there and yet my body was asleep at my house.
>
> I awoke moments later and called my boyfriend. I immediately began to describe his bedroom in detail—the red shirt I had bought him crumpled next to his pillow, the position of the dog, the half-drunk glass of water on the night stand—details that I never would have known had I not been there. And they

were all true. We were both terrified and yet had never felt closer. I had had an out-of-body experience, where my mind journeyed to its own destination and my body was left behind.

OBEs tend to be life-affirming experiences for those who have had them, although for 40% of those who have had OBEs, they can be associated with strange sounds and bodily vibrations that can be extreme and frightening (Steffen, Wilde, & Cooper, 2017). Robert Monroe (1972/1975) experienced a "'vibration,' steady and unvarying in frequency" (p. 30), accompanied by a roaring sound that sent him to his physician, a psychiatrist, and a psychologist seeking an explanation. Eventually the vibrations presaged journeys out of the body (Monroe, 1972/1975).

If it is possible that we really can leave our bodies while we are alive, then it is plausible that that may also be what happens when we die. That is the relevance of research concerning OBEs to the *survival hypothesis*, which is the hypothesis "that a disembodied consciousness or some such discarnate element of human personality might survive bodily death at least for a time" (Irwin, 1994, p. 183).

Perceptions During Out-of-Body Experiences

In keeping with our third thematic thread, perhaps the most obvious question that comes to mind, upon reading an account such as that of my student, is whether perceptions during OBEs are delusional or veridical. In considering that question, we need to note that only some OBEs pertain to the physical world. Robert Monroe (1994) maintained that OBEs are a way of exploring nonphysical aspects of the universe in which he has encountered intelligent beings, most of whom were not human. Validation of such explorations would require some means of access to events in nonphysical domains. In part, this could be done through the perceptions of others who claim to have similar abilities. Usually the question of validity is confined to OBEs taking place in environments corresponding to the physical world. Based on aggregated data from a number of studies, an average of 19% of experiencers have claimed to have made observations during their OBEs that were verified, although there is reason to distrust that prevalence figure (Alvarado, 2000). Did they really see what was happening? In some cases, such as the example given previously, experiencers can satisfy themselves regarding the accuracy of their perceptions. The overall results of formal investigations, however, have been ambiguous.

The obvious type of experiment to test the idea that veridical perceptions can occur during OBEs would be to have a participant induce an OBE and then identify targets set out by the experimenter. Tart has conducted a number of such studies. In one case he had encountered a woman who claimed that, since childhood, occasionally when she was asleep, she felt that she had awakened mentally and "was floating near the ceiling, looking down on her physical body" (Tart, 1998, pp. 78–79). Tart suggested to her that she make up 10 slips of paper numbered from 1 through 10 to keep in a box beside her bed. Upon retiring for the night, she was to randomly choose one to place facing upward on a bedside table without looking at it. If she found herself outside her body during the night, she was to observe the number on the piece of paper and check in the morning to see if she had got it right. Subsequently "she reported that she had tried the experiment seven times" (Tart, 1998, p. 79) and had been right about the number each time.

After her successful OBE self-experiment, Tart was able to have the woman spend four nights in his sleep laboratory. Once the participant was lying in bed and the polysomnograph was running smoothly, Tart would go to his office, randomly select a five-digit number from a table of random numbers, write it on a piece of paper, carry the paper in a folder back into the participant's room, and, without exposing the number to the participant, place the paper on a shelf with the number facing upward so that it could only be seen by someone at least 6 feet above the floor. Although she said that she had occasionally been "out" on the first three nights, the participant "had not been able to control her experiences enough to be in position to see the target number" (Tart, 1998, p. 81). However, on the fourth night she awakened at one point and gave the number as 25132, which was, indeed, the correct number. The participant had also thought that the target piece of paper was to have been propped up against the wall but "correctly reported that it was lying flat" (Tart, 1998, p. 81). This is probably the best known of the studies getting positive results (Alvarado, 2000).

There have been studies other than Tart's in which participants with induced OBEs "have been able to identify remote targets to a statistically significant degree" (Irwin, 1994, p. 232) but still others in which no statistically significant effect was found (Alvarado, 2000). In another study conducted by Tart (1998), hypnotized participants who fell in the "upper 10% of hypnotic susceptibility" (p. 91) were given the suggestion that they would have an OBE during which they were to go to another room across the hall and view some target materials that had been placed on a table. "All the participants reported vivid OBEs that seemed like real experiences to them" (Tart, 1998, p. 91), but none of them could identify the target materials.

It may well be that not all OBEs are alike. In particular, the experience of someone who has had spontaneous OBEs on an ongoing basis since childhood is likely to be different from the experience of someone who has been given a hypnotic suggestion to have an OBE. However, we should not be surprised that in some cases targets have been correctly identified by participants, since there is good evidence for extrasensory perception in some situations such as in the Ganzfeld studies reviewed in Chapter 1. The question is, are participants actually outside of their physical bodies in cases of correct identification in OBE studies, or is some other mechanism at work? Given the difficulty in trying to establish the veridicality of out-of-body perceptions, it is not surprising that studies concerning the mechanism by which they take place are even less conclusive (cf. Irwin, 1994). However, as we shall see shortly, there are some features of OBEs in the context of some near-death experiences that provide interesting material for speculation.

A Cognitive Theory of Out-of-Body Experiences

Susan Blackmore, who herself has had OBEs, has advanced a cognitive theory to explain them. The idea is that we are always creating a cognitive model of the world with ourselves in it based on sensory information from the environment surrounding us and from our own bodies. Most of the time, because we engage in various physical activities, we imagine ourselves to be inside our bodies. However, sometimes our images of the world and of ourselves break down. Without sensory input, for example, we are forced to rely upon our memory and imagination to supply us with "a body image and a world" (Blackmore, 1993, p. 177). When that happens, rather than imaging ourselves located within our bodies we may tend to adopt a "bird's-eye view" (Blackmore, 1993, p. 177) that then appears to us to be real. Hence, we think that we are outside of our bodies looking at them.

Support for Blackmore's theory comes from examining the characteristics of those who have frequent OBEs. For example, "people who dream in bird's-eye view or see themselves in their dreams are more likely to have OBEs" (Blackmore, 1993, p. 180). In fact, in some studies but not others, various dream variables such as the presence of vivid dreams, lucid dreams, and flying dreams have been correlated with the incidence of OBEs. In general, researchers have found that the best predictors of someone having OBEs are absorption in imaginal activity, fantasy proneness, high hypnotizability, and dissociative tendencies (Alvarado, 2000; see also Steffen et al., 2017). In other words, those with apparently the most flexible models of the world are those most likely to report having had OBEs. However, it should be noted that because these are correlational studies they do not prove that OBEs are just the product of memory and the imagination. It just may be that those with greater imaginative skills are also those more likely to actually find themselves outside their bodies if there is any sense in which that could actually occur. So this raises our fourth thematic thread: Is there anything extraordinary about OBEs?

NEAR-DEATH EXPERIENCES

A *near-death experience* (*NDE*) is an experience that a person reports having had around the time that they were close to death or thought that they were close to death (cf. Greyson, 2000), with about 9% to 18% of those who have been demonstrably close to death having had an NDE (Greyson, 1998; see also Craffert, 2019; Parnia, Waller, Yeates, & Fenwick, 2001; Zingrone & Alvarado, 2009). Let us examine the characteristics of NDEs, give some examples of NDEs, then look at NDEs of those who are blind, distressing NDEs, and, finally, some explanations for what might be happening.

Characteristics of Near-Death Experiences

By the early 1970s, improvements in resuscitation technology had made it possible to bring people back to life after cardiac arrest so that increasing numbers of people were reporting having had NDEs (Holden, Greyson, & James, 2009). There were two notable physicians who independently identified the occurrence of NDEs among their patients: Elisabeth Kübler-Ross and Raymond Moody. Kübler-Ross had already become famous for improving the care of individuals who were dying (Kübler-Ross, 1997). Raymond Moody, a medical student at the time (Holden, Greyson, & James, 2009), wrote a book *Life After Life*, in which he named, identified, and characterized NDEs on the basis of interviews with people who had come close to physical death in the course of injury or illness, and people who had been resuscitated after they had been thought to be dead (Moody, 1975).

The following are among the features that Moody has found. After a period of intense pain a person may feel a "very real sense of peace and painlessness" (Moody, 1988, p. 7). Forty-eight percent of the time an OBE is reported in which the experiencer sees their own body (Greyson, 2010). They may be "propelled into darkness," for instance, by entering a tunnel, going through a door, or ascending a staircase, only to find that it is a "passageway toward an intense light" (Moody, 1988, p. 9) that does not hurt their eyes. They may meet friends and relatives who have died, as well as, perhaps, a being of light who may be identified as a spiritual figure consistent with their religious tradition (Moody, 1988). There may be a life review in which the events of their life are replayed forward or backward, sometimes in detail that is equivalent to physically living one's life (Atwater, 2007; Ring & Valarino, 1998). Then at some point, they would end up back in their body (Moody, 1988). Note that there are two apparently different locales for NDE events: one that corresponds to the location of the physical body, and a second, more otherworldly environment, sometimes separated from the first by a transition that could take the form of a tunnel.

Do NDEs have anything to do with actual death? After all, experiences similar to NDEs have been reported from people who were nowhere near physical death (Moody, 1977; see also Ring, 1992; van Quekelberghe, Göbel, & Hertweck, 1995). However, one of the most striking aftereffects of NDEs is that many of those who have had them have a dramatically reduced fear of death (Greyson, 1994; see also van Lommel, van Wees, Meyers, & Elfferich, 2001). While this reduced fear of death can occur without belief in an afterlife, in one study 48% of 350 experiencers reported having become convinced of the survival of life after death. Sometimes experiencers have characterized their NDEs as previews of death (Fenwick & Fenwick, 1995).

Loss of the fear of death is just one of the common aftereffects of NDEs that is part of a constellation of changes resulting from an experiencer's feeling that their life has been radically transformed, with the NDE itself redefining their sense of self (Cassol, D'Argembeau, Charland-Verville, Laureys, & Martial, 2019; Noyes, Fenwick, Holden, & Christian, 2009). Scores on existential meaning are higher for those who have had an NDE. An experiencer may feel that they have a mission to accomplish, even if they are not sure exactly what that is. There can be increased compassion toward others (Noyes et al., 2009) although the divorce rate for experiencers is 75% (Atwater, 2007). And there can be a newfound search for knowledge about the nature of consciousness and reality (Noyes et al., 2009).

There can also be anomalous aftereffects. For instance, typically experiencers cannot wear wristwatches because the timepieces will not function when they wear them. More generally, many experience the Pauli effect, whereby mechanical and electrical equipment of various sorts ceases to function in the person's physical presence (Atwater, 2007; cf. Moody, 1975; Noyes et al., 2009). Sometimes various anomalous abilities appear to be turned on as a result of the NDE, including clairvoyance, precognition, and healing abilities (Noyes et al., 2009). There have been cases of anomalous healing apparently resulting from the NDE itself (Atwater, 2007; Khanna, Moore, & Greyson, 2018; Rivas, Dirven, & Smit, 2016). For instance, Anita Moorjani lost 70% of her cancer tumor mass within several days following an NDE in which she saw that if she returned to life, she would be healthy (Moorjani, 2012; Rivas et al., 2016). Let us consider a couple of famous examples of NDEs.

Pam Reynolds's Near-Death Experience

Michael Sabom (1998) studied the case of Pam Reynolds, a woman in the United States who underwent a "surgical procedure known as hypothermic cardiac arrest" (p. 37) to excise an aneurysm in her brain. Among other things, after she was anaesthetized, her eyes were taped shut, molded speakers were placed in her ears, and electroencephalogram (EEG) electrodes were attached to her head to record her brain activity. The speakers were used to expose Pam to 100-decibel clicks that would ordinarily show up on the EEG as auditory-evoked potentials, which are indicative of the brain's capacity to respond to sensory stimulation. A bone saw was used to cut out "a large section of Pam's skull" (Sabom, 1998, p. 41). The blood from her body was routed through a machine used to circulate and cool it. Her heart was stopped, her brain waves flattened, and her body temperature was lowered to 60°F. There was no response to the auditory clicks. Then "the head of the operating table was tilted up" (Sabom, 1998, p. 43) and the bypass machine was switched off so that the blood drained from Pam's brain. The aneurysm was excised and then the process was reversed with the bypass machine turned on, the blood warmed, and the heart restarted. The EEG signals gradually returned, indicating the resumption of brain activity. Seven hours after being brought into it, with about four of those taken up with the surgery itself, Pam was taken from the operating room (Sabom, 1998). Although it can be argued about how little brain activity there must be in order to consider a person dead (Brody, 1999), it is clear in this case that, at least for a period of time, Pam's physical condition was such that she could reasonably have been considered dead were it not for the surgical environment in which she found herself.

According to Pam, she remembers being brought into the operating room and then experiencing "a loss of time" (Sabom, 1998, p. 38). Eventually she became aware of a sound that felt as though it were pulling her out of the top of her head. She could apparently see what was happening in the operating room with vision that was "brighter and more focused and clearer than normal vision" (Sabom, 1998, p. 41). She realized that the sound was coming from the bone saw that the surgeon was using. And although she did not see the saw being used on her head, she did give what turned out to be a somewhat accurate description of the saw and the container that held its blades. She also apparently heard a conversation about her veins and arteries being small, and indeed, the small size of her veins and arteries did become a matter of concern during the surgery. Then at one point, she felt that she was being pulled into a "tunnel vortex" (Sabom, 1998, p. 44) and found herself ascending rapidly. While she was in the vortex she heard her grandmother calling her, so she continued moving through a dark shaft, at the end of which was a "very little tiny pinpoint of light that kept getting bigger and bigger and bigger" (Sabom, 1998, p. 44). It became so bright that she put her hands up in front of her face. However, she could not see her hands even though she knew that they were there. There were different figures in the light that resolved themselves into people, many of whom were deceased relatives whom she recognized, such as her grandmother, uncle, cousin, and grandfather (Sabom, 1998).

During the encounter with her relatives, it was made clear to Pam that she could not go further into the light, as then she would be unable to go back into her body. Her relatives fed her "something sparkly" (Sabom, 1998, p. 45), making her feel strong. Eventually her uncle took her back through the tunnel. When she got to the end of the tunnel, she saw that her body looked "like a train wreck" (Sabom, 1998, p. 46), and she did not want to get back into it. Her uncle communicated to her "that it was like jumping into a swimming pool" (Sabom, 1998, p. 46). Pam saw her body lurch twice. Then her uncle pushed her and she found herself back in her body with the song "Hotel California" playing in the background as the chief surgeon's assistants closed her surgical wounds (Rivas et al., 2016).

We need to look at the timing in this case. First of all, the account of Pam's experience was not documented until more than 3 years after its occurrence, during which time she may have learned details of the events that occurred from those who were familiar with them (Hyman, 2001). Hence, there is more credibility in accounts collected within days of a person's having had an NDE (e.g., van Lommel et al., 2001). Second, Pam's apparent perception of coming out of her body to the sound of the bone saw and hearing the comment about her veins allows us to pin those phenomenological events to the time at which the bone saw was used, given that those events actually did occur in the operating room. At that point Pam was anaesthetized, and the brain should not have been capable of subjective consciousness$_2$. Third, can any of Pam's NDE be attributed to the time during the hypothermic cardiac arrest, when there clearly was no brain activity? Perhaps. It turns out that Pam's heart did have to be restarted twice, and the song "Hotel California" really was being played during the operation. Those phenomenological events could be timed to the tail-end of the hypothermic cardiac arrest (Rivas et al., 2016). But this raises a question: Have there been any NDEs that occurred during a time when there was no brain activity? The answer appears to be yes.

Lloyd Rudy's Patient

Lloyd William Rudy, Jr., and Roberto Amado-Cattaneo were cardiac surgeons who had completed heart surgery for a patient in the late 1990s or early 2000s but could not get his body to function without being connected to the heart–lung machine that they were using, so they pronounced him dead, turned off the machine, left the operating theater, and told the man's wife that he had died. The surgeons took off their gowns, masks, and gloves and returned to the operating theater, where they stood in the doorway in short-sleeved shirts discussing whether there could have been anything else that they could have done to save the patient. No one had turned off the various types of equipment monitoring the patient's blood pressure and pulse, so they continued to create a pile of paper on the floor. A surgical assistant had just closed the body so as to prepare it for an autopsy when the cardiac surgeons noticed some electrical activity of the heart on the monitors after at least 20 and possibly closer to 25 minutes of there not having been any heartbeat or blood pressure. They called the anaesthesiologist and nurses back into the operating theater and were able to resuscitate the man, who had no neurological deficits in spite of the severe insult to his brain from the lack of oxygen (Rivas et al., 2016).

Over the following 2 weeks the surgeons and other hospital staff talked to the patient about any experiences that he may have had during the procedure. According to Rudy, the patient described seeing a tunnel with a bright light at the end of it. And, to the surgeons' surprise, the patient claimed to have floated around the operating room and correctly described various details, including having seen the two cardiac surgeons standing in the doorway with their arms folded and the anaesthesiologist running back into the room. According to Rudy, "He was up there. He described the scene, things that there is no way he knew. I mean, he didn't wake up in the operating room and see all this stuff" (Rivas et al., 2016, p. 74). So now we appear to have a time anchor that ties an NDE narrative to the physical surroundings in which the NDE takes place at a point in time when we can be reasonably confident that the experiencer's brain was essentially silent (cf. Holden, 2009). This raises our third, second, 10th, and ninth thematic threads: Is this veridical perception, as it appears to be? Is there something truly transcendent about this NDE? Is the psyche open or closed? Are we humans more than information-processing devices encased in physical bodies?

Near-Death Experiences of Blind Individuals

There is a group of NDEs that is interesting to consider, namely, the NDEs of people who are blind. Kenneth Ring and Sharon Cooper carried out a retrospective study of NDEs and OBEs of 31 blind participants, 14 of whom had been blind since birth (Ring & Cooper, 1997; Ring & Valarino, 1998). The NDEs of the 21 participants who had had them turned out to be "indistinguishable from those of sighted persons" with regard to the typical features of NDEs such as feelings of peace, OBEs, "traveling through a tunnel" (Ring & Cooper, 1997, p. 108), encountering a light, and experiencing a life review. In particular with regard to visual elements, 15 of the 21 participants "claimed to have had some kind of sight" (Ring & Cooper, 1997, p. 115), with all but one of the remainder having been blind from birth. It is possible that some of the congenitally blind who did not report having had sight may nonetheless have experienced some kind of seeing without having recognized it for what it was. For example, one of the participants said that he did not know how to explain the perceptions that he had had, since he did not know what was meant by "seeing" (Ring & Cooper, 1997, p. 115).

Sight that occurs during an NDE can be particularly clear and detailed, as attested to by both those who had been able to see and then had lost their sight, thereby allowing them to have a basis for comparison, as well as by those who were congenitally blind. For example, one of the participants who had been blind from birth maintained that he could clearly see billions of books in a library during a "transcendental phase of his NDE" (Ring & Cooper, 1997, p. 116), even though he reminded himself at the time that he could not see. The visual impressions of those blind from birth are particularly striking because their brains have never had the opportunity to be properly developed for visual processing (cf. Hirsch & Spinelli, 1971). Thus, for example, those blind from birth or who lost their sight before 5 years of age generally do not report having any "visual imagery in their dreams" (Kerr, 2000, p. 488), although their dreams are otherwise indistinguishable from those of sighted people. Indeed, some of the congenitally blind participants who had had NDEs said that their NDEs were radically different from their dreams precisely because of the presence of visual imagery (Ring & Cooper, 1997).

Closer analysis of the reports of vision during NDEs of the blind participants revealed that the visual aspects of NDEs may not have much to do with seeing as sighted individuals ordinarily do with the eyes, but may be some form of direct knowing that the investigators have called *transcendental awareness*. "In this type of awareness, it is not of course that the eyes see anything; it is rather that the mind itself sees, but more in the sense of 'understanding' or 'taking in' than of visual perception as such" (Ring & Cooper, 1997, p. 140). In a separate study of NDEs, a sighted woman reported that during her NDE she could simultaneously see everything in detail all at once, including the tiles on the ceiling, the tiles on the floor, and "every single hair and the follicle out of which it grew on the head of the nurse standing beside the stretcher" (Ring & Cooper, 1997, p. 139). Transcendental awareness is not confined to those who are blind but in fact may be a manner of perception that occurs more generally during NDEs, OBEs, and transcendent states.

Distressing Near-Death Experiences

Most NDEs that have been reported have been characterized by "profound feelings of peace or bliss, joy, and a sense of cosmic unity" (Greyson & Bush, 1992, p. 95). Indeed, Ring has maintained that "in their essence, *NDEs have nothing inherently to do with death at all*, much less with life after death" (Ring, 1987, p. 174; emphasis in original) but that they are, instead, instances of cosmic consciousness during which a person can become aware of their expanded eternal nature. However, there have also been reports of distressing NDEs.

Bruce Greyson and Nancy Bush, who herself has had a distressing NDE (Bush, 2009), analyzed a sample of 50 accounts of distressing NDEs and classified them into three types. The first type is a prototypical NDE that is interpreted as being terrifying. For example, a man said that he had screamed that he was not ready and asked God to help him after having been drawn through a funnel at the end of which was a blinding light and flashing crystal into which it appeared that he would fall. In some cases the terror has been replaced with peace partway through an NDE, apparently as the experiencer "stops fighting the experience and accepts it" (Greyson & Bush, 1992, p. 100), reminding us of the balance of volition and surrender of our 10th thematic thread.

The second type of distressing NDE is one in which a person has a "paradoxical sensation of ceasing to exist entirely, or of being condemned to a featureless void for eternity" (Greyson & Bush, 1992, p. 101). One woman, for example, during the delivery of her child, found herself "rocketing through space" until she encountered a group of black-and-white circles that "made a clicking sound as they snapped black to white, white to black"; their message was that she had never existed, that she had been "allowed to make it up," that "it was all a joke" (Greyson & Bush, 1992, p. 102), and that that was all that there was to reality. Her experience had been "more than real: absolute reality," and she had been absolutely convinced that she "had seen what the other side was" (Greyson & Bush, 1992, p. 102). This experience is reminiscent of the perturbing experience of the woman who encountered the cosmic diamond cat during DMT intoxication, as recounted in Chapter 7.

A third type of distressing NDE is one involving explicitly hellish imagery. For example, one man who hung himself from a utility shed in an attempt to commit suicide believed that he was surrounded by demons chattering "like blackbirds" (Greyson & Bush, 1992, p. 105), waiting to drag him to hell to torment him. He decided he needed help, so, in his out-of-body state, he ran into the house to alert his wife. When she could not hear him, he "went right into her body" until he "made contact" and "she grabbed a knife from the kitchen" (Greyson & Bush, 1992, p. 105) and ran outdoors to cut him down.

Following upon this research, Bush found that there were three ways in which experiencers responded to their distressing NDEs. For some, these were warnings that functioned as conversion experiences that motivated them to modify their lives toward healthier lifestyles. Others took a reductionistic approach and dismissed them by rationalizing them as some sort of transient brain misbehavior. A third group consisted of people who continued to struggle with the existential implications of their experiences and continued to fear death years later (Bush, 2009). Our eighth thematic thread surfaces: Are NDEs sometimes dangerous? But we have seen this before. This is, on the face of it, an encounter with the shadow, which can occur in dreams, shamanic journeying, possession, alien abduction phenomena, psychedelic trips, transcendent experiences, and, apparently, experiences associated with death.

Explanations of Near-Death Experiences

Overall, explanations of NDEs fall into one of two categories: the dying brain hypothesis and the exosomatic hypothesis. The *dying brain hypothesis* is the proposal that the phenomenological events that occur during an NDE are the result of physiological processes taking place in a brain as it dies. The *exosomatic hypothesis* is the proposal that the phenomenological events that occur during an NDE are the result of subjective aspects of consciousness along with some personality elements leaving the physical body and encountering other realms of existence. In the first theory, the psyche is closed; in the second, it is open, so this discussion directly engages our 10th thematic thread.

Last semester I taught a third-year undergraduate psychology course about NDEs. In addition to the students, there were three other individuals sitting in on the discussions: a former student who had had a profound NDE when her car was hit by a bus, a doctoral student writing her dissertation about the veridicality of NDEs with me, and a resident in psychiatry at our medical school who could explain the details of the medical procedures that are frequently part of NDE narratives. Already after several weeks of immersing ourselves in the details of NDEs, it became clear that the dying brain hypothesis fell woefully short of explaining them and that some sort of exosomatic theory was going to be necessary. I present an exosomatic theory in the final chapter. Here, let me try to mount the best dying brain hypothesis argument to illustrate the problems that one encounters.

As we have already noted, not all NDEs occur when the brain is dying, such as in cases in which a person falls from a mountain and lands without injury. In such cases, there is nothing wrong with the brain, so brain pathology cannot explain the NDE. So, we need to start by saying that NDEs are not a homogeneous phenomenon, split off the ones that occur where a person is actually dying, and, furthermore, for good measure, fragment those into components, offering different explanations for different types of NDEs and their various components (Craffert, 2019; Lake, 2017). Notice that such a strategy can also be applied to the ordinary waking state, so that we need to justify why waking state experiences can be regarded as unitary whereas those in altered states cannot. Nonetheless, let us proceed. Now we are down to explaining the NDEs that occur when the brain really is dying.

Experiencers have frequently claimed that the events that occurred during their NDEs were as real or more real than physical events, and that their cognitive capacity was increased rather than decreased during the NDE (Stevenson & Cook, 1995). For instance, in one study of NDE experiencers, 29% claimed that their thinking was more logical than usual, and 45% reported that it was clearer than usual (E. W. Kelly, Greyson, & Kelly, 2007/2010, p. 386). Furthermore, some life reviews that occur in the context of NDEs are sensorially rich re-enactments of a person's entire life that are experienced as being more real than ordinary physical life (Ring & Valarino, 1998). In other words, there are complex events occurring with a vividness that matches or surpasses that of the ordinary waking state.

Now here is the challenge. Blood flow to the brain stops within seconds of cardiac arrest, and any meaningful cortical activity ends within 20 seconds of cardiac arrest (van Lommel, 2013). This does not give us much time. There has recently been considerable excitement around findings that some transient neural activity can persist for possibly minutes after cardiac arrest (Lake, 2017; Norton et al., 2017; van Rijn, Krijnen, Menting-Hermeling, & Coenen, 2011). But careful examination of the data reveals that it is *too little, too soon*. At least in the human cases, none of it appears to have sufficient power to rise to the level necessary for awareness (Norton et al., 2017), nor can it account for events that occur after a few minutes of cardiac arrest. So the brain is going to have to do whatever it is going to do within about 20 seconds.

There is another, obvious problem with trying to account for NDEs with a dying brain hypothesis and that is that the brain is dying (Fenwick & Fenwick, 1995). This is contrary to the neuroscientistic thesis that experience arises from neural activity. We talked about how mind wandering is correlated with activity in the default mode network. But the default mode network is a sophisticated network that includes the healthy functioning of multiple structures finely balanced to produce the metacognitive sense of a self-interacting with friends in the past or the future, or whatever it is that we mind-wander about. If we shut off oxygen to the brain, we could expect momentary delirium, perhaps, before oblivion ensues, but how could any neural activity be sustained that could produce mind wandering, let alone the sensorially rich content of some NDEs? So we need to posit some sort of special mechanism that creates a surge of activity around the time of cardiac arrest that could account for the phenomenology of the NDEs (Lake, 2017).

Given the similarities between NDEs and some psychedelic experiences, both DMT (Timmermann et al., 2018) and ketamine, a dissociative anaesthetic (Greyson, Kelly, & Kelly, 2009), have been separately proposed as surge agents. We have already seen that it is highly unlikely that DMT could be synthesized in sufficient amounts in the brain to produce psychedelic effects, let alone in less than 20 seconds, and no endogenous ketamines have ever been found that could suddenly surge at the time of cardiac arrest (Atwater, 2007). This is where evidence from cases, such as that of Pam Reynolds, become important. Reynolds was massively sedated and her neural activity monitored from the beginning of the procedure to the end. There were no surges or, in fact, any other types of neural activity that could explain having any experiences at all during the procedure (Rivas et al., 2016).

There is another problem with the dying brain hypothesis. Recall, from Chapter 3, that individuals have impaired memory for what happened within 3 minutes of falling asleep, as a result of an attenuated ability to consolidate information from short-term memory into long-term memory once they have fallen asleep. Brain death is clearly less capable of consolidating short-term memory into long-term memory than nonrapid eye movement sleep, so if an NDE occurs within the 20 seconds in which the brain is dying, how would we ever remember that? So there is a need to propose and verify a physiological mechanism for remembering these events.

There is something else, of course, and that is the presence of anomalous features that occur during some NDEs that we need to be explain with our dying brain hypothesis. The usual explanation is silence (Bush, 2009): not addressing them, pretending that whatever happened did not happen. That is, of course, not science. So we could explain them as coincidences, exaggerations, misperceptions, misrememberings, false statements, and so on. However, there is lots of explaining to do. Titus Rivas and his colleagues collected 104 cases of NDEs with anomalous features that were independently confirmed by doctors, nurses, family members, friends, and medical records (Rivas et al., 2016, p. 215), one of which, for instance, was the case of Lloyd Rudy's patient.

Furthermore, just because we can imagine some speculative physiological mechanisms that could create the NDE phenomenology does not mean that our theory is the most reasonable explanation. We still need to produce evidence to support it. And, to date, *none of the physiological theories of NDEs has been empirically verified* (Greyson, 2014).

There is a final, logical point that I want to make; it has to do with the manner in which truth is assigned to statements about the nature of reality. It is difficult to prove a universal contention such as the neuroscientistic assertion that all phenomena are the result of physiological processes because one has to show that it applies to all possible cases. On the other hand, to disprove such a contention, only a single counterexample is necessary. Not two, three, or a preponderance of counterexamples, or some statistical average, *but only one*. That means that if only one of the claims of veridical anomalous perception during an OBE turns out to be correct, then not all perception is mediated by the physical senses. If only one NDE actually occurred during the time that a person's brain was incapable of coherent cognitive functioning, then the brain is not the cause of all experience. And if only one experiencer's consciousness really did persist while her physical body was functionally dead, then consciousness does not end with death. Of course, many experiencers who have had an NDE believe that their experience is the needed counterexample to a materialist interpretation of reality (Barušs, 1996). I will let the reader decide for themself where the truth of the matter lies.

PAST-LIFE EXPERIENCES

Past life experiences are a person's impressions of themself as a particular person in a previous lifetime (cf. Mills & Lynn, 2000). These impressions can occur spontaneously or through alterations of consciousness whose purpose is to regress a person into the past. Let us first consider the spontaneous past-life experiences of children and then the past-life experiences of adults. Even more so than NDEs, perhaps, such experiences engage our ninth thematic thread, that about the nature of the self.

Children's Past-Life Experiences

Sometimes children, from the time that they first learn to speak until about 7 years of age, spontaneously report having lived previous lives. Ian Stevenson (2013), who, along with colleagues, has collected about 2,500 such cases (Mills & Tucker, 2015), noted that apparent recall of a previous life by a child can be accompanied by statements made by that child about the previous personality's life that are consistent with an actual deceased person's life but have no referents "in the current life," by behavioral traits such as phobias "that are uncharacteristic of the person's current life but are meaningful in the context of a past-life identity" (Mills & Lynn, 2000, p. 289), by the presence of skills identified with the previous personality that are not related to a child's current life, and by birthmarks or birth defects that the child or others have attributed to physical conditions or markings of the deceased person (Mills & Lynn, 2000). Some of these features are illustrated in the following case.

While she was pregnant with him, Süleyman Çapar's mother had a dream in which a man, whom she claims she did not know at the time, had approached her on horseback and told her that he had been killed by a blow from a shovel and that he wanted to stay with her. When Süleyman was born in 1966 in the village of Madenli, Turkey, the back of his head "was depressed and soft" (Stevenson, 1997a, p. 1438). The "bone of the skull" in that area was still "noticeably depressed" in 1973, with the surface of the skin being uneven and having "the appearance of a healed scar" (Stevenson, 1997a, p. 1439). Shortly after he began to speak, Süleyman "pointed away from his house and said that he wanted to go to 'the stream'" (Stevenson, 1997a, p. 1429). He began to allude to a previous lifetime in which he had been a miller who had been killed by a customer during a quarrel. His mother allowed him to lead her to the village of Ekber, which is about 5 or 6 kilometers by road, where he pointed out a house in which he said that he had lived in a previous life. On a separate trip when Süleyman was about two and a half years old, his father took him to Ekber, at which time he identified "the mother of the man whose life he seemed to be remembering" (Stevenson, 1997a, p. 1429).

It became clear to Süleyman's parents that the man whose life he was apparently remembering was that of a miller in Ekber, named Mehmet Bekler, who had been killed in 1965 during a quarrel by a blow to the head with a flour shovel wielded by Mehmet Bayrakdar. Although the details of the quarrel are unclear, a hospital postmortem report included the information that "a portion of the skull of the approximate size of the palm of the hand was fractured and depressed about a centimeter" (Stevenson, 1997a, p. 1432) and that death had occurred as a result of trauma to the head. Süleyman appeared to have identified with Mehmet Bekler, given that Süleyman used the present tense to refer to the people from his previous life, that after his initial visits he liked to visit with members of Mehmet Bekler's family, exhibiting a "somewhat possessive attitude toward their property" (Stevenson, 1997a, p. 1433), and that "when Süleyman saw Mehmet Bayrakdar once in Madenli, he pointed to him and said angrily: 'He killed me'" (p. 1438). By 1977, Süleyman was "gradually forgetting" (Stevenson, 1997a, p. 1442) the details of his previous life, and, although he still liked to visit with surviving members of Mehmet Bekler's family in Ekber, his father discouraged him from doing so.

Was Süleyman Çapar the reincarnation of Mehmet Bekler? While Stevenson (1997a) considered "that reincarnation is at least a plausible interpretation" (p. 2066) for cases such as this one, he has never encountered a perfect case, nor has he been able to eliminate all other explanations (Stevenson, 1997b). One of the flaws with this case is that Stevenson did not find and investigate it until 1973, at which time Süleyman was about 7 years old and had met with the previous personality's family. Of 18 statements about the previous personality attributed to Süleyman by his father, 14 were verified to be true. Ideally, investigators would arrive at the time that a child begins to make statements about a previous personality before there had been any contact with the previous personality's family, rather than having to rely on retrospective attributions at the time of a later investigation. Another flaw in the case is that it is likely that Süleyman's father had known of the murder of Mehmet Bekler at the time that it occurred, and his mother had identified the man in her dream as Mehmet Bekler 6 months after its occurrence, so we could speculate that his parents may have influenced Süleyman to identify himself with Mehmet Bekler. In part, the argument for reincarnation in this case rests on the apparent association between the manner of Mehmet Bekler's death and Süleyman's birth defect. Given that "the best overall estimate of the incidence of birth defects is about 2% of births" (Stevenson, 1997b, p. 115), such an association would be a statistically rare event.

In Süleyman Çapar's case, even if normal means of information transfer could be ruled out and the birth defect persuasively tied to the manner of death of the previous personality, we would still not have evidence for reincarnation, just the contention that aspects of Mehmet Bekler's personality and condition at the time of death had somehow become impressed on young Süleyman's psyche and physiology. While children with past-life experiences rarely develop dissociative identity disorder (DID) in adulthood (Mills & Lynn, 2000), nonetheless, we have seen in Chapters 6 and 8 that a person's identity is not always fixed, so that the cause of past-life experiences could be more complex than a simple transmigration of souls.

Past-Life Regression

In Chapter 5, we saw that people have been hypnotically regressed back to childhood for psychotherapeutic purposes. Brian Weiss (1992) had regressed a woman back to her childhood during psychotherapy using hypnosis, but her symptoms did not improve as much as he had expected. Perhaps a traumatic incident lay even earlier in her childhood than the ones that had already been uncovered. To explore this possibility, Weiss gave the woman the suggestion that she would "go back to the time from which [her] symptoms [arose]" (Weiss, 1992, p. 19). But instead of going back once again to her early childhood, the woman ended up going back 4,000 years into a previous lifetime. Weiss was "shocked and skeptical" (Weiss, 1992, p. 19). This had never happened to him before. But the woman's condition improved dramatically with continued regression to past lives so that "within a few months she was totally cured, without the use of any medicines" (Weiss, 1992, p. 20). Not surprisingly, "anyone who is a good hypnotic subject can be almost guaranteed to produce at least one past life, and often a string of them, when given a past-life regression" (Fenwick & Fenwick, 1999, p. 27).

Past-life experiences can occur in contexts other than those that are labeled as hypnosis. Various guided imagery techniques have been used in which a person is led through a process of relaxation and then told to imagine themself symbolically being transported to a previous life, for example, by going down a stairway, being taken back in time by a spaceship, or finding themself at the bottom of a clear pool (Lucas, 1993; see also Harman, 1994). The *christos technique* is one such guided imagery procedure. It begins by having a person lie with eyes closed on the floor while their forehead and ankles are rubbed vigorously. Next, they are asked to visualize themself progressively expanding beyond the confines of their physical body. Then they are asked to imagine and describe the outside of the front door of their house, then to describe their surroundings from the roof of the house, and then to describe what they see from increasingly greater heights above the roof. Finally, the person is told to land feet first, to describe their feet upon landing, and then to describe the details of their appearance and the appearance of the environment in which they find themself. After that the person can be asked questions about events in that lifetime and told to move forward or backward in time as necessary (Glaskin, 1976). I have used this technique a number of times and have yet to encounter anyone who would not find themself apparently experiencing a previous lifetime or, in rare cases, a future lifetime.

The question, of course, is whether these past-life experiences refer to real events in real past lives. The answer is, probably not. Or at least, not most of them. Most are probably just fantasies (cf. Schumaker, 1995; Stevenson, 1994; Venn, 1986). It has been argued that past-life regression phenomena result from suggestions on the part of hypnotists, expectations of participants, and the demands of the social situation within which hypnosis takes place (R. A. Baker, 1982), with participants in one study developing identities that reflected the expectations of the hypnotist (Spanos, Menary, Gabora, DuBreuil, & Dewhirst, 1991). However, as we have seen, not all past-life regression involves hypnosis. Also, in addition to the work of Stevenson and his colleagues there have been other cases in which the details of purported previous lifetimes, which the experiencers could not reasonably have known, have apparently matched the descriptions of their past-life experiences (e.g., Bowman, 2001; Cockell, 1993; Glaskin, 1974, 1979; Goldberg, 1997; Grof, 1987; Mills & Tucker, 2015).

Perhaps the most striking case of a past-life experience by an adult is that of an American woman, Laurel Dilmen, who in the 1970s apparently recalled, through hypnosis, dreams, flashbacks, and self-hypnosis, a previous lifetime as a woman named Antonia who lived in 16th-century Spain. This is not strictly an adult case because, as a child, Dilmen had already claimed to have lived as an adult, including, possibly, a life as Antonia. Not only did Dilmen, as an adult, recall a lifetime as Antonia but she also gave hundreds of specific details of the circumstances of Antonia's life. Linda Tarazi (1990), who spent 3 years investigating the validity of these statements, was struck by their accuracy. For example, Dilmen referred to the presence of a college in Cuenca whose faculty and students, she insisted, had "met regularly at Antonia's inn" (Tarazi, 1990, p. 321). Tarazi could find no such college listed in encyclopedias, history books, or travel books. During a visit to Cuenca, "the archivist at the Municipal Archives . . . said he had never heard of one" (Tarazi, 1990, p. 321). It was only after inquiries at a couple of universities that Tarazi found an "old seven-volume work in Spanish" in which "the founding of a college in Cuenca in the mid-16th century" (Tarazi, 1990, p. 321) was mentioned. Dilmen also correctly provided details such as the "date of the first publication of the Edict of Faith on the Island of Hispaniola" (Tarazi, 1990, p. 316) and the "dates and contents of the Spanish indexes of prohibited books and how they differed from the Roman Index" (p. 317). In fact, Tarazi has said that, while no record of Antonia herself could be found, she could not find any errors in Dilmen's account of the circumstances in which Antonia's life could have been lived, nor did it appear that Dilmen had acquired that information through normal means during her current lifetime. Is it possible that Dilmen had lived a life as Antonia?

Past-Life Therapy

One of our thematic threads, the third, is concerned with whether or not phenomena in alterations of consciousness are delusional or veridical. Another, the eighth, is concerned with their dangers and benefits. Irrespective of whether or not past lives are fictional or actual, regression to past lives may serve a therapeutic purpose, perhaps through projecting a person's psychological conflicts onto a historical pastiche. When used as a therapeutic strategy, *past-life therapy* has been said to be useful primarily "with clients who are ready to assume greater responsibility for their lives and who are open to exploring how repressed emotional response patterns are related to current difficulties" (Jue, 1996, p. 378). Conditions that are thought to respond to past-life therapy include "unexplained phobias, psychosomatic problems lacking any known cause, and anomalous experiences" (Jue, 1996, p. 378; see also Knight, 1995; Lucas, 1993). The woman who was treated by Weiss got better. Tarazi's client, Dilmen, on the other hand, appeared to become obsessed with the life of Antonia, and therapeutic strategies were needed to reorient her to her current life (Tarazi, 1990). The problem is that there have been almost no outcome studies of past-life therapy (e.g., T. B. Freedman, 1997) so that its effectiveness as a therapeutic strategy is unknown (cf. Stevenson, 1994).

One of my students, Kellye Woods, addressed the paucity of research by conducting a laboratory study with 24 healthy volunteers to see whether past-life regression would produce greater psychological well-being than regression to the present lifetime. However, as the experiment proceeded, we found that the induction was not reliably producing past-life regression, so we lost the ability to randomly assign participants to conditions. Subsequent ad hoc analyses showed that there were no differences in changes to psychological well-being for those who received the past-life suggestion and had at least some past-life imagery and those who received the past-life suggestion and did not have any past-life imagery. The only overall result was that participants, as a group, were more likely to report that they had had an extraordinary experience at the 14-day follow-up than they had prior to the induction. Perhaps not surprisingly, we also found that, for participants who reported past-life imagery, greater absorption during the imagery exercise as measured by the Phenomenology of Consciousness Inventory was correlated with higher scores on some of the subscales of the Beliefs About Consciousness and Reality Questionnaire. In other words, the depth of alteration of experience was not associated with an increase in well-being, but it was associated with more transcendent beliefs (Woods & Barušs, 2004).

Let us consider one last question about past-life experiences. Could unexplained phobias be traced to events in previous lives? In his study of children's spontaneous past-life experiences, Stevenson found a correspondence between the presence of phobias and the manner of death of the purported previous personality. Thus, for example, "a child who claims to remember a life that ended in drowning may have a phobia of being immersed in water [and] one who claims to remember a life that ended in stabbing may have a fear of bladed weapons" (Stevenson, 1990, p. 247). Phobias have occurred more frequently when violent deaths were recalled than when natural deaths were recalled. "In a series of 240 cases in India phobias occurred in 53 (39%) of the 135 cases with violent death, but in only 3 (3%) of the 105 cases having a natural death" (Stevenson, 1990, p. 247). Sometimes fears have generalized to stimuli similar to those at the time of the purported previous personality's death, and sometimes they have been isolated to specific stimuli that were present at death, both of which would be expected in phobias following traumatic events. For example, a Turkish boy who claimed to have remembered a previous life in which he had been killed when a van in which he had been riding had "crashed against the abutment of a narrow bridge" had both a generalized fear of automobiles and a specific fear of "the bridge where the accident had occurred" (Stevenson, 1990, p. 247). As with the benefits of past-life therapy in general, it is not clear that finding past-life associations to phobias has any therapeutic value.

THE QUESTION OF LIFE AFTER DEATH

We have looked at OBEs, NDEs, and past-life experiences. These are interesting alterations of consciousness in their own right. But what, if anything, do they tell us about the question of life after death? All three are certainly consistent with the survival hypothesis. In fact, as we have seen, it takes some effort to squeeze them into the materialist straightjacket. Let us briefly touch upon one other relevant avenue of investigation, that of *after-death communication*, namely, the ostensible interaction of the dead with the living. I will do so by summarizing a bit of what happened in the Scole experiment.

The Scole Experiment

In Scole, England, three researchers attended 32 meetings from October 1995 to August 1997 of a group of four people who met twice a week in the basement of a house for the purpose of contacting spirits. Two of the group were *mediums* who would enter and remain in a "trance state" (Keen, Ellison, & Fontana, 1999, p. 180) for the 2- to 22-hour duration of a session. Ten different spirits apparently spoke through the two mediums, sometimes in a manner that was uncharacteristic of the mediums. The sessions included conversations between the spirits and those present as well as the manifestation of various anomalous physical phenomena. Among the physical phenomena were markings on 15 rolls of film that had usually been left unopened in their cases during the sessions but nonetheless were often found afterward to contain a variety of phrases written in English, German, French, Latin, and Greek, as well as various drawings including Chinese ideograms (Foy, 2008; Keen et al., 1999).

During the final session attended by the regular investigators, an audiotape recorder with the microphone removed was connected to a "primitive semiconductor (germanium) apparatus" (Keen et al., 1999, p. 297) that one of the investigators had built to the specification of the purported spirits. The investigators had brought their own packet of audiocassette tapes, removed one at random, marked the surface of the cassette on four locations, and inserted it into the microphoneless tape recorder, which was turned on Record and kept under the control of one of the investigators throughout the session. During the session, music with an overriding voice message could be heard coming from the microphoneless cassette recorder. The music was Rachmaninoff's *Piano Concerto No. 2 in C Minor*, which, according to the spirits, was being played by the composer himself. After the session, the tape was inspected and found to have the four identifying marks. When the tape was played, it was found to contain the piano concerto with the overriding voice along with a great deal of white noise but none of the background sounds that had been present in the room at the time, as evidenced by a normal tape recording that had also been made during the session. "In the course of over 20 sittings the investigators were unable to detect any direct indication of fraud or deception" and concluded that the evidence favored the hypothesis that "intelligent forces, whether originating in the human psyche or from discarnate sources" (Keen et al., 1999, p. 157) were responsible for the anomalous Scole phenomena.

There is overlap between trance channeling and *poltergeist experiences* in which sounds occur and objects are moved around without apparent human agency (Irwin, 1994). The apparent tampering by spirits with electronic devices, such as the music and voice on tape in the Scole experiment, has become a field of investigation of its own that started with *electronic voice phenomenon*, consisting of apparently anomalous voices on tape, and has diversified to *instrumental transcommunication*, which, in addition to voices on tape, has included apparently anomalous telephone, television, computer, and cell phone messages. Much of this investigation, however, has been done outside mainstream scientific and academic institutions and has been difficult to evaluate (Barušs, 2001b, 2007a; Cardoso, 2010; M. R. Leary & Butler, 2015).

The Evidence for Survival

Is there life after death? What does the evidence reveal? Scientific evidence for and against the survival hypothesis has been slowly accumulating since the founding of the Society for Psychical Research in England in 1882 (Irwin, 1994). It literally takes years to become familiar with the relevant research and the nature of the arguments, which are philosophically complex (Barušs & Mossbridge, 2017). There have been a number of thorough evaluations of that research, some of which find that the evidence tips in favor of survival (Braude, 2003; Fontana, 2005) and some of which do not (Sudduth, 2016).

Here is the problem with evaluating the evidence for survival. Those of us having this discussion are alive. So anything that is ostensibly happening in other dimensions of reality has to enter our realm of the living so that we can talk about it. As soon as that happens, if we are sufficiently creative, we can imagine ways in which whatever it is that is happening originated from the realm of the living. This brings us back to the hockey-game-in-the-television analogy. Of course, speculation that the game is inside the television set itself is insufficient. There also needs to be evidence to support the speculation. In the meantime, we are left wondering whether consciousness survives the demise of the body.

SUMMARY

We started this chapter by considering OBEs, then NDEs, then past-life experiences, and we then turned to complex forms of mediumship and after-death communication. Are experiences in altered states of consciousness associated with death meaningless or meaningful (our fifth thematic thread)? Are they what they appear to be? Are they delusional or veridical (our third thread)? Are they mundane or extraordinary (our fourth thread)? Can materialist theories adequately account for them (our second thread)? Are they beneficial (our eighth thread)? What do they tell us about our self-identity (our ninth thread)? Is the psyche closed or open (our 10th thread)? Is there life after death (our second thread)? Do we surrender to death (our 11th thread)? As usual, I will leave the reader to decide the answers to these questions for themself.

10

Conclusion

We have surveyed the spectrum of alterations of consciousness, from the ordinary waking state, through sensory restriction, sleep, dreams, hypnosis, trance, drug-induced states, transcendence, and experiences associated with death. What is striking about the ground that we have covered is the amount of polarization in this area of investigation: The mind is a by-product of the brain versus the brain is a vehicle for the mind; dreams are meaningless versus dreams are messages; hypnosis is just ordinary behavior in a social situation labeled as hypnosis versus hypnosis is a special state of trance; shamanism is just schizophrenia versus shamanism is a means of communicating with spirits; dissociative identity disorder (DID) does not exist versus multiple personalities are present in DID; people who believe they have been abducted by aliens are crazy versus people really are being abducted by aliens; psychedelics are dangerous versus psychedelics are divine sacraments; mystical experiences are nothing but aberrant brain activity versus enlightenment is conferred in mystical experiences; death is oblivion versus personal consciousness continues after death. Perhaps the best way to tie together some of the material in this book would be to use our thematic threads as the basis for a summary discussion. In the process of doing so, let me take the opportunity to make some comments about directions for further research. And then let me outline some of the features of a possible postmaterialist way of thinking about the material in this book.

http://dx.doi.org/10.1037/0000200-010
Alterations of Consciousness: An Empirical Analysis for Social Scientists, Second Edition,
by I. Baruš

REVISITING OUR THEMATIC THREADS

In Chapter 1, the following 11 thematic threads, associated with fundamental questions about the nature of reality, were introduced, with the idea that they would help us to discuss alterations of consciousness.

1. Physiological, Cognitive, and Experiential Perspectives

Our first thread was that of the three perspectives taken when approaching consciousness. Although all three were used throughout the book, the physiological perspective underlaid our discussions of sleep and psychedelic states, the cognitive perspective was most evident in cognitive theories such as those for dreaming and out-of-body experiences (OBEs), and the experiential perspective became particularly significant for unusual phenomena such as transcendence and near-death experiences (NDEs). All three perspectives need to be considered as much as possible in any further research, and the interactions between them need to be established more fully. For instance, what is the connection between a person's mind when they are cycling and the cancer that they are trying to eradicate? What physiological changes accompany the perceptual changes associated with hypnotic suggestions of analgesia? What is the nature of the knowledge associated with the noetic quality of transcendent states of consciousness? What exactly is happening in the brain during an NDE?

2. Material Versus Transcendent Beliefs

It is hard to overemphasize the importance of the material–transcendent dimension of beliefs about consciousness and reality for the understanding of alterations of consciousness. Consciousness and reality are entirely physical in nature versus physical nature is a by-product of consciousness. And there are variations between those two poles. The ways in which phenomena are conceptualized, the kinds of research programs that are carried out and the interpretation of the results of research depend on the beliefs of investigators. For example, if the world is conceptualized as a physical place in a naive sense and consciousness as just an emergent property of processes in the brain, then there is no point in research aimed at looking for life after death. It is important for scientists to examine their own beliefs, to learn to rely on the data rather than their predilections, and to go wherever the evidence leads them.

3. Delusional Versus Veridical Experiences

Remaining open to transcendental interpretations of reality involves taking into greater account phenomenological data. But that raises the question of whether the events occurring in people's experiences are what they appear to be. Do we really know what is in our minds? Are there really presences that can be sensed? Do some dreams really foretell the future? Did hypnotically recalled trauma really happen? Are people really being abducted by aliens? Do we really see into other dimensions during intoxication with N,N-dimethyltryptamine (DMT)? Are insights that reveal the nature of reality during transcendent states really true? Can people really see what is happening in the environment around them during OBEs? Is an NDE really a preview of death? Are there previous lives to be remembered? Or are these all delusions? Or are some of them delusions and some of them veridical? If some of them are veridical, which ones? Our beliefs about consciousness and reality will likely determine our answers to these questions. We need to follow the empirical evidence as far as it will take us. But we also need to learn more about introspection to determine if there are ways of discriminating between that which is imaginary and that which is real. Maybe some of what we think is imaginary will turn out to be real, and some of what we think is real may turn out to be imaginary. Is the ordinary, everyday world actually real, or is it imaginary?

4. Mundane Versus Extraordinary Phenomena

Directly related to the question of the veridical nature of experiences is that of whether the phenomena occurring in alterations of consciousness are mundane or extraordinary. Are sensed presences just imaginary impressions, or are we actually encountering invisible beings? Are the correspondences between precognitive dreams and subsequent events incidental or actual? Is hypnosis just more ordinary cognition triggered by a particular social situation, or is it a special state? Are the phenomena associated with mediumship the result of hoaxes, or is there some other explanation? Sometimes it seems to me that there is an attitude within conventional scientific approaches that the world is a boring place and that anything interesting that appears to be happening can be explained in mundane terms. That may often be true, but it should not be used as a judgmental heuristic for evaluating individual events.

5. Meaningless Versus Meaningful Events

Maybe something is not happening in the physical world, and maybe there is a mundane explanation for it, but is it nonetheless meaningful? Are fantasies during daydreaming meaningful? Are dreams meaningful? Are drug-induced states just drug states, or can they reveal something meaningful about reality? Those who have had NDEs are frequently profoundly affected by them, so are NDEs meaningful? Given that hypnagogic imagery appears to be autosymbolic, are there nonrational sources of information about ourselves? Do such images stem from the superconscious? Do we have a superconscious? We need more research to understand any ways in which nonrational meaningfulness and knowledge can occur. Can meaning extend beyond the human?

6. Lateral Versus Vertical Meaningfulness

Not only could we extend the boundary of what is meaningful laterally through consideration of the use of ways of knowing other than the rational but, in some cases, there could be an apparent vertical extension through the deepening of meaning, such as with Franklin Wolff's introception. Existential questions have apparently been resolved in some transcendent states of consciousness precisely because of the noetic quality of such states. But in what sense is such enlightenment really knowledge? We recall the cases of DMT intoxication and distressing NDEs in which there was absolute conviction that the world is a terrible place. What are the cognitive and physiological correlates of the deepening of meaning? Is it possible to develop meditation techniques analogous to those used in the Finders Course, perhaps, that scientists can use to facilitate the occurrence of transcendent states of consciousness for themselves as an investigative method? Are there other ways in which vertical meaningfulness could be understood?

7. Psychopathology Versus Well-Being

We have considered actual psychopathology in this book, such as schizophrenia, sleep disorders, DID, and impairments associated with drug use. There has been a tendency in the past to regard some altered states as pathological, such as shamanic soul journeying and transcendence, even though they are quite different in character from psychological disorders. And some alterations of consciousness that look as though they should be some kind of psychopathology, such as alien abduction experiences, cannot be accounted for in terms of known mental disorders. It is important in trying to understand alterations of consciousness not to instinctively label as pathological that which we do not understand but to leave the question open as to whether or not some form of mental disease is present until more is known about it.

We have also considered alterations that are characterized by exceptional well-being. Most notable among these are transcendent states such as flow, peak experiences, mystical experiences, and persistent transcendent states of consciousness. In many cases, it is not the type of alteration but the nature of an individual's experience in an alteration of consciousness that determines whether that experience will be felicitous or not. We have seen that occur with daydreams, sensory deprivation, hypnagogic imagery, dreams, trance, drug-induced states, and NDEs.

8. Dangerous Versus Beneficial Alterations

Related to questions of psychopathology and well-being are those concerned with the dangerousness and benefits of phenomena in alterations of consciousness. Are psychoactive drugs such as fluoxetine and LSD dangerous or beneficial? Under what conditions does sensory restriction cease to be therapeutic and begin to be dangerous? Is stage hypnosis dangerous? Are alien abduction experiences dangerous, and if so, what can be done to stop them?

From an alternative perspective, many of the alterations of consciousness lend themselves to therapeutic efforts. Guided imagery has been used to try to improve physical and psychological functioning. Dreams have been interpreted for the sake of self-understanding and, in the form of lucid dreams, harnessed for self-development. Hypnosis has been used in a wide range of situations, such as analgesia during surgery. DID may in and of itself be a healthy response to an unhealthy situation. Psychedelics have been given to addicts to treat their addictions and to the dying to help them with intractable pain and existential fear. Meditation has been used to counteract stress. And past-life regression has been part of some psychotherapists' repertoires of therapeutic techniques. The volume of research concerning the effectiveness of these strategies is varied, with numerous studies for some of them, such as hypnosis, and almost none for others, such as past-life regression. It would make sense to carefully examine the therapeutic potential of all of the procedures that could be developed in any of these alterations of consciousness.

9. The Nature of the Self

The question of the nature of the self has certainly been opened up in this book. Is the self a thought that appropriates to itself previously aggregated ideas about what it is like? Is it just a representation of the biological organism within its own information-processing system? How is it that self-identity can change so readily for hypnotic virtuosos? What gets disconnected during dissociation? Does the self leave the body during soul-journeying and OBEs? Who is the self for a person with DID? Is the self eternal, as it appears to be during transcendent states of consciousness? Has the self itself disappeared, as self-referential thoughts disappear for those who are in persistent transcendent states of consciousness? Have we lived previous lives? Does the self survive death? I think that there needs to be research aimed at better understanding the nature of the self in light of the changes of self-identity in alterations of consciousness.

10. Closed Versus Open Psyche

At the root of much of the disparity concerning consciousness is the question of whether the psyche is open or closed. Is consciousness bound by the skull, or does it extend spatially and temporally? The answers to these questions depend upon the answers to questions about the extent to which phenomena associated with alterations of consciousness are what they appear to be. Are we being deluded, or are some of the events occurring in some of these alterations veridical? Are the results of the Ganzfeld studies valid? Do nonlocal healing effects actually occur? Are sensed presences objective in some sense? Do precognitive dreams foretell future events? Do shamans encounter spirits? Are aliens interdimensional travelers? Does intoxication with psychedelics lead to otherworldly adventures? Are NDEs a preview of death? Do mediums give voice to the dead? In other words, is consciousness a product of the brain, or is the brain a vehicle of expression for consciousness?

11. Volition Versus Surrender

Sometimes the exercise of control is an aspect of phenomena in altered states of consciousness, such as in some cases of guided imagery, lucid dreaming, flow, and meditation. There are other times when surrender seems to be an appropriate strategy, such as sleep, channeling, psychedelic drug intoxication, transcendent experiences, and NDEs. In fact, releasing self-determination and surrendering to a psychological process could lead from the ordinary waking state into altered states or from the occurrence of dysphoric events to euphoric ones. Determining the nature of self-determination and surrender, and their optimal balance, is another of the research programs that are necessary for understanding not only alterations of consciousness but the psyche itself.

AN EXOSOMATIC THEORY OF CONSCIOUSNESS

Where does pondering these thematic threads leave us? We are used to thinking that the only objective reality that exists is whatever it is that we encounter through our sensory modalities. Of course, we know intellectually that there is more to physical reality than what we can perceive, since our physical senses are only attuned to a narrow range of physical events. Visible light, for instance, is only a fraction of the spectrum of electromagnetic radiation. Just as there is more physical reality out there than we can see, so there could be more reality out there that is not physical than we can perceive. So, what if some of the experiences that we have during altered states of consciousness are what they appear to be—perceptions of other worlds, journeys out of the body, encounters with discarnate beings, and so on? Let us think about that for minute.

Let me define an *exosomatic theory of consciousness* as a theory of consciousness in which consciousness has a fundamental existence apart from the physical body. In other words, consciousness is not a by-product of neural activity in the brain but exists as a double that can act through the brain. This places us into the transcendent versions of beliefs about consciousness and reality— conservatively transcendent if we think that physical manifestation has some sort of essential reality, and extraordinarily transcendent, if we think that physical manifestation itself is a by-product of consciousness.

First, there appear to be perceptual capabilities of consciousness that are not mediated by the physical senses. We saw that in the Ganzfeld studies, precognitive dreaming, and transcendental awareness. So, in addition to being able to perceive what is happening within physical manifestation, we may be able to turn on a nonlocal ability to perceive what is happening in other dimensions of reality. It may also be that, just as we have a perspective from which we perceive the physical world with our physical senses, so we may have a perspective, our interpretation of reality, from which we perceive other aspects of reality so that their appearance conforms, in part, to our expectations.

Second, if the body is just a vehicle of expression of myself, then I can leave the body and possibly encounter beings that inhabit whatever space I have entered. This could occur in shared dreaming. This could be what shamans do during soul journeying. This could happen during OBEs, for example, as reported by my student who saw her boyfriend asleep in his bed. This could explain why experiencers encounter deceased friends and relatives during NDEs.

Third, we can turn this around. There could be intrusions from other dimensions into our ordinary waking state. Discarnate entities could warn us during sensory restriction. Or they could come through during channeling. Or they could take over our bodies and possess us. Or they could present as alters that have the capability of switching the physiological characteristics of our bodies. Or they could drag our doubles away to their lairs to torment us, as in some cases of alien abduction experiences. Or they could create physical phenomena such as those in the Scole experiment.

Fourth, the physically embodied state is a restricted state for consciousness, which functions more naturally without having to drive a brain. The brain acts as a filter. This is suggested by the negative correlation between the clarity of events in NDEs and the deterioration of the brain. The more deteriorated the brain is during an NDE, the more the double has been freed from the constraints imposed by the brain. We can crack open the filter to allow more information to come down into the brain, as we do while asleep or during mental channeling. Or we can knock out the filter for a while so that we are released into the natural domain of the double, through the influence of psychedelic drugs or during an NDE.

Fifth, nonlocal consciousness may be able to influence what happens without conventional physical manipulation. We see this in Bengston's experiments in which mice are healed. This is implicated in the story of the fellow with a dysphoric NDE who hung himself from the shed and ostensibly manipulated his wife to cut him down. Anita Moorjani claims that she knew during her NDE that if she came back to life, she would be healed. The consciousness of the double appears to be capable of manipulating physical manifestation.

Phenomena that occur in alterations of consciousness strain materialist versions of reality to the breaking point. The materialist effort is like that of trying to row a sieve across a lake. Water keeps coming in, but you keep insisting that there is no water and keep trying to row. But in spite of all your effort, the water keeps entering the sieve. Anomalous phenomena cannot be stopped, and after a while, ignoring them or continuously labeling them as coincidences, mental diseases, delusions, misperceptions, misrememberings, exaggerations, false statements, and so on, is clearly maladaptive. It is time to reconsider what one is doing. In this way, alterations of consciousness raise deep questions, forcing us to reconsider our understanding of the fundamental nature of reality.

REFERENCES

Aanstoos, C. M. (1987). The psychology of computer models and the question of the imagination. In E. L. Murray (Ed.), *Imagination and phenomenological psychology* (pp. 48–77). Pittsburgh, PA: Duquesne University Press.

Abdalmalak, A., Milej, D., Norton, L., Debicki, D. B., Gofton, T., Diop, M., . . . St. Lawrence, K. (2017). Single-session communication with a locked-in patient by functional near-infrared spectroscopy. *Neurophotonics, 4*(4). http://dx.doi.org/10.1117/1.NPh.4.4.040501

Abraham, A. (2018). The wandering mind: Where imagination meets consciousness. *Journal of Consciousness Studies, 19*, 34–52.

Abraham, H. D., & Aldridge, A. M. (1993). Adverse consequences of lysergic acid diethylamide. *Addiction, 88*, 1327–1334. http://dx.doi.org/10.1111/j.1360-0443.1993.tb02018.x

Ader, R., & Cohen, N. (1975). Behaviorally conditioned immunosuppression. *Psychosomatic Medicine, 37*, 333–340. http://dx.doi.org/10.1097/00006842-197507000-00007

Ader, R., & Cohen, N. (1982). Behaviorally conditioned immunosuppression and murine systemic lupus erythematosus. *Science, 215*, 1534–1536. http://dx.doi.org/10.1126/science.7063864

Ader, R., & Cohen, N. (1993). Psychoneuroimmunology: Conditioning and stress. *Annual Review of Psychology, 44*, 53–85. http://dx.doi.org/10.1146/annurev.ps.44.020193.000413

Adler, N., & Matthews, K. (1994). Health psychology: Why do some people get sick and some stay well? *Annual Review of Psychology, 45*, 229–259. http://dx.doi.org/10.1146/annurev.ps.45.020194.001305

Aggernæs, A. (1972). The difference between the experienced reality of hallucinations in young drug abusers and schizophrenic patients. *Acta Psychiatrica Scandinavica, 48*, 287–299. http://dx.doi.org/10.1111/j.1600-0447.1972.tb04370.x

Alamir, Y. A., Zullig, K. J., Wen, S., Montgomery-Downs, H., Kristjansson, A. L., Misra, R., & Zhang, J. (2019). Association between nonmedical use of prescription drugs and sleep quality in a large college student sample. *Behavioral Sleep Medicine, 17*, 470–480. http://dx.doi.org/10.1080/15402002.2017.1403325

Alarcón, A., Capafons, A., Bayot, A., & Cardeña, E. (1999). Preference between two methods of active-alert hypnosis: Not all techniques are created equal. *The American Journal of Clinical Hypnosis, 41*, 269–276. http://dx.doi.org/10.1080/00029157.1999.10404218

Aldrich, M. S. (1999). *Sleep medicine*. New York, NY: Oxford University Press.

Allen, D. S. (1995). Schizophreniform psychosis after stage hypnosis. *The British Journal of Psychiatry, 166*, 680. http://dx.doi.org/10.1192/bjp.166.5.680a

Alvarado, C. S. (2000). Out-of-body experiences. In E. Cardeña, S. J. Lynn, & S. Krippner (Eds.), *Varieties of anomalous experience: Examining the scientific evidence* (pp. 183–218). Washington, DC: American Psychological Association. http://dx.doi.org/10.1037/10371-006

American Psychiatric Association. (2000). *Diagnostic and statistical manual of mental disorders* (4th ed.; text revision). Arlington, VA: Author.

American Psychiatric Association. (2013). *Diagnostic and statistical manual of mental disorders* (5th ed.). Arlington, VA: Author.

Ancoli-Israel, S., Martin, J. L., Blackwell, T., Buenaver, L., Liu, L., Meltzer, L. J., . . . Taylor, D. J. (2015). The SBSM guide to actigraphy monitoring: Clinical and research applications. *Behavioral Sleep Medicine, 13*(suppl. 1), S4–S38.

Andresen, J. (2000). Meditation meets behavioural medicine: The story of experimental research on meditation. *Journal of Consciousness Studies, 7*(11–12), 17–73.

Andrew, T. A., & Duval, J. V. (2017). Confronting an upsurge in opiate deaths with limited resources. *Academic Forensic Pathology, 7*, 7–18. http://dx.doi.org/10.23907/2017.002

Andrews-Hanna, J. R., Irving, Z. C., Fox, K. C. R., Spreng, R. N., & Christoff, K. (2018). The neuroscience of spontaneous thought: An evolving interdisciplinary field. In K. C. Fox & K. Christoff (Eds.), *The Oxford handbook of spontaneous thought: Mind-wandering, creativity, and dreaming* (pp. 143–163). Oxford, England: Oxford University Press.

Appelle, S. (1996). The abduction experience: A critical evaluation of theory and evidence. *Journal of UFO Studies, 6*, 29–78.

Appelle, S., Lynn, S. J., & Newman, L. (2000). Alien abduction experiences. In E. Cardeña, S. J. Lynn, & S. Krippner (Eds.), *Varieties of anomalous experience: Examining the scientific evidence* (pp. 253–282). Washington, DC: American Psychological Association. http://dx.doi.org/10.1037/10371-008

Appelle, S., Lynn, S. J., Newman, L., & Malaktaris, A. (2014). Alien abduction experiences. In E. Cardeña, S. J. Lynn, & S. Krippner (Eds.), *Varieties of anomalous experience: Examining the scientific evidence* (2nd ed., pp. 213–240). Washington, DC: American Psychological Association. http://dx.doi.org/10.1037/14258-008

Armitage, R., Emslie, G., & Rintelmann, J. (1997). The effect of fluoxetine on sleep EEG in childhood depression: A preliminary report. *Neuropsychopharmacology, 17*, 241–245. http://dx.doi.org/10.1016/S0893-133X(97)00048-1

Armitage, R., Trivedi, M., & Rush, A. J. (1995). Fluoxetine and oculomotor activity during sleep in depressed patients. *Neuropsychopharmacology, 12*, 159–165. http://dx.doi.org/10.1016/0893-133X(94)00075-B

Arnulf, I. (2018). Sleepwalking. *Current Biology, 28*(22), R1288–R1289. http://dx.doi.org/10.1016/j.cub.2018.09.062

Aserinsky, E. (1996). Memories of famous neuropsychologists: The discovery of REM sleep. *Journal of the History of the Neurosciences, 5*, 213–227. http://dx.doi.org/10.1080/09647049609525671

Aserinsky, E., & Kleitman, N. (1953). Regularly occurring periods of eye motility, and concomitant phenomena, during sleep. *Science, 118*, 273–274. http://dx.doi.org/10.1126/science.118.3062.273

Aspy, D. J., Delfabbro, P., Proeve, M., & Mohr, P. (2017). Reality testing and the mnemonic induction of lucid dreams: Findings from the national Australian lucid dream induction study. *Dreaming, 27,* 206–231. http://dx.doi.org/10.1037/drm0000059

Assagioli, R. (1965). *Psychosynthesis: A manual of principles and techniques.* New York, NY: Penguin.

Ataria, Y. (2018). Mindfulness and trauma: Some striking similarities. *Anthropology of Consciousness, 29,* 44–56. http://dx.doi.org/10.1111/anoc.12086

Atwater, P. M. H. (2007). *The big book of near-death experiences: The ultimate guide to what happens when we die.* Charlottesville, VA: Hampton Roads.

Bailey, T. D., & Brand, B. L. (2017). Traumatic dissociation: Theory, research, and treatment. *Clinical Psychology: Science and Practice, 24,* 170–185. http://dx.doi.org/10.1111/cpsp.12195

Baird, B., Mota-Rolim, S. A., & Dresler, M. (2019). The cognitive neuroscience of lucid dreaming. *Neuroscience & Biobehavioral Reviews, 100,* 305–323. http://dx.doi.org/10.1016/j.neubiorev.2019.03.008

Baker, D. (1977). *The spiritual diary.* Potters Bar, England: The College of Spiritual Enlightenment and Esoteric Knowledge.

Baker, D., & Hansen, C. (1977). *In the steps of the master.* Essendon, England: Douglas Baker.

Baker, R. A. (1982). The effect of suggestion on past-lives regression. *American Journal of Clinical Hypnosis, 25,* 71–76. http://dx.doi.org/10.1080/00029157.1982.10404067

Banaji, M. R., & Kihlstrom, J. F. (1996). The ordinary nature of alien abduction memories. *Psychological Inquiry, 7,* 132–135. http://dx.doi.org/10.1207/s15327965pli0702_3

Banks, S., Dorrian, J., Basner, M., & Dinges, D. F. (2017). Sleep deprivation. In M. Kryger, T. Roth, & W. C. Dement (Eds.), *Principles and practice of sleep medicine* (6th ed., pp. 49–55). Philadelphia, PA: Elsevier. http://dx.doi.org/10.1016/B978-0-323-24288-2.00005-2

Barabasz, A. F. (2000). EEG markers of alert hypnosis: The induction makes a difference. *Sleep and Hypnosis, 2,* 164–169.

Barabasz, A. F., Baer, L., Sheehan, D. V., & Barabasz, M. (1986). A three-year follow-up of hypnosis and restricted environmental stimulation therapy for smoking. *International Journal of Clinical and Experimental Hypnosis, 34,* 169–181. http://dx.doi.org/10.1080/00207148608406983

Barabasz, A. F., & Barabasz, M. (2016). Induction technique: Beyond simple response to suggestion. *American Journal of Clinical Hypnosis, 59,* 204–213. http://dx.doi.org/10.1080/00029157.2016.1209456

Barabasz, A. F., Barabasz, M., & Bauman, J. (1993). Restricted environmental stimulation technique improves human performance: Rifle marksmanship. *Perceptual and Motor Skills, 76,* 867–873. http://dx.doi.org/10.2466/pms.1993.76.3.867

Barabasz, M., Barabasz, A. F., & Dyer, R. (1993). Chamber REST reduces alcohol consumption: 3, 6, 12, and 24 hour sessions. In A. F. Barabasz & M. Barabasz (Eds.), *Clinical and experimental restricted environmental stimulation: New developments and perspectives* (pp. 163–173). New York, NY: Springer-Verlag. http://dx.doi.org/10.1007/978-1-4684-8583-7_19

Barber, J. (1998a). The mysterious persistence of hypnotic analgesia. *International Journal of Clinical and Experimental Hypnosis, 46,* 28–43. http://dx.doi.org/10.1080/00207149808409988

Barber, J. (1998b). When hypnosis causes trouble. *International Journal of Clinical and Experimental Hypnosis, 46,* 157–170. http://dx.doi.org/10.1080/00207149808409997

Barber, K. (2004). *Canadian Oxford dictionary* (2nd ed.). Oxford, England: Oxford University Press.

Barber, T. X. (1999). A comprehensive three-dimensional theory of hypnosis. In I. Kirsch, A. Capafons, E. Cardeña-Buelna, & S. Amigó (Eds.), *Clinical hypnosis and self-regulation: Cognitive–behavioral perspectives* (pp. 21–48). Washington, DC: American Psychological Association. http://dx.doi.org/10.1037/10282-001

Baron, P. H. (1989). Fighting cancer with images. In H. Wadeson, J. Durkin, & D. Perach (Eds.), *Advances in art therapy* (pp. 148–168). New York, NY: Wiley.

Barrett, D. (1993). The "committee of sleep": A study of dream incubation for problem solving. *Dreaming, 3,* 115–122. http://dx.doi.org/10.1037/h0094375

Barrett, D. (1996a). Dreams in multiple personality disorder. In D. Barrett (Ed.), *Trauma and dreams* (pp. 68–81). Cambridge, MA: Harvard University Press.

Barrett, D. (1996b). Fantasizers and dissociaters: Two types of high hypnotizables, two different imagery styles. In R. G. Kunzendorf, N. P. Spanos, & B. Wallace (Eds.), *Hypnosis and imagination* (pp. 123–135). Amityville, NY: Baywood.

Barrett, D. (1996c). Introduction. In D. Barrett (Ed.), *Trauma and dreams* (pp. 1–6). Cambridge, MA: Harvard University Press.

Barrett, D. (2017). Dreams and creative problem-solving. *Annals of the New York Academy of Sciences, 1406,* 64–67. http://dx.doi.org/10.1111/nyas.13412

Baruss, I. (1986). Quantum mechanics and human consciousness. *Physics in Canada/ La Physique au Canada, 42,* 3–5.

Baruss, I. (1987). Metanalysis of definitions of consciousness. *Imagination, Cognition and Personality, 6,* 321–329. http://dx.doi.org/10.2190/39X2-HMUL-WB7B-B1A1

Baruss, I. (1990). *The personal nature of notions of consciousness: A theoretical and empirical examination of the role of the personal in the understanding of consciousness.* Lanham, MD: University Press of America.

Baruss, I. (1993). Can we consider matter as ultimate reality? Some fundamental problems with a materialist interpretation of reality. *Ultimate Reality and Meaning: Interdisciplinary Studies in the Philosophy of Understanding, 16,* 245–254.

Baruss, I. (1996). *Authentic knowing: The convergence of science and spiritual aspiration.* West Lafayette, IN: Purdue University Press.

Baruss, I. (2000a). Overview of consciousness research. *Informatica: An International Journal of Computing and Informatics, 24,* 269–273.

Baruss, I. (2000b). Psychopathology of altered states of consciousness. *Journal of Baltic Psychology, 1,* 12–26.

Baruss, I. (2001a). The art of science: Science of the future in light of alterations of consciousness. *Journal of Scientific Exploration, 15,* 57–68.

Baruss, I. (2001b). Failure to replicate electronic voice phenomenon. *Journal of Scientific Exploration, 15,* 355–367.

Baruss, I. (2006). Quantum theories of consciousness. *Baltic Journal of Psychology, 7,* 39–45.

Baruss, I. (2007a). An experimental test of instrumental transcommunication. *Journal of Scientific Exploration, 21,* 89–98.

Baruss, I. (2007b). Franklin Wolff's mathematical resolution of existential issues. *Journal of Scientific Exploration, 21,* 751–756.

Baruss, I. (2007c). *Science as a spiritual practice.* Exeter, England: Imprint Academic.

Baruss, I. (2008a). Beliefs about consciousness and reality: Clarification of the confusion concerning consciousness. *Journal of Consciousness Studies, 15,* 277–292.

Baruss, I. (2008b). Characteristics of consciousness in collapse-type quantum mind theories. *Journal of Mind and Behavior, 29,* 255–265.

Baruss, I. (2008c). Quantum mind: Conscious intention in the context of quantum mechanics. *Dydaktyka Literatury, 28,* 31–40.

Baruss, I. (2009). Speculations about the direct effects of intention on physical manifestation. *Journal of Cosmology, 3,* 590–599.

Baruss, I. (2012). What we can learn about consciousness from altered states of consciousness. *Journal of Consciousness Exploration & Research, 3,* 805–819.

Barušs, I. (2013). *The impossible happens: A scientist's personal discovery of the extraordinary nature of reality*. Alresford, England: Iff Books.

Barušs, I. (2018a). Meaning fields: Meaning beyond the human as a resolution of boundary problems introduced by nonlocality. *EdgeScience, 35*, 8–11.

Barušs, I. (2018b). Transition to transcendence: Franklin Merrell-Wolff's mathematical yoga. *Journal of Conscious Evolution, 1*, Article 3. Retrieved September 14, 2000, from https://digitalcommons.ciis.edu/cgi/viewcontent.cgi?article=1002&context=cejournal

Barušs, I., & Moore, R. J. (1989). Notions of consciousness and reality. In J. E. Shorr, P. Robin, J. A. Connella, & M. Wolpin (Eds.), *Imagery: Current perspectives* (pp. 87–92). New York, NY: Plenum Press. http://dx.doi.org/10.1007/978-1-4899-0876-6_8

Barušs, I., & Moore, R. J. (1992). Measurement of beliefs about consciousness and reality. *Psychological Reports, 71*, 59–64. http://dx.doi.org/10.2466/pr0.1992.71.1.59

Barušs, I., & Moore, R. J. (1997, Spring). Beliefs about consciousness and reality: Highlights of Tucson II consciousness survey. *Consciousness Bulletin*, pp. 5–6.

Barušs, I., & Moore, R. J. (1998). Beliefs about consciousness and reality of participants at 'Tucson II.' *Journal of Consciousness Studies, 5*, 483–496.

Barušs, I., & Mossbridge, J. (2017). *Transcendent mind: Rethinking the science of consciousness*. Washington, DC: American Psychological Association. http://dx.doi.org/10.1037/15957-000

Barwise, J. (1986). Information and circumstance. *Notre Dame Journal of Formal Logic, 27*, 324–338. http://dx.doi.org/10.1305/ndjfl/1093636678

Basterfield, K. (1994). Abductions: The Australian experience. In A. Pritchard, D. E. Pritchard, J. E. Mack, P. Kasey, & C. Yapp (Eds.), *Alien discussions: Proceedings of the Abduction Study Conference held at MIT, Cambridge, MA* (pp. 178–186). Cambridge, MA: North Cambridge Press.

Bauer, I. L. (2018). Ayahuasca: A risk for travellers? *Travel Medicine and Infectious Disease, 21*, 74–76. http://dx.doi.org/10.1016/j.tmaid.2018.01.002

Beauregard, M. (2011). Transcendent experiences and brain mechanisms. In E. Cardeña & M. Winkelman (Eds.), *Altering consciousness: Multidisciplinary perspectives: Vol. 2. Biological and psychological perspectives* (pp. 63–84). Santa Barbara, CA: Praeger.

Beauregard, M. (2012). *Brain wars: The scientific battle over the existence of the mind and the proof that will change the way we live our lives*. Toronto, Ontario, Canada: HarperCollins.

Beischel, J. (2007). Contemporary methods used in laboratory-based mediumship research. *Journal of Parapsychology, 71*, 37–68.

Beischel, J. (2013). *Among mediums: A scientist's quest for answers*. Tucson, AZ: Windbridge Institute.

Beischel, J., Boccuzzi, M., Biuso, M., & Rock, A. J. (2015). Anomalous information reception by research mediums under blinded conditions II: Replication and extension. *EXPLORE, 11*, 136–142. http://dx.doi.org/10.1016/j.explore.2015.01.001

Beischel, J., & Schwartz, G. E. (2007). Anomalous information reception by research mediums demonstrated using a novel triple-blind protocol. *EXPLORE, 3*, 23–27. http://dx.doi.org/10.1016/j.explore.2006.10.004

Bem, D. J. (1994). "Anomaly or artifact? Comments on Bem and Honorton": Response to Hyman. *Psychological Bulletin, 115*, 25–27. http://dx.doi.org/10.1037/0033-2909.115.1.25

Bem, D. J. (2011). Feeling the future: Experimental evidence for anomalous retroactive influences on cognition and affect. *Journal of Personality and Social Psychology, 100*, 407–425. http://dx.doi.org/10.1037/a0021524

Bem, D. J., & Honorton, C. (1994). Does psi exist? Replicable evidence for an anomalous process of information transfer. *Psychological Bulletin, 115*, 4–18. http://dx.doi.org/10.1037/0033-2909.115.1.4

Benedetti, F. (2009). *Placebo effects: Understanding the mechanisms in health and disease*. Oxford, England: Oxford University Press.

Bengston, W. F. (2007). Commentary: A method used to train skeptical volunteers to heal in an experimental setting. *Journal of Alternative and Complementary Medicine, 13,* 329–332. http://dx.doi.org/10.1089/acm.2007.6403

Bengston, W. F., & Krinsley, D. (2000). The effect of the "laying on of hands" on transplanted breast cancer in mice. *Journal of Scientific Exploration, 14,* 353–364.

Benson, H. (1975). *The relaxation response.* New York, NY: William Morrow.

Benson, H. (1983). The relaxation response: Its subjective and objective historical precedents and physiology. *Trends in Neurosciences, 6,* 281–284. http://dx.doi.org/10.1016/0166-2236(83)90120-0

Bentall, R. P. (2000). Hallucinatory experiences. In E. Cardeña, S. J. Lynn, & S. Krippner (Eds.), *Varieties of anomalous experience: Examining the scientific evidence* (pp. 85–120). Washington, DC: American Psychological Association. http://dx.doi.org/10.1037/10371-003

Beseme, S., Bengston, W., Radin, D., Turner, M., & McMichael, J. (2018). Transcriptional changes in cancer cells induced by exposure to a healing method. *Dose–Response, 16*(3), 1559325818782843. Advance online publication. http://dx.doi.org/10.1177/1559325818782843

Blackmore, S. (1993). *Dying to live: Near-death-experiences.* Buffalo, NY: Prometheus Books.

Blewett, D. B. (1969). *The frontiers of being.* New York, NY: Award Books.

Bliwise, D. L. (1996). Historical change in the report of daytime fatigue. *Sleep, 19,* 462–464. http://dx.doi.org/10.1093/sleep/19.6.462

Bonnet, M. H. (2000). Sleep deprivation. In M. H. Kryger, T. Roth, & W. C. Dement (Eds.), *Principles and practice of sleep medicine* (3rd ed., pp. 53–71). Philadelphia, PA: W. B. Saunders.

Borbély, A. A., & Achermann, P. (2000). Sleep homeostasis and models of sleep regulation. In M. H. Kryger, T. Roth, & W. C. Dement (Eds.), *Principles and practice of sleep medicine* (3rd ed., pp. 377–390). Philadelphia, PA: W. B. Saunders.

Botta, S. A. (1999). Self-hypnosis as anesthesia for liposuction surgery. *American Journal of Clinical Hypnosis, 41,* 299–301. http://dx.doi.org/10.1080/00029157.1999.10404227

Bourguignon, E. (1979). *Psychological anthropology: An introduction to human nature and cultural differences.* New York, NY: Holt, Rinehart and Winston.

Boutros, N. N., & Bowers, M. B., Jr. (1996). Chronic substance-induced psychotic disorders: State of the literature. *The Journal of Neuropsychiatry and Clinical Neurosciences, 8,* 262–269. http://dx.doi.org/10.1176/jnp.8.3.262

Bowers, K. S. (1976). *Hypnosis for the seriously curious.* New York, NY: W. W. Norton.

Bowers, K. S., & Woody, E. Z. (1996). Hypnotic amnesia and the paradox of intentional forgetting. *Journal of Abnormal Psychology, 105,* 381–390. http://dx.doi.org/10.1037/0021-843X.105.3.381

Bowman, C. (2001). *Return from heaven: Beloved relatives reincarnated within your family.* New York, NY: HarperCollins.

Braid, J. (1960). *Braid on hypnotism: The beginnings of modern hypnosis* (Rev. ed.; A. E. Waite, Ed.). New York, NY: Julian Press. (Original work published 1842–1883)

Brand, B. L., Sar, V., Stavropoulos, P., Krüger, C., Korzekwa, M., Martínez-Taboas, A., & Middleton, W. (2016). Separating fact from fiction: An empirical examination of six myths about dissociative identity disorder. *Harvard Review of Psychiatry, 24,* 257–270. http://dx.doi.org/10.1097/HRP.0000000000000100

Branger, P., Arenaza-Urquijo, E. M., Tomadesso, C., Mézenge, F., André, C., de Flores, R., . . . Rauchs, G. (2016). Relationships between sleep quality and brain volume, metabolism, and amyloid deposition in late adulthood. *Neurobiology of Aging, 41,* 107–114. http://dx.doi.org/10.1016/j.neurobiolaging.2016.02.009

Braude, S. E. (2003). *Immortal remains: The evidence for life after death.* Lanham, MD: Rowman & Littlefield.

Braude, S. E. (2007). *The gold leaf lady and other parapsychological investigations.* Chicago, IL: University of Chicago Press. http://dx.doi.org/10.7208/chicago/9780226071534.001.0001

Bravo, G., & Grob, C. (1996). Psychedelic psychotherapy. In B. W. Scotton, A. B. Chinen, & J. R. Battista (Eds.), *Textbook of transpersonal psychiatry and psychology* (pp. 335–343). New York, NY: Basic Books.

Breakey, W. R., Goodell, H., Lorenz, P. C., & McHugh, P. R. (1974). Hallucinogenic drugs as precipitants of schizophrenia. *Psychological Medicine, 4,* 255–261. http://dx.doi.org/10.1017/S0033291700042938

Brentano, F. (1960). The distinction between mental and physical phenomena (D. B. Terrell, Trans.). In R. M. Chisholm (Ed.), *Realism and the background of phenomenology* (pp. 39–61). Glencoe, IL: The Free Press. (Reprinted from *Psychologie vom empirischen standpunkt,* 1874, Vol. I, Book II, Chap. i.)

Bressler, S. L., & Menon, V. (2010). Large-scale brain networks in cognition: Emerging methods and principles. *Trends in Cognitive Sciences, 14,* 277–290. http://dx.doi.org/10.1016/j.tics.2010.04.004

Brody, B. A. (1999). How much of the brain must be dead? In S. J. Youngner, R. M. Arnold, & R. Schapiro (Eds.), *The definition of death: Contemporary controversies* (pp. 71–82). Baltimore, MD: The Johns Hopkins University Press.

Brogaard, B., & Gatzia, D. E. (2016). What can neuroscience tell us about the hard problem of consciousness? *Frontiers in Neuroscience, 10,* 395. http://dx.doi.org/10.3389/fnins.2016.00395

Broughton, R. [Richard] S. (1991). *Parapsychology: The controversial science.* New York, NY: Ballantine Books.

Broughton, R. [Roger]. (1986). Human consciousness and sleep/waking rhythms. In B. B. Wolman & M. Ullman (Eds.), *Handbook of states of consciousness* (pp. 461–484). New York, NY: Van Nostrand Reinhold.

Broughton, R. J. [Roger] (2000). NREM arousal parasomnias. In M. H. Kryger, T. Roth, & W. C. Dement (Eds.), *Principles and practice of sleep medicine* (3rd ed., pp. 693–706). Philadelphia, PA: W. B. Saunders.

Brown, B. M., Rainey-Smith, S. R., Villemagne, V. L., Weinborn, M., Bucks, R. S., Sohrabi, H. R., . . . the AIBL Research Group. (2016). The relationship between sleep quality and brain amyloid burden. *Sleep, 39,* 1063–1068. http://dx.doi.org/10.5665/sleep.5756

Brown, D., Scheflin, A. W., & Hammond, D. C. (1998). *Memory, trauma treatment, and the law.* New York, NY: W. W. Norton.

Brown, M. F. (1997). *The channeling zone: American spirituality in an anxious age.* Cambridge, MA: Harvard University Press.

Bryan, C. D. B. (1995). *Close encounters of the fourth kind: A reporter's notebook on alien abduction, UFOs, and the conference at M.I.T.* New York, NY: Arkana.

Bucke, R. M. (1991). *Cosmic consciousness: A study in the evolution of the human mind.* New York, NY: Arkana. (Original work published 1901)

Burkes, J., & Dennett, P. (2018). Medical healings reported by UAP contact experiencers: An Analysis of the FREE data. In R. Hernandez, J. Klimo, & R. Schild (Eds.), *Beyond UFOs: The science of consciousness and contact with non-human intelligence* (Vol. 1, pp. 391–446). CreateSpace Independent Publishing Platform.

Bush, N. E. (2009). Distressing western near-death experiences: Finding a way through the abyss. In J. M. Holden, B. Greyson, & D. James (Eds.), *The handbook of near-death experiences: Thirty years of investigation* (pp. 63–86). Santa Barbara, CA: Praeger.

Butler, D. C., & Batalis, N. I. (2017). Opioid-associated deaths in South Carolina, 2013–2016: A retrospective review. *Academic Forensic Pathology, 7,* 640–648. http://dx.doi.org/10.23907/2017.054

Callicott, C. (2016). Introduction to the special issue: Ayahuasca, plant-based spirituality, and the future of Amazonia. *Anthropology of Consciousness, 27,* 113–120. http://dx.doi.org/10.1111/anoc.12059

Cao, M. T., & Guilleminault, C. (2017). Narcolepsy: Diagnosis and management. In M. Kryger, T. Roth, & W. C. Dement (Eds.), *Principles and practice of sleep medicine* (6th ed., pp. 873–882). Philadelphia, PA: Elsevier. http://dx.doi.org/10.1016/B978-0-323-24288-2.00090-8

Cardeña, E. (1996). "Just floating on the sky." A comparison of hypnotic and shamanic phenomena. In D. Eigner & R. van Quekelberghe (Eds.), *Jahrbuch für transkulturelle medizin und psychotherapie* [Yearbook of cross-cultural medicine and psychotherapy]: *Vol. 1994. Trance, Besessenheit, Heilrituale und Psychotherapie* [Trance, possession, healing rituals, and psychotherapy] (pp. 85–98). Berlin, Germany: Verlag für Wissenschaft und Bildung.

Cardeña, E. (2018). The experimental evidence for parapsychological phenomena: A review. *American Psychologist, 73,* 663–677. http://dx.doi.org/10.1037/amp0000236

Cardeña, E., & Krippner, S. (2018). Some needed psychological clarifications on the experience(s) of shamanism. *Behavioral and Brain Sciences, 41,* e72. http://dx.doi.org/10.1017/S0140525X17002035

Cardeña, E., Lynn, S. J., & Krippner, S. (Eds.). (2000). *Varieties of anomalous experience: Examining the scientific evidence.* Washington, DC: American Psychological Association. http://dx.doi.org/10.1037/10371-000

Cardoso, A. (2010). *Electronic voices: Contact with another dimension.* Winchester, England: O-Books.

Carlson, N. R. (1994). *Physiology of behavior* (5th ed.). Boston, MA: Allyn and Bacon.

Carskadon, M. A., & Dement, W. C. (2000). Normal human sleep: An overview. In M. H. Kryger, T. Roth, & W. C. Dement (Eds.), *Principles and practice of sleep medicine* (3rd ed., pp. 15–25). Philadelphia, PA: W. B. Saunders.

Carskadon, M. A., & Dement, W. C. (2017). Normal human sleep: An overview. In M. Kryger, T. Roth, & W. C. Dement (Eds.), *Principles and practice of sleep medicine* (6th ed., pp. 15–24). Philadelphia, PA: Elsevier. http://dx.doi.org/10.1016/B978-0-323-24288-2.00002-7

Carskadon, M. A., & Rechtschaffen, A. (2000). Monitoring and staging human sleep. In M. H. Kryger, T. Roth, & W. C. Dement (Eds.), *Principles and practice of sleep medicine* (3rd ed., pp. 1197–1215). Philadelphia, PA: W. B. Saunders.

Carson, R. C., Butcher, J. N., & Mineka, S. (1996). *Abnormal psychology and modern life* (10th ed.). New York, NY: HarperCollins.

Cassol, H., D'Argembeau, A., Charland-Verville, V., Laureys, S., & Martial, C. (2019). Memories of near-death experiences: Are they self-defining? *Neuroscience of Consciousness, 2019*(1), niz002. Advance online publication. http://dx.doi.org/10.1093/nc/niz002

Cavallero, C., Cicogna, P., Natale, V., Occhionero, M., & Zito, A. (1992). Slow wave sleep dreaming. *Sleep, 15,* 562–566. http://dx.doi.org/10.1093/sleep/15.6.562

Cavanna, F., Vilas, M. G., Palmucci, M., & Tagliazucchi, E. (2018). Dynamic functional connectivity and brain metastability during altered states of consciousness. *NeuroImage, 180*(Pt. B), 383–395. http://dx.doi.org/10.1016/j.neuroimage.2017.09.065

Cebolla, A., Campos, D., Galiana, L., Oliver, A., Tomás, J. M., Feliu-Soler, A., . . . Baños, R. M. (2017). Exploring relations among mindfulness facets and various meditation practices: Do they work in different ways? *Consciousness and Cognition, 49,* 172–180. http://dx.doi.org/10.1016/j.concog.2017.01.012

Chadwick, M. J., Anjum, R. S., Kumaran, D., Schacter, D. L., Spiers, H. J., & Hassabis, D. (2016). Semantic representations in the temporal pole predict false memories. *Proceedings of the National Academy of Sciences of the United States of America, 113,* 10180–10185. http://dx.doi.org/10.1073/pnas.1610686113

Chalker, B. (2005). *Hair of the alien: DNA and other forensic evidence of alien abduction.* New York, NY: Paraview Pocket Books.

Chalmers, D. J. (1995). Facing up to the problem of consciousness. *Journal of Consciousness Studies, 2,* 200–219.

Child, I. L. (1985). Psychology and anomalous observations: The question of ESP in dreams. *American Psychologist, 40,* 1219–1230. http://dx.doi.org/10.1037/0003-066X.40.11.1219

Churchland, P. S. (1980). A perspective on mind-brain research. *The Journal of Philosophy, 77,* 185–207.

Cialdini, R. B. (1988). *Influence: Science and practice* (2nd ed.). New York, NY: HarperCollins.

Cockell, J. (1993). *Across time and death: A mother's search for her past life children.* New York, NY: Fireside Books.

Colman, A. M. (2015). *A dictionary of psychology* (4th ed.). Oxford, England: Oxford University Press.

Combs, A. (2009). *Consciousness explained better: Towards an integral understanding of the multifaceted nature of consciousness.* St. Paul, MN: Paragon House.

Cook, C. M., & Persinger, M. A. (1997). Experimental induction of the "sensed presence" in normal subjects and an exceptional subject. *Perceptual and Motor Skills, 85,* 68–693.

Coons, P. M. (1993). The differential diagnosis of possession states. *Dissociation, 6,* 213–221.

Council, J. R., Chambers, D., Jundt, T. A., & Good, M. D. (1991). Are the mental images of fantasy-prone persons really more "real"? *Imagination, Cognition and Personality, 10*(4), 319–327. http://dx.doi.org/10.2190/9JXW-Y16H-JUA5-A7NP

Craffert, P. F. (2019). Making sense of near-death experience research: Circumstance specific alterations of consciousness. *Anthropology of Consciousness, 30,* 64–89. http://dx.doi.org/10.1111/anoc.12111

Creppage, K. E., Yohannan, J., Williams, K., Buchanich, J. M., Songer, T. J., Wisniewski, S. R., & Fabio, A. (2018). The rapid escalation of fentanyl in illicit drug evidence in Allegheny County, Pennsylvania, 2010–2016. *Public Health Reports, 133*(2), 142–146. http://dx.doi.org/10.1177/0033354917753119

Cresswell, J., Wagoner, B., & Hayes, A. (2017). Rediscovering James' *Principles of Psychology. New Ideas in Psychology, 46,* A1–A6. http://dx.doi.org/10.1016/j.newideapsych.2017.03.001

Csikszentmihalyi, M. (1988). The flow experience and its significance for human psychology. In M. Csikszentmihalyi & I. S. Csikszentmihalyi (Eds.), *Optimal experience: Psychological studies of flow in consciousness* (pp. 15–35). Cambridge, England: Cambridge University Press. http://dx.doi.org/10.1017/CBO9780511621956.002

Csikszentmihalyi, M. (1990). *Flow: The psychology of optimal experience.* New York, NY: HarperPerennial.

Csikszentmihalyi, M., & Csikszentmihalyi, I. (1988). Introduction to Part IV. In M. Csikszentmihalyi & I. S. Csikszentmihalyi (Eds.), *Optimal experience: Psychological studies of flow in consciousness* (pp. 251–265). Cambridge, England: Cambridge University Press. http://dx.doi.org/10.1017/CBO9780511621956.015

Csikszentmihalyi, M., & Nakamura, J. (2018). Flow, altered states of consciousness, and human evolution. *Journal of Consciousness Studies, 25*(11–12), 102–114.

Damgaard, J. A. (1987). The inner self helper: Transcendent life within life? *Noetic Sciences Review, 5,* 24–28.

d'Aquili, E. G., & Newberg, A. B. (1999). *The mystical mind: Probing the biology of religious experience.* Minneapolis, MN: Fortress.

d'Aquili, E. G., & Newberg, A. B. (2000a). The neuropsychology of aesthetic, spiritual, and mystical states. *Zygon, 35,* 39–51.

d'Aquili, E., & Newberg, A. (2000b, May/June). Wired for ultimate reality: The neuro-psychology of religious experience. *Science & Spirit Magazine, 11*(2), pp. 12–13.

Dass, R. (1979). *Miracle of love: Stories about Neem Karoli Baba.* New York, NY: E. P. Dutton.

De Koninck, J. (2000). Waking experiences and dreaming. In M. H. Kryger, T. Roth, & W. C. Dement (Eds.), *Principles and practice of sleep medicine* (3rd ed., pp. 502–509). Philadelphia, PA: W. B. Saunders.

Dell, P. F. (2017). What is the essence of hypnosis? *International Journal of Clinical and Experimental Hypnosis, 65,* 162–168.

Dell, P. F. (2019). Reconsidering the autohypnotic model of the dissociative disorders. *Journal of Trauma & Dissociation, 20,* 48–78. http://dx.doi.org/10.1080/15299732. 2018.1451806

Dement, W. C. (2000). History of sleep physiology and medicine. In M. H. Kryger, T. Roth, & W. C. Dement (Eds.), *Principles and practice of sleep medicine* (3rd ed., pp. 1–14). Philadelphia, PA: W. B. Saunders.

Demertzi, A., Tagliazucchi, E., Dehaene, S., Deco, G., Barttfeld, P., Raimondo, F., . . . Sitt, J. D. (2019). Human consciousness is supported by dynamic complex patterns of brain signal coordination. *Science Advances, 5*(2), eaat7603. http://dx.doi.org/10.1126/sciadv.aat7603

Demirci, K., Akgönül, M., & Akpinar, A. (2015). Relationship of smartphone use severity with sleep quality, depression, and anxiety in university students. *Journal of Behavioral Addictions, 4,* 85–92. http://dx.doi.org/10.1556/2006.4.2015.010

Dennett, D. C. (1978). *Brainstorms: Philosophical essays on mind and psychology.* Montgomery, VT: Bradford.

Dinges, D. F., Whitehouse, W. G., Orne, E. C., Bloom, P. B., Carlin, M. M., Bauer, N. K., . . . Orne, M. T. (1997). Self-hypnosis training as an adjunctive treatment in the management of pain associated with sickle cell disease. *International Journal of Clinical and Experimental Hypnosis, 45,* 417–432. http://dx.doi.org/10.1080/00207149708416141

Doblin, R. (1991). Pahnke's "Good Friday experiment": A long-term follow-up and methodological critique. *Journal of Transpersonal Psychology, 23,* 1–28.

Doblin, R. E., Christiansen, M., Jerome, L., & Burge, B. (2019). The past and future of psychedelic science: An introduction to this issue. *Journal of Psychoactive Drugs, 51,* 93–97. http://dx.doi.org/10.1080/02791072.2019.1606472

Dobyns, Y. (2015). The PEAR laboratory: Explorations and observations. In D. Broderick & B. Goertzel (Eds.), *Evidence for psi: Thirteen empirical research reports* (pp. 213–236). Jefferson, NC: McFarland.

Dodd, S., Dean, O. M., Vian, J., & Berk, M. (2017). A review of the theoretical and biological understanding of the nocebo and placebo phenomena. *Clinical Therapeutics, 39,* 469–476. http://dx.doi.org/10.1016/j.clinthera.2017.01.010

Dokic, J., & Martin, J.-R. (2017). Felt reality and the opacity of perception. *Topoi, 36,* 299–309. http://dx.doi.org/10.1007/s11245-015-9327-2

Domhoff, G. W. (2000). Methods and measures for the study of dream content. In M. H. Kryger, T. Roth, & W. C. Dement (Eds.), *Principles and practice of sleep medicine* (3rd ed., pp. 463–471). Philadelphia, PA: W. B. Saunders.

Domhoff, G. W. (2018a). Dreaming is an intensified form of mind-wandering, based in an augmented portion of the default network. In K. C. R. Fox & K. Christoff (Eds.), *The Oxford handbook of spontaneous thought: Mind-wandering, creativity, and dreaming* (pp. 355–370). Oxford, England: Oxford University Press.

Domhoff, G. W. (2018b). *The emergence of dreaming: Mind-wandering, embodied simulation, and the default network.* New York, NY: Oxford University Press.

Domínguez-Clavé, E., Soler, J., Elices, M., Pascual, J. C., Álvarez, E., de la Fuente Revenga, M., . . . Riba, J. (2016). Ayahuasca: Pharmacology, neuroscience and therapeutic potential. *Brain Research Bulletin, 126*(Pt 1), 89–101. http://dx.doi.org/10.1016/j.brainresbull.2016.03.002

Donderi, D. (2013). *UFOs, ETs, and alien abductions: A scientist looks at the evidence.* Charlottesville, VA: Hampton Roads.

Dorsey, C. M., & Bootzin, R. R. (1997). Subjective and psychophysiologic insomnia: An examination of sleep tendency and personality. *Journal of Psychiatric Research, 41,* 209–216. http://dx.doi.org/10.1016/0006-3223(95)00659-1

Dorsey, C. M., Lukas, S. E., & Cunningham, S. L. (1996). Fluoxetine-induced sleep disturbance in depressed patients. *Neuropsychopharmacology, 14,* 437–442. http://dx.doi.org/10.1016/0893-133X(95)00148-7

DuPre, E., & Spreng, N. R. (2018). Rumination is a sticky form of spontaneous thought. In K. C. R. Fox & K. Christoff (Eds.), *The Oxford handbook of spontaneous thought: Mind-wandering, creativity, and dreaming* (pp. 509–520). Oxford, England: Oxford University Press.

Dyck, E. (2019). Psychedelics and dying care: A historical look at the relationship between psychedelics and palliative care. *Journal of Psychoactive Drugs, 51,* 102–107. http://dx.doi.org/10.1080/02791072.2019.1581308

Dywan, J., & Bowers, K. (1983). The use of hypnosis to enhance recall. *Science, 222,* 184–185. http://dx.doi.org/10.1126/science.6623071

Eason, A. D., & Parris, B. A. (2019). Clinical applications of self-hypnosis: A systematic review and meta-analysis of randomized controlled trials. *Psychology of Consciousness, 6,* 262–278. http://dx.doi.org/10.1037/cns0000173

Eccles, J. C. (Ed.). (1966). *Brain and conscious experience: Study week September 28 to October 4, 1964, of the Pontificia Academia Scientiarum.* New York, NY: Springer-Verlag.

Eifring, H. (2018). Spontaneous thought in contemplative traditions. In K. C. R. Fox & K. Christoff (Eds.), *The Oxford handbook of spontaneous thought: Mind-wandering, creativity, and dreaming* (pp. 529–538). Oxford, England: Oxford University Press.

Eischens, P., & Atherton, W. L. (2019). Psychedelic therapy as a complementary treatment approach for alcohol use disorders. In M. Winkelman & B. Sessa (Eds.), *Advances in psychedelic medicine: State-of-the-art therapeutic applications* (pp. 170–190). Santa Barbara, CA: Praeger.

Elkins, G. R., Roberts, R. L., & Simicich, L. (2018). Mindful self-hypnosis for self-care: An integrative model and illustrative case example. *American Journal of Clinical Hypnosis, 61,* 45–56. http://dx.doi.org/10.1080/00029157.2018.1456896

Erickson, M. H. (1979). Self-exploration in the hypnotic state. In D. Goleman & R. J. Davidson (Eds.), *Consciousness: Brain, states of awareness, and mysticism* (pp. 155–158). New York, NY: Harper & Row.

Everson, C. A. (1997). Clinical manifestations of prolonged sleep deprivation. In M. Fisher (Series Ed.) & W. J. Schwartz (Vol. Ed.), *Monographs in clinical neuroscience: Vol. 15. Sleep science: Integrating basic research and clinical practice* (pp. 34–59). Basel, Switzerland: Karger. http://dx.doi.org/10.1159/000061563

Ewin, D. M., Levitan, A. A., & Lynch, D. F., Jr. (1999). Comment on "Self-hypnosis as anesthesia for liposuction surgery." *American Journal of Clinical Hypnosis, 41,* 302. http://dx.doi.org/10.1080/00029157.1999.10404228

Facco, E. (2017). Meditation and hypnosis: Two sides of the same coin? *International Journal of Clinical and Experimental Hypnosis, 65,* 169–188.

Facco, E., Agrillo, C., & Greyson, B. (2015). Epistemological implications of near-death experiences and other non-ordinary mental expressions: Moving beyond the concept of altered state of consciousness. *Medical Hypotheses, 85,* 85–93. http://dx.doi.org/10.1016/j.mehy.2015.04.004

Facco, E., Pasquali, S., Zanette, G., & Casiglia, E. (2013). Hypnosis as sole anaesthesia for skin tumour removal in a patient with multiple chemical sensitivity. *Anaesthesia, 68,* 961–965. http://dx.doi.org/10.1111/anae.12251

Farthing, G. W. (1992). *The Psychology of consciousness*. Englewood Cliffs, NJ: Prentice Hall.

Feinberg-Moss, B. B., & Oatley, K. (1990). Guided imagery in brief psychodynamic therapy: Outcome and process. *British Journal of Medical Psychology, 63,* 117–129. http://dx.doi.org/10.1111/j.2044-8341.1990.tb01605.x

Feinstein, J. S., Khalsa, S. S., Yeh, H., Al Zoubi, O., Arevian, A. C., Wohlrab, C., . . . Paulus, M. P. (2018). The elicitation of relaxation and interoceptive awareness using floatation therapy in individuals with high anxiety sensitivity. *Biological Psychiatry: Cognitive Neuroscience and Neuroimaging, 3,* 555–562.

Fenwick, P., & Fenwick, E. (1995). *The truth in the light: An investigation of over 300 near-death experiences*. New York, NY: Berkeley Books.

Fenwick, P., & Fenwick, E. (1999). *Past lives: An investigation into reincarnation memories*. London, England: Headline.

Ferracuti, S., Sacco, R., & Lazzari, R. (1996). Dissociative trance disorder: Clinical and Rorschach findings in ten persons reporting demon possession and treated by exorcism. *Journal of Personality Assessment, 66,* 525–539. http://dx.doi.org/10.1207/s15327752jpa6603_4

Ferrucci, P. (1982). *What we may be: Techniques for psychological and spiritual growth through psychosynthesis*. Los Angeles, CA: Jeremy P. Tarcher.

Fiacconi, C. M., Kouptsova, J. E., & Köhler, S. (2017). A role for visceral feedback and interoception in feelings-of-knowing. *Consciousness and Cognition, 53,* 70–80. http://dx.doi.org/10.1016/j.concog.2017.06.001

Fields, R. D. (2009). *The other brain: The scientific and medical breakthroughs that will heal our brains and revolutionize our health*. New York, NY: Simon & Schuster.

Flanagan, O. (1992). *Consciousness reconsidered*. Cambridge, MA: MIT Press.

Fontana, D. (2005). *Is there an afterlife? A comprehensive overview of the evidence*. Winchester, England: O-Books.

Forte, R. (1997). Introduction. In R. Forte (Ed.), *Entheogens and the future of religion* (pp. 1–5). San Francisco, CA: Council on Spiritual Practices.

Fotiou, E. (2016). The globalization of ayahuasca shamanism and the erasure of indigenous shamanism. *Anthropology of Consciousness, 27,* 151–179. http://dx.doi.org/10.1111/anoc.12056

Foulkes, D. (1966). *The psychology of sleep*. New York, NY: Charles Scribner's Sons.

Foulkes, D. (1985). *Dreaming: A cognitive-psychological analysis*. Hillsdale, NJ: Erlbaum.

Foulkes, D. (1990). Dreaming and consciousness. *The European Journal of Cognitive Psychology, 2,* 39–55. http://dx.doi.org/10.1080/09541449008406196

Foulkes, D. (1996). Dream research: 1953–1993. *Sleep, 19,* 609–624. http://dx.doi.org/10.1093/sleep/19.8.609

Fox, C. (2000, March). The search for extraterrestrial life. *Life,* pp. 46–51, 54, 56.

Fox, K. C. R., & Christoff, K. (2018). Introduction: Toward an interdisciplinary science of spontaneous thought. In K. C. R. Fox & K. Christoff (Eds.), *The Oxford handbook of spontaneous thought: Mind-wandering, creativity, and dreaming* (pp. 1–8). Oxford, England: Oxford University Press.

Fox, O. (1975). *Astral projection: A record of out-of-the-body experiences*. Secaucus, NJ: Citadel Press.

Foy, R. P. (2008). *Witnessing the impossible*. Diss, England: Torcal.

Frank, N. C., Spirito, A., Stark, L., & Owens-Stively, J. (1997). The use of scheduled awakenings to eliminate childhood sleepwalking. *Journal of Pediatric Psychology, 22,* 345–353. http://dx.doi.org/10.1093/jpepsy/22.3.345

Frankel, F. H., & Covino, N. A. (1997). Hypnosis and hypnotherapy. In P. S. Appelbaum, L. A. Uyehara, & M. R. Elin (Eds.), *Trauma and memory: Clinical and legal controversies* (pp. 344–359). New York, NY: Oxford University Press.

Frankl, V. E. (1984). *Man's search for meaning* (Rev. & updated ed.). New York, NY: Washington Square Press. (Original work published 1946)

Frankl, V. E. (1997a). *Man's search for ultimate meaning.* New York, NY: Insight Books. (Original work published 1948)

Frankl, V. E. (1997b). *Victor Frankl—Recollections: An autobiography.* (J. Fabry & J. Fabry, Trans.). New York, NY: Insight. (Original work published 1995)

Freedman, N. (2017). Positive airway pressure treatment for obstructive sleep apnea. In M. Kryger, T. Roth, & W. C. Dement (Eds.), *Principles and practice of sleep medicine* (6th ed., pp. 1125–1137). Philadelphia, PA: Elsevier. http://dx.doi.org/10.1016/B978-0-323-24288-2.00115-X

Freedman, T. B. (1997). Past life and interlife reports of phobic people: Patterns and outcome. *The Journal of Regression Therapy, 11,* 91–94.

French, C. C., Santomauro, J., Hamilton, V., Fox, R., & Thalbourne, M. A. (2008). Psychological aspects of the alien contact experience. *Cortex, 44,* 1387–1395. http://dx.doi.org/10.1016/j.cortex.2007.11.011

Freud, S. (1950). *The interpretation of dreams* (A. A. Brill, Trans.). New York, NY: Random House. (Original work published 1900)

Gentile, J. P., Dillon, K. S., & Gillig, P. M. (2013). Psychotherapy and pharmacotherapy for patients with dissociative identity disorder. *Innovations in Clinical Neuroscience, 10*(2), 22–29.

Giannelli, P. C. (1995). The admissibility of hypnotic evidence in U.S. courts. *International Journal of Clinical and Experimental Hypnosis, 43,* 212–233. http://dx.doi.org/10.1080/00207149508409962

Gifford-May, D., & Thompson, N. L. (1994). "Deep states" of meditation: Phenomenological reports of experience. *Journal of Transpersonal Psychology, 26,* 117–138.

Gillig, P. M. (2009). Dissociative identity disorder: A controversial diagnosis. *Psychiatry, 6*(3), 24–29.

Gilson, T. P., Shannon, H., & Freiburger, J. (2017). The evolution of the opiate/opioid crisis in Cuyahoga County. *Academic Forensic Pathology, 7,* 41–49. http://dx.doi.org/10.23907/2017.005

Glaskin, G. M. (1974). *Windows of the mind: Discovering your past and future lives through massage and mental exercise.* New York, NY: Delacorte Press.

Glaskin, G. M. (1976). *Worlds within: Probing the Christos experience.* London, England: Wildwood House.

Glaskin, G. M. (1979). *A door to eternity: Proving the Christos experience.* London, England: Wildwood House.

Goertzel, T., & Goertzel, B. (2015). Skeptical responses to psi research. In D. Broderick & B. Goertzel (Eds.), *Evidence for psi: Thirteen empirical research reports* (pp. 291–301). Jefferson, NC: McFarland.

Goldberg, B. (1997). *The search for Grace.* St. Paul, MN: Llewellyn.

Goldblatt, R. (1979). *Topoi: The categorial analysis of logic.* Amsterdam, Netherlands: North-Holland.

Goleman, D. (1988). *The meditative mind: The varieties of meditative experience.* Los Angeles, CA: Jeremy P. Tarcher. (Original work published 1977)

González-Díaz, S. N., Arias-Cruz, A., Elizondo-Villarreal, B., & Monge-Ortega, O. P. (2017). Psychoneuroimmunoendocrinology: Clinical implications. *World Allergy Organization Journal, 10,* 19. http://dx.doi.org/10.1186/s40413-017-0151-6

Graff, D. E. (2000). *River dreams: The case of the missing general and other adventures in psychic research.* Boston, MA: Element.

Gravitz, M. A. (1995). Inability to dehypnotize—Implications for management: A brief communication. *International Journal of Clinical and Experimental Hypnosis, 43,* 369–374. http://dx.doi.org/10.1080/00207149508409981

Greer, S. M. (2001). *Disclosure: Military and government witnesses reveal the greatest secrets in modern history*. Crozet, VA: Crossing Point.

Greyson, B. (1994). Reduced death threat in near-death experiencers. In R. A. Neimeyer (Ed.), *Death anxiety handbook: Research, instrumentation, and application* (pp. 169–179). Washington, DC: Taylor & Francis.

Greyson, B. (1998). The incidence of near-death experiences. *Medicine & Psychiatry, 1*, 92–99.

Greyson, B. (2000). Near-death experiences. In E. Cardeña, S. J. Lynn, & S. Krippner (Eds.), *Varieties of anomalous experience: Examining the scientific evidence* (pp. 315–352). Washington, DC: American Psychological Association. http://dx.doi.org/10.1037/10371-010

Greyson, B. (2010). Implications of near-death experiences for a postmaterialist psychology. *Psychology of Religion and Spirituality, 2*, 37–45. http://dx.doi.org/10.1037/a0018548

Greyson, B. (2014). Near-death experiences. In E. Cardeña, S. J. Lynn, & S. Krippner (Eds.), *Varieties of anomalous experience: Examining the scientific evidence* (2nd ed., pp. 333–367). http://dx.doi.org/10.1037/14258-012

Greyson, B., & Bush, N. E. (1992). Distressing near-death experiences. *Psychiatry: Interpersonal and Biological Processes 55*, 95–110. http://dx.doi.org/10.1080/00332747.1992.11024583

Greyson, B., Kelly, E. W., & Kelly, E. F. (2009). Explanatory models for near-death experiences. In J. M. Holden, B. Greyson, & D. James (Eds.), *The handbook of near-death experiences: Thirty years of investigation* (pp. 213–234). Santa Barbara, CA: Praeger.

Griffiths, R., Richards, W., Johnson, M., McCann, U., & Jesse, R. (2008). Mystical-type experiences occasioned by psilocybin mediate the attribution of personal meaning and spiritual significance 14 months later. *Journal of Psychopharmacology, 22*, 621–632. http://dx.doi.org/10.1177/0269881108094300

Griffiths, R. R., Richards, W. A., McCann, U., & Jesse, R. (2006). Psilocybin can occasion mystical-type experiences having substantial and sustained personal meaning and spiritual significance. *Psychopharmacology, 187*, 268–283. http://dx.doi.org/10.1007/s00213-006-0457-5

Grinspoon, L., & Bakalar, J. B. (1979). *Psychedelic drugs reconsidered*. New York, NY: Basic Books.

Grinspoon, L., & Bakalar, J. B. (1997). *Psychedelic drugs reconsidered*. New York, NY: Lindesmith Center. (Original work published 1979)

Grob, C., & Harman, W. (1995). Making sense of the psychedelic issue. *Noetic Sciences Review, 35*, 4–9, 37–41.

Grof, S. (1987). Survival of consciousness after death: Myth and science. In J. S. Spong (Ed.), *Consciousness and survival: An interdisciplinary inquiry into the possibility of life beyond biological death* (pp. 135–164). Sausalito, CA: Institute of Noetic Sciences.

Grof, S., & Halifax, J. (1978). *The human encounter with death*. New York, NY: E. P. Dutton.

Grossinger, R. (1989). Giving them a name. *ReVision: The Journal of Consciousness and Change, 11*(4), 43–48.

Grosso, M. (2014). Two perspectives on possession. *Journal of Scientific Exploration, 28*, 509–517.

Grunstein, R., & Sullivan, C. (2000). Continuous positive airway pressure for sleep breathing disorders. In M. H. Kryger, T. Roth, & W. C. Dement (Eds.), *Principles and practice of sleep medicine* (3rd ed., pp. 894–912). Philadelphia, PA: W. B. Saunders.

Guiley, R. E. (1991). *Harper's encyclopedia of mystical & paranormal experience*. New York, NY: HarperSanFrancisco.

Guilleminault, C., & Anagnos, A. (2000). Narcolepsy. In M. H. Kryger, T. Roth, & W. C. Dement (Eds.), *Principles and practice of sleep medicine* (3rd ed., pp. 676–686). Philadelphia, PA: W. B. Saunders.

Halaris, A., Bechter, K., Haroon, E., Leonard, B. E., Miller, A., Pariante, C., & Zunszain, P. (2019). The future of psychoneuroimmunology: Promises and challenges. In A. Javed & K. N. Fountoulakis (Eds.), *Advances in Psychiatry* (pp. 235–266). Springer International Publishing AG. http://dx.doi.org/10.1007/978-3-319-70554-5_15

Halifax, J. (1990). The shaman's initiation. *ReVision: The Journal of Consciousness and Change, 13*(2), 53–58.

Hall, J. A. (1977). *Clinical uses of dreams: Jungian interpretations and enactments.* New York, NY: Grune & Stratton.

Hameroff, S. R. (1994). Quantum coherence in microtubules: A neural basis for emergent consciousness? *Journal of Scientific Exploration, 10,* 91–118.

Hanson, S. J., & Burr, D. J. (1990). What connectionist models learn: Learning and representation in connectionist networks. *Behavioral and Brain Sciences, 13,* 471–489. http://dx.doi.org/10.1017/S0140525X00079760

Hardy, J. (1987). *A psychology with a soul: Psychosynthesis in evolutionary context.* London, England: Arkana.

Harman, W. (1994). Past lives put to present use. *Noetic Sciences Review, 29,* 20–22.

Harrison, J. R., & Barabasz, A. F. (1991). Effects of restricted environmental stimulation therapy on the behavior of children with autism. *Child Study Journal, 21,* 153–166.

Hasenkamp, W. (2018). Catching the wandering mind: Meditation as a window into spontaneous thought. In K. C. R. Fox & K. Christoff (Eds.), *The Oxford handbook of spontaneous thought: Mind-wandering, creativity, and dreaming* (pp. 539–551). Oxford, England: Oxford University Press.

Hastings, A. (1988). Exceptional abilities in channeling. *Noetic Sciences Review, 6,* 27–29.

Hastings, A. (1991). *With the tongues of men and angels: A study of channeling.* Fort Worth, TX: Holt, Rinehart and Winston.

Hauri, P. J. (2000). Primary insomnia. In M. H. Kryger, T. Roth, & W. C. Dement (Eds.), *Principles and practice of sleep medicine* (3rd ed., pp. 633–639). Philadelphia, PA: W. B. Saunders.

Havlík, M. (2017). Missing piece of the puzzle in the science of consciousness: Resting state and endogenous correlates of consciousness. *Consciousness and Cognition, 49,* 70–85. http://dx.doi.org/10.1016/j.concog.2017.01.006

Haye, A., & Torres-Sahli, M. (2017). To feel is to know relations: James' concept of stream of thought and contemporary studies on procedural knowledge. *New Ideas in Psychology, 46,* 46–55. http://dx.doi.org/10.1016/j.newideapsych.2017.02.001

Heap, M. (1995). A case of death following stage hypnosis: Analysis and implications. *Contemporary Hypnosis, 12,* 99–110.

Hernandez, R., Davis, R., Scalpone, R., & Schild, R. (2018). A study on reported contact with non-human intelligence associated with unidentified aerial phenomena. *Journal of Scientific Exploration, 32,* 298–348. http://dx.doi.org/10.31275/2018.1282

Hibler, N. S. (1995). Using hypnosis for investigative purposes. In M. I. Kurke & E. M. Scrivner (Eds.), *Police psychology into the 21st century* (pp. 319–336). Hillsdale, NJ: Erlbaum.

Hilgard, E. R. (1973a). The domain of hypnosis. With some comments on alternative paradigms. *American Psychologist, 28,* 972–982. http://dx.doi.org/10.1037/h0035452

Hilgard, E. R. (1973b). A neodissociation interpretation of pain reduction in hypnosis. *Psychological Review, 80,* 396–411. http://dx.doi.org/10.1037/h0020073

Hilgard, E. R. (1979). The hypnotic state. In D. Goleman & R. J. Davidson (Eds.), *Consciousness: Brain, states of awareness, and mysticism* (pp. 147–150). New York, NY: Harper & Row.

Hilgard, E. R. (1987). *Psychology in America: A historical survey*. San Diego, CA: Harcourt Brace Jovanovich.

Hill, C. E. (1996). Dreams and therapy. *Psychotherapy Research, 6*, 1–15. http://dx.doi.org/10.1080/10503309612331331538

Hill, C. E., & Rochlen, A. B. (1999). A cognitive-experiential model for working with dreams in psychotherapy. In L. Vandecreek & T. L. Jackson (Eds.), *Innovations in clinical practice: A source book* (pp. 467–480). Sarasota, FL: Professional Resource Press.

Hirsch, H. V. B., & Spinelli, D. N. (1971). Modification of the distribution of receptive field orientation in cats by selective visual exposure during development. *Experimental Brain Research, 12*, 509–527. http://dx.doi.org/10.1007/BF00234246

Hirshkowitz, M., Moore, C. A., & Minhoto, G. (1997). The basics of sleep. In M. R. Pressman & W. C. Orr (Eds.), *Understanding sleep: The evaluation and treatment of sleep disorders* (pp. 11–34). Washington, DC: American Psychological Association. http://dx.doi.org/10.1037/10233-001

Hobson, J. A. (1988). *The dreaming brain*. New York, NY: Basic Books.

Hobson, J. A. (1990). Dreams and the brain. In S. Krippner (Ed.), *Dreamtime and dreamwork: Decoding the language of the night* (pp. 215–223). Los Angeles, CA: Jeremy P. Tarcher.

Hobson, J. A. (1997). Consciousness as a state-dependent phenomenon. In J. D. Cohen & J. W. Schooler (Eds.), *Scientific approaches to consciousness* (pp. 379–396). Mahwah, NJ: Erlbaum.

Hobson, J. A., & McCarley, R. W. (1977). The brain as a dream state generator: An activation–synthesis hypothesis of the dream process. *The American Journal of Psychiatry, 134*, 1335–1348. http://dx.doi.org/10.1176/ajp.134.12.1335

Hobson, J. A., Pace-Schott, E. F., & Stickgold, R. (2000). Consciousness: Its vicissitudes in waking and sleep. In M. S. Gazzaniga (Ed.), *The new cognitive neurosciences* (2nd ed., pp. 1341–1354). Cambridge, MA: MIT Press.

Hock, R. R. (1999). *Forty studies that changed psychology: Explorations into the history of psychological research* (3rd ed.). Upper Saddle River, NJ: Prentice Hall.

Hoffman, D. D. (1998). *Visual intelligence: How we create what we see*. New York, NY: W. W. Norton.

Hofmann, A. (1980). *LSD: My problem child* (J. Ott, Trans.). New York, NY: McGraw-Hill. (Original work published 1979)

Hofstadter, D. R. (1979). *Gödel, Escher, Bach: An eternal golden braid*. New York, NY: Basic Books.

Holden, J. M. (2009). Veridical perception in near-death experiences. In J. M. Holden, B. Greyson, & D. James (Eds.), *The handbook of near-death experiences: Thirty years of investigation* (pp. 185–211). Santa Barbara, CA: Praeger.

Holden, J. M., Greyson, B., & James, D. (Eds.). (2009). *The handbook of near-death experiences: Thirty years of investigation*. Santa Barbara, CA: Praeger.

Hollister, L. E., & Sjoberg, B. M. (1964). Clinical syndromes and biochemical alterations following mescaline, lysergic acid diethylamide, psilocybin and a combination of the three psychotomimetic drugs. *Comprehensive Psychiatry, 5*, 170–178. http://dx.doi.org/10.1016/S0010-440X(64)80030-4

Holman, C. (2011). Surfing for a shaman: Analyzing an ayahuasca website. *Annals of Tourism Research, 38*, 90–109. http://dx.doi.org/10.1016/j.annals.2010.05.005

Holvenstot, C. (2011). Toward a science of consciousness 2011: The greatest show on earth. *Journal of Consciousness Exploration & Research, 2*, 656–665.

Holyoak, K. J., & Spellman, B. A. (1993). Thinking. *Annual Review of Psychology, 44*, 265–315. http://dx.doi.org/10.1146/annurev.ps.44.020193.001405

Honorton, C. (1974). Tracing ESP through altered states of consciousness. In J. White (Ed.), *Frontiers of consciousness: The meeting ground between inner and outer reality* (pp. 159–168). New York, NY: Julian Press.

Hood, R. W., Jr., Spilka, B., Hunsberger, B., & Gorsuch, R. (1996). *The psychology of religion: An empirical approach* (2nd ed.). New York, NY: Guilford Press.

Hopkins, B. (2000). Hypnosis and the investigation of UFO abduction accounts. In D. M. Jacobs (Ed.), *UFOs and abductions: Challenging the borders of knowledge* (pp. 215–240). Lawrence, KS: University Press of Kansas.

Horstmann, S., Hess, C. W., Bassetti, C., Gugger, M., & Mathis, J. (2000). Sleepiness-related accidents in sleep apnea patients. *Sleep, 23,* 383–389. http://dx.doi.org/10.1093/sleep/23.3.1e

Houran, J., & Lange, R. (1998). Modeling precognitive dreams as meaningful coincidences. *Psychological Reports, 83,* 1411–1414.

Hove, M. J., & Stelzer, J. (2018). Biological foundations and beneficial effects of trance. *Behavioral and Brain Sciences, 41,* e76. http://dx.doi.org/10.1017/S0140525X17002072

Howard, H. A. (2017). Promoting safety in hypnosis: A clinical instrument for the assessment of alertness. *American Journal of Clinical Hypnosis, 59,* 344–362. http://dx.doi.org/10.1080/00029157.2016.1203281

Howe, R. B. K. (1991a). Introspection: A reassessment. *New Ideas in Psychology, 9,* 25–44. http://dx.doi.org/10.1016/0732-118X(91)90038-N

Howe, R. B. K. (1991b). Reassessing introspection: A reply to Natsoulas, Lyons, and Ericsson and Crutcher. *New Ideas in Psychology, 9,* 383–394. http://dx.doi.org/10.1016/0732-118X(91)90011-A

Hughes, D. J. (1992). Differences between trance channeling and multiple personality disorder on structured interview. *Journal of Transpersonal Psychology, 24,* 181–192.

Hunt, H. T. (1986). Some relations between the cognitive psychology of dreams and dream phenomenology. *Journal of Mind and Behavior, 7,* 213–228.

Hurley, T. J., III. (1985a). Etiology of multiple personality: From abuse to alter personalities. *Institute of Noetic Sciences: Investigations: A Research Bulletin, 1*(3/4), 11–13.

Hurley, T. J., III. (1985b). Glossary of key concepts. *Institute of Noetic Sciences: Investigations: A Research Bulletin, 1*(3/4), 22.

Hurley, T. J., III. (1985c). Inner faces of multiplicity: Contemporary look at a classic mystery. *Institute of Noetic Sciences: Investigations: A Research Bulletin, 1*(3/4), 3–6.

Hurley, T. J., III. (1985d). Multiplicity & the mind-body problem: New windows to natural plasticity. *Institute of Noetic Sciences: Investigations: A Research Bulletin, 1*(3/4), 7–9.

Hurley, T. J., III. (1985e). Possession, dynamic psychiatry & science: The historical fortunes of MPD. *Institute of Noetic Sciences: Investigations: A Research Bulletin, 1*(3/4), 19–21.

Huxley, A. (1945). *The perennial philosophy.* New York, NY: Harper & Brothers.

Hyman, R. (1994). Anomaly or artifact? Comments on Bem and Honorton. *Psychological Bulletin, 115,* 19–24. http://dx.doi.org/10.1037/0033-2909.115.1.19

Hyman, R. (2001). Anomalous experiences in a mundane world. *Contemporary Psychology, 46,* 453–456. http://dx.doi.org/10.1037/002399

Irving, Z. C., & Thompson, E. (2018). The philosophy of mind-wandering. In K. C. R. Fox & K. Christoff (Eds.), *The Oxford handbook of spontaneous thought: Mind-wandering, creativity, and dreaming* (pp. 87–96). Oxford, England: Oxford University Press.

Irwin, H. J. (1994). *An introduction to parapsychology* (2nd ed.). Jefferson, NC: McFarland.

Isaacs, T. C. (1987). The possessive states disorder: The diagnosis of demonic possession. *Pastoral Psychology, 35,* 263–273. http://dx.doi.org/10.1007/BF01760734

Jackendoff, R. (1987). *Consciousness and the computational mind.* Cambridge, MA: MIT Press.

Jacobs, B. L. (1987). How hallucinogenic drugs work. *American Scientist, 75,* 386–392.

Jacobs, D. M. (1998). *The threat.* New York, NY: Simon & Schuster.

Jahn, R. G. (2001). 20th and 21st century science: Reflections and projections. *Journal of Scientific Exploration, 15,* 21–31.

Jahn, R. G., & Dunne, B. J. (1987). *Margins of reality: The role of consciousness in the physical world*. San Diego, CA: Harcourt Brace Jovanovich.

James, E. (2001). *Personality correlates of beliefs about consciousness and reality*. (Unpublished bachelor's thesis). University of Regina, Regina, Canada.

James, W. (1904a). Does "consciousness" exist? *The Journal of Philosophy, Psychology and Scientific Methods, 1*, 477–491. http://dx.doi.org/10.2307/2011942

James, W. (1904b). A world of pure experience. I. *The Journal of Philosophy, Psychology and Scientific Methods, 1*, 533–543. http://dx.doi.org/10.2307/2011912

James, W. (1904c). A world of pure experience. II. *The Journal of Philosophy, Psychology and Scientific Methods, 1*, 561–570. http://dx.doi.org/10.2307/2011356

James, W. (1983). *The principles of psychology*. Cambridge, MA: Harvard University Press. (Original work published 1890)

Jeans, J. (1937). *The mysterious universe* (New rev. ed.). New York, NY: MacMillan.

Jensen, M. P., Jamieson, G. A., Lutz, A., Mazzoni, G., McGeown, W. J., Santarcangelo, E. L., . . . Terhune, D. B. (2017). New directions in hypnosis research: Strategies for advancing the cognitive and clinical neuroscience of hypnosis. *Neuroscience of Consciousness, 3*(1), nix004. Advance online publication. http://dx.doi.org/10.1093/nc/nix004

Jewkes, S., & Baruš, I. (2000). Personality correlates of beliefs about consciousness and reality. *Advanced Development: A Journal on Adult Giftedness, 9*, 91–103.

Johnson, C. P. L., & Persinger, M. A. (1994). The sensed presence may be facilitated by interhemispheric intercalation: Relative efficacy of the Mind's Eye, Hemi-Sync Tape, and bilateral temporal magnetic field stimulation. *Perceptual and Motor Skills, 79*, 351–354. http://dx.doi.org/10.2466/pms.1994.79.1.351

Jones, R. T. (1971). Tetrahydrocannabinol and the marijuana-induced social "high," or the effects of the mind on marijuana. In A. J. Singer (Vol. Ed.), *Annals of the New York Academy of Sciences: Vol. 191. Marijuana: Chemistry, pharmacology, and patterns of social use* (pp. 155–165). New York, NY: The New York Academy of Sciences.

Jonsson, K. (2018). *Flotation-REST (Restricted Environmental Stimulation Technique) in the age of anxiety: Exploring the role and treatment applications of sensory isolation in the modern world* (Unpublished doctoral dissertation). Karlstad University, Karlstad, Sweden.

Josipovic, Z. (2014). Neural correlates of nondual awareness in meditation. *Annals of the New York Academy of Sciences, 1307*, 9–18. http://dx.doi.org/10.1111/nyas.12261

Jouvet, M. (1999). *The paradox of sleep: The story of dreaming* (L. Garey, Trans.). Cambridge, MA: Bradford. (Original work published 1993)

Jue, R. W. (1996). Past-life therapy. In B. W. Scotton, A. B. Chinen, & J. R. Battista (Eds.), *Textbook of transpersonal psychiatry and psychology* (pp. 377–387). New York, NY: Basic Books.

Jung, C. G. (1965). *Memories, dreams, reflections* (Rev. ed.; A. Jaffé, Recorder & Ed.; R. Winston & C. Winston, Trans.). New York, NY: Vintage Books.

Jung, C. G. (1971). *Psychological types*. In W. McGuire (Exec. Ed.), H. Read, M. Fordham, & G. Adler (Eds.), H. G. Baynes (Trans.) & R. F. C. Hull (Revisor of English translation), *The collected works of C. G. Jung: Vol. 6*. Princeton, NJ: Princeton University Press. (Original work without appendix published 1921)

Kahn, D. (2016). The dream as a product of an emergent process. *Emergence: Complexity & Organization, 18*, 1–5.

Kahn, D., Krippner, S., & Combs, A. (2000). Dreaming and the self-organizing brain. *Journal of Consciousness Studies, 7*(7), 4–11.

Kalas, P. (2018). *The Oneironauts: Using dreams to engineer our future*. Author.

Kales, A., & Kales, J. D. (1984). *Evaluation and treatment of insomnia*. New York, NY: Oxford University Press.

Kanda, T., Tsujino, N., Kuramoto, E., Koyama, Y., Susaki, E. A., Chikahisa, S., & Funato, H. (2016). Sleep as a biological problem: An overview of frontiers in sleep research. *The Journal of Physiological Sciences; JPS, 66*, 1–13. http://dx.doi.org/10.1007/s12576-015-0414-3

Katz, S. T. (1978). Language, epistemology, and mysticism. In S. T. Katz (Ed.), *Mysticism and philosophical analysis* (pp. 22–74). New York, NY: Oxford University Press.

Kauders, A. D. (2017). The social before sociocognitive theory: Explaining hypnotic suggestion in German-speaking Europe, 1900–1960. *American Journal of Clinical Hypnosis, 59*, 422–439. http://dx.doi.org/10.1080/00029157.2016.1239062

Keen, M., Ellison, A., & Fontana, D. (1999). The Scole report: An account of an investigation into the genuineness of a range of physical phenomena associated with a mediumistic group in Norfolk, England. *Proceedings of the Society for Psychical Research, 58*(Pt. 220), 149–392.

Keenan, S., & Hirshkowitz, M. (2017). Sleep stage scoring. In M. Kryger, T. Roth, & W. C. Dement (Eds.), *Principles and practice of sleep medicine* (6th ed., pp. 1567–1575). Philadelphia, PA: Elsevier. http://dx.doi.org/10.1016/B978-0-323-24288-2.00161-6

Kellehear, A. (1996). *Experiences near death: Beyond medicine and religion.* New York, NY: Oxford University Press.

Kelly, E. W., Greyson, B., & Kelly, E. F. (2010). Unusual experiences near death and related phenomena. In E. F. Kelly, E. W. Kelly, A. Crabtree, A. Gauld, M. Gross, & B. Greyson (Eds.), *Irreducible mind: Toward a psychology for the 21st century* (pp. 367–421). Lanham, MD: Rowman & Littlefield. (Original work published 2007)

Kelly, S. F., & Kelly, R. J. (1995). *Imagine yourself well: Better health through self-hypnosis.* New York, NY: Plenum Press.

Kerr, N. H. (2000). Dreaming, imagery, and perception. In M. H. Kryger, T. Roth, & W. C. Dement (Eds.), *Principles and practice of sleep medicine* (3rd ed., pp. 482–490). Philadelphia, PA: W. B. Saunders.

Khanna, S., Moore, L. E., & Greyson, B. (2018). Full neurological recovery from *Escherichia coli* meningitis associated with near-death experience. *The Journal of Nervous and Mental Disease, 206*, 744–747. http://dx.doi.org/10.1097/NMD.0000000000000874

Kihlstrom, J. F. (1985). Hypnosis. *Annual Review of Psychology, 36*, 385–418. http://dx.doi.org/10.1146/annurev.ps.36.020185.002125

Kihlstrom, J. F. (2018). Hypnosis: Applications. In *Reference Module in Neuroscience and Biobehavioral Psychology.* Elsevier. http://dx.doi.org/10.1016/B978-0-12-809324-5.21772-0

Kilduff, T. S., & Mendelson, W. B. (2017). Hypnotic medications: Mechanisms of action and pharmacologic effects. In M. Kryger, T. Roth, & W. C. Dement (Eds.), *Principles and practice of sleep medicine* (6th ed., pp. 424–431). Philadelphia, PA: Elsevier. http://dx.doi.org/10.1016/B978-0-323-24288-2.00041-6

King, W., Jr., & Ellison, G. (1989). Long-lasting alterations in behavior and brain neurochemistry following continuous low-level LSD administration. *Pharmacology Biochemistry and Behavior, 33*, 69–73. http://dx.doi.org/10.1016/0091-3057(89)90431-0

Kirmayer, L. J. (2015). Mindfulness in cultural context. *Transcultural Psychiatry, 52*, 447–469. http://dx.doi.org/10.1177/1363461515598949

Kirsch, I., & Lynn, S. J. (1995). The altered state of hypnosis: Changes in the theoretical landscape. *American Psychologist, 50*, 846–858. http://dx.doi.org/10.1037/0003-066X.50.10.846

Klimo, J. (1987). *Channeling: Investigations on receiving information from paranormal sources.* Los Angeles, CA: Jeremy P. Tarcher.

Klinger, E. (1978). Modes of normal conscious flow. In K. S. Pope & J. L. Singer (Eds.), *The stream of consciousness: Scientific investigations into the flow of human experience* (pp. 225–258). New York, NY: Plenum Press. http://dx.doi.org/10.1007/978-1-4684-2466-9_9

Klinger, E. (1990). *Daydreaming: Using waking fantasy and imagery for self-knowledge and creativity.* Los Angeles, CA: Jeremy P. Tarcher.

Klinger, E., & Cox, W. M. (1987). Dimensions of thought flow in everyday life. *Imagination, Cognition and Personality, 7,* 105–128. http://dx.doi.org/10.2190/7K24-G343-MTQW-115V

Klinger, E., & Kroll-Mensing, D. (1995). Idiothetic assessment experience sampling and motivational analysis. In J. N. Butcher (Ed.), *Clinical personality assessment: Practical approaches* (pp. 267–277). New York, NY: Oxford University Press.

Klinger, E., Marchetti, I., & Koster, E. H. W. (2018). Spontaneous thought and goal pursuit: From functions such as planning to dysfunctions such as rumination. In K. C. R. Fox & K. Christoff (Eds.), *The Oxford handbook of spontaneous thought: Mind-wandering, creativity, and dreaming* (pp. 215–232). Oxford, England: Oxford University Press.

Kluft, R. P. (1996). Dissociative identity disorder. In L. K. Michelson & W. J. Ray (Eds.), *Handbook of dissociation: Theoretical, empirical, and clinical perspectives* (pp. 337–366). New York, NY: Plenum. http://dx.doi.org/10.1007/978-1-4899-0310-5_16

Knight, Z. (1995). The healing power of the unconscious: How can we understand past life experiences in psychotherapy? *South African Journal of Psychology. Suid-Afrikaanse Tydskrif vir Sielkunde, 25,* 90–98. http://dx.doi.org/10.1177/008124639502500204

Knox, V. J., Morgan, A. H., & Hilgard, E. R. (1974). Pain and suffering in ischemia. The paradox of hypnotically suggested anesthesia as contradicted by reports from the "hidden observer." *Archives of General Psychiatry, 30,* 840–847. http://dx.doi.org/10.1001/archpsyc.1974.01760120090013

Koch, C. (2012). *Consciousness: Confessions of a romantic reductionist.* Cambridge, MA: MIT Press. http://dx.doi.org/10.7551/mitpress/9367.001.0001

Koriat, A. (2000). The feeling of knowing: Some metatheoretical implications for consciousness and control. *Consciousness and Cognition, 9,* 149–171. http://dx.doi.org/10.1006/ccog.2000.0433

Krippner, S. (1981). Access to hidden reserves of the unconscious through dreams in creative problem solving. *The Journal of Creative Behavior, 15,* 11–22. http://dx.doi.org/10.1002/j.2162-6057.1981.tb00270.x

Krippner, S. (1993). The Maimonides ESP-dream studies. *Journal of Parapsychology, 57,* 39–54.

Krippner, S. (1994). Cross-cultural treatment perspectives on dissociative disorders. In S. J. Lynn & J. W. Rhue (Eds.), *Dissociation: Clinical and theoretical perspectives* (pp. 338–361). New York, NY: Guilford Press.

Krippner, S. (1997). The varieties of dissociative experience. In S. Krippner & S. M. Powers (Eds.), *Broken images, broken selves: Dissociative narratives in clinical practice* (pp. 336–361). Bristol, PA: Brunner/Mazel.

Krippner, S. (1999). The varieties of hypnotic experience. *Contemporary Hypnosis, 16,* 157–159. http://dx.doi.org/10.1002/ch.169

Krippner, S., & Combs, A. (2002). The neurophenomenology of shamanism: An essay review. *Journal of Consciousness Studies, 9,* 77–82.

Krippner, S., & Dillard, J. (1988). *Dreamworking: How to use your dreams for creative problem-solving.* Buffalo, NY: Bearly.

Krippner, S., & Faith, L. (2001). Exotic dreams: A cross-cultural study. *Dreaming, 11,* 73–82. http://dx.doi.org/10.1023/A:1009480404011

Krippner, S., & George, L. (1986). Psi phenomena as related to altered states of consciousness. In B. B. Wolman & M. Ullman (Eds.), *Handbook of states of consciousness* (pp. 332–364). New York, NY: Van Nostrand Reinhold.

Krouwel, M., Jolly, K., & Greenfield, S. (2017). What the public think about hypnosis and hypnotherapy: A narrative review of literature covering opinions and attitudes of the general public 1996–2016. *Complementary Therapies in Medicine, 32,* 75–84. http://dx.doi.org/10.1016/j.ctim.2017.04.002

Kryger, M. H. (2000). Monitoring respiratory and cardiac function. In M. H. Kryger, T. Roth, & W. C. Dement (Eds.), *Principles and practice of sleep medicine* (3rd ed., pp. 1217–1230). Philadelphia, PA: W. B. Saunders.

Krystal, J. H., Bennett, A., Bremner, J. D., Southwick, S. M., & Charney, D. S. (1996). Recent developments in the neurobiology of dissociation: Implications for post-traumatic stress disorder. In L. K. Michelson & W. J. Ray (Eds.), *Handbook of dissociation: Theoretical, empirical, and clinical perspectives* (pp. 163–190). New York, NY: Plenum Press. http://dx.doi.org/10.1007/978-1-4899-0310-5_8

Kübler-Ross, E. (1997). *The wheel of life: A memoir of living and dying*. New York, NY: Touchstone Books.

Kurtz, P. (Ed.). (1985). *A skeptic's handbook of parapsychology*. Buffalo, NY: Prometheus Books.

LaBerge, S. (1990a). Lucid dreaming: Psychophysiological studies of consciousness during REM sleep. In R. R. Bootzin, J. F. Kihlstrom, & D. L. Schacter (Eds.), *Sleep and cognition* (pp. 109–126). Washington, DC: American Psychological Association. http://dx.doi.org/10.1037/10499-008

LaBerge, S. (1990b, Winter). Naps: The best time for lucid dreaming? *NightLight: The Lucidity Institute Newsletter, 2,* 5–8.

LaBerge, S., & Gackenbach, J. (1986). Lucid dreaming. In B. B. Wolman & M. Ullman (Eds.), *Handbook of states of consciousness* (pp. 159–198). New York, NY: Van Nostrand Reinhold.

LaBerge, S., & Gackenbach, J. (2000). Lucid dreaming. In E. Cardeña, S. J. Lynn, & S. Krippner (Eds.), *Varieties of anomalous experience: Examining the scientific evidence* (pp. 151–182). Washington, DC: American Psychological Association. http://dx.doi.org/10.1037/10371-005

LaBerge, S., LaMarca, K., & Baird, B. (2018). Pre-sleep treatment with galantamine stimulates lucid dreaming: A double-blind, placebo-controlled, crossover study. *PloS ONE, 13*(8), e0201246. 1–16. http://dx.doi.org/10.1371/journal.pone.0201246

LaBerge, S., & Rheingold, H. (1990). *Exploring the world of lucid dreaming*. New York, NY: Ballantine Books.

Lake, J. (2017). The near-death experience: A testable neural model. *Psychology of Consciousness: Theory, Research, and Practice, 4,* 115–134. http://dx.doi.org/10.1037/cns0000099

Lambert, S. A. (1996). The effects of hypnosis/guided imagery on the postoperative course of children. *Journal of Developmental & Behavioral Pediatrics, 17,* 307–310. http://dx.doi.org/10.1097/00004703-199610000-00003

Lambie, J. A., & Marcel, A. J. (2002). Consciousness and the varieties of emotion experience: A theoretical framework. *Psychological Review, 109,* 219–259. http://dx.doi.org/10.1037/0033-295X.109.2.219

Landry, M., Lifshitz, M., & Raz, A. (2017). Brain correlates of hypnosis: A systematic review and meta-analytic exploration. *Neuroscience and Biobehavioral Reviews, 81,* 75–98. http://dx.doi.org/10.1016/j.neubiorev.2017.02.020

Langer, E. J. (1989). *Mindfulness*. Reading, MA: Addison-Wesley.

Laughlin, C. D., & Rock, A. J. (2014). What can we learn from shamans' dreaming? A cross-cultural exploration. *Dreaming, 24,* 233–252. http://dx.doi.org/10.1037/a0038437

Leary, M. R., & Butler, T. (2015). Electronic voice phenomena. In E. Cardeña, J. Palmer, & D. Marcusson-Clavertz (Eds.), *Parapsychology: A handbook for the 21st century* (pp. 341–349). Jefferson, NC: McFarland.

Leary, T. (1970). *The politics of ecstasy*. St. Albans, England: Paladin. (Original work published 1965)

Lee, R. L. M. (2015). When is dreaming waking? Continuity, lucidity and transcendence in modern contexts of dreaming. *International Journal of Dream Research, 8,* 66–71.

Lenz, K. L., & Dunlap, D. S. (1998). Continuous fentanyl infusion: Use in severe cancer pain. *Annals of Pharmacotherapy, 32,* 316–319. http://dx.doi.org/10.1345/aph.17285

Leonard, L., & Dawson, D. (2018). The marginalisation of dreams in clinical psychological practice. *Sleep Medicine Reviews, 42,* 10–18. http://dx.doi.org/10.1016/j.smrv.2018.04.002

Lester, D. S., Felder, C. C., & Lewis, E. N. (Eds.). (1997). *Annals of the New York Academy of Sciences: Vol. 820. Imaging brain structure and function: Emerging technologies in the neurosciences.* New York, NY: The New York Academy of Sciences.

Levinthal, C. F. (1996). *Drugs, behavior, and modern society.* Boston, MA: Allyn & Bacon.

Levitan, L., & LaBerge, S. (1990, Fall). Beyond nightmares: Lucid resourcefulness vs. helpless depression. *NightLight: The Lucidity Institute Newsletter, 2,* 1–3, 9–11.

Libet, B., Freeman, A., & Sutherland, K. (1999). Editors introduction: The volitional brain: Towards a neuroscience of free will. [ix–xxii.]. *Journal of Consciousness Studies, 6,* 8–9.

Lilly, J. C. (1978). *The scientist: A novel autobiography.* Philadelphia, PA: J. B. Lippincott.

Lindbergh, C. A. (1953). *The Spirit of St. Louis.* New York, NY: Charles Scribner's Sons.

Lingpa, D. (2016). The foolish dharma of an idiot clothed in mud and feathers. (B. A. Wallace, Trans.) In *Heart of the great perfection: Düdjom Lingpa's visions of the great perfection,* by D. Lingpa and P. Tashi (Vol. 1, pp. 139–161). Somerville, MA: Wisdom Publications.

Lipson, M. (1987). Objective experience. *Noûs, 21,* 319–343. http://dx.doi.org/10.2307/2215185

Liu, X., Lauer, K. K., Douglas Ward, B., Roberts, C., Liu, S., Gollapudy, S., . . . Hudetz, A. G. (2017). Propofol attenuates low-frequency fluctuations of resting-state fMRI BOLD signal in the anterior frontal cortex upon loss of consciousness. *NeuroImage, 147,* 295–301. http://dx.doi.org/10.1016/j.neuroimage.2016.12.043

Lockwood, M. (1989). *Mind, brain & the quantum: The compound 'I'.* Oxford, England: Blackwell.

Lotti, T., & França, K. (2019). Psycho-neuro-endocrine-immunology: A psychobiological concept. In K. França & T. Lotti (Eds.), *Advances in integrative dermatology* (pp. 9–23). Hoboken, NJ: Wiley. http://dx.doi.org/10.1002/9781119476009.ch2

Louchakova-Schwartz, O. (2017). Qualia of God: Phenomenological materiality in introspection, with a reference to Advaita Vedanta. *Open Theology, 3*(1), 257–273. http://dx.doi.org/10.1515/opth-2017-0021

Lucas, W. B. (1993). *Regression therapy: A handbook for professionals: Vol. 1. Past-life therapy.* Crest Park, CA: Deep Forest.

Ludwig, A. M. (1966). Altered states of consciousness. *Archives of General Psychiatry, 15,* 225–234. http://dx.doi.org/10.1001/archpsyc.1966.01730150001001

Ludwig, A. M., Levine, J., & Stark, L. H. (1970). *LSD and alcoholism: A clinical study of treatment efficacy.* Springfield, IL: Charles C Thomas.

Luke, D. (2011). Anomalous phenomena, psi, and altered consciousness. In E. Cardeña & M. Winkelman (Eds.), *Altering consciousness: Multidisciplinary perspectives: Vol. 2. Biological and psychological perspectives* (pp. 355–374). Santa Barbara, CA: Praeger.

Lukey, N., & Barušs, I. (2005). Intelligence correlates of transcendent beliefs: A preliminary study. *Imagination, Cognition and Personality, 24,* 259–270. http://dx.doi.org/10.2190/5H80-2PCY-02YB-F7HN

Lukoff, D. (1985). The diagnosis of mystical experiences with psychotic features. *Journal of Transpersonal Psychology, 17,* 15–181.

Lukoff, D., & Everest, H. C. (1985). The myths in mental illness. *Journal of Transpersonal Psychology, 17,* 123–153.

Lycan, W. G. (1987). *Consciousness.* Cambridge, MA: MIT Press.

Lydic, R., Keifer, J. C., Baghdoyan, H. A., Craft, R., & Angel, C. (2017). Opiate action on sleep and breathing. In M. Kryger, T. Roth, & W. C. Dement (Eds.), *Principles and practice of sleep medicine* (6th ed., pp. 250–259). Philadelphia, PA: Elsevier. http://dx.doi.org/10.1016/B978-0-323-24288-2.00024-6

Lynn, S. J., Green, J. P., Kirsch, I., Capafons, A., Lilienfeld, S. O., Laurence, J.-R., & Montgomery, G. H. (2015). Grounding hypnosis in science: The "new" APA Division 30 definition of hypnosis as a step backward. *American Journal of Clinical Hypnosis, 57*, 390–401. http://dx.doi.org/10.1080/00029157.2015.1011472

Lynn, S. J., Kirsch, I., Barabasz, A., Cardeña, E., & Patterson, D. (2000). Hypnosis as an empirically supported clinical intervention: The state of the evidence and a look to the future. *International Journal of Clinical and Experimental Hypnosis, 48*, 239–259. http://dx.doi.org/10.1080/00207140008410050

Lynn, S. J., Pintar, J., & Rhue, J. W. (1997). Fantasy proneness, dissociation, and narrative construction. In S. Krippner & S. M. Powers (Eds.), *Broken images, broken selves: Dissociative narratives in clinical practice* (pp. 274–302). Bristol, PA: Brunner/Mazel.

Lynn, S. J., & Rhue, J. W. (1988). Fantasy proneness. Hypnosis, developmental antecedents, and psychopathology. *American Psychologist, 43*, 35–44. http://dx.doi.org/10.1037/0003-066X.43.1.35

Lyons, W. (1986). *The disappearance of introspection*. Cambridge, MA: MIT Press.

Mac Lane, S., & Moerdijk, I. (1992). *Sheaves in geometry and logic: A first introduction to topos theory*. New York, NY: Springer-Verlag.

Mack, J. E. (1994a). *Abduction: Human encounters with aliens* (Rev. ed.). New York, NY: Ballantine Books.

Mack, J. E. (1994b). Why the abduction phenomenon cannot be explained psychiatrically. In A. Pritchard, D. E. Pritchard, J. E. Mack, P. Kasey, & C. Yapp (Eds.), *Alien discussions: Proceedings of the abduction study conference held at MIT, Cambridge, MA* (pp. 372–374). Cambridge, MA: North Cambridge Press.

Mack, J. E. (1999). *Passport to the cosmos: Human transformation and alien encounters*. New York, NY: Three Rivers Press.

MacMartin, C., & Yarmey, A. D. (1999). Rhetoric and the recovered memory debate. *Canadian Psychology/Psychologie Canadienne, 40*, 343–358. http://dx.doi.org/10.1037/h0086852

Magallón, L. L. (1997). *Mutual dreaming: When two or more people share the same dream*. New York, NY: Pocket Books.

Malmgren, J. (1994, November 27). Tune in, turn on, get well? *St. Petersburg Times*, p. 1F.

Mandelbaum, W. A. (2000). *The psychic battlefield: A history of the military-occult complex*. New York, NY: St. Martin's Press.

Mandell, A. J. (1980). Toward a psychobiology of transcendence: God in the brain. In J. M. Davidson & R. J. Davidson (Eds.), *The psychobiology of consciousness* (pp. 379–464). New York, NY: Plenum Press. http://dx.doi.org/10.1007/978-1-4684-3456-9_14

Mangini, M. (1998). Treatment of alcoholism using psychedelic drugs: A review of the program of research. *Journal of Psychoactive Drugs, 30*, 381–418. http://dx.doi.org/10.1080/02791072.1998.10399714

Markman, A. B., & Gentner, D. (2001). Thinking. *Annual Review of Psychology, 52*, 223–247. http://dx.doi.org/10.1146/annurev.psych.52.1.223

Martin, J. A. (2017, June). *Clusters of individual experiences form a continuum of persistent non-symbolic experiences in adults*. Paper presented at the Society for Consciousness Studies Annual Conference, Yale University, New Haven, CT.

Martin, J. A. (2019). *The finders*. Jackson, WY: Integration Press.

Maslow, A. H. (1968). *Toward a psychology of being* (2nd ed.). New York, NY: Van Nostrand Reinhold.

Mason, P. (1994). *The Maharishi: The biography of the man who gave transcendental meditation to the world*. Shaftesbury, England: Element Books.

Masters, R. E. L., & Houston, J. (1966). *The varieties of psychedelic experience*. New York, NY: Holt, Rinehart and Winston.

Mateos, D. M., Guevara Erra, R., Wennberg, R., & Perez Velazquez, J. L. (2018). Measures of entropy and complexity in altered states of consciousness. *Cognitive Neurodynamics*, *12*, 73–84. http://dx.doi.org/10.1007/s11571-017-9459-8

Mauer, M. H., Burnett, K. F., Ouellette, E. A., Ironson, G. H., & Dandes, H. M. (1999). Medical hypnosis and orthopedic hand surgery: Pain perception, postoperative recovery, and therapeutic comfort. *International Journal of Clinical and Experimental Hypnosis*, *47*, 144–161. http://dx.doi.org/10.1080/00207149908410027

Mavromatis, A. (1987a). *Hypnagogia: The unique state of consciousness between wakefulness and sleep*. London, England: Routledge & Kegan Paul.

Mavromatis, A. (1987b). On shared states of consciousness and objective imagery. *Journal of Mental Imagery*, *11*, 125–130.

Maxwell, M., & Tschudin, V. (1990). *Seeing the invisible: Modern religious and other transcendent experiences*. London, England: Arkana.

May, E. C. (1996). The American Institutes for Research review of the Department of Defense's STAR GATE program: A commentary. *Journal of Scientific Exploration*, *10*(1), 89–107.

McAleney, P., & Barabasz, A. (1993). Effects of flotation REST and visual imagery on athletic performance: Tennis. In A. F. Barabasz & M. Barabasz (Eds.), *Clinical and experimental restricted environmental stimulation: New developments and perspectives* (pp. 79–85). New York, NY: Springer-Verlag. http://dx.doi.org/10.1007/978-1-4684-8583-7_10

McAleney, P. J., Barabasz, A., & Barabasz, M. (1990). Effects of flotation restricted environmental stimulation on intercollegiate tennis performance. *Perceptual and Motor Skills*, *71*, 1023–1028. http://dx.doi.org/10.2466/pms.1990.71.3.1023

McCall Smith, A., & Shapiro, C. M. (1997). Sleep disorders and the criminal law. In C. Shapiro & A. McCall Smith (Eds.), *Forensic aspects of sleep* (pp. 29–64). Chichester, England: Wiley.

McConkey, K. M., Wende, V., & Barnier, A. J. (1999). Measuring change in the subjective experience of hypnosis. *International Journal of Clinical and Experimental Hypnosis*, *47*, 23–39. http://dx.doi.org/10.1080/00207149908410020

McFarlane, A. C., & van der Kolk, B. A. (1996). Conclusions and future directions. In B. A. van der Kolk, A. C. McFarlane, & L. Weisaeth (Eds.), *Traumatic stress: The effects of overwhelming experience on mind, body, and society* (pp. 559–575). New York, NY: Guilford Press.

McGinty, D., & Szymusiak, R. (2017). Neural control of sleep in mammals. In M. Kryger, T. Roth, & W. C. Dement (Eds.), *Principles and practice of sleep medicine* (6th ed., pp. 62–77). Philadelphia, PA: Elsevier. http://dx.doi.org/10.1016/B978-0-323-24288-2.00007-6

McKenna, D. J. (2004). Clinical investigations of the therapeutic potential of ayahuasca: Rationale and regulatory challenges. *Pharmacology & Therapeutics*, *102*, 111–129. http://dx.doi.org/10.1016/j.pharmthera.2004.03.002

McKenna, T. (1989). A conversation over saucers. *ReVision: The Journal of Consciousness and Change*, *11*(3), 23–30.

McKenna, T. (1993). *True hallucinations: Being an account of the author's extraordinary adventures in the devil's paradise*. New York, NY: HarperSanFrancisco.

McLeod, C. C., Corbisier, B., & Mack, J. E. (1996). A more parsimonious explanation for UFO abduction. *Psychological Inquiry*, *7*, 156–168. http://dx.doi.org/10.1207/s15327965pli0702_9

McNally, R. J. (2012). Explaining "memories" of space alien abduction and past lives: An experimental psychopathology approach. *Journal of Experimental Psychopathology*, *3*, 2–16. http://dx.doi.org/10.5127/jep.017811

McNamara, P. (2011). *Spirit possession and exorcism: History, psychology, and neurobiology* (Vol. 1 & 2). Santa Barbara, CA: Praeger.

McNamara, P., Dietrich-Egensteiner, L., & Teed, B. (2017). Mutual dreaming. *Dreaming, 27,* 87–101. http://dx.doi.org/10.1037/drm0000048

Mellman, T. A. (2018). Sleep and PTSD. In C. B. Nemeroff & C. R. Marmar (Eds.), *Post-traumatic stress disorder* (pp. 409–419). New York, NY: Oxford University Press.

Merrell-Wolff, F. (1994). *Franklin Merrell-Wolff's experience and philosophy: A personal record of transformation and a discussion of transcendental consciousness.* Albany: State University of New York Press. (Contains *Pathways Through to Space* and *The Philosophy of Consciousness Without an Object: Vol. 1.*)

Merrell-Wolff, F. (1995a). *Mathematics, philosophy & yoga: A lecture series presented at the Los Olivos Conference Room in Phoenix, Arizona, in 1966.* Phoenix, AZ: Phoenix Philosophical Press.

Merrell-Wolff, F. (1995b). *Transformations in consciousness: The metaphysics and epistemology.* Albany, NY: State University of New York Press. (Contains *The Philosophy of Consciousness Without an Object: Vol. 2. Introceptualism*)

Metcalfe, J. (2000). Feelings and judgments of knowing: Is there a special noetic state? *Consciousness and Cognition, 9,* 178–186. http://dx.doi.org/10.1006/ccog.2000.0451

Metcalfe, J., & Shimamura, A. P. (Eds.). (1994). *Metacognition: Knowing about knowing.* Cambridge, MA: MIT Press. http://dx.doi.org/10.7551/mitpress/4561.001.0001

Meyerson, J. (2010). Memory focused interventions (MFI) as a therapeutic strategy in hypnotic psychotherapy. *American Journal of Clinical Hypnosis, 52,* 189–203. http://dx.doi.org/10.1080/00029157.2010.10401719

Mignot, E. (2017). Narcolepsy: Genetics, immunology, and pathophysiology. In M. Kryger, T. Roth, & W. C. Dement (Eds.), *Principles and practice of sleep medicine* (6th ed., pp. 855–872). Philadelphia, PA: Elsevier. http://dx.doi.org/10.1016/B978-0-323-24288-2.00089-1

Miller, G. E., Chen, E., Armstrong, C. C., Carroll, A. L., Ozturk, S., Rydland, K. J., . . . Nusslock, R. (2018). Functional connectivity in central executive network protects youth against cardiometabolic risks linked with neighborhood violence. *Proceedings of the National Academy of Sciences of the United States of America, 115*(47), 12063–12068. http://dx.doi.org/10.1073/pnas.1810067115

Miller, I. (2013). Pineal gland, DMT & altered state of consciousness. *Journal of Consciousness Exploration & Research, 4,* 214–233.

Miller, J. G. (1994). Envelope epidemiology. In A. Pritchard, D. E. Pritchard, J. E. Mack, P. Kasey & C. Yapp (Eds.), *Alien discussions: Proceedings of the abduction study conference held at MIT, Cambridge, MA* (pp. 232–235). Cambridge, MA: North Cambridge Press.

Miller, J. J. (1993). The unveiling of traumatic memories and emotions through mindfulness and concentration meditation: Clinical implications and three case reports. *Journal of Transpersonal Psychology, 25*(2), 169–180.

Miller, M. F., Barabasz, A. F., & Barabasz, M. (1991). Effects of active alert and relaxation hypnotic inductions on cold pressor pain. *Journal of Abnormal Psychology, 100,* 223–226. http://dx.doi.org/10.1037/0021-843X.100.2.223

Mills, A., & Lynn, S. J. (2000). Past-life experiences. In E. Cardeña, S. J. Lynn, & S. Krippner (Eds.), *Varieties of anomalous experience: Examining the scientific evidence* (pp. 283–313). Washington, DC: American Psychological Association. http://dx.doi.org/10.1037/10371-009

Mills, A., & Tucker, J. B. (2015). Reincarnation: Field studies and theoretical issues today. In E. Cardeña, J. Palmer, & D. Marcusson-Clavertz (Eds.), *Parapsychology: A handbook for the 21st century* (pp. 314–326). Jefferson, NC: McFarland.

Milton, J. (1999). Should ganzfeld research continue to be crucial in the search for a replicable psi effect? Part I. Discussion paper and introduction to an electronic-mail discussion. *Journal of Parapsychology, 63,* 309–333.

Milton, J., & Wiseman, R. (1999). Does psi exist? Lack of replication of an anomalous process of information transfer. *Psychological Bulletin, 125,* 387–391. http://dx.doi.org/10.1037/0033-2909.125.4.387

Mistlberger, R. E., & Rusak, B. (2000). Circadian rhythms in mammals: Formal properties and environmental influences. In M. H. Kryger, T. Roth, & W. C. Dement (Eds.), *Principles and practice of sleep medicine* (3rd ed., pp. 321–333). Philadelphia, PA: W. B. Saunders.

Mitchell, E. (with Williams, D.). (1996). *The way of the explorer: An Apollo astronaut's journey through the material and mystical worlds.* New York, NY: G. P. Putnam's Sons.

Mitchell, S. (Producer). (2006). *The view from space: A message of peace* [DVD]. US: SMPI.

Monroe, R. A. (1975). *Journeys out of the body.* London, England: Corgi Books. (Original work published 1972)

Monroe, R. A. (1994). *Ultimate journey.* New York, NY: Doubleday.

Montgomery, G. H., DuHamel, K. N., & Redd, W. H. (2000). A meta-analysis of hypnotically induced analgesia: How effective is hypnosis? *International Journal of Clinical and Experimental Hypnosis, 48,* 138–153. http://dx.doi.org/10.1080/00207140008410045

Monti, M. M., Vanhaudenhuyse, A., Coleman, M. R., Boly, M., Pickard, J. D., Tshibanda, L., . . . Laureys, S. (2010). Willful modulation of brain activity in disorders of consciousness. *The New England Journal of Medicine, 362,* 579–589. http://dx.doi.org/10.1056/NEJMoa0905370

Montplaisir, J., Nicolas, A., Godbout, R., & Walters, A. (2000). Restless legs syndrome and periodic limb movement disorder. In M. H. Kryger, T. Roth, & W. C. Dement (Eds.), *Principles and practice of sleep medicine* (3rd ed., pp. 742–752). Philadelphia, PA: W. B. Saunders.

Moody, R. A., Jr. (1975). *Life after life: The investigation of a phenomenon—Survival of bodily death.* Covington, GA: Bantam/Mockingbird.

Moody, R. A., Jr. (1977). *Reflections on life after life.* Covington, GA: Bantam/Mockingbird.

Moody, R. A., Jr. (1988). *The light beyond.* New York, NY: Bantam Books.

Moorjani, A. (2012). *Dying to be me: My journey from cancer, to near death, to true healing.* Carlsbad, CA: Hay House.

Moraes, L. J., Miranda, M. B., Loures, L. F., Mainieri, A. G., & Mármora, C. H. C. (2018). A systematic review of psychoneuroimmunology-based interventions. *Psychology Health and Medicine, 23,* 635–652. http://dx.doi.org/10.1080/13548506.2017.1417607

Morehouse, D. (1996). *Psychic warrior: Inside the CIA's Stargate program; The true story of a soldier's espionage and awakening.* New York, NY: St. Martin's Press.

Morris, S. (1984, January). Games. *Omni, 6,* 82, 128–129.

Muldoon, S. J., & Carrington, H. (1929). *The projection of the astral body.* London, England: Rider Books.

Mutz, J., & Javadi, A. H. (2017). Exploring the neural correlates of dream phenomenology and altered states of consciousness during sleep. *Neuroscience of Consciousness, 2017*(1), nix009. Advance online publication. http://dx.doi.org/10.1093/nc/nix009

Nadel, L., & Jacobs, W. J. (1998). Traumatic memory is special. *Current Directions in Psychological Science, 7*(5), 154–157. http://dx.doi.org/10.1111/1467-8721.ep10836842

Naiman, R. R. (2014). *Healing night: The science and spirit of sleeping, dreaming, and awakening* (2nd ed.). Tucson, AZ: New Moon Media.

Nashida, T., Yabe, H., Sato, Y., Hiruma, T., Sutoh, T., Shinozaki, N., & Kaneko, S. (2000). Automatic auditory information processing in sleep. *Sleep, 23,* 821–828. http://dx.doi.org/10.1093/sleep/23.6.1i

Natsoulas, T. (1983a). Concepts of consciousness. *Journal of Mind and Behavior, 4,* 13–59.

Natsoulas, T. (1983b). The experience of a conscious self. *Journal of Mind and Behavior, 4,* 451–478.

Natsoulas, T. (1999). A rediscovery of presence. *Journal of Mind and Behavior, 20,* 17–41.

Nelson, R. D., Dunne, B. J., Dobyns, Y. H., & Jahn, R. G. (1996). Precognitive remote perception: Replication of remote viewing. *Journal of Scientific Exploration, 10*(1), 109–110.

Netter, F. H. (1986). *The CIBA collection of medical illustrations: Vol. 1. Nervous system. Part I: Anatomy and physiology*. West Caldwell, NJ: CIBA.

Newman, L. S. (1997). Intergalactic hostages: People who report abduction by UFOs. *Journal of Social and Clinical Psychology, 16*, 151–177. http://dx.doi.org/10.1521/jscp.1997.16.2.151

Newman, L. S., & Baumeister, R. F. (1996). Toward an explanation of the UFO abduction phenomenon: Hypnotic elaboration, extraterrestrial sadomasochism, and spurious memories. *Psychological Inquiry, 7*, 99–126. http://dx.doi.org/10.1207/s15327965pli0702_1

Nguyen, J., & Brymer, E. (2018). Nature-based guided imagery as an intervention for state anxiety. *Frontiers in Psychology, 9*, 1858. http://dx.doi.org/10.3389/fpsyg.2018.01858

Nichols, D. (1999). From Eleusis to PET scans: The mysteries of psychedelics. *MAPS: Bulletin of the Multidisciplinary Association for Psychedelic Studies, 9*(4), 50–55.

Nichols, D. E. (2018). *N,N*-dimethyltryptamine and the pineal gland: Separating fact from myth. *Journal of Psychopharmacology, 32*, 30–36. http://dx.doi.org/10.1177/0269881117736919

Nichols, D. E., & Chemel, B. R. (2011). LSD and the serotonin system's effects on human consciousness. In E. Cardeña & M. Winkelman (Eds.), *Altering consciousness: Multidisciplinary perspectives: Vol. 2. Biological and psychological perspectives* (pp. 121–146). Santa Barbara, CA: Praeger.

Nielsen, T. (2017). Microdream neurophenomenology. *Neuroscience of Consciousness, 2017*(1), nix001. Advance online publication. http://dx.doi.org/10.1093/nc/nix001

Nisbett, R. E., & Wilson, T. D. (1977). Telling more than we can know: Verbal reports on mental processes. *Psychological Review, 84*, 231–259. http://dx.doi.org/10.1037/0033-295X.84.3.231

Noble, J., & McConkey, K. M. (1995). Hypnotic sex change: Creating and challenging a delusion in the laboratory. *Journal of Abnormal Psychology, 104*, 69–74. http://dx.doi.org/10.1037/0021-843X.104.1.69

Northrop, F. S. C. (1966). *The meeting of East and West: An inquiry concerning world understanding*. New York, NY: Collier. (Original work published 1946)

Norton, L., Gibson, R. M., Gofton, T., Benson, C., Dhanani, S., Shemie, S. D., . . . Young, G. B. (2017). Electroencephalographic recordings during withdrawal of life-sustaining therapy until 30 minutes after declaration of death. *Canadian Journal of Neurological Sciences, 44*(2), 139–145. http://dx.doi.org/10.1017/cjn.2016.309

Noyes, R., Fenwick, P., Holden, J. M., & Christian, S. (2009). Aftereffects of pleasurable western adult near-death experiences. In J. M. Holden, B. Greyson, & D. James (Eds.), *The handbook of near-death experiences: Thirty years of investigation* (pp. 41–62). Santa Barbara, CA: Praeger.

Nutt, D. J., King, L. A., & Phillips, L. D. (2010). Drug harms in the UK: A multicriteria decision analysis. *The Lancet, 376*, 1558–1565. http://dx.doi.org/10.1016/S0140-6736(10)61462-6

Nutt, D., King, L. A., Saulsbury, W., & Blakemore, C. (2007). Development of a rational scale to assess the harm of drugs of potential misuse. *The Lancet, 369*, 1047–1053. http://dx.doi.org/10.1016/S0140-6736(07)60464-4

O'Regan, B. (1983). Psychoneuroimmunology: The birth of a new field. *Investigations: A Bulletin of the Institute of Noetic Sciences, 1*, 1–2.

Orne, M. T. (1959). The nature of hypnosis: Artifact and essence. *Journal of Abnormal and Social Psychology, 58*, 277–299. http://dx.doi.org/10.1037/h0046128

Ornstein, R. E. (1972). *The psychology of consciousness*. New York, NY: Viking.

Owen, A. M., Coleman, M. R., Boly, M., Davis, M. H., Laureys, S., & Pickard, J. D. (2006). Detecting awareness in the vegetative state. *Science, 313*, 1402–1402. http://dx.doi.org/10.1126/science.1130197

Oxman, T. E., Rosenberg, S. D., Schnurr, P. P., Tucker, G. J., & Gala, G. (1988). The language of altered states. *The Journal of Nervous and Mental Disease, 176*, 401–408. http://dx.doi.org/10.1097/00005053-198807000-00002

Pahnke, W. N. (1963). *Drugs and mysticism: An analysis of the relationship between psychedelic drugs and the mystical consciousness* (Unpublished doctoral dissertation). Harvard University.

Pahnke, W. N., & Richards, W. A. (1972). Implications of LSD and experimental mysticism. In C. T. Tart (Ed.), *Altered states of consciousness* (pp. 409–439). Garden City, NY: Anchor Books.

Parnia, S., Waller, D. G., Yeates, R., & Fenwick, P. (2001). A qualitative and quantitative study of the incidence, features and aetiology of near death experiences in cardiac arrest survivors. *Resuscitation, 48*, 149–156. http://dx.doi.org/10.1016/S0300-9572(00)00328-2

Parrino, L., & Terzano, M. G. (2017). Central nervous system arousals and cyclic alternating patterns. In M. Kryger, T. Roth, & W. C. Dement (Eds.), *Principles and practice of sleep medicine* (6th ed., pp. 1576–1587). Philadelphia, PA: Elsevier. http://dx.doi.org/10.1016/B978-0-323-24288-2.00162-8

Parry, S., Lloyd, M., & Simpson, J. (2018). "It's not like you have PSTD with a touch of dissociation": Understanding dissociative identity disorder through first person accounts. *European Journal of Trauma & Dissociation, 2*, 31–38. http://dx.doi.org/10.1016/j.ejtd.2017.08.002

Partinen, M., & Hublin, C. (2000). Epidemiology of sleep disorders. In M. H. Kryger, T. Roth, & W. C. Dement (Eds.), *Principles and practice of sleep medicine* (3rd ed., pp. 558–579). Philadelphia, PA: W. B. Saunders.

Patihis, L., Frenda, S. J., & Loftus, E. L. (2018). False memory tasks do not reliably predict other false memories. *Psychology of Consciousness, 5*, 140–160. http://dx.doi.org/10.1037/cns0000147

Patihis, L., & Younes Burton, H. J. (2015). False memories in therapy and hypnosis before 1980. *Psychology of Consciousness, 2*, 153–169. http://dx.doi.org/10.1037/cns0000044

Pekala, R. J. (1991). *Quantifying consciousness: An empirical approach.* New York, NY: Plenum Press. http://dx.doi.org/10.1007/978-1-4899-0629-8

Pekala, R. J., & Cardeña, E. (2000). Methodological issues in the study of altered states of consciousness and anomalous experiences. In E. Cardeña, S. J. Lynn, & S. Krippner (Eds.), *Varieties of anomalous experience: Examining the scientific evidence* (pp. 47–82). Washington, DC: American Psychological Association. http://dx.doi.org/10.1037/10371-002

Pekala, R. J., & Kumar, V. K. (2000). Operationalizing "trance" I: Rationale and research using a psychophenomenological approach. *American Journal of Clinical Hypnosis, 43*, 107–135. http://dx.doi.org/10.1080/00029157.2000.10404265

Pelayo, R., & Dement, W. C. (2017). History of sleep physiology and medicine. In M. Kryger, T. Roth, & W. C. Dement (Eds.), *Principles and practice of sleep medicine* (6th ed., pp. 3–14). Philadelphia, PA: Elsevier. http://dx.doi.org/10.1016/B978-0-323-24288-2.00001-5

Penrose, R. (1994). Mechanisms, microtubules and the mind. *Journal of Scientific Exploration, 10*, 241–249.

Penzel, T. (2017). Home sleep testing. In M. H. Kryger, T. Roth, & W. C. Dement (Eds.), *Principles and practice of sleep medicine* (6th ed., pp. 1610–1614). Philadelphia, PA: Elsevier.

Persinger, M. A. (1987). *Neuropsychological bases of God beliefs.* New York, NY: Praeger.

Persinger, M. A. (2001). The neuropsychiatry of paranormal experiences. *The Journal of Neuropsychiatry and Clinical Neurosciences, 13*, 515–524.

Persinger, M. A. (with Carrey, N. J., & Suess, L. A.). (1980). *TM and cult mania.* North Quincy, MA: Christopher.

Peters, L. G. (1981). An experiential study of Nepalese shamanism. *Journal of Transpersonal Psychology, 13*, 1–26.

Peters, L. G. (1989). Shamanism: Phenomenology of a spiritual discipline. *Journal of Transpersonal Psychology, 21*, 115–137.

Petit, D., Montplaisir, J., St. Louis, E. K., & Boeve, B. F. (2017). Alzheimer disease and other dementias. In M. Kryger, T. Roth, & W. C. Dement (Eds.), *Principles and practice of sleep medicine* (6th ed., pp. 935–943). Philadelphia, PA: Elsevier. http://dx.doi.org/10.1016/B978-0-323-24288-2.00096-9

Petrie, K. J., Booth, R. J., & Pennebaker, J. W. (1998). The immunological effects of thought suppression. *Journal of Personality and Social Psychology, 75*, 1264–1272. http://dx.doi.org/10.1037/0022-3514.75.5.1264

Phillips, O. (2005). *Astral projection, plain & simple: The out-of-body experience.* Woodbury, MN: Llewellyn.

Picker, W., Lerman, A., & Hajal, F. (1992). Potential interaction of LSD and fluoxetine. *American Journal of Psychiatry, 149*, 843–844. http://dx.doi.org/10.1176/ajp.149.6.843b

Pigeon, W. R., & Mellman, T. A. (2017). Dreams and nightmares in posttraumatic stress disorder. In M. Kryger, T. Roth, & W. C. Dement (Eds.), *Principles and practice of sleep medicine* (6th ed., pp. 561–566). Philadelphia, PA: Elsevier. http://dx.doi.org/10.1016/B978-0-323-24288-2.00055-6

Pollan, M. (2018). *How to change your mind: What the new science of psychedelics teaches us about consciousness, dying, addiction, depression, and transcendence.* New York, NY: Penguin Press.

Privette, G. (1983). Peak experience, peak performance, and flow: A comparative analysis of positive human experiences. *Journal of Personality and Social Psychology, 45*, 1361–1368. http://dx.doi.org/10.1037/0022-3514.45.6.1361

Puthoff, H. E. (1996). CIA-initiated remote viewing program at Stanford Research Institute. *Journal of Scientific Exploration, 10*(1), 63–76.

Puthoff, H. E. (2018, June). *The Department of Defense Unidentified Aerial Phenomena program: The back story, the forward story.* Paper presented at the meeting of The Society for Scientific Exploration and The International Remote Viewing Association Joint Conference, Las Vegas, NV.

Putnam, F. W. (1984). The psychophysiologic investigation of multiple personality disorder: A review. *Psychiatric Clinics of North America, 7*, 31–39. http://dx.doi.org/10.1016/S0193-953X(18)30778-0

Radin, D. I. (1997). *The conscious universe: The scientific truth of psychic phenomena.* New York, NY: HarperEdge.

Rayl, A. J. S. (1989, June). Encyclopedia psychedelia. *Omni, 11*(9), 30, 96.

Rechtschaffen, A., & Kales, A. (Eds.). (1968). *A manual of standardized terminology, techniques and scoring system for sleep stages of human subjects.* Bethesda, MD: U.S. Department of Health, Education, and Welfare; Public Health Service—National Institutes of Health; National Institute of Neurological Diseases and Blindness; Neurological Information Network.

Reddan, M. C., Wager, T. D., & Schiller, D. (2018). Attenuating neural threat expression with imagination. *Neuron, 100*, 994–1005.e4. http://dx.doi.org/10.1016/j.neuron.2018.10.047

Reggia, J. A., Huang, D. W., & Katz, G. (2015). Beliefs concerning the nature of consciousness. *Journal of Consciousness Studies, 22*(5–6), 146–171.

Register, P. A., & Kihlstrom, J. F. (1986). Finding the hypnotic virtuoso. *International Journal of Clinical and Experimental Hypnosis, 34*, 84–97. http://dx.doi.org/10.1080/00207148608406974

Reich, D. (1989a, October 14). Multiple personality disorder. *The London Free Press*, p. A6.

Reich, D. (1989b, October 14). The 29 lives of Brenda. *The London Free Press*, pp. A6–A7.

Revonsuo, A., Kallio, S., & Sikka, P. (2009). What is an altered state of consciousness? *Philosophical Psychology, 22*, 187–204. http://dx.doi.org/10.1080/09515080902802850

Rex, E. (2013). Calming a turbulent mind. *Scientific American Mind, 24*(2), 58–66. http://dx.doi.org/10.1038/scientificamericanmind0513-58

Richards, W. A. (2016). *Sacred knowledge: Psychedelics and religious experiences.* New York, NY: Columbia University Press.

Ring, K. (1987). Near-death experiences: Intimations of immortality? In J. S. Spong (Ed.), *Consciousness and survival: An interdisciplinary inquiry into the possibility of life beyond biological death* (pp. 165–176). Sausalito, CA: Institute of Noetic Sciences.

Ring, K. (1989). Near-death and UFO encounters as shamanic initiations: Some conceptual and evolutionary implications. *ReVision: The Journal of Consciousness and Change, 11*, 14–22.

Ring, K. (1992). *The omega project: Near-death experiences, UFO encounters, and mind at large.* New York, NY: William Morrow.

Ring, K., & Cooper, S. (1997). Near-death and out-of-body experiences in the blind: A study of apparent eyeless vision. *Journal of Near-Death Studies, 16*, 101–147. http://dx.doi.org/10.1023/A:1025010015662

Ring, K., & Valarino, E. E. (1998). *Lessons from the light: What we can learn from the near-death experience.* Portsmouth, NH: Moment Point.

Ripinsky-Naxon, M. (1993). *The nature of shamanism: Substance and function of a religious metaphor.* Albany: State University of New York Press.

Rivas, T., Dirven, A., & Smit, R. H. (2016). *The self does not die: Verified paranormal phenomena from near-death experiences* (J. M. Holden, Series Ed.; W. J. Boeke, Ed. & Trans.). Durham, NC: IANDS.

Roberts, B. (1993). *The experience of no-self: A contemplative journey* (Rev. ed.). Albany, NY: State University of New York Press.

Roberts, J. (1978). *The afterdeath journal of an American philosopher: The world view of William James.* Englewood Cliffs, NJ: Prentice-Hall.

Roe, C. A. (1999). Critical thinking and belief in the paranormal: A re-evaluation. *British Journal of Psychology, 90*, 85–98. http://dx.doi.org/10.1348/000712699161288

Roe, C. A., Sonnex, C., & Roxburgh, E. C. (2015). Two meta-analyses of noncontact healing studies. *EXPLORE: The Journal of Science and Healing, 11*, 11–23. http://dx.doi.org/10.1016/j.explore.2014.10.001

Roehrs, T., Carskadon, M. A., Dement, W. C., & Roth, T. (2000). Daytime sleepiness and alertness. In M. H. Kryger, T. Roth, & W. C. Dement (Eds.), *Principles and practice of sleep medicine* (3rd ed., pp. 43–52). Philadelphia, PA: W. B. Saunders.

Rosch, E. (1999). Is wisdom in the brain? *Psychological Science, 10*, 222–224. http://dx.doi.org/10.1111/1467-9280.00140

Rosen, C., Jones, N., Chase, K. A., Melbourne, J. K., Grossman, L. S., & Sharma, R. P. (2017). Immersion in altered experience: An investigation of the relationship between absorption and psychopathology. *Consciousness and Cognition, 49*, 215–226. http://dx.doi.org/10.1016/j.concog.2017.01.015

Rosenthal, D. M. (2000). Consciousness, content, and metacognitive judgments. *Consciousness and Cognition, 9*, 203–214. http://dx.doi.org/10.1006/ccog.2000.0437

Ross, C. A. (1996). History, phenomenology, and epidemiology of dissociation. In L. K. Michelson & W. J. Ray (Eds.), *Handbook of dissociation: Theoretical, empirical, and clinical perspectives* (pp. 3–24). New York, NY: Plenum Press. http://dx.doi.org/10.1007/978-1-4899-0310-5_1

Ross, C. A., Norton, G. R., & Wozney, K. (1989). Multiple personality disorder: An analysis of 236 cases. *Canadian Journal of Psychiatry/La Revue Canadienne de Psychiatrie, 34*, 413–418. http://dx.doi.org/10.1177/070674378903400509

Ross, C. A., Somer, E., & Goode, C. (2018). Reliability of the Dissociative Trance Disorder Interview Schedule: A preliminary report. *Journal of Trauma & Dissociation, 19*, 176–184. http://dx.doi.org/10.1080/15299732.2017.1329774

Ross, R. M., & McKay, R. (2018). Shamanism and the psychosis continuum. *Behavioral and Brain Sciences, 41*, e84. http://dx.doi.org/10.1017/S0140525X17002151

Ruffini, G. (2017). An algorithmic information theory of consciousness. *Neuroscience of Consciousness, 2017*(1), nix019. Advance online publication. http://dx.doi.org/10.1093/nc/nix019

Rumelhart, D. E., Hinton, G. E., & McClelland, J. L. (1986). A general framework for parallel distributed processing. In D. E. Rumelhart, J. L. McClelland, & the PDP Research Group (Eds.), *Parallel distributed processing: Explorations in the microstructure of cognition: Volume 1: Foundations* (pp. 45–76). Cambridge, MA: MIT Press.

Ruzyla-Smith, P., & Barabasz, A. (1993). Effects of flotation REST on the immune response: T-cells, B-cells, helper and suppressor cells. In A. F. Barabasz & M. Barabasz (Eds.), *Clinical and experimental restricted environmental stimulation: New developments and perspectives* (pp. 223–237). New York, NY: Springer-Verlag. http://dx.doi.org/10.1007/978-1-4684-8583-7_24

Ryff, C. D. (1995). Psychological well-being in adult life. *Current Directions in Psychological Science, 4*, 99–104. http://dx.doi.org/10.1111/1467-8721.ep10772395

Sabom, M. (1998). *Light & death: One doctor's fascinating account of near-death experiences.* Grand Rapids, MI: Zondervan.

Sadzot, B., Baraban, J. M., Glennon, R. A., Lyon, R. A., Leonhardt, S., Jan, C.-R., & Titeler, M. (1989). Hallucinogenic drug interactions at human brain 5-HT$_2$ receptors: Implications for treating LSD-induced hallucinogenesis. *Psychopharmacology, 98*, 495–499. http://dx.doi.org/10.1007/BF00441948

Sanders, M. H. (2000). Medical therapy for obstructive sleep apnea-hypopnea syndrome. In M. H. Kryger, T. Roth, & W. C. Dement (Eds.), *Principles and practice of sleep medicine* (3rd ed., pp. 879–893). Philadelphia, PA: W. B. Saunders.

Saniotis, A. (2019). Becoming animals: Neurobiology of shamanic shapeshifting. *NeuroQuantology: An Interdisciplinary Journal of Neuroscience and Quantum Physics, 17*(5), 81–86. http://dx.doi.org/10.14704/nq.2019.17.5.2258

Şar, V., Dorahy, M. J., & Krüger, C. (2017). Revisiting the etiological aspects of dissociative identity disorder: A biopsychosocial perspective. *Psychology Research and Behavior Management, 10*, 137–146. http://dx.doi.org/10.2147/PRBM.S113743

Saver, J. L., & Rabin, J. (1997). The neural substrates of religious experience. *The Journal of Neuropsychiatry and Clinical Neurosciences, 9*, 498–510. http://dx.doi.org/10.1176/jnp.9.3.498

Schacter, D. L. (1995). Memory distortion: History and current status. In D. L. Schacter (Ed.), *Memory distortion: How minds, brains, and societies reconstruct the past* (pp. 1–43). Cambridge, MA: Harvard University Press.

Schatzman, M. (1983). Solve your problems in your sleep. *New Scientist, 99*, 416–417.

Schifano, F., Orsolini, L., Duccio Papanti, G., & Corkery, J. M. (2015). Novel psychoactive substances of interest for psychiatry. *World Psychiatry, 14*, 15–26.

Schmidt, T. T., & Berkemeyer, H. (2018). The Altered States Database: Psychometric data of altered states of consciousness. *Frontiers in Psychology, 9*, 1028. http://dx.doi.org/10.3389/fpsyg.2018.01028

Schnabel, J. (1997). *Remote viewers: The secret history of America's psychic spies.* New York, NY: Dell.

Schneider, J., Smith, C. W., Minning, C., Whitcher, S., & Hermanson, J. (1990). Guided imagery and immune system function in normal subjects: A summary of research findings. In R. G. Kunzendorf (Ed.), *Mental imagery* (pp. 179–191). New York, NY: Plenum Press. http://dx.doi.org/10.1007/978-1-4899-2623-4_20

Schredl, M. (2017). Incorporation of waking experiences into dreams. In M. Kryger, T. Roth, & W. C. Dement (Eds.), *Principles and practice of sleep medicine* (6th ed., pp. 555–560). Philadelphia, PA: Elsevier. http://dx.doi.org/10.1016/B978-0-323-24288-2.00054-4

Schredl, M., Brennecke, J., & Reinhard, I. (2013). Does training increase NREM dream recall? A pilot study. *International Journal of Dream Research, 6,* 54–68. http://dx.doi.org/10.11588/ijodr.2013.1.9963

Schredl, M., Stumbrys, T., & Erlacher, D. (2016). Dream recall, nightmare frequency, and spirituality. *Dreaming, 26,* 1–9. http://dx.doi.org/10.1037/drm0000015

Schreiber, E. H. (1997). Use of group hypnosis to improve college students' achievement. *Psychological Reports, 80,* 636–638. http://dx.doi.org/10.2466/pr0.1997.80.2.636

Schueler, H. E. (2017). Emerging synthetic fentanyl analogs. *Academic Forensic Pathology, 7,* 36–40. http://dx.doi.org/10.23907/2017.004

Schultes, R. E. (1982). The beta-carboline hallucinogens of South America. *Journal of Psychoactive Drugs, 14,* 205–220. http://dx.doi.org/10.1080/02791072.1982.10471930

Schultes, R. E., & Winkelman, M. (1996). The principal American hallucinogenic plants and their bioactive and therapeutic properties. In M. Winkelman & W. Andritzky (Eds.), *Jahrbuch für transkulturelle Medizin und Psychotherapie* [Yearbook of cross-cultural medicine and psychotherapy]: *Vol. 1995. Sakrale Heilpflanzen, Bewußtsein und Heilung: Transkulturelle und interdisziplinäre Perspektiven* [Sacred plants, consciousness and healing: Cross-cultural and interdisciplinary perspectives] (pp. 205–239). Berlin, Germany: Verlag für Wissenschaft und Bildung.

Schumaker, J. F. (1995). *The corruption of reality: A unified theory of religion, hypnosis, and psychopathology.* Amherst, NY: Prometheus Books.

Schwartz, G. E., Woollacott, M., Schwartz, S. A., Baruš, I., Beauregard, M., Dossey, L., . . . Tart, C. (2018). The Academy for the Advancement of Postmaterialist Sciences: Integrating consciousness into mainstream science. *EXPLORE: The Journal of Science and Healing, 14,* 111–113. http://dx.doi.org/10.1016/j.explore.2017.12.006

Schwartz, S. A. (2015). Through time and space: The evidence for remote viewing. In D. Broderick & B. Goertzel (Eds.), *Evidence for psi: Thirteen empirical research reports* (pp. 168–212). Jefferson, NC: McFarland.

Schwartz, W. J. (1997). Introduction: On the neurobiology of sleep and sleep disorders not yet known. In M. Fisher (Series Ed.) & W. J. Schwartz (Vol. Ed.), *Monographs in clinical neuroscience: Vol. 15. Sleep science: Integrating basic research and clinical practice* (pp. 1–8). Basel, Switzerland: Karger.

Schweitzer, P. K. (2000). Drugs that disturb sleep and wakefulness. In M. H. Kryger, T. Roth, & W. C. Dement (Eds.), *Principles and practice of sleep medicine* (3rd ed., pp. 441–461). Philadelphia, PA: W. B. Saunders.

Schweitzer, P. K., & Randazzo, A. C. (2017). Drugs that disturb sleep and wakefulness. In M. Kryger, T. Roth, & W. C. Dement (Eds.), *Principles and practice of sleep medicine* (6th ed., pp. 480–498). Philadelphia, PA: Elsevier. http://dx.doi.org/10.1016/B978-0-323-24288-2.00045-3

Schwitzgebel, E. (2016). Introspection. In E. N. Zalta (Ed.), *The Stanford encyclopedia of philosophy.* Retrieved from https://plato.stanford.edu/archives/win2016/entries/introspection/

Scott, R. D. (1978). *Transcendental misconceptions.* San Diego, CA: Beta.

Searle, J. R. (2000). Consciousness, free action and the brain. *Journal of Consciousness Studies, 7*(10), 3–22.

Sell, C., Möller, H., & Taubner, S. (2018). Effectiveness of integrative imagery- and trance-based psychodynamic therapies: Guided imagery psychotherapy and hypno-psychotherapy. *Journal of Psychotherapy Integration, 28,* 90–113. http://dx.doi.org/10.1037/int0000073

Sferios, E. (1999). Report from DanceSafe: Laboratory analysis program reveals DXM tablets sold as "Ecstasy." *MAPS: Bulletin of the Multidisciplinary Association for Psychedelic Studies, 9*(4), 47–48.

Shaffer, J. B. P. (1978). *Humanistic psychology.* Englewood Cliffs, NJ: Prentice-Hall.

Shanon, B. (2001). Altered temporality. *Journal of Consciousness Studies, 8*(1), 35–58.

Shanon, B. (2002). *The antipodes of the mind: Charting the phenomenology of the ayahuasca experience.* Oxford, England: Oxford University Press.

Shear, J. (1996). The hard problem: Closing the empirical gap. *Journal of Consciousness Studies, 3*(1), 54–68.

Shor, R. E., & Orne, E. C. (1962). *Manual: Harvard Group Scale of Hypnotic Susceptibility: Form A*. Palo Alto, CA: Consulting Psychologists Press.

Siegel, R. K. (1975). Introduction. In R. K. Siegel & L. J. West (Eds.), *Hallucinations: Behavior, experience, and theory* (pp. 1–7). New York, NY: Wiley.

Siegel, R. K. (1977). Hallucinations. *Scientific American, 237*(4), 132–140. http://dx.doi.org/10.1038/scientificamerican1077-132

Siegel, R. K., & Jarvik, M. E. (1975). Drug-induced hallucinations in animals and man. In R. K. Siegel & L. J. West (Eds.), *Hallucinations: Behavior, experience, and theory* (pp. 81–161). New York, NY: Wiley.

Simons, J. S., Garrison, J. R., & Johnson, M. K. (2017). Brain mechanisms of reality monitoring. *Trends in Cognitive Sciences, 21*, 462–473. http://dx.doi.org/10.1016/j.tics.2017.03.012

Sio, U. N., Monaghan, P., & Ormerod, T. (2013). Sleep on it, but only if it is difficult: Effects of sleep on problem solving. *Memory & Cognition, 41*, 159–166. http://dx.doi.org/10.3758/s13421-012-0256-7

Slavova, S., O'Brien, D. B., Creppage, K., Dao, D., Fondario, A., Haile, E., . . . Wright, D. (2015). Drug overdose deaths: Let's get specific. *Public Health Reports, 130*, 339–342. http://dx.doi.org/10.1177/003335491513000411

Smallwood, J., Margulies, D., Bernhardt, B. C., & Jefferies, E. (2018). Investigating the elements of thought: Toward a component process account of spontaneous cognition. In K. C. R. Fox & K. Christoff (Eds.), *The Oxford handbook of spontaneous thought: Mind-wandering, creativity, and dreaming* (pp. 71–83). Oxford, England: Oxford University Press.

Smith, A. L., & Tart, C. T. (1998). Cosmic consciousness experience and psychedelic experiences: A first person comparison. *Journal of Consciousness Studies, 5*, 97–107.

Smith, H. (2000). *Cleansing the doors of perception: The religious significance of entheogenic plants and chemicals*. New York, NY: Jeremy P. Tarcher/Putnam.

Smith, J. C., Amutio, A., Anderson, J. P., & Aria, L. A. (1996). Relaxation: Mapping an uncharted world. *Biofeedback & Self-Regulation, 21*, 63–90. http://dx.doi.org/10.1007/BF02214150

Smith, J. T., Barabasz, A., & Barabasz, M. (1996). Comparison of hypnosis and distraction in severely ill children undergoing painful medical procedures. *Journal of Counseling Psychology, 43*, 187–195. http://dx.doi.org/10.1037/0022-0167.43.2.187

Smith, P. H. (2011). Remote viewing: State of the field. *EdgeScience, 8*, 13–16.

Smolensky, P. (1988). On the proper treatment of connectionism. *Behavioral and Brain Sciences, 11*, 1–23. http://dx.doi.org/10.1017/S0140525X00052432

Sommer, A. (2014). Psychical research in the history and philosophy of science. An introduction and review. *Studies in History and Philosophy of Biological and Biomedical Sciences, 48*, 38–45. http://dx.doi.org/10.1016/j.shpsc.2014.08.004

Spanos, N. P. (1982). Hypnotic behavior: A cognitive, social psychological perspective. *Research Communications in Psychology, Psychiatry & Behavior, 7*, 199–213.

Spanos, N. P. (1986). Hypnotic behavior: A social–psychological interpretation of amnesia, analgesia, and "trance logic." *Behavioral and Brain Sciences, 9*, 449–467. http://dx.doi.org/10.1017/S0140525X00046537

Spanos, N. P. (1991). A sociocognitive approach to hypnosis. In S. J. Lynn & J. W. Rhue (Eds.), *Theories of hypnosis: Current models and perspectives* (pp. 324–361). New York, NY: Guilford Press.

Spanos, N. P., Menary, E., Gabora, N. J., DuBreuil, S. C., & Dewhirst, B. (1991). Secondary identity enactments during hypnotic past-life regression: A sociocognitive perspective. *Journal of Personality and Social Psychology, 61*, 308–320. http://dx.doi.org/10.1037/0022-3514.61.2.308

Spanos, N. P., Radtke, H. L., Hodgins, D. C., Bertrand, L. D., Stam, H. J., & Dubreuil, D. L. (1983). The Carleton University Responsiveness to Suggestion Scale: Stability, reliability, and relationships with expectancy and "hypnotic experiences." *Psychological Reports, 53*, 555–563. http://dx.doi.org/10.2466/pr0.1983.53.2.555

Spanos, N. P., Radtke, H. L., Hodgins, D. C., Stam, H. J., & Bertrand, L. D. (1983). The Carleton University Responsiveness to Suggestion Scale: Normative data and psychometric properties. *Psychological Reports, 53*, 523–535. http://dx.doi.org/10.2466/pr0.1983.53.2.523

Sparrow, G., Hurd, R., Carlson, R., & Molina, A. (2018). Exploring the effects of galantamine paired with meditation and dream reliving on recalled dreams: Toward an integrated protocol for lucid dream induction and nightmare resolution. *Consciousness and Cognition, 63*, 74–88. http://dx.doi.org/10.1016/j.concog.2018.05.012

Speth, J., Speth, C., Kaelen, M., Schloerscheidt, A. M., Feilding, A., Nutt, D. J., & Carhart-Harris, R. L. (2016). Decreased mental time travel to the past correlates with default-mode network disintegration under lysergic acid diethylamide. *Journal of Psychopharmacology, 30*, 344–353. http://dx.doi.org/10.1177/0269881116628430

Spiegel, D. (2003). Hypnosis and traumatic dissociation: Therapeutic opportunities. *Journal of Trauma & Dissociation, 4*(3), 73–90. http://dx.doi.org/10.1300/J229v04n03_05

Spiegel, D., Bierre, P., & Rootenberg, J. (1989). Hypnotic alteration of somatosensory perception. *The American Journal of Psychiatry, 146*, 749–754. http://dx.doi.org/10.1176/ajp.146.6.749

Spiegel, H., & Spiegel, D. (1978). *Trance and treatment: Clinical uses of hypnosis.* Washington, DC: American Psychiatric Press.

Spielman, A. J., Yang, C.-M., & Glovinsky, P. B. (2000). Assessment techniques for insomnia. In M. H. Kryger, T. Roth, & W. C. Dement (Eds.), *Principles and practice of sleep medicine* (3rd ed., pp. 1239–1250). Philadelphia, PA: W. B. Saunders.

Sripada, C. S. (2018). An exploration/exploitation trade-off between mind-wandering and goal-directed thinking. In K. C. R. Fox & K. Christoff (Eds.), *The Oxford handbook of spontaneous thought: Mind-wandering, creativity, and dreaming* (pp. 23–34). Oxford, England: Oxford University Press.

Stace, W. T. (1960). *Mysticism and philosophy.* Los Angeles, CA: Jeremy P. Tarcher.

Stan, D., & Christoff, K. (2018). The mind wanders with ease: Low motivational intensity is an essential quality of mind-wandering. In K. C. R. Fox & K. Christoff (Eds.), *The Oxford handbook of spontaneous thought: Mind-wandering, creativity, and dreaming* (pp. 47–53). Oxford, England: Oxford University Press.

Stawarczyk, D. (2018). Phenomenological properties of mind-wandering and daydreaming: A historical overview and functional correlates. In K. C. R. Fox & K. Christoff (Eds.), *The Oxford handbook of spontaneous thought: Mind-wandering, creativity, and dreaming* (pp. 193–214). Oxford, England: Oxford University Press.

Steffen, E. M., Wilde, D. J., & Cooper, C. E. (2017). Affirming the positive in anomalous experiences: A challenge to dominant accounts of reality, life, and death. In N. J. L. Brown, T. Lomas, & F. J. Eiroa-Orosa (Eds.), *The Routledge international handbook of critical positive psychology* (pp. 227–244). London, England: Routledge. http://dx.doi.org/10.4324/9781315659794-18

Steriade, M. (2000). Brain electrical activity and sensory processing during waking and sleep states. In M. H. Kryger, T. Roth, & W. C. Dement (Eds.), *Principles and practice of sleep medicine* (3rd ed., pp. 93–111). Philadelphia, PA: W. B. Saunders.

Stevens, A. (1995). *Private myths: Dreams and dreaming.* Cambridge, MA: Harvard University Press.

Stevenson, I. (1990). Phobias in children who claim to remember previous lives. *Journal of Scientific Exploration, 4*, 243–254.

Stevenson, I. (1994). A case of the psychotherapist's fallacy: Hypnotic regression to "previous lives." *American Journal of Clinical Hypnosis, 36*, 188–193. http://dx.doi.org/10.1080/00029157.1994.10403068

Stevenson, I. (1997a). *Reincarnation and biology: A contribution to the etiology of birthmarks and birth defects.* Westport, CT: Praeger.

Stevenson, I. (1997b). *Where reincarnation and biology intersect.* Westport, CT: Praeger.

Stevenson, I. (2013). *Science, the self, and survival after death: Selected writings of Ian Stevenson* (E. W. Kelly, Ed.). Lanham, MD: Rowman & Littlefield.

Stevenson, I., & Cook, E. W. (1995). Involuntary memories during severe physical illness or injury. *The Journal of Nervous and Mental Disease, 183,* 452–458. http://dx.doi.org/10.1097/00005053-199507000-00005

Stevenson, I., Pasricha, S., & McClean-Rice, N. (1989). A case of the possession type in India with evidence of paranormal knowledge. *Journal of Scientific Exploration, 3,* 81–101.

Stevner, A. B. A., Vidaurre, D., Cabral, J., Rapuano, K., Nielsen, S. F. V., Tagliazucchi, E., . . . Kringelbach, M. L. (2019). Discovery of key whole-brain transitions and dynamics during human wakefulness and non-REM sleep. *Nature Communications, 10,* 1035. Advance online publication. http://dx.doi.org/10.1038/s41467-019-08934-3

Stone, K. L., & Ancoli-Israel, S. (2017). Actigraphy. In M. Kryger, T. Roth, & W. C. Dement (Eds.), *Principles and practice of sleep medicine* (6th ed., pp. 1671–1678). Philadelphia, PA: Elsevier. http://dx.doi.org/10.1016/B978-0-323-24288-2.00171-9

Storm, L., & Ertel, S. (2001). Does psi exist? Comments on Milton and Wiseman's (1999) meta-analysis of ganzfeld research. *Psychological Bulletin, 127,* 424–433. http://dx.doi.org/10.1037/0033-2909.127.3.424

Strassman, R. J. (1996). Human psychopharmacology of N,N-dimethyltryptamine. *Behavioural Brain Research, 73,* 121–124. http://dx.doi.org/10.1016/0166-4328(96)00081-2

Strassman, R. J. (1997). Biomedical research with psychedelics: Current models and future prospects. In R. Forte (Ed.), *Entheogens and the future of religion* (pp. 153–162). San Francisco, CA: Council on Spiritual Practices.

Strassman, R. J. (2001). *DMT: The spirit molecule.* Rochester, VT: Park Street Press.

Strauch, I., & Meier, B. (1996). *In search of dreams: Results of experimental dream research.* Albany, NY: State University of New York Press. (Original work published 1992)

Sudduth, M. (2016). *A philosophical critique of empirical arguments for postmortem survival.* Basingstoke, England: Palgrave Macmillan. http://dx.doi.org/10.1057/9781137440945

Suedfeld, P., & Borrie, R. A. (1999). Health and therapeutic applications of chamber and flotation restricted environmental stimulation therapy (REST). *Psychology & Health, 14,* 545–566. http://dx.doi.org/10.1080/08870449908407346

Suedfeld, P., & Coren, S. (1989). Perceptual isolation, sensory deprivation, and REST: Moving introductory psychology texts out of the 1950s. *Canadian Psychology/Psychologie Canadienne, 30*(1), 17–29. http://dx.doi.org/10.1037/h0079795

Suedfeld, P., & Mocellin, J. S. P. (1987). The "sensed presence" in unusual environments. *Environment and Behavior, 19,* 33–52. http://dx.doi.org/10.1177/0013916587191002

Suedfeld, P., Rank, A. D., & Maluš, M. (2018). Spontaneous mental experiences in extreme and unusual environments. In K. C. R. Fox & K. Christoff (Eds.), *The Oxford handbook of spontaneous thought: Mind-wandering, creativity, and dreaming* (pp. 553–571). Oxford, England: Oxford University Press.

Tabatabaeian, S., & Jennings, C. D. (2018). Toward a neurophysiological foundation for altered states of consciousness. *Behavioral and Brain Sciences, 41,* 36–37. http://dx.doi.org/10.1017/S0140525X17002187

Tafur, J. (2017). *The fellowship of the river: A medical doctor's exploration into traditional Amazonian plant medicine.* Phoenix, AZ: Espiritu Books.

Tarazi, L. (1990). An unusual case of hypnotic regression with some unexplained contents. *Journal of the American Society for Psychical Research, 84,* 309–344.

Targ, R. (1996). Remote viewing at Stanford Research Institute in the 1970s: A memoir. *Journal of Scientific Exploration, 10,* 77–88.

Tart, C. T. (1971). A psychologist's experience with transcendental meditation. *Journal of Transpersonal Psychology, 3,* 135–140.

Tart, C. T. (Ed.). (1972a). *Altered states of consciousness* (2nd ed.). Garden City, NY: Anchor Books.

Tart, C. T. (1972b). Introduction. In C. T. Tart (Ed.), *Altered states of consciousness* (pp. 1–6). Garden City, NY: Anchor Books.

Tart, C. T. (1972c). States of consciousness and state-specific sciences. *Science, 176*(4040), 1203–1210. http://dx.doi.org/10.1126/science.176.4040.1203

Tart, C. T. (1975). *States of consciousness*. New York, NY: Dutton.

Tart, C. T. (1988). Meditation and consciousness: A dialogue between a meditation teacher and a psychologist: An interview with Shinzen Young. *Noetic Sciences Review, 8*, 14–21.

Tart, C. T. (1991). Influences of previous psychedelic drug experiences on students of Tibetan Buddhism: A preliminary exploration. *Journal of Transpersonal Psychology, 23*, 139–173.

Tart, C. T. (1998). Six studies of out-of-body experiences. *Journal of Near-Death Studies, 17*, 73–99. http://dx.doi.org/10.1023/A:1022932505993

Tart, C. T. (2009). *The end of materialism: How evidence of the paranormal is bringing science and spirit together*. Oakland, CA: New Harbinger.

Taylor, E. (1981). The evolution of William James's definition of consciousness. *ReVISION: Journal of Knowledge and Consciousness, 4*(2), 40–47.

Taylor, E. (1997). Introduction. In M. Murphy & S. Donovan (Authors) and E. Taylor (Ed.), *The physical and psychological effects of meditation: A review of contemporary research with a comprehensive bibliography 1931–1996*. Sausalito, CA: Institute of Noetic Sciences.

Taylor, S. (2017). *The leap: The psychology of spiritual awakening*. Novato, CA: New World Library.

Terhune, D. B., Cleeremans, A., Raz, A., & Lynn, S. J. (2017). Hypnosis and top-down regulation of consciousness. *Neuroscience and Biobehavioral Reviews, 81*, 59–74. http://dx.doi.org/10.1016/j.neubiorev.2017.02.002

Thomas, L. E., & Cooper, P. E. (1980). Incidence and psychological correlates of intense spiritual experiences. *Journal of Transpersonal Psychology, 12*, 75–85.

Thompson, C. (2019). *Coders: The making of a new tribe and the remaking of the world*. New York, NY: Penguin Press.

Thompson, T., Terhune, D. B., Oram, C., Sharangparni, J., Rouf, R., Solmi, M., . . . Stubbs, B. (2019). The effectiveness of hypnosis for pain relief: A systematic review and meta-analysis of 85 controlled experimental trials. *Neuroscience and Biobehavioral Reviews, 99*, 298–310. http://dx.doi.org/10.1016/j.neubiorev.2019.02.013

Timmermann, C., Roseman, L., Williams, L., Erritzoe, D., Martial, C., Cassol, H., . . . Carhart-Harris, R. (2018). DMT models the near-death experience. *Frontiers in Psychology, 9*(1424), 1424. Advance online publication. http://dx.doi.org/10.3389/fpsyg.2018.01424

Tompkins, P. (1990). *This tree grows out of hell: Mesoamerica and the search for the magical body*. New York: HarperSanFrancisco.

Trethowan, W. H. (1976). Exorcism: A psychiatric viewpoint. *Journal of Medical Ethics, 2*, 127–137.

Trichter, S. (2010). Ayahuasca beyond the Amazon: The benefits and risks of a spreading tradition. *Journal of Transpersonal Psychology, 42*, 131–148.

Tupper, K. W. (2009). Ayahuasca healing beyond the Amazon: The globalization of a traditional indigenous entheogenic practice. *Global Networks, 9*, 117–136. http://dx.doi.org/10.1111/j.1471-0374.2009.00245.x

Ullman, M. (1999). Dreaming consciousness: More than a bit player in the search for answers to the mind/body problem. *Journal of Scientific Exploration, 13*, 91–112.

Ullman, M., & Krippner, S. (with Vaughan, A.). (1973). *Dream telepathy*. New York, NY: Macmillan.

Urbain, C., De Tiège, X., Op De Beeck, M., Bourguignon, M., Wens, V., Verheulpen, D., . . . Peigneux, P. (2016). Sleep in children triggers rapid reorganization of memory-related brain processes. *NeuroImage, 134,* 213–222. http://dx.doi.org/10.1016/j.neuroimage.2016.03.055

Vallée, J. F. (1990). Five arguments against the extraterrestrial origin of unidentified flying objects. *Journal of Scientific Exploration, 4,* 105–117.

Vallée, J. F. (1991). *Revelations: Alien contact and human deception.* New York, NY: Ballantine Books.

van der Kolk, B. A. (1996). Trauma and memory. In B. A. van der Kolk, A. C. McFarlane, & L. Weisaeth (Eds.), *Traumatic stress: The effects of overwhelming experience on mind, body, and society* (pp. 279–302). New York, NY: Guilford Press.

van Eeden, F. (1913). A study of dreams. *Proceedings of the Society for Psychical Research, 26*(Pt. 67), 431–461.

van Lommel, P. (2013). Non-local consciousness: A concept based on scientific research on near-death experiences during cardiac arrest. *Journal of Consciousness Studies, 20*(1–2), 7–48.

van Lommel, P., van Wees, R., Meyers, V., & Elfferich, I. (2001). Near-death experience in survivors of cardiac arrest: A prospective study in the Netherlands. *The Lancet, 358,* 2039–2045. http://dx.doi.org/10.1016/S0140-6736(01)07100-8

van Quekelberghe, R., Göbel, P., & Hertweck, E. (1995). Simulation of near-death and out-of-body experiences under hypnosis. *Imagination, Cognition and Personality, 14,* 151–164. http://dx.doi.org/10.2190/GDFW-XLEL-ENQL-5WQ6

van Rijn, C. M., Krijnen, H., Menting-Hermeling, S., & Coenen, A. M. L. (2011). Decapitation in rats: Latency to unconsciousness and the 'wave of death'. *PLoS ONE, 6*(1), e16514. http://dx.doi.org/10.1371/journal.pone.0016514

Vaughan, F. E. (1979). Transpersonal psychotherapy: Context, content and process. *Journal of Transpersonal Psychology, 11,* 101–110.

Venn, J. (1986). Hypnosis and the reincarnation hypothesis: A critical review and intensive case study. *Journal of the American Society for Psychical Research, 80,* 409–425.

Vieten, C., Wahbeh, H., Cahn, B. R., MacLean, K., Estrada, M., Mills, P., . . . Delorme, A. (2018). Future directions in meditation research: Recommendations for expanding the field of contemplative science. *PLoS ONE, 13*(11), e0205740. http://dx.doi.org/10.1371/journal.pone.0205740

Vollenweider, F. X., Leenders, K. L., Scharfetter, C., Maguire, P., Stadelmann, O., & Angst, J. (1997). Positron emission tomography and fluorodeoxyglucose studies of metabolic hyperfrontality and psychopathology in the psilocybin model of psychosis. *Neuropsychopharmacology, 16,* 357–372. http://dx.doi.org/10.1016/S0893-133X(96)00246-1

Vollenweider, F. X., Vollenweider-Scherpenhuyzen, M. F. I., Bäbler, A., Vogel, H., & Hell, D. (1998). Psilocybin induces schizophrenia-like psychosis in humans via a serotonin-2 agonist action. *Neuroreport, 9,* 3897–3902. http://dx.doi.org/10.1097/00001756-199812010-00024

Wagaman, J., & Barabasz, A. (1993). Flotation REST and imagery in the improvement of collegiate athletic performance: Basketball. In A. F. Barabasz & M. Barabasz (Eds.), *Clinical and experimental restricted environmental stimulation: New developments and perspectives* (pp. 87–92). New York, NY: Springer-Verlag. http://dx.doi.org/10.1007/978-1-4684-8583-7_11

Wagaman, J. D., Barabasz, A. F., & Barabasz, M. (1991). Flotation REST and imagery in the improvement of collegiate basketball performance. *Perceptual and Motor Skills, 72,* 119–122. http://dx.doi.org/10.2466/pms.1991.72.1.119

Waggoner, R. (2009). *Lucid dreaming: Gateway to the inner self.* Needham, MA: Moment Point Press.

Waldron, J. L. (1998). The life impact of transcendent experiences with a pronounced quality of *noesis. Journal of Transpersonal Psychology, 30,* 103–134.

Walker, E. H. (1970). The nature of consciousness. *Mathematical Biosciences, 7,* 131–Wich178. http://dx.doi.org/10.1016/0025-5564(70)90046-5

Walker, E. H. (2000). *The physics of consciousness: Quantum minds and the meaning of life.* Cambridge, MA: Perseus Books.

Walker, M. (2017). *Why we sleep: Unlocking the power of sleep and dreams.* New York: Scribner.

Wallace, B. A. (1998). *The bridge of quiescence: Experiencing Tibetan Buddhist meditation.* Chicago, IL: Open Court.

Wallace, B. A. (2017). Introduction to Dzogchen [Online course]. Retrieved from https://wisdomexperience.org/courses/intro-dzogchen/

Walling, D. P., & Baker, J. M. (1996). Hypnosis training in psychology intern programs. *American Journal of Clinical Hypnosis, 38,* 219–223. http://dx.doi.org/10.1080/00029157.1996.10403341

Walsh, R. (1989). What is a shaman? Definition, origin and distribution. *Journal of Transpersonal Psychology, 21,* 1–11.

Walsh, R. (1995). Phenomenological mapping: A method for describing and comparing states of consciousness. *Journal of Transpersonal Psychology, 27,* 25–56.

Walsh, R. (2007). *The world of shamanism: New views of an ancient tradition.* Woodbury, MN: Llewellyn.

Walter, W. G., & Dovey, V. J. (1944). Electro-encephalography in cases of subcortical tumour. *Journal of Neurology, Neurosurgery and Psychiatry, 7,* 57–65.

Wammes, M., & Baruss, I. (2009). Characteristics of spontaneous musical imagery. *Journal of Consciousness Studies, 16,* 37–61.

Ware, J. C., & Hirshkowitz, M. (2000). Assessment of sleep-related erections. In M. H. Kryger, T. Roth, & W. C. Dement (Eds.), *Principles and practice of sleep medicine* (3rd ed., pp. 1231–1237). Philadelphia, PA: W. B. Saunders.

Warren, J. (2007). *The head trip: Adventures on the wheel of consciousness.* New York, NY: Random House.

Watkins, J. G., & Watkins, H. H. (1986). Hypnosis, multiple personality, and ego states as altered states of consciousness. In B. B. Wolman & M. Ullman (Eds.), *Handbook of states of consciousness* (pp. 133–158). New York, NY: Van Nostrand Reinhold.

Watson, J. B. (1919). *Psychology from the standpoint of a behaviorist.* Philadelphia, PA: J. B. Lippincott. http://dx.doi.org/10.1037/10016-000

Watt, C. (2014). Precognitive dreaming: Investigating anomalous cognition and psychological factors. *Journal of Parapsychology, 78,* 115–125.

Watt, C., & Tierney, I. (2014). Psi-related experiences. In E. Cardeña, S. J. Lynn, & S. Krippner (Eds.), *Varieties of anomalous experience: Examining the scientific evidence* (2nd ed., pp. 241–272). Washington, DC: American Psychological Association. http://dx.doi.org/10.1037/14258-009

Watt, C., & Vuillaume, L. (2015). Dream precognition and sensory incorporation: A controlled sleep laboratory study. *Journal of Consciousness Studies, 22*(5–6), 172–190.

Wehr, T. A. (1992). In short photoperiods, human sleep is biphasic. *Journal of Sleep Research, 1,* 103–107. http://dx.doi.org/10.1111/j.1365-2869.1992.tb00019.x

Weil, A., & Rosen, W. (1993). *From chocolate to morphine: Everything you need to know about mind-altering drugs* (Rev. ed.). Boston, MA: Houghton Mifflin.

Weiss, B. L. (1992). *Through time into healing.* New York, NY: Simon & Schuster.

Weitzenhoffer, A. M., & Hilgard, E. R. (1962). *Stanford Hypnotic Susceptibility Scale: Form C.* Palo Alto, CA: Consulting Psychologists Press.

Wenzlaff, R. M., & Wegner, D. M. (2000). Thought suppression. *Annual Review of Psychology, 51,* 59–91. http://dx.doi.org/10.1146/annurev.psych.51.1.59

West, V., Fellows, B., & Easton, S. (1995). The British Society of Experimental and Clinical Hypnosis: A national survey. *Contemporary Hypnosis, 12,* 143–147. http://dx.doi.org/10.1002/ch.62

White, P. A. (1988). Knowing more about what we can tell: 'Introspective access' and causal report accuracy 10 years later. *British Journal of Psychology, 79,* 13–45. http://dx.doi.org/10.1111/j.2044-8295.1988.tb02271.x

Wichniak, A., Wierzbicka, A., Walęcka, M., & Jernajczyk, W. (2017). Effects of anti-depressants on sleep. *Current Psychiatry Reports, 19*(9), 63. http://dx.doi.org/10.1007/s11920-017-0816-4

Wilbur, C. B., & Kluft, R. P. (1989). Multiple personality disorder. In *Treatments of psychiatric disorders: A task force report of the American Psychiatric Association* (pp. 2197–2216). Washington, DC: American Psychiatric Association.

Wilson, S. C., & Barber, T. X. (1981). Vivid fantasy and hallucinatory abilities in the life histories of excellent hypnotic subjects ("somnambules"): Preliminary report with female subjects. In E. Klinger (Ed.), *Imagery: Vol. 2. Concepts, results, and applications* (pp. 133–149). New York, NY: Plenum Press.

Windt, J. M., Nielsen, T., & Thompson, E. (2016). Does consciousness disappear in dreamless sleep? *Trends in Cognitive Sciences, 20*, 871–882. http://dx.doi.org/10.1016/j.tics.2016.09.006

Winkelman, M. (2011). Shamanism and the alteration of consciousness. In E. Cardeña & M. Winkelman (Eds.), *Altering consciousness: Multidisciplinary perspectives: Vol. 1. History, culture, and the humanities* (pp. 159–180). Santa Barbara, CA: Praeger.

Wood, D. P., & Sexton, J. L. (1997). Self-hypnosis training and captivity survival. *American Journal of Clinical Hypnosis, 39*, 201–211.

Woods, K., & Baruš, I. (2004). Experimental test of possible psychological benefits of past-life regression. *Journal of Scientific Exploration, 18*, 597–608.

Woody, E. Z. (1997). Have the hypnotic susceptibility scales outlived their usefulness? *International Journal of Clinical and Experimental Hypnosis, 45*, 226–238. http://dx.doi.org/10.1080/00207149708416125

Woody, E. Z., & Bowers, K. S. (1994). A frontal assault on dissociated control. In S. J. Lynn & J. W. Rhue (Eds.), *Dissociation: Clinical and theoretical perspectives* (pp. 52–79). New York, NY: Guilford Press.

Woody, E. Z., Drugovic, M., & Oakman, J. M. (1997). A reexamination of the role of nonhypnotic suggestibility in hypnotic responding. *Journal of Personality and Social Psychology, 72*, 399–407. http://dx.doi.org/10.1037/0022-3514.72.2.399

Woody, E. Z., & Sadler, P. (2016). What can a hypnotic induction do? *American Journal of Clinical Hypnosis, 59*, 138–154. http://dx.doi.org/10.1080/00029157.2016.1185004

Wren-Lewis, J. (1988). The darkness of God: A personal report on consciousness transformation through an encounter with death. *Journal of Humanistic Psychology, 28*, 105–122. http://dx.doi.org/10.1177/0022167888282011

Wren-Lewis, J. (1991). A reluctant mystic: God-consciousness not guru worship. *Self and Society, 19*, 4–11. http://dx.doi.org/10.1080/03060497.1991.11085159

Wren-Lewis, J. (1994). Aftereffects of near-death experiences: A survival mechanism hypothesis. *Journal of Transpersonal Psychology, 26*, 107–115.

Wulff, D. M. (2000). Mystical experience. In E. Cardeña, S. J. Lynn, & S. Krippner (Eds.), *Varieties of anomalous experience: Examining the scientific evidence* (pp. 397–440). Washington, DC: American Psychological Association. http://dx.doi.org/10.1037/10371-012

Wyatt, J. K., Bootzin, R. R., Anthony, J., & Stevenson, S. (1992). Does sleep onset produce retrograde amnesia? *Sleep Research, 21*, 113.

Xie, L., Kang, H., Xu, Q., Chen, M. J., Liao, Y., Thiyagarajan, M., . . . Nedergaard, M. (2013). Sleep drives metabolite clearance from the adult brain. *Science, 342*, 373–377. http://dx.doi.org/10.1126/science.1241224

Yaden, D., Le Nguyen, K. D., Kern, M. L., Wintering, N. A., Eichstaedt, J. C., Schwartz, H. A., . . . Newberg, A. B. (2017). The noetic quality: A multimethod exploratory study. *Psychology of Consciousness, 4*, 54–62. http://dx.doi.org/10.1037/cns0000098

Yan, W. (2019). The nuclear sins of the Soviet Union live on in Kazakhstan. *Nature, 568*, 22–24. http://dx.doi.org/10.1038/d41586-019-01034-8

Yang, E. H., Hla, K. M., McHorney, C. A., Havighurst, T., Badr, M. S., & Weber, S. (2000). Sleep apnea and quality of life. *Sleep, 23*(4), 1–7. http://dx.doi.org/10.1093/sleep/23.4.1g

Yram. (1967). *Practical astral projection*. New York, NY: Samuel Weiser.

Zarcone, V. P., Jr. (2000). Sleep hygiene. In M. H. Kryger, T. Roth, & W. C. Dement (Eds.), *Principles and practice of sleep medicine* (3rd ed., pp. 657–661). Philadelphia, PA: W. B. Saunders.

Zilbergeld, B. (1983). *The shrinking of America: Myths of psychological change*. New York, NY: Little, Brown.

Zingrone, N. L., & Alvarado, C. S. (2009). Pleasurable Western adult near-death experiences: Features, circumstances, and incidence. In J. M. Holden, B. Greyson, & D. James (Eds.), *The handbook of near-death experiences: Thirty years of investigation* (pp. 17–40). Santa Barbara, CA: Praeger.

Zusne, L., & Jones, W. H. (1989). *Anomalistic psychology: A study of magical thinking* (2nd ed.). Hillsdale, NJ: Erlbaum.

INDEX

and surrender, 220
and thinking, 33
and transcendent experiences, 178
and well-being, 218
Nedergaard, Maiken, 64
Negative hallucinations (hypnosis), 107
Negative symptoms of schizophrenia, 128
Neodissociation theory, 116
Neophytes, 127
Nerve cells, 52, 53
Nervous system, 52
Network approach to cognitive functioning, 188
Neural correlates of consciousness (NCC), 8
Neurons, 53
Neuropharmacology, 161–162
Neuroscience of consciousness, 52–54
    as component of physiological
        perspective, 6
    and hypnosis, 112–114
    and meditation, 188–189
    and near-death experiences, 204–206
    overview, 8–9
    and sleep, 53–54
Neurotransmitters, 53
Neutrophils, 42
Nicotine, 70
Nicotinic acid, 167
Nightmare disorder, 71
Nightmares, 82–83, 92. *See also* Dreams
Nisbett, R. E., 28
Noble, J., 101, 109–110
Nocebo effects, 43
Nocturnal lucidity, 88
Noetic quality, 175, 177, 180, 190, 191, 216, 218
Noncontact healing, 43–44
Nonduality, 184, 186, 188, 189
"Non-immersive imagery and sleep thinking," 62
"Non-insane automatism," 72
Nonlocal consciousness, 43, 76, 221
Nonrapid eye movement (NREM) sleep
    and benefits of sleep, 64, 66
    and dreaming, 62
    and dream theories, 77
    and effects of drugs, 60
    and insomnia, 70
    and lucid dreaming, 91
    overview, 55–58
    and parasomnias, 71
    and sleep state misperception, 70
    stages of. *See specific headings*
Noradrenaline, 82
Northrop, F. S. C., 186
NovaDreamer device, 93
NREM sleep. *See* Nonrapid eye movement sleep
Nutt, David, 150–151

O

OBEs. *See* Out-of-body experiences
Obesity, 122
Obstructive sleep apnea hypopnea, 68–69
Oneirology, 75
Oneironauts, 75
Ontological shock, 147
Open monitoring meditation, 184
Openness, 19–20
Open psyche, 23, 219–220
Opioids, 150
Opium, 150
Ordinary waking state, 5, 10–14, 22, 23, 25, 26, 34, 44, 51, 55, 62, 63, 76, 98, 118, 123, 149, 171, 180, 183, 191, 204, 205, 215, 220, 221
    as baseline, 11–12
    changes away from, 10
    and death, 204, 205
    and dreams, 76, 98
    examination of events during, 13
    factors leading to, 5
    and hypnosis, 123
    interest in, 14
    and psychedelics, 149, 171
    and sleep, 51, 55, 62, 63
    and transcendence, 180, 183, 191
    unawareness of, 118
Orexins, 68
Orne, Martin, 106–107, 109, 110
Osmond, Humphry, 151, 155, 165
Out-of-body experiences (OBEs), 194–197
    characteristics of, 194–195
    cognitive theory of, 197, 216
    and dreams, 99
    and exosomatic theory of consciousness, 221
    perception during, 194–197, 203
    and trance states, 129
Overdose deaths, 150
Overwhelming experiences, 135

P

Pacemakers (nerve cells), 53
Pahnke, Walter, 167–169, 175, 190
Pain
    and dreaming, 62
    and hypnotic analgesia, 121, 122
    and meditation, 182
    and psychedelic drugs, 166
Palliative care, 166–167
Paradoxicality, 176
Paradoxical sleep, 57
Parapsychology, 194
Parasomnias, 71–72
Parks, Kenneth, 72
Parrino, L., 57